On the People's Terms

According to republican political theory, people's freedom as persons requires that they be publicly protected against subjection or domination in the exercise of basic liberties. But there is no public protection without a coercive state and that raises a problem since, by all accounts, coercion takes away from the freedom of the coerced. In addressing this problem, Philip Pettit argues that state coercion does not involve subjection or domination if people share equally in democratic control of the direction it takes. He proposes a normative theory of democracy under which the goal is to ensure that political coercion is non-dominating and, linking philosophy with policy, he supplements the theory with a realistic model of institutions that might promote that goal. *On the People's Terms* is an original account of the rationale and organization of democracy, offering a new direction for democratic thought. It fully lives up to the high ideals of the Seeley Lectures.

PHILIP PETTIT is L. S. Rockefeller University Professor of Politics and Human Values at Princeton University and also Distinguished Professor of Philosophy at the Australian National University. His books include *The Common Mind*; *Republicanism*; *Rules, Reasons and Norms*; and *Made with Words: Hobbes on Language, Mind and Politics*. Amongst his recent co-authored books are *The Economy of Esteem*, with Geoffrey Brennan; *A Political Philosophy in Public Life*, with Jose Marti; and *Group Agency*, with Christian List. A collection of papers on his work, *Common Minds: Themes from the Philosophy of Philip Pettit*, appeared in 2007.

T0382147

THE SEELEY LECTURES

The John Robert Seeley Lectures have been established by the University
of Cambridge as a biennial lecture series in social and political studies,
sponsored jointly by the Faculty of History and the University Press. The
Seeley Lectures provide a unique forum for distinguished scholars of
international reputation to address, in an accessible manner, themes of
broad and topical interest in social and political studies. Subsequent to their
public delivery in Cambridge the University Press publishes suitably
modified versions of each set of lectures. Professor James Tully delivered the
inaugural series of Seeley Lectures in 1994 on the theme of *Constitutionalism
in an Age of Diversity*.

The Seeley Lectures include

(1)   Strange Multiplicity: Constitutionalism in an Age of Diversity
JAMES TULLY
ISBN 978 0 521 47694 2 (paperback)
Published 1995

(2)   The Dignity of Legislation
JEREMY WALDRON
ISBN 978 0 521 65092 2 (hardback) 978 0 521 65883 6 (paperback)
Published 1999

(3)   Woman and Human Development: The Capabilities Approach
MARTHA NUSSBAUM
ISBN 978 0 521 66086 0 (hardback) 978 0 521 00385 8 (paperback)
Published 2000

(4)   Value, Respect and Attachment
JOSEPH RAZ
ISBN 978 0 521 80180 5 (hardback) 978 0 521 00022 2 (paperback)
Published 2001

(5)   The Rights of Others: Aliens, Residents and Citizens
SEYLA BENHABIB

ISBN 978 0 521 83134 5 (hardback) 978 0 521 53860 2 (paperback)
Published 2004

(6)   Laws of Fear: Beyond the Precautionary Principle
CASS R. SUNSTEIN
ISBN 978 0 521 84823 7 (hardback) 978 0 521 61512 9 (paperback)
Published 2005

(7)   Counter Democracy: Politics in an Age of Distrust
PIERRE ROSANVALLON
ISBN 978 0 521 86622 2 (hardback) 978 0 521 71383 2 (paperback)
Published 2008

(8)   On the People's Terms: A Republican Theory and Model of Democracy
PHILIP PETTIT
ISBN 978 1 107 00511 2 (hardback) 978 0 521 18212 6 (paperback)
Published 2012

ON THE PEOPLE'S TERMS

A Republican Theory and Model of Democracy

PHILIP PETTIT

CAMBRIDGE
UNIVERSITY PRESS

CAMBRIDGE
UNIVERSITY PRESS

University Printing House, Cambridge CB2 8BS, United Kingdom

Cambridge University Press is part of the University of Cambridge.

It furthers the University's mission by disseminating knowledge in the pursuit of education, learning and research at the highest international levels of excellence.

www.cambridge.org
Information on this title: www.cambridge.org/9780521182126

First published 2012
3rd printing 2014

A catalogue record for this publication is available from the British Library

Library of Congress Cataloguing in Publication data
Pettit, Philip, 1945–
On the people's terms : a republican theory and model of democracy / Philip Pettit.
    p.   cm. – (The Seeley lectures)
ISBN 978-1-107-00511-2 (hardback)
1. Republicanism.   2. Political science – Philosophy.   3. Democracy.   4. State, The.   I. Title.
JC423.P432   2012
321.8′6–dc23

                                                                2012020514

ISBN 978-0-521-18212-6 Hardback

For Rory and Owen, in another season.

Contents

Tables

Acknowledgements

This book has been long in the making. I decided to give more attention to the relationship between republican political theory and democratic theory soon after publishing *Republicanism: A Theory of Freedom and Government* in 1997 (Pettit 1997c) and I wrote some papers on the topic in the years immediately following. I worked at developing an overall view of republicanism and democracy in the Pufendorf Lectures in Philosophy at the University of Lund in 2005, in the Albertus Magnus Lectures in Philosophy at the University of Cologne in 2009 and, finally, in the Seeley Lectures in Political Theory at the University of Cambridge in 2010. I wrote up a final draft of the book while on a year's research leave at the Center for Advanced Study in the Behavioral Sciences at Stanford in 2010–11 and I reworked the text in the course of a graduate seminar in Philosophy and Politics at Princeton University in Fall Semester 2011. Late in the piece I presented related material in the Frankfurt Lectures in Political Theory at the Goethe University in Frankfurt, and in the Quain Lecture in Jurisprudence at University College, London, and the intense discussions on each occasion led to some final alterations. I am grateful to all those institutions for their support, as well as to the John Guggenheim Foundation for the award of a fellowship in 2010–11.

In the course of the years working on the text I built up an enormous number of personal, as well as institutional, debts. Since I cannot hope to acknowledge all my creditors, I hope just a few words of thanks will suffice. I am grateful for the valuable contributions of my audiences and hosts at the institutions where I lectured or gave seminars on the topic, for the contributions of the graduate students with whom I have been fortunate to work on related topics, and for the wholly invaluable commentary and criticism that was provided week after week by the students who participated in the Princeton seminar in 2011. I must also thank those who took the trouble to read the full text and sent often extremely insightful and helpful comments: David Plunkett, who used it in a course at UCLA; my colleague, Annie

Stilz, who was a selfless, illuminating critic; and especially Niko Kolodny, who wrote as a temporarily anonymous reviewer for Cambridge University Press and forced me to reconsider a long list of issues.[1]

Sustained interaction with those Princeton colleagues associated with the University Center for Human Values has been absolutely crucial in shaping my views; the relevant players, on any count, have to include Anthony Appiah, Chuck Beitz, Marc Fleurbaey, Dan Garber, Liz Harman, Nan Keohane, Melissa Lane, Stephen Macedo, Victoria McGeer, Jan Werner Mueller, Alan Patten, Gideon Rosen, Kim Scheppele, Peter Singer, Michael Smith and Jeff Stout. There are many others with whom I have had exchanges, some of them quite extended, on the topics covered. The list includes John Braithwaite, Geoffrey Brennan, Annabel Brett, Ian Carter, John Ferejohn, Rainer Forst, John Gardner, Moira Gatens, Bob Goodin, Alan Hayek, Kinch Hoekstra, Istvan Hont, Duncan Ivison, Frank Jackson, Susan James, Matthew Kramer, Martin Krygier, Chandran Kukathas, Cecile Laborde, Niki Lacey, George Letsas, Christian List, Frank Lovett, Jenny Mansbridge, Jose Marti, Josh Ober, Michael Otsuka, Paul Patton, Joseph Raz, Magnus Ryan, Wojciech Sadurski, Tim Scanlon, Amartya Sen, Ian Shapiro, Quentin Skinner, David Soskice, Nic Southwood, John Tasioulas, Larry Temkin, Richard Tuck, Laura Valentini, Miguel Vatter, Jeremy Waldron, Albert Weale, Barry Weingast, Jo Wolff and the late Iris Marion Young.

The various people listed have each played an important role in pushing and pulling me around the arena of debates covered in the book. My thanks to all for their interest and their engagement and my apologies, of course, for what many of them will take – or, as I would naturally like to think, mistake – for sheer obstinacy. I owe a special debt to Quentin Skinner, who is responsible for having introduced me to the potential of republican ideas. And I owe an extra-special debt to Victoria McGeer, with whom conversation and life never flag. Finally, I should express my gratitude to Richard Fisher of Cambridge University Press for the enormous encouragement and support that he offered from the time I was first invited to present the Seeley Lectures.

---

[1] N. Kolodny, in his unpublished paper, 'Rule Over None: Social Equality and the Value of Democracy', offers an alternative way of developing some of the ideas that are basic to the approach taken in this book and this was a source of constant challenges as I prepared the final version of my own text.

Introduction. The republic, old and new

Every philosophy of the good society starts with an account of the canonical complaint that the state should help to put right: the evil that the society should drive out by means of political organization and initiative. The complaints targeted for political rectification come in two broad families. On the one side, personal afflictions like misery or poverty or inequality; on the other, social failures like division or disorder or perhaps an excess of customary restriction.

The more personal complaints generate a powerfully motivating agenda, since most of us would rejoice in a state that silenced them. But these complaints are liable to seem politically over-demanding. While it would be good to be rid of misery or poverty or inequality, not everyone will agree that the state could, or should, be given the job of dealing with them. The removal of the less personal evils is not politically over-demanding in the same way, for most people will think that the state is able to remedy such failures. But these complaints may fail to motivate appropriately: their rectification falls short of what many of us feel that we in a politically organized society can and should collectively provide for our members.

Republican philosophy identifies a complaint that is meant to be at once personally motivating and politically feasible. It indicts the evil of subjection to another's will – particularly in important areas of personal choice – as an ill that we all recognize and recoil from and at the same time as an ill that the state is well placed to deal with. I shall be arguing in the course of this book that such subjection can be effectively corralled and reduced, though certainly not wholly eliminated, by means of political initiative. And yet it takes only a little imagination to realize just how repellent this subjection can be.

Think, by way of exercising such imagination, of how you would feel as a student if you depended for not failing a course on the whim of an instructor. Or as a wife if you had to rely on the mood of your husband for whether you could enjoy an unmolested day. Or as a worker if you hung on the favour of a manager for whether you retained your job. Or as a debtor if you were dependent on the goodwill of a creditor for whether you had to face public ignominy. Or as someone destitute if you had to cast yourself on the mercy of others just to survive or maintain your family. Or think about how you would feel as the member of a cultural minority if you had to rely on the humour of majority groups for whether you escaped humiliation; or as an elderly person if you depended on escaping the notice of youth gangs for walking safely home; or as a citizen if you were dependent on winning the favour of some insider group for whether you or your kind ever caught the eye of government.

It is a commonplace in most cultures that such involuntary exposure to the will of others is inherently troubling and objectionable. Even when those others do not exercise their power in actual interference, the very dependency involved is something from which we naturally recoil. The possible modes of subjection are many and diverse, as these examples already testify, but it should be clear that the state is capable of curtailing them in various ways. Without assuming the cast of a Leviathan in their lives, it can assure its people of a level of protection, support and status that frees them from at least the more egregious forms that such dependency can take.

Already in classical, republican Rome, the evil of subjection to the will of others, whether or not such subjection led to actual interference, was identified and indicted as the iconic ill from which political organization should liberate people, in particular those in the fortunate position of citizens. It was described as the evil of being subject to a master, or *dominus* – suffering *dominatio* – and was contrasted with the good of *libertas*, or 'liberty'. The accepted wisdom was that people could enjoy liberty, both in relation to one another and to the collectivity, only by being invested with the power and status of the *civis*, or 'citizen'. Being a free person became synonymous with being sufficiently empowered to stand on equal terms with others, as a citizen amongst citizens (Wirszubski 1968: Chapter 1).

The idea that citizens could enjoy this equal standing in their society, and not have to hang on the benevolence of their betters, became the signature theme in the long and powerful tradition of republican thought. Familiar from its instantiation in classical Rome, the idea was reignited in medieval and Renaissance Italy; spread throughout Europe in the modern era, sparking the English Civil War and the French Revolution; and inflamed the passions of England's American colonists in the late eighteenth century, leading to the foundation of the world's first modern democracy. With citizenship becoming more and more inclusive as a category, the idea was that the state could provide for all citizens in such a measure that they would each be able to walk tall, live without shame or indignity, and look one another in the eye without any reason for fear or deference.

The recent revival of republican thought is built on this idea that there is an ideal for the state to promote – freedom understood as non-domination – that is both personally motivating and politically implementable. Freedom in this sense is not meant to be the only value in life, or the only value that ultimately matters. The claim is merely that it is a gateway good, suited to guide the governments that people form and sustain. Let government look after the freedom of citizens in this sense, so the line goes, and it will also have to look after a plausible range of other goods and do so at a plausible level of provision. It will have to guard against division and disorder and intrusive regulation and it will have to provide in a decent measure against misery and poverty, unfairness and inequality.

This book joins a growing body of contributions in political theory that are guided by the republican ideal and more generally by the republican tradition of thought.[1] While the volume offers an outline history of the tradition, an analysis of freedom as non-domination, and an account of what the ideal requires by way of social justice in people's relationships with one another, the main focus is elsewhere. It is on what the ideal demands by way of political legitimacy in the relationships between citizens and their state. The book argues that while the state has to guard people against private domination – that is, the requirement of social justice – it also needs to guard against itself practising a form of public domination. The requirement of guarding against public domination, thereby delivering political legitimacy, turns out to demand a rich array of popular controls over government: in effect, a distinctive form of democracy. It enables us to explain why and how government should be forced, in the title of the volume, to operate on the people's terms.

---

[1] The recent movement, as I think of it, began from the historical work of Quentin Skinner (1978) on the medieval foundations of modern political thought, and from his subsequent articles in the 1980s on figures like Machiavelli, who wrote within the republican tradition identified by John Pocock (1975). An up-to-date list of English works in contemporary republican thinking should include these books: Pettit (1997c); Skinner (1998); Brugger (1999); Honohan (2002); Viroli (2002); Maynor (2003); Lovett (2010); Marti and Pettit (2010); McGilvray (2011); these collections of papers: Van Gelderen and Skinner (2002); Weinstock and Nadeau (2004); Honohan and Jennings (2006); Laborde and Maynor (2007); Besson and Marti (2008); Niederberger and Schink (2012); and a number of studies that deploy the conception of freedom as non-domination, broadly understood: Braithwaite and Pettit (1990); Richardson (2002); Slaughter (2005); Bellamy (2007); Bohman (2007); Laborde (2008); White and Leighton (2008).

This theory of democracy, which takes final shape in Chapter 3, will not be very persuasive unless we can offer at least a rough model of how it might be institutionally realized. That is what the final two chapters provide. While the model developed there may be rejected or amended by many who still want to stick with the basic republican theory, it should at least help to show that the theory is not institutionally infeasible.

The model developed in chapters 4 and 5 suggests that democracy operates at its best in a dual process involving, in the short haul, the exercise of popular influence over government and, in the long haul, the imposition of a popular direction on government. As a result of the short-term electoral and contestatory influence that democracy can give them, so the idea goes, the people gain the power to force government over the longer term to conform to widely accepted norms of policy-making. The combination of these two processes, each with its own temporal register, can ensure that the *demos*, or 'people', enjoy a significant degree of *kratos*, or 'power', over the laws that govern and shape their lives, thereby avoiding public domination. The model offers a picture of how public institutions might serve to implement the republican version of the democratic ideal, giving people channels of influence that conjoin to form a river of popular control. Readers who are interested in this model, rather than in the republican theory on which it is based, might go directly to the final two chapters, using the propositional summary offered in the Conclusion to orientate their reading.

In the remainder of this Introduction, I outline the main ideas in the historical tradition of republican thought, distinguishing them from liberal and communitarian ideas, and explaining how I make use of them in the philosophical argument that follows. That argument begins in Chapter 1 with an account of the republican ideal of freedom as non-domination, and continues in the following two chapters with the theory of social justice and political legitimacy that republicanism would support. As already suggested, social justice constrains the relations that the members of a society should have with one another, and political legitimacy the relations that they should have with their government and, more broadly, their state. The theory of republican legitimacy turns out to offer a theory of democracy, since it requires a very specific form of equally shared, popular control over government. Having developed that theory in Chapter 3, I then go on in chapters 4 and 5 to outline the dual-aspect model of the sort of democracy required.

Even where it covers ground that I have traversed elsewhere, my presentation of republican history and theory has shifted somewhat as a result of the many recent discussions of these topics. The historical outline in this Introduction coheres with the story of republican development that I have presented in earlier writings, building on the work of Quentin Skinner, but it sharpens the contrast between the Italian–Atlantic republicanism with which I identify and the form of republican thought introduced by Rousseau. The argument in the first three chapters is broadly faithful to lines of thinking I have defended in other works but is novel on a number of counts. It builds the discussion around the distinction between freedom of choice and freedom of the person. It uses an analysis of the fundamental liberties, and of their grounding in public norm and law, to articulate the ideal of freedom as a person and the requirements of republican justice. And it develops a theory of republican legitimacy at proper length, marking it off from the theory of republican justice on the one side and non-republican theories of legitimacy on the other.

THREE CORE IDEAS

Three ideas stand out as landmarks on the terrain of traditional republican thought. While the ideas received different interpretations and emphases in different periods and amongst different authors, they constitute points of reference that were recognized and authorized by almost everyone down to the late eighteenth century who has a claim to belong to the tradition.

The first idea, unsurprisingly, is that the equal freedom of its citizens, in particular their freedom as non-domination – the freedom that goes with not having to live under the potentially harmful power of another – is the primary concern of the state or republic. The second is that if the republic is to secure the freedom of its citizens then it must satisfy a range of constitutional constraints associated broadly with the mixed constitution. And the third idea is that if the citizens are to keep the republic to its proper business then they had better have the collective and individual virtue to track and contest public policies and initiatives: the price of liberty, in the old republican adage, is eternal vigilance.

The mixed constitution was meant to guarantee a rule of law – a constitutional order – under which each citizen would be equal with others and a separation and sharing of powers – a mixed order – that would deny control over the law to any one individual or body. The contestatory citizenry was the civic complement to this constitutional ideal: it was to be a citizenry committed to interrogating all the elements of government and imposing itself in the determination of law and policy. These institutional measures were taken to be essential for organizing a government that would promote the equal freedom of citizens without itself becoming a master in their lives – in other words, that would protect against private forms of domination without perpetrating public forms.[2]

Freedom as non-domination, the mixed constitution and the contestatory citizenry were all represented in Roman republican thought and practice, and they were articulated in different ways amongst the many writers who identified with Roman institutions. These authors included the Greek-born historian, Polybius, the orator and lawyer, Marcus Tullius Cicero, and the native Roman historian, Titus Livius or, as we know him, Livy. While they drew freely on earlier Greek sources, including Plato and Aristotle, they were united in the belief that it was Rome that first gave life and recognition to the key republican ideas.[3]

Leading thinkers in medieval and Renaissance Italy drew heavily on Polybius, Cicero and Livy when, more than a thousand years later, they reworked the republican ideas in seeking a political philosophy that would reflect the organization and experience of independent city-states like Florence and Venice (Skinner 1978). The neo-Roman framework of thought that they crafted in the course of this exercise – in particular the framework outlined in Nicolo Machiavelli's *Discourses on Livy* – served in turn to provide terms of political self-understanding for northern European countries that resisted or overthrew absolute monarchs.[4] These included the Polish republic of the nobles in the sixteenth and seventeenth centuries, the seventeenth- and eighteenth-century Dutch republic and the English republic of the 1640s and 1650s.

While the English republic was the shortest lived of these regimes, it had the widest influence and the deepest impact. The republican ideas

[2] There are three ways, according to most contemporary normative theories, in which a government and state might fail to be satisfactory (Fukuyama 2011). It might fail to operate impartially by systematically favouring members of a particular grouping, like a family or tribe. It might operate impartially but fail to operate according to established, stable rules in decision-making; that is, it might be ad hoc or capricious, rather than constitutional. Or it might operate impartially and constitutionally but fail to be accountable to its subjects. The first danger introduces partial, as distinct from impartial, rule; the second particularistic rule, as distinct from constitutional rule – the rule of law; and the third paternalistic rule, rather than accountable rule. We might say that in the republican tradition the mixture of the mixed constitution is meant to ensure impartial rule, the constitutionalism of the mixed constitution to ensure constitutional rule, and the contestatory character of the citizenry to ensure accountable rule.
[3] Eric Nelson (2004) has identified a Greek tradition in later republican thought that coexisted with the neo-Roman tradition in which I am interested. I do not give attention to this tradition here.
[4] For a vigorous and impressive argument that Machiavelli gave the contestatory element such emphasis that he should be seen as a distinctive figure in the tradition – a radical democrat rather than an aristocratic republican – see McCormick (2011). Chapter 6 of that book takes me to task for not being more Machiavellian in that sense and I hope that the current work may help to counter its depiction of the republicanism I espouse as being aristocratic in character.

that emerged in the thought of defenders such as James Harrington, John Milton and Algernon Sidney became a staple of political thought in eighteenth-century Britain and America, albeit often adapted to make room for a constitutional monarchy (Raab 1965). And they were incorporated deeply, if not always overtly, into the enormously influential work of the Baron de Montesquieu (1989) on *The Spirit of the Laws*. However differently interpreted or applied, the ideas were more or less common property to the Whig establishment in eighteenth-century Britain; to their Tory opposition, at least as that was formulated by the 1st Viscount Bolingbroke (Skinner 1974); to radical Whigs who were a constant sting in the side of every establishment (Robbins 1959); and, of course, to the American colonists, and their British apologists, who came to feel that the Westminster Parliament ruled its colonies in a manner that betrayed the 'commonwealthman' or republican heritage (Bailyn 1967; Reid 1988; Sellers 1995). Republican ideas provided the framework for the arguments made in support of the cause of American independence over the 1760s and 1770s – including arguments made by contemporary English supporters such as Richard Price (1991) and Joseph Priestley (1993) – and for the arguments put forward in the constitutional debates of the 1780s between federalists and anti-federalists (Madison, Hamilton and Jay 1987; Ketcham 2003).

Amongst the three ideas associated with the republican tradition, the conception of freedom as non-domination is the most distinctive. If you are to enjoy freedom as non-domination in certain choices, so the idea went, then you must not be subject to the will of others in how you make those choices; you must not suffer *dominatio*, in the word established in Roman republican usage (Lovett 2010: Appendix 1). That means that you must not be exposed to a power of interference on the part of any others, even if they happen to like you and do not exercise that power against you. The mere fact that I can interfere at little cost in your choices – the mere fact that I can track those choices and intervene when I like – means that you depend for your ability to choose as you wish on my will remaining a goodwill. You are not *sui juris* – or not 'your own person' – in the expression from Roman law. You are unfree, as the eighteenth-century republican Richard Price (1991: 26) explained, because your access to the options will depend on an 'indulgence' or an 'accidental mildness' on my part. To quote from a seventeenth-century republican, Algernon Sidney (1990: 17, 304), freedom in this tradition requires 'independency upon the will of another' – an 'exemption from dominion' in relations with others. In an equivalent slogan from a popular eighteenth-century tract, 'Liberty is, to live upon one's own terms; slavery is, to live at the mere mercy of another' (Trenchard and Gordon 1971: II, 249–50).

In arguing that the state should be concerned in the first place with the equal freedom of its citizens, republicans held that citizens should each be assured of enjoying non-domination in a sphere of choice that came to be described as that of the fundamental or basic liberties (Libourne 1646; Pettit 2008a). This might be identified, in contemporary terms, with the sphere of choice required for being able to function in the local society (see Sen 1985; Nussbaum 2006). They thought that a state organized under a mixed constitution, and disciplined by a contestatory citizenry, was the best hope of promoting this ideal.

The citizenry was traditionally restricted to mainstream, usually pro-pertied, males and, under the republican vision, a citizen would be a *liber*, or a 'free-man', insofar as he enjoyed sufficient power and protection in the sphere of the basic liberties to be able to walk tall amongst others and look any in the eye without reason for fear or deference. John Milton (1953–82: VIII, 424–5) captured the idea nicely in arguing that, in a 'free Commonwealth', 'they who are greatest . . . are not elevated above their brethren; live soberly in their families, walk the streets as other men, may be spoken to freely, familiarly, friendly, without adoration'. In the vision of contemporary republicans, this ideal ought to be extended to an inclusive citizenry; freedom as non-domination ought to be secured for all more or less permanent residents, independently of gender or property or religion.

THE LIBERAL OPPOSITION

These remarks constitute the broadest of brush strokes but the pattern that they project on to the intellectual and institutional swirl of political history is not a capricious imposition; it is not like the figures that we may think we see in the snow, or the clouds, or the stars. The Italian–Atlantic tradition that we have been describing constitutes a firm reality that endured across classical, medieval and modern times (Pocock 1975). The best sign of its independent importance is that the set of ideas described constituted a vivid and salient target of attack for those who espoused a rival way of thinking about liberty – a way of thinking that eventually gave rise to classical liberalism – in the later eighteenth century. The main figures here were utilitarian thinkers like Jeremy Bentham and William Paley (Pettit 1997c: Chapter 1).[5]

---

[5] For a somewhat divergent reading see Kalyvas and Katznelson (2008).

Hobbes had already set himself against the republican way of thinking about freedom in the 1640s, offering a somewhat complex alternative – though not one that had a lasting influence – in its place (Pettit 2008c: Chapter 8; Skinner 2008b). Without explicitly drawing on that earlier precedent, Bentham reported in the 1770s 'a kind of discovery I had made, that the idea of liberty, imported nothing in it that was positive: that it was merely a negative one: and ... accordingly I defined it "the absence of restraint"' (Long 1977: 54). On this definition you are free in a given choice just insofar as others do not restrain the selection of any option: not the option you actually prefer, for sure, but also – at least on what came to be the standard reading (Berlin 1969: xxxix; Pettit 2011b) – not any option you might have preferred but didn't. This conception makes the absence of actual interference on the part of others enough for the freedom of a choice; it does not require the absence of a power of interference on their part. Even though you avoid interference only because of my being good-willed and indulgent, then – even though you can choose as you wish only because I permit it – still, on this new approach, that is enough to make you free.

Bentham and Paley and their ilk were reformers, committed to having the state cater for the freedom – and more generally for the utility or happiness – of the whole population, not just the freedom of mainstream, propertied males that government had traditionally protected. So why would they have weakened the ideal of freedom so that it is not compromised by having to live under the power of another, only by active interference? My own hunch is that it was more realistic to argue for universal freedom if freedom was something that a wife could enjoy at the hands of a kind husband, a worker under the rule of a tolerant employer – in other words, if it was an ideal that, unlike universal freedom as non-domination, did not require redressing the power imbalances allowed under contemporary family and master–servant law (Pettit 1997b: Chapter 1). It may be for this reason that Paley (2002: 315) described freedom in broadly the republican sense – an idea that 'places liberty in security', in accord with 'common discourse' (313) – as one of those versions of 'civil freedom' that are 'unattainable in experience, inflame expectations that can never be gratified, and disturb the public content with complaints, which no wisdom or benevolence of government can remove'.

The rejection of freedom as non-domination raised a question about the linked ideas of a mixed constitution and a contestatory citizenry. Those devices were required on the traditional, republican way of viewing things because they were supposed to ensure that when the republic makes laws that protect its citizens against private domination, it does not impose those laws in a publicly dominating manner. The idea was that if the interference imposed by the state is not under the control of any single agency, as the mixed constitution more or less guarantees, and if it is itself subject to the control of those on whom it is imposed, as a contestatory citizenry would ideally ensure, then it will not be dominating. It will not involve subjecting people to the unchecked will of a distinct, independent agent. It will be a non-dominating – or, as it was often called, a non-arbitrary – form of interference.

Once freedom came to be construed as non-interference, however, it was no longer clear why such constraints were necessary. Every system of law coerces and penalizes its subjects – and every system of law presup-poses taxation – so that there is no law without interference. If freedom means non-interference, therefore, then there is no freedom-based requirement to make the interference non-dominating, as the mixed constitution and the contestatory citizenry promised to do. The best system will be that in which there is the least overall interference, public or private. And it may just be that the best system is one in which a benevolent despot coerces people so that they don't interfere with one another, yet keeps the coercion it perpetrates to a minimum. William Paley (2002: 314), surely Bentham's most clear-headed associate, embraced the point when he noted as early as 1785 that the cause of liberty as non-interference might be as well served, in some circumstances, by 'the edicts of a despotic prince, as by the resolutions of a popular assem-bly'. In such conditions, he said, 'would an absolute form of government be no less free than the purest democracy' – and, by his lights, no less free than the most classical republic.

While Bentham and Paley were mainly interested in advancing the utilitarian programme, they shaped the way in which early nineteenth-century liberals thought about freedom and the requirements of freedom. We might define liberalism – somewhat tendentiously, in view of the many meanings given to the term – as any approach to government that makes freedom as non-interference paramount or central. And in that sense it contrasts quite sharply with the republican approach in which freedom as non-domination plays the central role. Liberalism in this sense may be right-of-centre, as classical liberals or libertarians generally were, making freedom as non-interference into the only concern of government. Or it may be left-of-centre, making freedom as non-interference into just one of government's goals: perhaps a goal derived from the broader concern with happiness, as in the case of utilitarians; perhaps a goal that is paired with a separate concern like equality, as in the case of John Rawls (1971, 1993, 2001), Ronald Dworkin (1978, 1986) and other egalitarians.[6]

No matter which form liberalism takes, it contrasts with republicanism on how to understand freedom, a value to which each approach gives a prominent place. On the republican construal, the real enemy of freedom is the power that some people may have over others, whereas on the liberal understanding, asymmetries in interpersonal power are not in themselves objectionable. Right-of-centre liberalism is happy to tolerate such imbalances, so long as active interference is avoided. And left-of-centre liberalism rejects them only insofar as they have unwelcome effects on equality or welfare or whatever other value is invoked to supplement the ideal of freedom.

Although there is a deep difference between the guiding ideals of the approaches, the conflict between republicanism and liberalism should not be overdrawn. For while Paley and others had seen that freedom as non-interference does not strictly require a mixed constitution or a contestatory citizenry, almost every form of liberalism has endorsed the main elements in the idea of the mixed constitution and given some recognition to the contestatory role of citizens.[7] Liberal ideals like the rule of law, the separation of powers, and the liberties of speech and expression are reflections of such earlier institutional ideals. Republicanism differs from liberalism in espousing a more radical ideal of freedom, in arguing for a distinctive connection between freedom in that sense and its twin institutional ideals, and in giving a distinctive interpretation of those ideals, particularly that of a contestatory citizenry. But nonetheless there are definite, discernible continuities between the traditions.[8]

In the late eighteenth century the republican tradition was opposed, not just by the emerging liberal approach to politics, but also by a tradition that

---

[6] A further distinction within liberal doctrines in this sense is that between those in which freedom is taken as a goal – I think, as indicated at the end of Chapter 1, that freedom as non-domination should be taken in this way (Pettit 1997c: Chapter 3) – and those in which the rights associated with freedom are taken in non-consequentialist form as side-constraints; the best example of the latter approach is Nozick (1974). For a discussion of consequentialist and non-consequentialist approaches in political philosophy, see Pettit (2001d, 2012a).

[7] Indeed Paley (2002: 331) himself embraced the 'combination of the three regular species of government' that he claimed to find in England in the 1780s.

[8] There might be some merit, for this reason, in adopting Richard Dagger's (1997) usage and speaking of the approach defended here – which resembles Dagger's own – as republican liberalism or liberal republicanism.

originates with Jean Jacques Rousseau. I describe this approach as communitarian, for reasons that will become clear shortly, though it is often described as republican; it represents a broadly Continental form of republicanism, as distinct from the Italian–Atlantic tradition that I have been characterizing.[9]

It is easy to mistake the two versions of republicanism, for as liberalism came to displace traditional republicanism as the main ideology of the English-speaking world, the name 'republicanism' came to designate the new Rousseauvian doctrine. It is primarily with the Continental, communitarian version of the doctrine, rather than the Italian–Atlantic tradition, that critics of liberalism like Hannah Arendt (1958, 1973) and Michael Sandel (1996) seem to identify, for example.[10] It is this version of republicanism that is rejected, along with liberalism, in the work of Juergen Habermas (1994, 1995).[11] And it is this doctrine that self-described liberals often focus on in arguing for the merits of their own approach (Brennan and Lomasky 2006).

Rousseau espoused a version of freedom as non-domination or non-dependency, giving it pride of place in the concerns of the state. He says that if people are to be free, each must be 'perfectly independent of all the others' (Rousseau 1997: 11.2.2). And he maintains that that 'which ought to be the end of every system of legislation is ... freedom and equality', where freedom is understood in the sense of non-dependency and equality is valued 'because freedom cannot subsist without it' (Rousseau 1997: 11.11.1). But while he remained faithful to Italian–Atlantic republicanism in this respect, he broke dramatically with it in arguing against the mixed constitution and the contestatory image of the citizenry.

Rousseau rejects the idea of the mixed constitution under the lead of absolutists like Jean Bodin (1967) in the sixteenth century, and Thomas Hobbes (1994a, 1994b, 1998) in the seventeenth.[12] He accepted their argument that every state has to have a single, absolute sovereign, individual or corporate, and that no such agency can operate, as envisaged in the mixed

---

[9] For a fuller discussion of this communitarian form of republicanism, with reference to Kant as well as Rousseau, see Pettit (2012b).

[10] In discussing this conception of the republic in earlier work, in particular the conception as it appears in Sandel, I have sometimes described it as neo-Athenian (Pettit 1998). I regret that usage now, since as a matter of history – if not in later representations, which were deeply influenced by Polybius – Athens had many of the characteristics of a mixed constitution; it was not a city ruled by an assembly with Rousseauvian powers. See Hansen (1991), and for a summary account that emphasizes this mixture see Chapter 2 of Dowlen (2008).

[11] For the record, I think that Habermas's own views come close to republican views, as I conceptualize and defend them.

[12] For a wonderful overview of the French tradition in the background of Rousseau's thinking see Keohane (1980).

constitution, on the basis of coordination between different, mutually checking centres of power. Hobbes had argued that the mixed constitution supports 'not one independent commonwealth, but three independent factions; nor one representative person, but three' (Hobbes 1994b: 29.16. See too 1998: 7.4, 1994a: 20.15). Rousseau strikes a similar note of derision in attacking the champions of this centrepiece of republican thought: 'they turn the Sovereign into a being that is fantastical and formed of disparate parts; it is as if they were putting together man out of several bodies one of which had eyes, another arms, another feet, and nothing else' (1997: 11.2.2).

Bodin and Hobbes had argued that the sovereign could be a monarch, which was their own favourite candidate, an aristocratic committee, or a committee-of-the-whole. But they allowed that such a sovereign might delegate much of the work of government to another agency. Rousseau held that only a unanimously endorsed committee-of-the-whole could serve in the sovereign role, on the grounds that an aristocracy or a monarchy would impose an alien will on people (1997: 1.4.4). And he argued that while the members of the sovereign assembly have to rely on majority voting in order to make their decisions (iv.2.7), they should deliberate and vote, at least in the ideal, on the basis of the common interest. Only if the members act in that way, he thought, can the assembly claim to be enacting a general will in which all figure as equal objects of concern. The members of Rousseau's assembly are to think as citizens, focused impartially on their common interest, and they are to vote for any measure they support, not out of personal or factional motives, but on the impersonal, deliberative basis that 'it is advantageous to the State ... that this or that opinion pass' (iv.1.6).[13]

How is this impartiality likely to be achieved? Rousseau thinks that insofar as the people in assembly have to decide only on matters of general law – and not on administrative or adjudicative measures involving individuals (1997: 111.17.5) – they will operate under a veil of abstraction that keeps personal or factional concerns out of the picture. They will consider 'the subjects in a body and their actions in the abstract, never any man as an individual or a particular action' (Rousseau 1997: 11.6.6). And so they will tend to be moved, he hopes, not by particularistic motives, but by an impartial, egalitarian concern 'with their common preservation, and the general welfare' (Rousseau 1997: iv.1.1). They will form their minds and cast

---

[13] On this reading of Rousseau, the common good is not defined procedurally as whatever good is supported by suitably motivated majority voting; rather it is the good that suitably motivated majority voting might be expected to track. See Cohen (2010).

their votes on the basis of open deliberation and debate about the requirements of the common good.[14]

Rousseau betrayed the earlier tradition of republicanism in this conception of popular sovereignty. In his idealized republic, individuals are confronted by the single powerful presence of 'the public person', which 'formerly assumed the name *City* and now assumes that of *Republic* or *body politic*' (1997: 1.6.10). While he envisages an ideal under which people are independent of one another as private persons, in line with the republican conception of freedom, he thinks that this mutual independence is attainable only at the cost of a form of submission to the public person – specifically, to the general or corporate will of the public person – that would have been wholly at odds with Italian–Atlantic sentiments. While every citizen should 'be perfectly independent of all the others', he says, this is only going to be possible insofar as each is 'excessively dependent on the City' (Rousseau 1997: 11.12.3). The totally novel, consciously outrageous assumption Rousseau introduces is that 'each, by giving himself to all, gives himself to no one' (1997: 1.6.8).

The rejection of the mixed constitution in favour of a popular, majoritarian sovereign led Rousseau to reject also the contestatory role that was given to citizens under traditional republicanism. Following Bodin and Hobbes he emphasizes that the sovereign assembly of the people has to have absolute power and not be subject to interrogation by citizens, at least when they speak outside the assembly on the basis of their rights as individuals. Hobbes (1994b: 18.4) had said if subjects could 'pretend a breach of the covenant made by the sovereign . . . there is in this case no judge to decide the controversy'. And in the same vein, Rousseau claims that 'if individuals were left some rights . . . there would be no common power who might adjudicate between them and the public' (1997: 1.6.7). The idea is that there has to be one, final, spokesperson on what the law is and that if the people could individually contest the legislature's decisions outside the assembly, there would have to be another body to rule between them. Once the legislative assembly has spoken, according to this picture, it falls to individuals to comply, not complain.[15] Citizens are no longer invigilators of government, alert to any possible

---

[14] Rousseau makes some remarks that seem to cast doubt on the value of public deliberation, but in general, as Joshua Cohen (2010: 75–7, 171–2) argues, he clearly expects deliberation to have a major role in the proceedings of the assembly.

[15] But how, Rousseau asks, 'are the opponents both free and subject to laws to which they have not consented'? His response is 'that the question is badly framed. The citizen consents to all the laws, even to those passed in spite of him, and even to those that punish him when he dares to violate any of them' (IV.2.8).

misdoing and ready to challenge and contest the legislative, executive and judicial authorities. They are law-makers, not law-checkers, generators of law, not testers of law. They serve in the production of public decisions, not in controlling for the quality of decisions proposed or made.

This viewpoint is deeply opposed to accepted republican doctrine and in adopting it Rousseau is moved by a thought first floated by that great enemy of the doctrine, Thomas Hobbes (1994b: 18.6). This is the idea that no law supported by the general impartial will 'can be unjust, since no man can be unjust towards himself' (Rousseau 1997: 11.6.7). Far from every law being a fair target for civic critique and challenge, each comes draped in an authority and majesty that brooks no individual opposition. Having been party to the creation of the popular sovereign no one as an individual retains the right of contesting the decisions of the collectivity, even if those decisions are ones that the person argued against in assembly. In an extraordinary reversal of received ideas, the cause of freedom as non-domination, from which Rousseau starts, is now linked with a new, communitarian form of the very absolutism that republican doctrine had always challenged. The people or community gets to be sacralized, as it assumes the role of the popular, incontestable sovereign, incapable of doing wrong to its own members.

While Rousseau's wider theory is deeply at odds with Italian–Atlantic republicanism, however – and while, as I believe, it is normatively unattractive – it has one powerfully appealing element. This is his ideal of a deliberative assembly in which everyone is able to speak and vote on an equal basis, and yet is required to speak and vote on the basis of a concern with the common good.[16] Elaborated influentially in the work of Juergen Habermas (1984–9, 1994, 1995), the constraint requires participants in a deliberative assembly to argue for their different proposals on the basis of 'reasons that are persuasive to all who are committed to acting on the results of a free and reasoned assessment of alternatives by equals' (Cohen 1989: 23). Such considerations will include general reasons to do with what promises more peace or order or prosperity for the society as a whole. But they can also include reasons

---

[16] While Rousseau does not address the issue of how precisely the parties should deliberate with one another, his insistence on their abstracting from personal and factional considerations can be taken to mandate something like this constraint. In any case, the constraint ought to be congenial from a Rousseauvian point of view. Setting it up as a formal requirement would serve as a defence against the intrusion of personal and factional concerns in the decisions of the assembly. If the participants are explicitly required to seek out mutually acceptable reasons in support of their proposals, that in itself may serve to elicit an attachment to the viewpoint of the public (Elster 1986). And once it is salient to everyone that everyone is expected to do this, it may become shameful for participants to display concerns of a more personal or factional character (Brennan and Pettit 2004). The topic is central to the discussion in Chapter 5.

put forward on behalf of a particular subgroup or individual. The consideration in this case will not be just that the subgroup or individual is unsatisfied, as if all others should be moved by that thought, but that the group or individual suffers a disadvantage to which – purportedly by general criteria that are endorsed across the society – no one should be exposed.

This deliberative constraint will play a role in our later discussions and, to that extent, the position taken in this book has Rousseauvian linkages. But the point I want to emphasize here is that the communitarian vision he sponsored is nonetheless hostile to the central tenets of Italian–Atlantic republicanism. Rousseau himself remained faithful to that tradition in his continuing to embrace something like the ideal of equal freedom as non-domination. But even this connection was broken amongst those who identified with his vision in later generations. As his ideas washed around political circles, this last vestige of republican thought was swept away in the flood. It became natural to think, in a vulgarization of Rousseau's own analysis (Spitz 1995), that freedom is nothing more or less than the possession or exercise of the right to participate in popular decision-making.

Benjamin Constant was probably the major figure in accomplishing this final step, although he did so as a critic, not a defender. Himself attracted to what was seen as a brand of liberalism – although one that in many respects kept close to the older republicanism – he gave a famous lecture in 1819 that described the supposedly ancient way of thinking about politics and freedom with which the liberal view has to compete (Constant 1988). According to this ancient way of thinking, he says, the people in a commonwealth constitute the sovereign, the role of citizens is to participate as officials or electors in sovereign decision-making and – this is the alteration from the strict Rousseauvian picture – freedom consists in nothing more or less than the right to participate in such communal self-determination: the right to live under a regime of law that you have a certain participatory or electoral role in creating.[17]

With this twist, Rousseau became associated with a set of ideas that contrasts in every dimension with the Italian–Atlantic tradition. This new ideology replaced freedom as non-domination with freedom as participation. It replaced the institutional ideal of the mixed constitution with that of a popular, absolutely sovereign assembly. And it replaced the ideal of a contestatory people with that of a participatory legislature against which

---

[17] Yiftah Elazar has persuaded me that while the eighteenth-century thinker, Richard Price (1991), preserves other aspects of the Italian–Atlantic tradition, he had also begun to emphasize this self-legislative theme.

individuals had no rights in their own name. This broadly communitarian family of ideas assumed many different forms, for example in Kant's political philosophy (Pettit 2012b), as it became associated with the nation-state rather than a city-state like Rousseau's Geneva, as the body of citizens proper was taken to be less inclusive than Rousseau imagined and, in a final departure, as participation was allowed to become electoral rather than legislative in character. But no matter what form it assumed, the approach remained decidedly at odds with the Italian–Atlantic tradition from which it had sprung.

The contrast between the approaches shows up nicely in their different images of the free person or citizen. The free-man in the Italian–Atlantic tradition, the *liber* of Roman thought, was someone who lived in his own domain – the masculine form fits with the habits of the time – on terms that he himself set. Within that domain he lived *sui juris*, as it was put in Roman law, 'under his own jurisdiction'. He did not operate *in potestate domini*, 'in the power of a master', and he did not have to make his choices *cum permissu*, 'with permission'. He could act without fear or deference, being protected and empowered in relation to others, and even in relation to the very law that helped establish his position.[18]

The tradition emphasized, of course, that no one can expect to enjoy this status outside a community in which citizens are powerful and vigilant enough to keep tabs and impose checks on government. It is because they 'attain unto liberty' on the basis of such political engagement, as James Harrington (1992: 75) puts it in the seventeenth century, that free citizens are 'able to live of themselves'. But while the status of the free person can exist only in the presence of such public virtue, it consists, according to this way of thinking, in the enjoyment of equal freedom as non-domination across a range of significant, personal choices: the fundamental or basic liberties. These choices have to be available in common to all citizens, and available on the common basis of a protective and empowering law and culture.

---

[18] Although self-described liberals do not ordinarily emphasize the need for contestatory virtue, they do often endorse this ideal of the free person, preserving a deep commonality with Italian–Atlantic republicanism. Isaiah Berlin (1969: lx) embraces the ideal when he says that freedom requires 'an area ... in which one is one's own master'; a domain where one 'is not obliged to account for his activities to any man so far as this is compatible with the existence of organized society'. This domain is to constitute 'a certain minimum area of personal freedom which must on no account be violated' (Berlin 1969: 123). It is not clear how you can be your own master without enjoying non-domination; to enjoy non-interference by grace of just the goodwill of another would seem to leave you well short of the independence required (Pettit 2011b). But putting that problem aside, it is clear that on this issue republicanism and liberalism may often converge.

The image of the free person assumes a different cast in the Rousseauvian tradition. According to the new, communitarian, way of thinking, the free person is the active political figure whose highest fulfilment consists in participating with others, at whatever level of community, in activities of shared deliberation and decision-making. In Hannah Arendt's (1958) favourite phrase, it is the citizen who embraces the *vita activa* rather than the *vita contemplativa* – the active rather than the contemplative life – and in particular an active life in the realm of public affairs. This rather romantic picture of the tirelessly engaged public figure stands in stark opposition to the image of the free-man in older republican thought, though it may echo the emphasis on the need for a contestatory citizenry. Whereas Italian–Atlantic thought hails the enjoyment of a publicly protected freedom in the domain of private life – a freedom, in the republican picture, that enables you to stand equal with others, not depending on anyone's grace or favour – this new vision tends to downplay private life in favour of public engagement.

BUILDING PHILOSOPHICALLY ON REPUBLICAN HISTORY

As already mentioned, this book joins a growing body of literature in seeking to build a contemporary political philosophy with ideas drawn from the Italian–Atlantic tradition (for an overview see Lovett and Pettit 2009). The main idea employed in the construction is that of freedom as non-domination, which is more fully explicated in the first chapter. But the ideas of a mixed constitution and a contestatory citizenry also play a role, as we shall see, at various stages in the unfolding argument.

Two of the three main topics addressed in normative political theory have already been introduced: social justice in the relations amongst the citizens of a state; and political legitimacy in the relations between the state and its citizens. The third topic, which is not addressed in this book, is the sovereignty that ought to be available to each of the different peoples that states ideally represent.[19] Republican political theory, understood as an approach built around the ideas reviewed here, offers a distinctive approach on all three fronts (Pettit 2013).

The republican theory of social justice would argue that the state should establish equal non-domination for its citizens in relation to one another. The republican theory of political legitimacy would argue that in the course of providing for them in this way the state ought not to dominate its

---

[19] This description of the ideals may not appeal to all. Other accounts would cast them as ideals of social justice, political justice and international justice.

citizens. And the republican theory of global sovereignty would argue that the state ought to help establish an international order under which it and its people are not dominated from without, whether by other states or by multinational organizations (see Pettit 2010a, 2010c). In a slogan, the state ought to be an internationally undominated, domestically undominating defender of its citizens' freedom as non-domination. In this book I shall be looking in outline at the republican theory of social justice and in greater detail at the republican theory of political legitimacy or, as it turns out to be, the republican theory of democracy. But I shall have little or nothing to say on the republican theory of international sovereignty.

Since the theory presented in the book is primarily philosophical in character, it may seem surprising that I should link it closely with a historical tradition, commenting at various points on the positions maintained by the champions and the critics of that tradition. After all, the fashion in most contemporary philosophical work is to emulate the sciences and cut free from the baggage of history. So why emphasize the traditional provenance of the ideas developed within the theory?

I try to sustain the historical linkage for a number of reasons. Construing the ideal of freedom in terms of non-domination is likely to be more widely acceptable if the construal can be given historical credentials, particularly credentials in the work of writers admired on all sides of politics. Building a political philosophy out of the demands of such an ideal in the context of a contemporary, inclusive, society is likely to be more persuasive if the enterprise can be linked with similar enterprises by other thinkers in other times. And, more generally, the existence of a historical pedigree for an approach taken in political philosophy is bound to give the approach more intellectual plausibility. How likely is it, after all, that any one of us would discover afresh a wholly novel ideal for political life?

While the tradition within which I pursue political philosophy is important to me, however, the philosophical use of historical ideas should not be mistaken for the proper historical investigation of those ideas and of the context in which they arose. I think of what I am doing as interacting with intellectual history by drawing on the work of experts in the area and sometimes challenging them with philosophically motivated hypotheses as to what was in the minds of their subjects. I do not think of the exercise as history proper, or even history improper.[20]

---

[20] The closest I have come to doing intellectual history is in my work on Hobbes's theory of language, thought and politics (Pettit 2008c). But even there I think of what I do as proposing a reading or

REFLECTIVE EQUILIBRIUM

The normative claims defended in the book should not be judged by historical criteria, therefore, but rather by philosophical. The philosophical methodology I follow is that which John Rawls (1971) described as reflective equilibrium. The idea is to set out general principles for the domain investigated, whether it be justice or legitimacy or sovereignty; to use empirical assumptions to derive their implications for specific cases; to see how those implications fit with what we find credible on reflection; and to go back and forth in the search for adjustments at either end that can promote overall coherence.

The methodology is even relevant to the interpretation of freedom as non-domination. I do not suppose that this is the only conception of freedom in common usage, as Chapter 1 should make clear (on different conceptions, see Schmidtz and Brennan 2010). My claim rather is that this way of thinking about freedom has serious payoffs in normative thought. It enables us to develop theories of social justice, political legitimacy and international sovereignty that stand up well to the tests that reflective equilibrium would support.[21]

This point is worth emphasizing because ordinary talk of freedom offers us a network of flexible and, it may often seem, wayward idioms. We say that if you can't enact a certain option then it's not a matter of your free choice. And yet we also say that you may be free to do something – say, go and vote – even when you are confined to bed and cannot get to the polling station. We say

---

hypothesis – that Hobbes was the first to think of language as an invention that transformed the nature of its inventors – that others are better qualified to test. That also is how I think of the idea, as it was formulated for example in Pettit (1996a, 1997c), that the main figures in the republican tradition conceptualize freedom as non-domination; that idea was stimulated, of course, by the work of Quentin Skinner, though it gave a somewhat different twist to what he had been saying (Pettit 2002b).

[21] When we follow the method of reflective equilibrium, I assume that we share general ideas about the nature of values like freedom, justice and legitimacy – the ideas come to us as connotations of the terms – and that a normative theory should try to respect these in the interpretation of what the values demand. I also assume that an overall normative theory will force us to weight these values against each other and to try to reconcile their rival demands. And I assume, finally, that the demands of values in this or that context – the demands of freedom-in-the-face-of-power, for example, or the demands of justice-in-the-face-of-reasonable-disagreement – do not have to be derived from the pure or abstract theory of freedom or justice, whatever that might be. I hope that in good part these assumptions will be justified, *arguendo*, by the role they play in my argument. The first two assumptions put me at loggerheads with the 'more ambitious and hazardous' holism that Ronald Dworkin (2011: 263) supports, under which the demands of all values whatsoever are to be construed, so that there are 'no genuine conflicts' (119) between them. For critical remarks on Dworkin's methodology see Pettit (2011a). The third assumption puts me at a distance from G. A. Cohen's (2008) foundationalist claim that the demands of justice under a contingent condition like reasonable disagreement are to be derived from their demands in abstraction from any such contingent fact. For a critique see Larmore (2012).

that even if something is not permitted, you may still have the freedom to choose it. And yet we also say that you do not have the freedom to act in a certain way – say, steal someone's property – because it is forbidden. We say that you may do something freely even if other options, unbeknownst to you, are all closed. And yet we also say that you do not enjoy freedom in a certain choice if there is only one alternative available: if, in effect, you are forced to take that particular path. We say that you have a free choice between two alternatives in a certain domain if those in charge there leave the decision up to you. And yet we also say that you do not enjoy freedom in a choice if you can make the decision only because others give you permission.

This variety of usage should not suggest that freedom-related words and idioms are unconstrained and that like Humpty Dumpty we can make them mean what we like. Describing a choice or action as free is always meant to mark a contrast with some other choice or action. But one and the same act may count as free in relation to one contrast and unfree in relation to another. And so, as different contexts put different contrasts in play, we may find ourselves ascribing freedom in the one case, unfreedom in the other. Take the example where you are confined to bed on election day. By contrast with another citizen who is not confined in that manner, you are not free to vote. But by contrast with a non-citizen it remains perfectly sensible to say that you are indeed free to vote. The predication of freedom is a useful way of marking a contrast in each case, yet the contrast it marks differs from one case to the other. And so we find ourselves saying what appear to be contradictory things when, as a matter of fact, they are perfectly consistent.

These observations about the idioms of freedom mean that if we are to build a political theory around the idea of freedom, then we have to regiment things a little and rule on exactly how we are using the term and its cognates. That is precisely what I do in Chapter 1, setting out the regimented, republican understanding of freedom with which I shall be working. While the regimentation builds on connotations of freedom that are recognized in ordinary talk – otherwise it would not count as a theory of freedom – the final case for preferring it to alternatives shows up in its capacity to underpin an independently attractive theory of justice, democracy and indeed sovereignty.

THE EMERGING VIEW OF DEMOCRACY

As already advertised, I offer a characterization of freedom as non-domination in the first chapter, introducing a range of clarifications prompted by various critics. I sketch a republican theory of social justice in the second chapter, showing what would be broadly required for the members of a society to enjoy equal freedom as non-domination in relation to one another. And that then sets the scene for asking after what might ensure that the state which supports its people's equal enjoyment of freedom as non-domination is not itself dominating – in other words, is a politically legitimate, freedom-respecting entity.

My analysis of the requirements for such legitimacy gives us a theory of democracy in the sense of a job specification for democratic institutions. According to that theory, a state will be legitimate just insofar as it gives each citizen an equal share in a system of popular control over government – that is, a democratic system in which the *demos*, or 'people', enjoy *kratos*, or 'power'. Chapter 3 outlines that theory, arguing that a system of equally shared control over government requires that people should enjoy a suitable form of equally accessible influence and that this influence should move the state in a direction that people find equally acceptable. And then the following two chapters develop a model of how this theory might be satisfied, giving a sketch of the sorts of institutions that would meet the job specification. Chapter 4 looks at the system of popular influence that might serve in the required role and Chapter 5 at how it might impose a suitable direction on the state and constitute a system of popular control. The book ends with a conclusion in which I offer a summary of the main propositions defended; this is meant to make it easier to use a volume that is longer and sometimes more complex than I would have wished.

The view of democracy that emerges from this argument is marked by three sharp contrasts with positions maintained in the current literature. It conflicts, first of all, with the approach of those like Paley who think that democracy has little or nothing to do with freedom. Amongst contemporary theorists, that viewpoint is well represented by Isaiah Berlin (1969: 7) when he says that 'there is no necessary connection between individual liberty and democratic rule' (see too Berlin 1969: 130–1). Against this point of view, I argue that if we start from the republican conception of freedom as non-domination, then we can derive the need for democracy, under a suitable characterization, from the requirements of freedom. That conception of freedom makes it clear that when people live under a government they do not control, then they live in unfreedom.

The view defended in the book contrasts, secondly, with the view of democracy that has become more or less standard in political science, under the impact of the Austrian–American economist and social theorist, Joseph Schumpeter. In his discussion of democracy in *Capitalism, Socialism and Democracy*, first published in 1942, Schumpeter (1984: 272) argued that democracy does not enable the people to 'control their political leaders' and that it merely serves to give them a potentially wayward form of influence that need not impose any controlling direction. I argue by contrast that while a system of non-directive influence might do a little to protect citizens – it would guard against dynastic regimes – it would not enable them to enjoy freedom as non-domination in their relationship with government. Democracy has to promote popular control, and it has to put in place the institutions that such control requires, if it is to serve the cause of freedom as non-domination.

The thesis defended in the fourth and fifth chapters, as I mentioned earlier, is that democracy can provide for such control by mobilizing a dual process. It has to provide for people's electoral and contestatory influence over who is in power, what processes of decision-making they follow, and what actual decisions they make. And it has to shape that short-haul influence so that over the longer haul it forces those in power to conform to widely shared norms in selecting the processes they follow and in determining the policies they adopt. This popular control may leave a good deal of discretion to the authorities within the state but it will only do so when such discretion does not entail domination.

The third big contrast that marks out the view of democracy defended here is with the very common assumption that democratic institutions are more or less exclusively majoritarian and electoral and that they operate in essential conflict with institutions that give constitutional protection to certain rights, authorizing the judiciary – or some other unelected body – to override legislation. While this distinction between democracy and constitutionalism is widely maintained, it is often linked with William Riker (1982), who argues that democratic populism has to be tempered with a constitutional liberalism. I maintain against this sort of view that the institutions required to give people control over government are likely to include many of those associated with constitutional protection. There is no need for the dichotomy that many current thinkers accept between the two institutional forms.[22]

Any plausible model of the form that democracy ought to take is bound to support many of the institutions that are actually in place in existing democracies. But no model will have normative bite unless it can be used as a base for arguing for reform. I hope it will be clear by the end of the book that the republican theory on offer here has a critical, reformist edge and is not designed merely to vindicate democracy as we know it. While it

---

[22] For other views on which democracy requires a degree of constitutional protection see Cohen (1989); Habermas (1995); Holmes (1995). For concerns about the extent to which any degree of constitutional protection can hamper democratic initiative, see Schwartzberg (2007) and Tully (2009). And for an outright defence of the adequacy of electoral, majoritarian democracy see Waldron (1999a, 1999b).

supports constitutional as well as electoral measures, then there is no reason why it should support the precise sorts of institutions that characterize extant regimes. Which precise measures it should support in any area will be determined by empirical considerations, as well as the more abstract, philosophical arguments advanced here; that is in the nature of institutional design. But even the broad-brush strokes offered by way of sketching possible institutional designs should make it absolutely clear that the agenda supported by the republican argument is reformist and progressive in its implications.

JUSTICE AND DEMOCRACY

In the course of the argument developed in the book I suggest, without offering any precise guidelines on how to conduct the exercise, that it is possible to use the ideals of republican justice and republican democracy to make judgements on how existing, imperfect, regimes compare in their realization. But one issue I do not address is the relative importance of those ideals. Suppose we had a choice between two regimes, one scoring better on democracy, the other on justice. The question is whether there is any reason in the abstract to be predisposed towards one or the other or whether, depending on context, our answer might go either way.

For the record, my own view is that in general we should prefer the more democratic alternative in any such choice. Freedom as non-domination, whether in the social or political arena, requires not just the absence of interference, as we have seen, but its robust absence: its absence over a range of scenarios in which there are variations in what we ourselves want to do and, crucially, in what others would want us to do. A failure in political legitimacy would compromise the robustness of freedom more deeply than a failure only in social justice. Where a lack of social justice alone would make us vulnerable only to our fellow citizens, a lack of political legitimacy would make us vulnerable on two fronts.

The reason is easy to see. If we are subject to a government that can dominate us, as in an illegitimate regime, then we are going to lack control over changes in that government's will towards us and towards those of our kind. But this lack of political control means that any social controls we enjoy over changes in the will of our fellow citizens towards us are also likely to be somewhat precarious. While the law may put social controls in place, guarding us against private domination, those safeguards will only be as reliable as the will of the government that establishes and maintains them. Let legitimacy fail, therefore – let the government be a law unto itself – and we will be vulnerable both in relation to the state and in relation to our fellow citizens. Public domination has costs that run deeper than those of private domination alone.

I conclude that the republican ideal of freedom as non-domination is bound to put a certain premium on the value of legitimacy and on the democratic control that it requires. Whatever policies the government supports, and whatever policies any one of us wills on government, none should be put in place unless it is implemented under a form of popular control in which we all equally share. That is the only guarantee against the doubly disabling effect of public domination.

Much contemporary political philosophy focuses on the requirements of justice where, bar a few references to the importance of certain political rights, this is more or less tantamount to social justice. From the republican perspective of this book, that is an unfortunate priority. The most important demand we can make on our state is that it should deliver policy under a system of control to which we each have equal access. Recognizing our equal claims as citizens, and our divergent views on political ideals, we should accept that whatever the proposals any one of us makes on public matters, they should only be implemented or maintained under the proviso that, however democracy is institutionally realized, they command democratic support.

This position entails a commitment to democracy that, paradoxically, is not itself subject to that democratic proviso. A society that makes decisions on a democratic basis, with everyone sharing equally in control of government, could in principle decide on a permanent renunciation of democratic rule, denying future generations the right to shape their institutions on an equally shared basis. The population might vote unanimously, to take an extreme example, to deny votes to women. Since such a possibility would be anathema from a republican viewpoint, it follows that we ought to exempt the recommendation to do things democratically, and that recommendation alone, from the democratic proviso. We ought not to recommend that our society should give people an equal share in control of government, provided this proposal is itself democratically endorsed. We ought to recommend that our society should give people an equal share of control, period. This, in Wittgenstein's image, is where the spade turns. This is bedrock.[23]

---

[23] Michael Walzer's (1981) complaint about the way in which philosophers ignore democracy, speaking as if they had the authority of the sage, is fully consistent, I believe, with my viewpoint here. Like him, I allow that most recommendations in normative political theory – all but the commitment to a fallback democracy – are democratically negotiable.

CHAPTER I

Freedom as non-domination

In order to gain a good understanding of the concept of freedom as non-domination it will be useful to focus first on what is required for freedom in one or another choice. As we saw, republicans traditionally concentrated on the freedom of the person, period – the free status of the *liber*, or 'free-man' or citizen – rather than on the freedom of a person's particular choices (Pettit 2007e; Skinner 2008a). But once we know what freedom of choice requires, we can represent people's status freedom as a function of their freedom over a common range of choices, secured on the basis of common norms and laws. We will return to that issue in the next chapter.

A choice is identified by a set of mutually exclusive, jointly exhaustive options, as in the choice you may have between doing X, doing Y and doing Z. The options are available insofar as two conditions hold, one objective, the other cognitive. Objectively, it is true that you can do X, or you can do Y, or you can do Z, and that's it: there is nothing else you can do instead. And this truth registers cognitively: it holds according to your own perceptions of the scenario.[1] Thus if you have a choice between X, Y and Z, then you must understand each of those options under its relevant aspect, as a case of X-ing or Y-ing or Z-ing; realize that you can choose any one of them, taking it under that aspect; and recognize that there is no further alternative. Whether you do X or Y or Z is up to you and you only; you can think truly 'I can do X', 'I can do Y' and 'I can do Z'. It may not be the case that any option chosen is logically guaranteed to materialize as a result of your decision – the letter you

---

[1] The ability or capacity to perform any option may be represented as coming in degrees, depending on how easy the choice of the option is. Or it may be taken to have an on–off character, with the degree of ease being registered at least implicitly in the characterization of the option. On the first approach we would speak of the ability at a certain level of ease, L, to do X; on the second we would speak of the ability in an on–off sense to do X-at-level-of-ease-L. While I avoid addressing this issue explicitly in the current text, I follow broadly the second approach. Thus I argue that imposing an ease-reducing penalty on doing X involves replacing the original option, X, by a different option, penalized-X. Such a replacement may be more or less invasive, as I shall put it, depending on how large the penalty is. I am grateful to Raffi Krut-Landau for a discussion of this point.

mail may not reach its destination because of problems at the post office – but it is enough that as a matter of contingent fact there are no obstacles in the way. Sending a letter to your correspondent is an option for you just to the extent that the world happens to be compliant – there are no postal problems – and success is in your hands.

There is a metaphysical issue about what has to be true of you as an agent in order for it to be true that a choice is up to you: that you can make it the case that the world in a moment from now is an X-world or a Y-world or a Z-world – a world where a letter is on its way to your friend, or a world where it isn't. The question in particular is whether you can play this choice-resolving role and yet be constituted, like every other natural entity, out of physical constituents that conform to physical laws. This is the issue of whether you have metaphysical freedom of will and it falls well outside our concerns here. I shall just assume that you have the power of free will, however that is to be understood, and ask about what social and other factors can impact on your exercise of the power in such a way that, intuitively, they reduce your freedom of choice.[2]

Almost all schools of thought agree that any factor that can reduce your freedom of choice in that sense constitutes a hindrance that makes one or another option unavailable: it removes some of the objective or cognitive resources required for accessing the option, or it restricts your use of those resources; it impairs or impedes the capacity that those resources establish. But there is disagreement on two broad fronts: first, on the issue of what has to be hindered in order for the freedom of a choice to be reduced; and second, on what sorts of hindrances can impose a reduction of freedom. I address the first issue in Section 1 and discuss different aspects of the second issue in the three sections following.

In Section 1 I argue that your freedom of choice will be reduced by a hindrance to any one of the options that characterize it, not just by a hindrance to the option you prefer. In Section 2 I argue that your free choice of an option may be hindered in either of two significantly different ways: one involves vitiating factors, as I shall call them, the other factors of an invasive kind. In the following two sections I then go on to explore the ways in which you may

---

[2] For the record, my own view is that we should identify free will in the metaphysical sense with conversability: a capacity to register and respond to reasons, as they are presented in interpersonal conversation (Pettit and Smith 1996; Pettit 2001b, 2005b, 2007a). This, broadly, is the commonality shared by those who are fit to be negotiated with from within what Peter Strawson (1962) calls the participant as distinct from the objective stance. 'Orthonomy', which I mention later, is the virtue displayed by someone to the extent that they successfully exercise conversability across the normal human range. It constitutes free will in the psychological, as distinct from the metaphysical, sense.

suffer a loss of freedom through invasion, as distinct from vitiation. I argue in Section 3 that domination – exposure to another's power of uncontrolled interference – is necessary for invasion: interference in the absence of dominating power is not enough. And I argue in Section 4 that domination is sufficient for invasion: you can suffer invasion without actually suffering interference. Section 5 looks in the light of this discussion at what we others can do to ensure your freedom in any choice, guarding you against vitiation and invasion.

Assuming that vitiation is not a problem, the lesson of the chapter is that freedom in a choice requires just the absence of domination; it is equivalent to the freedom that was hailed as an ideal in the long tradition of republican thought. While this equation of freedom with non-domination allows us to say that domination with interference is worse in various ways than domination without interference, it marks the threshold where freedom begins to fail at the point where domination, even domination without interference, kicks in. With the argument for this understanding of freedom in place, we can go on in the next chapter to ask after what it would mean to establish equality for people in the enjoyment of freedom: that is, to ensure an equal status for them as free citizens. This ideal amounts, as we shall see, to a republican ideal of social justice.

1. WHAT HAS TO BE HINDERED TO REDUCE FREEDOM OF CHOICE?

We saw that any choice is characterized by a set of options that are available in virtue of the objective and cognitive resources that you can access and use. What does a hindrance have to affect if you are not to enjoy freedom in that choice? There are two answers in the literature. The first is that the hindrance need only affect your preferred option. The second is that a hindrance to any option, preferred or unpreferred, will reduce your freedom. I shall argue in favour of the second answer.[3]

Hobbes's position

The best-known defender of the first answer is Thomas Hobbes. His view of freedom – corporal freedom, to be exact (Pettit 2008c: Chapter 8) – is

---

[3] I ignore a third possible answer, that in order to reduce your freedom every option other than at least one has to be hindered – that you have to be more or less forced to perform the remaining option. This answer hardly makes an appearance in the literature.

summed up in his famous, consciously anti-republican definition of a free-man (Skinner 2008b): 'a free-man is he that in those things which by his strength and wit he is able to do is not hindered to do what he has a will to' (Hobbes 1994b: 21.2). According to this definition, a hindrance takes away from your freedom in a choice only if it hinders an option that you have 'a will to'; only if you prefer the option that is subject to hindrance.

This claim is not just an implication of his definition that may have escaped Hobbes's attention. It is a thesis that he explicitly defends in a debate with Bishop Bramhall about the preconditions for having a free choice between playing tennis or not. Bramhall suggests that if you are considering whether or not to play tennis – we assume a willing partner – and you decide against doing so, then you may still have been wrong to think that you had a free choice. After all, unbeknownst to you, someone may have shut the door of the ('real') tennis court against you. Hobbes is undaunted by the claim, asserting that for anyone in your position 'it is no impediment to him that the door is shut till he have a will to play' (Hobbes and Bramhall 1999: 91).

The line that Hobbes takes here is that your freedom in a choice is reduced only when there is a hindrance that frustrates you in the attempt to satisfy your final preference between the options. There is no frustration if a hindrance blocks you taking an option that, as it happens, you do not want to take anyhow; and so in that case there is no loss of freedom either. We may all agree that you freely decided against playing tennis and that you might therefore be held responsible for this decision; after all, you thought you could act on your preference, whatever that turned out to be, and as a matter of fact you did act on the preference you formed (Frankfurt 1969).[4] But is managing to choose in accordance with the preference you form, even managing to do so in the manner illustrated by the tennis example, all that freedom in a choice requires? I argue not.[5]

There is a clear contrast between a case like that of the tennis example and the case where all of the options, and not just the option preferred, are unhindered. In the tennis-type case we can say that you made a choice freely, but not that you had a choice between the option preferred and the alternative, a choice between playing tennis and not playing tennis. In the contrast case, both things are true: whatever you choose, you choose freely and, moreover, you have a choice between the given options. The question to consider is whether in fostering freedom of choice we ought to try to

---

[4] In such a case the action you take is voluntary, in ordinary usage, being taken for reasons other than that you have no (acceptable) alternative; on this conception of voluntariness see Olsaretti (2004).

[5] For a different point of view, in which 'voluntary' is equated with 'willing', see Otsuka (2003: Chapter 5).

ensure that both things are true or just the one. Ought we to try to give agents choice over which of the options to realize? Or ought we to try just to ensure that their preference between the different options is satisfied?

These are distinct ideals and they have different ramifications for policy. If we seek the richer goal, trying to keep all your options open, we will want to invest resources in making each available, independently of what you are likely to prefer. If we seek the more austere goal, trying merely to avoid preference-frustration, we will want to invest resources in making an option available only to the extent that it is likely that you will choose that option. The richer ideal is more expensive in the resources required, the poorer more economical. Where we do not have the resources to support the first ideal, of course, it will make sense to focus on the second. But this does not yet tell us which ideal is the more appealing, nor which answers better to the ordinary notion of freedom of choice.

Berlin's critique

Other things being equal, the richer ideal is certainly the more appealing, since its satisfaction entails the satisfaction of the more austere counterpart: if you can do whatever you might prefer, you will be able to do what you happen actually to prefer. More importantly, however, that ideal also answers better to our shared ideas about freedom of choice. It sustains the natural assumption that if you enjoy freedom in a choice between certain options, then it must be up to you whether one or another option is realized. And it enables us to avoid some counter-intuitive results that plague the Hobbesian view.

If we say that preference-satisfaction is enough for freedom of choice, as Hobbes implies, then you may count as free in a choice, even when you are forced to choose as you do; the force won't matter so long as the action you are forced to take is the one you prefer. We might choose to live with that counter-intuitive result, arguing that other virtues in the Hobbesian approach outweigh the cost of doing so. But there is still worse in store for us if we stick with that approach, as Isaiah Berlin (1969: xxxix) has pointed out (Pettit 2011b).[6]

---

[6] Berlin clearly focuses on this point only in the 1969 Introduction to the collection in which his 1958 lecture on 'Two Concepts of Liberty' was published and acknowledges doing so as a result of criticism by an anonymous reviewer of the 1958 lecture in the *Times Literary Supplement*. That reviewer, it appears, was Richard Wollheim. I am grateful to Albert Weale and Jonathan Wolff for throwing light on this for me.

If we say that preference-satisfaction is enough for freedom of choice, then we have to acknowledge that there are two distinct ways in which you can make yourself free in a choice between two options, X and Y, where you want X and it happens to be obstructed. You may remove the hindrance so that you can get what you want, i.e. X. Or you may work at changing your preference, so that you come to want what you can get, i.e. Y. But, as Berlin (1969: xxxix) argues, it is quite absurd to think that you might make yourself free in this second manner: 'to teach a man that, if he cannot get what he wants, he must learn to want only what he can get may contribute to his happiness or his security; but it will not increase his civil or political freedom'.

Berlin's argument is worth setting out in detail.

1. Suppose with Hobbes that you enjoy freedom in a choice between X and Y just in case you avoid hindrance in the option that you actually choose; suppose that non-frustration is enough for freedom.
2. By that supposition, you do not enjoy freedom of choice in the case where I hinder X, not Y, and you choose X.
3. But, by supposition, you would enjoy freedom of choice in that case, if you were to choose Y.
4. If you know the situation, therefore, it appears that you can give yourself freedom of choice, without constraining my hindrance, just by adapting your preferences and choosing Y.
5. But this is absurd. You cannot make yourself free in the choice just by accommodating yourself to my disposition to hinder your choice.
6. Thus the original supposition that non-frustration is enough for freedom of choice must be false.

In order to illustrate the problem, imagine that you are a prisoner who, being forcibly imprisoned, does not have freedom of choice between staying behind bars and living in the outside world. Do you lack freedom just because the option you happen to prefer is living outside prison, as the Hobbesian approach implies? If so, then you can make yourself free – you can give yourself freedom in the choice between living in prison or outside – just by adapting your preferences and coming to want to stay in prison. As Berlin (1969: 139) expresses the thought, 'I need only contract or extinguish my wishes and I am made free.' But this is patently absurd and argues powerfully for rejecting the Hobbesian approach. Adaptation to a constraint cannot count on any plausible way of thinking as a form of liberation from that constraint.[7]

---

[7] While adaptation cannot plausibly make you free in the sense required, there is an independent sense in which it may serve freedom: it can expand the range of choices available to you. Suppose you would like to be able to choose between spending or not spending the odd weekend with me, where you can

Think of each option in a choice as a door, where an option is available just when the door is open (Berlin 1969: xlviii). The lesson of this argument is that it is not enough for freedom of choice in the ordinary sense that the door you actually choose to push on happens to be open. It must also be the case that any other option in the choice, any door that you might have pushed on instead, is also open. Suppose we are considering whether you are free in a choice between two options, X and Y. If you are truly to count as having a free choice in the actual world, then you must not be hindered in the actual world where you prefer X but equally you must not be hindered in the possible world where you prefer Y.[8] You must get what you actually want but it must also be the case that you would have got the other option had you wanted it instead.[9] All doors must be open.

As against this point of view, a partisan of the Hobbesian position might argue that it would be irrational to care about what happens should you choose a particular option, say Y, when you think it vanishingly unlikely that you might choose Y. And, building on that observation, the opponent might urge that you should care about the hindrance to an option only in a way that reflects the probability that you assign to choosing it.

This objection is misdirected. When you perform as a deliberative agent, you think of yourself as someone able to choose between the available options, someone on whom the choice depends. You conceive of yourself, in other words, as the arbiter and author of whether the world will be one in which this option materializes or one in which some alternative materializes. This self-conception is inconsistent with indifference to the prospect of any option

---

only spend a weekend with me if you are prepared to go hiking, a prospect that is currently unattractive. You might provide yourself with such a choice by working on your preferences and making hiking into a tolerable prospect.

[8] Is it enough that you enjoy the absence of hindrance in the actual world where you prefer X and in the nearest possible world in which you choose the other option, Y? Or is it required that you can get X in any of a wider range of worlds, including the actual one, in which you prefer X; and can get Y in any of a wider range of possible worlds, including the nearest possible one, in which you prefer Y? My own view is that you must escape hindrance for each option in a wider range of worlds; that this range of worlds is discernible only on an intuitive, context-sensitive basis; and that it does not include all possible worlds. These issues about the relationship between non-hindrance and freedom – about how robust non-hindrance must be (Pettit 2001a; List 2004, 2006b) – are parallel to issues in epistemology about the relation between true belief and knowledge; see for example Williamson (2000). I abstract from them in the current discussion.

[9] Strictly, there is a problem in saying that to be free in the choice of X, it must be the case that you could have chosen the alternative, Y, had you wanted to – had you preferred that option. This condition might be incapable of fulfilment because you are the sort of person who would only want to do Y if it was not an available option; the possibility will be salient from Groucho Marx's quip that he would only want to join a club that would not accept him as a member. The problem can be overcome if what is required is that you could have chosen Y had you tried to do so, where it is not required in that eventuality that you actually prefer Y. For expressive convenience, I shall ignore this complication in the text. I am grateful to Lara Buchak for alerting me to the problem.

being hindered, even one you are unlikely to take. Any such hindrance will compromise your status as an agent, pre-empting the capacity that you take yourself – we assume, correctly – to possess. And so the prospect of any such hindrance is bound to be unattractive.

This discussion began with the question as to what has to be hindered in a given choice in order for the hindrance to reduce the agent's freedom. Following Berlin, I propose to understand freedom in such a way that in a choice between given options, say X, Y and Z, or just X and Y, your freedom can be reduced by the hindrance of any one of those options, regardless of which you happen to prefer. Such a hindrance will make one or more of the options unavailable, undermining your objective or cognitive resources. It will mean that you are no longer in a position to say or think truly 'I can do X, or I can do Y, or I can do Z'. One or another of those disjuncts will be false as a matter of fact or false as a matter of your perceptions.

Freedom, robustness and probability

Given this account of the hindrances that can reduce the freedom of a choice, we might ask about what is required to promote the prospect of your freedom in a particular choice between X and Y: roughly, to maximize expected freedom in this sense. The most plausible answer is that we should minimize two probabilities: the probability of your being hindered in the event of choosing X and the probability of your being hindered in the event of choosing Y. If X is to be an open door, then the probability of hindrance in the event of your taking X should be low, and if Y is to be an open door, then the probability of hindrance in the event of your taking Y should also be low. Thus, we should minimize a function that reflects the two probabilities in some way: say, to take an over-simple proposal, we should minimize the sum that we get by adding them together.[10] Adopting this additive proposal

[10] If we go with the adding proposal, we ought to stipulate that neither probability should go to 1 or 0; this is reasonable since under standard probability axioms only logical necessities attract 1, only logical impossibilities 0. The reason for imposing the stipulation is, as Emily Chapman pointed out to me, that the probability of freedom will be intuitively much smaller in the first than in the second of the following cases, though the sum is the same in each. First case: the probability of interference with one option is 1, with the other 0. Second case: the probability of interference with each option is 0.5. This observation may suggest that instead of adding the probabilities to find the number to be minimized we should conjoin them in a way that is sensitive to the variance between the probabilities of interference associated with the different options; for example, we might do this by taking the number to be minimized to be the sum of the square of $P(H \text{ if } X)$ and the square of $P(H \text{ if } Y)$. The idea would be that the greater the difference between the probabilities of interference associated with options, the more dangerous that is for the probability of freedom. This is an issue in the measurement of freedom that I ignore, as I ignore many other measurement issues.

for illustrative purposes, we should minimize P(H if X) + P(H if Y), where 'P' stands for probability and 'H' for hindrance.[11]

We should seek to minimize this sum, at any rate, if the resources available for reducing hindrances are not a problem. If resources are scarce, then we should obviously invest them with a view to minimizing the probability of hindrance with the option that you are more likely to choose. Since preference-satisfaction is desirable, other things being equal, you will endure a worse failure if you suffer hindrance with frustration than if you suffer hindrance without frustration; you will suffer, not just a loss of freedom, but also a loss of preference-satisfaction. And of course you will be worse off in the event of suffering interference without frustration, the more probable the frustration is. It would be irrational to invest scarce defensive resources where they are likely to do less good and so it would be irrational to seek to defend an option you are less likely to prefer rather than an option you are more likely to prefer.[12]

However plausible the claim that freedom requires us to minimize P(H if X) + P(H if Y), some writers take a different approach. They say that if we are concerned with minimizing hindrance then we should focus on minimizing the probability of hindrance for a given option only to the extent that that option is likely to be chosen (Goodin and Jackson 2007). We should try to minimize, not the sum of the probabilities given above, but the sum of those probabilities after they have each been discounted by the probability of the relevant option being actually chosen. In other words, we should seek to minimize the following sum: P(X)P(H if X) + P(Y)P(H if Y).

To take this line, however, would be to endorse the Hobbesian position described earlier, rejecting Berlin's open-doors view (Pettit 2008b). To see why the approach is Hobbesian, consider how it might lead you to think about what freedom demands of you in the choice between X and Y. If freedom requires minimizing the sum of the discounted probabilities, not the original sum, then it is likely to require that you should choose X or choose Y, depending on which is the less likely to attract hindrance: depending on which of the probabilities, P(H if X) and P(H if Y), is lower. If P(H if X) is higher, for example, then by choosing Y you will set P(X) at zero, so that

[11] For reasons familiar from the debate between evidential and causal decision theory, the hypothetical probabilities P(H if X) and P(H if Y) should be understood, not as conditional probabilities, but in one of the alternative modes consistent with causal decision theory. See Joyce (1999). Take the conditional probability P(H/X), the probability of H given X. This might be low, not because X is an open door, but because those who are capable of hindering you in the choice want you to choose X.

[12] Waldron (2007) uses the fact that it may be sensible to invest resources on the basis of probability of choice to argue, in effect, for linking freedom with the absence of frustration. For a response see Pettit (2007a). Waldron adopts a position similar to that taken by Goodin and Jackson (2007), which I go on to discuss in the text.

Table 1.1 *Variations in hindrance*

Hindrance is more probable	If you choose X	If you choose Y
You actually	1. choose X	2. choose X
You actually	3. choose Y	4. choose Y

P(X)(H if X) + P(Y)(H if Y) will reduce to P(Y)P(H if Y). That probability may be extremely low, say because those with a power of hindrance want you to choose Y. And so by adjusting so as to prefer and choose Y you will have lowered the probability of hindrance and, on this Hobbesian account, will have raised the probability of enjoying freedom of choice.

It may be helpful, using this probabilistic language, to set out schematically the contrast between the positions that the two sides to this debate adopt. I do this in Table 1.1.

The Hobbesian view entails that if scenario 2 or 3 obtains, then you are likely to escape frustration and so be free in the choice between X and Y. The open-doors view entails that the probability of your being free in the choice is independent of what you actually choose; it is determined, regardless of what you choose, by the probabilities, P(H if X) and P(H if Y).

While this contrast between the two positions is sharp and clear, it is consistent with allowing, as mentioned earlier, that a hindrance to a preferred option is worse than a hindrance to an unpreferred option. You will be unfree in either event but you will suffer a greater harm in the first. Should we register this greater harm in the measurement of freedom? That depends on whether we decide that frustration compounds the loss of freedom inherent in the hindrance of any option or whether it counts as a distinct sort of harm. I incline in the latter direction, but the issue is one of book-keeping and measurement and need not concern us greatly here. I mention some problems in the measurement of freedom in Section 2, but I generally skirt them in this book.[13]

2. VITIATING AND INVASIVE HINDRANCES

Having seen that the freedom of a choice can be reduced by a hindrance to any of the options by which it is characterized, we ask in this section about

---

[13] If we do decide that it is in some measure a freedom-relevant loss, then there will be a corresponding reason for weighting the harm associated with P(H if X) or P(H if Y) – say, on a scale between 0 and 1 – in a way that reflects the degree of preference and so the probability, P(X) or P(Y). So long as the weighting is suitably low, the proposal will be distinct from the proposal supported by Goodin and Jackson (2007).

the sorts of hindrances by which your freedom of choice may be reduced. In this section I argue that it is important to distinguish between hindrances that invade free choice, as I shall put it, and hindrances that vitiate free choice, and that there is a sense in which invasive hindrances are more serious. And then in the following two sections I look at the different ways in which freedom of choice can be invaded.

The resources required for free choice

All hindrances to free choice affect the resources, objective and cognitive, that freedom presupposes. And so it will be useful to begin with an overview of the resources that are required if you are to be free in a choice between any set of options such as X, Y and Z. These come in three broad varieties, personal, natural and social.

At the personal level you must have the mental and bodily wherewithal or know-how required for making the choice, and you must be aware of having such a capacity. You must be consciously able to raise your hand or not to raise your hand if you are to have a choice about which to do. You must be consciously able to send an email or post a letter if you are to have a choice between sending a message by one or the other medium.[14]

The natural resources required for being able to enact a certain option are those conditions in your environment that are required to make the action possible. You will not be able to raise your hand if it is so cold that you are frozen stiff; you will not be able to send an email if an electrical storm has knocked out the Internet. Thus you must avoid such problems in the natural environment, if you are to have freedom in the choice between raising or not raising your hand, sending or not sending an email. And you must also be in a position, of course, to know that you do not face such problems.

There are no particular social resources needed for being able to raise a hand, considered just as a physical movement. But such resources are going to be necessary for using the raised hand to signal something. You will be able to raise your hand to greet someone, or to call a foul in umpiring a game, only if your society establishes conventions that make such an act of communication possible and only if you are aware of the fact. And, even more obviously, you will be able to send an email or post a letter only if your society provides you

[14] In particular, you must be consciously able to do these things in the presence of a desire to raise or not raise your hand, to send an email or post a letter; you must have an ability that can serve your preference or will, whatever it should turn out to be, over the options. You would not have adequate personal resources for choosing an option if, perversely, you were able to enact it only in the event of not actually wanting to do so!

with the technology and infrastructure presupposed to such actions and, again, you are aware of the fact. You will depend on there being enough others in the society willing to supply such a service, and enough others willing to demand and pay for it, that you have the choice between emailing or posting a letter – or relying on some more pedestrian form of communication.

It may not be clear how far social resources extend. Consider a case where you are able to raise your hand only with the help of a physiotherapist who is coaching you back to health after an accident or where you are able to send an email only with the assistance of someone who understands computers. Do you have the ability in such a case to take the option mentioned? Does the voluntary assistance of another person count as a relevant social resource?

My response is to say that if you depend on the goodwill of a given individual or set of individuals for being able to take the relevant option, then you do not have the ability in the sense required for freedom. You will have the ability required for free choices if others are independently constrained or motivated to provide the assistance needed, or if there is a queue of people willing to provide it so that, should any assistants fail, there will be others willing to take their place. But you will not have that ability, on the line suggested, just because someone happens to be willing to help you out. The response is intuitive insofar as there is a clear distinction between the case where you depend on the goodwill of others for assistance and the case in which you can command such assistance, as we might say – the case where you can lay claim to it, as if it were yours to own. That distinction will be of relevance later when we consider the conditions under which domination occurs; the first case allows domination, as we shall see, the second does not.

Two kinds of hindrance

These observations show that if you are able to make a choice between any set of options, then you must have objective and cognitive access to the personal, natural and social resources required for selecting each. To make a free choice between options, X, Y and Z, is to use such resources in order to satisfy your preference or will over those options, whatever that will turns out to be. It is to exercise the capacity that the resources put in your possession in order to satisfy your will or preference over the options.

But if freedom of choice requires being able to use your resources in order to satisfy your will, then we can distinguish between two possible sorts of hindrances. On the one side, there will be hindrances that affect the use of your resources for any purpose and so, in particular, for the purpose of

satisfying your will. On the other there will be hindrances that affect the use
of your resources for the specific purpose of satisfying your will, and not in a
generic way.

Suppose that you have a car that can in principle serve you in various
ways, including for driving into the local city centre. You may be hindered
from using your car to drive into the city by either of two saliently distinct
sorts of hindrances, generic or specific. You may be hindered by generic
obstacles that prevent you from using the car for any purpose and, a fortiori,
for driving into the city; fuel may be short, the engine may fail, or the car
may be damaged. Or you may be hindered by obstacles that specifically
affect your driving it into the city centre, being triggered by your using it or
trying to use it for that purpose. There may be a law against driving into the
city centre; others may be tempted by your action to emulate you, thereby
causing traffic congestion; or an environmental group may be prompted to
respond by disabling your vehicle.

As there may be generic and specific obstacles to your using your car for a
certain purpose, so there are generic and specific hindrances that may affect
your using available resources, objective or cognitive, for the purpose of
satisfying your will in a given choice. I describe specific hindrances as invaders
of free choice and generic hindrances as vitiators.[15] Invaders are inherently
inimical to freedom of choice in the sense that they are only triggered by your
attempting – or by the prospect of your attempting – to satisfy your will by
using the resources at your disposal. Vitiators are incidentally rather than
inherently inimical, because they do not have to be triggered in this way;
they materialize for reasons that are not connected to your attempting, or
being able to attempt, to satisfy your will. Where vitiators affect the capacity
presupposed to your being able to satisfy your will, invaders target the capacity
to satisfy your will just as such: they are designed, as we might put it, to thwart
your will.

Whenever another person or body imposes their will on you, allowing
you to choose only within limits that they dictate or only on conditions that
they decide, their hindrance certainly targets your ability to satisfy your will
and constitutes an inherently inimical assault – an invasion of your choice.
Just by virtue of imposing their will on you, they affect the extent to which
you can act so as to satisfy your own will. The imposition of their will entails
the displacement of your will, as we might say; it competes with your will for

---

[15] In earlier work I relied, not on the distinction between invading and vitiating hindrances, but on the
closely connected distinction between hindrances that compromise, and hindrances that condition,
freedom (Pettit 1997c: Chapter 2).

control of what you do. It may amount to usurping your control over the choice, taking charge of what you do. Or it may amount to claiming a share in that control, establishing limits on the extent to which you can select an option according to your own preference.

This observation shows that subjection to the will of another, be it total or partial, represents one way in which your choice may be invaded, being subject to a specific rather than a generic hindrance. But such subjection to another agent's or agency's will also looks to be the only way in which a choice may be invaded. A hindrance that invades your choice between options has to be triggered by your seeking to satisfy your will in that choice, rather than materializing for independent reasons. And while that triggering condition can be fulfilled in the presence of a will that competes with your own will for control of what you do, it is hard to see how it could be met otherwise. Your seeking to satisfy your will in a choice is hardly likely, for example, to trigger the appearance of a natural obstacle to your getting your way. For these reasons we may identify invasive hindrances to choice with hindrances that reflect the will of another as to what you should do.

When we discuss the variety of invasive hindrances in the next section, we shall see that others may impose their will on you without deliberately hindering you – without, in that sense, interfering with you. But many thinkers treat the interference that another inflicts on you as the paradigm of an invasion of choice. They equate the invasion of choice with an intentional attempt to usurp or claim a share in your control, or perhaps with a quasi-intentional counterpart of such an attempt: say, the negligent failure to take an expected level of care not to undermine your control (Miller 1984). Isaiah Berlin (1969: 122) is one of this group, holding that the primary offence against freedom of choice is 'the deliberate interference of other human beings'.

What sorts of factors will count as vitiators rather than invaders of a free choice? The answer should now be obvious. Any factors that deprive you of resources required for freedom in that choice, or that limit the use to which you can put those resources, without imposing the will of another as to what you should do. Any factors, in other words, that impair or impede your capacity to use your resources for satisfying your will but without deriving from the intrusive will of another agent or agency. Thus any lack of personal, natural or indeed social resources will vitiate your freedom in a choice, provided it is not a lack deriving from the will of another agent or agency as to how you in particular, or those in your particular category, should make that choice. Such failures of resources may derive at any time from your own illness or disability, from the limits of your natural environment, from the continuing, damaging results on you or your environment of the invasion of earlier choices, from the aggregate consequences of independently motivated actions by others, or from the actions of another agent that are necessitated in some way and not a matter of voluntary choice (Olsaretti 2004).

The line drawn between invasive and vitiating hindrances runs bright and clear in most cases, but it is less salient with the hindrances that derive from the actions that others take. There is a big difference between the case where you deny me the option of reading the newspaper, as in invasive interference, and the case where that option ceases to be available because most other people come to rely on electronic sources of news, put the newspaper out of business, and thereby vitiate my choice of reading the newspaper. But what, for example, of the case where there is only one copy of the newspaper available, you and I both wish to read it and, recognizing the competition between us, you grab it first, thereby frustrating me? Or what about the case where the union of workers in the newspaper office calls a strike in order to punish the management but fully recognize that this will frustrate readers like me? Does such an act count as invasion or vitiation?

I say in each case that it counts as invasion. You may not wish to impose your will on me as such, lamenting the fact that we cannot both read the newspaper, but you impose your will on me – you actively and deliberately interfere with me – for the instrumental reason that that is the only way in which you can satisfy your own will. Equally, the union in the newspaper office may not wish to impose their will on readers like me just for its own sake; they may only impose their will on us for the instrumental reason that that is the best way in which they can pressurize management to improve wages or conditions. We may not take such a contingently motivated invasion to be as bad as an invasion pursued for its own sake. And, to anticipate the argument of the next chapter, we may not think that invasions of that type ought always to be prohibited in a free society. But on the line taken here we clearly have to say that nonetheless it counts as a straightforward case of invasion.

In invasions of these kinds, whether inherently or contingently hostile, you exercise a power of interfering or not interfering with me, depending on your will. Both forms of interference contrast, however, with the vitiating sort of constraint you impose on me when you have no choice, by whatever criteria, but to impose a certain constraint: you intervene in my choice, but out of necessity, not out of a will – a free will, as we might say – to intervene rather than not intervene. Thus, if we think that you have no choice but to seek your own preservation in a certain context, and if your doing so impacts negatively on me, then the constraint you impose constitutes a vitiating, not an invasive, hindrance to my choice. You impose more or less involuntarily on me.

The relevance of vitiating hindrances

Hobbes acknowledges the importance of vitiating hindrances when he says, as we saw, that a person makes a free choice in virtue of not being hindered 'in those things which by his strength and wit he is able to do'. He implies thereby that you can be free to choose an option only if you have the 'strength and wit' – in our terms, the objective and cognitive resources – to be able to enact it; only if it lies, as we say, within your capacity. And he contrasts the way in which you can be deprived of your freedom by a vitiating failure on this front – as, for example, when you are like 'a man fastened to his bed by sickness' – with the invasive way you may be deprived of freedom by 'external impediments' (Hobbes 1994b: 21.1). In the latter case you are made properly unfree, as we might put it; in the former you are made non-free, not being eligible as a candidate for the enjoyment of freedom (Pettit 2008c: Chapter 8).

Our distinction between invaders and vitiators of choice diverges from Hobbes's in two connected ways. First, it recognizes resources beyond the internal resources of strength and wit on which he focuses. And second, it breaks with his approach in associating invading resources only with will-imposing hindrances and not, as he does, with any external impediments.[16] Still, abstracting from those differences, our claim that there are two sharply divided kinds of hindrances to freedom is broadly faithful to the Hobbesian view.

Where the standpoint adopted in the last section put us on Berlin's side and against Hobbes, it turns out that the standpoint adopted in this not only puts us on Hobbes's side; it also puts us against Berlin. For Berlin (1969: 122) maintains, quite assertively, that freedom in a choice does not require the absence of vitiators, only the absence of invaders. 'Mere incapacity to attain a goal is not lack of political liberty,' he says, where he clearly means the sort of incapacity produced by vitiation. The observation behind his claim is that we can say that you are free to vote or not to vote, for example, just in case the government does not deny you the vote and regardless of whether you have the capacity to get to the polling station: regardless, for example, of whether you are fastened to your bed by sickness. Berlin generalizes this conception of liberty, arguing that the freedom to make a choice, even in the ordinary sense

---

[16] Despite these differences, it is not misleading to think of Hobbes as looking for a distinction, similar to ours, that will mark off inherently inimical from incidentally inimical deprivations of freedom. Given that he thinks of all resources as internal, and of failures that deprive an agent of those resources as incidental, he may think of external impediments as targeting the use of those resources – their use, necessarily, in the external forum – in an attempt to satisfy the agent's will.

in which we predicate such freedom, does not ever entail the capacity to make that choice: it does not require the presence of the resources that would make the choice feasible.

We do often speak of liberty in the sense in which it is enough for freedom of choice that the choice is not blocked by government or by any other agency. But, going back to a theme in the Introduction, I think that this usage is quite special, being useful only in certain contexts. Thus in the context of marking the person's citizenship it might serve a useful purpose to ascribe the freedom to vote to the person who is sick in bed. It would be highly misleading to say more generally, however, that you can enjoy the freedom to choose between certain options, even when you lack the capacity to exercise the choice (Van Parijs 1995). In most contexts to say that you are free to choose between the options – that in that sense you have freedom of choice – is to imply that the option to be realized is up to you. And it can be up to you only if you have the resources and capacity to make such a choice: only if you are free of vitiation, not just free of invasion.

The connection between freedom and responsibility reinforces this intuitive claim (Pettit 2001e). Suppose you believe that you have freedom of choice between options, X, Y and Z. Under standard assumptions about the connection between freedom and responsibility, you will have to think that you are fit to be held responsible for whatever you choose: you can be blamed or praised, as appropriate, depending on the merits of the option selected. But if you believe that you lacked the objective or cognitive resources needed for choosing one or another of the options, then you could not think that you are fit to be held responsible for choosing that option. Hence your belief that you have freedom of choice between the three options requires you to believe that you have all the resources required for choosing any of them.[17]

The difference between the view adopted here and that which Berlin espouses is of importance to how we keep the books on freedom but it need not mark a substantial divergence in ultimate commitments. The reason is that while Berlin thinks that strictly speaking the freedom to choose between certain options does not require the capacity to do so, he insists that freedom will be of little value in the absence of such a capacity. 'What is freedom to those who cannot make use of it?' he asks. 'Without adequate conditions for the use of freedom, what is the value of freedom?' (Berlin 1969: 124; see too lii). Treating freedom as a bundle of legal, not necessarily effective, liberties, John Rawls (1971) also distinguishes between what freedom requires, strictly

---

[17] I am grateful to Daniel Berntson for discussion on this point.

speaking, and what it requires if it is to be valuable. We shall see in the next chapter that this is an important feature of Rawls's view and that it is relevant to the comparison between his theory of justice and the theory that a republican approach would support.

The significance of invasive hindrances

We have been arguing that your freedom of choice may be reduced either by vitiating factors that are not inherently inimical to your freedom or by invasive factors that are. But invasive hindrances are naturally cast, in any accounting of freedom, as particularly objectionable and significant. To suffer the vitiation of choice is to be denied a precondition for enjoying freedom of choice: to lack required resources. To suffer invasion is to be denied the very condition by which freedom is identified: to be thwarted in making the choice according to your will.

The significance we ascribe to invasion, as distinct from vitiation, shows up in the difference between the reactions that we have to obstruction of the two kinds. You may be frustrated and exasperated by hindrances that do not impose another's will: say, by your lack of certain skills or knowledge, by the impact of the weather on your plans, by the growing level of traffic on the roads, or just by the way the dog soiled the carpet. But if you suffer will-imposed hindrances – hindrances that reflect subjection to the will of another – then you will feel all of that and something more. Unless you are possessed of a special degree of self-discipline, you will also burn with resentment and indignation (Strawson 1962).

Suppose that as you park your car in an unknown part of town, someone warns you that if you leave your car there, it is likely to be damaged by a coming hailstorm. Imagine the worry about the hailstorm – and the gratitude for the information provided – that the warning would trigger. And now think by contrast about the reaction that you would have in the parallel case where the person makes a threat, if you leave your car there, to impose a similar level of damage. You will be anxious about the damage of which you are warned in the first scenario but, unless you are not as other people, you will be outraged about the damage with which you are threatened in the second. The warning alerts you to a cost that it is certainly important to take into account in deciding whether to park your car. But while the threat reveals your exposure only to a similar cost, it also does more besides. It shows that you are not acting under your own will in adjusting to your environment; you are in a situation where another will presumes to rule over your actions. And that, intuitively, is much more objectionable.

The distinction between vitiating and invading obstacles to free choice, as we have drawn it here, maps onto this psychologically resonant distinction between restrictions that exasperate and restrictions that may also outrage. In view of their connection with such outrage, these are the hindrances that assume prominence in social life and that call out most urgently for rectification. Drawing on a tradition that long preceded him, Kant (2005: 11) emphasized the point in a comment prompted by reading Rousseau's *Social Contract*. 'Find himself in what condition he will, the human being is dependent on many external things . . . But what is harder and more unnatural than this yoke of necessity is the subjection of one human being under the will of another. No misfortune can be more terrifying to one who is accustomed to freedom.'[18]

This argues that the invasion of free choice is worse on the whole than its mere vitiation. But it is important not to downplay the impact of vitiating factors. Such factors affect the range of choices in which you can hope to enjoy the absence of invasion. And, more than that, they may put such limits on your range of choice that you are subject, as a result, to a greater degree of invasion on the part of others. Thus the way things are organized in a society may not be the work of will in a relevant sense and may not invade people's choices as such – it may be the unintended, aggregate consequence of how people are independently motivated to act – but it can impact on free choice in a way that is closely connected to invasion. It may constitute a structure or pattern that facilitates the invasion by some people of the choices available to others. It may amount to an indirect, structural form of invasion, we might even say, as distinct from the direct, personal form of invasion that it occasions.[19]

The measurement of freedom

The upshot of this discussion is that in charting hindrances to freedom we should distinguish between the vitiation that denies you a choice between

[18] The primacy of will-imposed hindrances – usually identified with acts of interference – is denied by Van Parijs (1995). Others are sympathetic with this viewpoint but concede that will-imposed hindrances should be given priority on the superficial grounds that they are more salient candidates for political remedy than other sorts of hindrances (Steiner 1994; Carter 1999; Kramer 2003). On the relevance of political salience see Carter (2008: 62). Most approaches, like that adopted here, take will-imposed hindrances to have priority over other hindrances on deeper, less contingent grounds.
[19] This comment explains why the theory of freedom developed here is capable of allowing for the systemic dangers to freedom that Clarissa Hayward (2011) rightly emphasizes. It provides a reason for recognizing what I later describe as structural domination. My thanks to Maeve Cook for a helpful exchange on this point.

certain options and the subjection to another's will, the invasion by another, that denies you the chance to make the choice according to your will. The emerging picture shows that there are two dimensions to freedom of choice: on the one side, the freedom that goes with the unvitiated range of choices available; and on the other the freedom that goes with not being invaded by others in the exercise of those choices. The unvitiated resources at your disposal define a range of effective opportunities, and to the extent to which that range is wider, you have greater latitude for choice, greater freedom of opportunity. Being in a position to use those resources without invasion – not being subject to the will of another, however partially, on the matter of how you exercise the capacity they give you – will enable you to exploit those opportunities more effectively.[20] Where the unvitiated resources ensure your freedom of opportunity, the absence of subjection and invasion ensures your freedom of exercise or control.[21]

This observation teaches an important lesson about measuring freedom of choice. Suppose we want to determine how two people fare in their freedom of choice. The most obvious way to do this will be to take a range of option-sets or choices as reference points – the choice between X and Y, the choice between V and W, and so on – and then to ask how the agents compare in opportunity-freedom and exercise-freedom, how they compare in latitude and control, with respect to those choices: how far they avoid vitiation, on the one side, and invasion on the other.[22]

Even if we think that comparisons of freedom of choice ought to be made by reference to the same range of option-sets, however, we may take any of a number of routes. One approach would be to assume equal unvitiated capacity across those option-sets – that is, to assume equal freedom of

---

[20] Here I make use of the notion of opportunity and exercise popularized by Charles Taylor (1985a) in his distinction between opportunity and exercise concepts of freedom.

[21] Eric McGilvray (2011) gives an illuminating account of how the traditional republican way of thinking about liberty came to be ousted by the new commercial or market conception of liberty in the nineteenth century; he links the latter with the earlier notion of natural liberty that figured prominently in the juristic tradition. Among the two conceptions he describes we might say that the republican tended to focus on the absence of servitude, the commercial on the presence of latitude.

[22] The most salient alternative to this approach would be to follow Hobbes and argue that how much freedom two people enjoy depends on how far they each enjoy exercise-freedom in respect of the different options within their personal, idiosyncratic capacity: how far each is unhindered in 'the things which by his wit and power he is able to do'. But this alternative would have the absurd consequence that the prince who can do lots of things – the prince who has enormous freedom of opportunity – may count as no more free than the pauper who has few if any opportunities for choice. The measurement of freedom of choice ought to be option-relative, as Hobbes would agree, but comparisons of freedom will make best sense if two people are measured against the same range of option-sets rather than each being measured against a different range: those that happen to lie within their own capacity and to constitute effective opportunities for choice.

opportunity – and to try to chart variations in the degree to which people are subject to invasion from others: that is, variations in their freedom of exercise or control. Another would be to assume equal freedom of exercise and to chart variations in their freedom of opportunity: variations in their unvitiated capacity to exercise choice across the different option-sets. And yet another would be to assume neither sort of freedom and to try to track variations in both dimensions across the same option-set. This project would require us to assign relative weights to vitiating and invasive hindrances.

Whichever of these paths we take, the measurement of freedom raises a daunting challenge. It is deeply unclear how exactly we should weight vitiating and invasive hindrances against one another, though my earlier comments argue for giving invasive hindrances some priority. And equally it is unclear how we should measure and compare different levels of freedom within the category of exercise on the one side or opportunity on the other.

We shall see in the next two sections that there are different ways in which your freedom of exercise or control may be hindered: that is, different ways in which your choices may be invaded. Your freedom to choose between X, Y and Z, to anticipate that discussion, may be reduced by suffering uncontrolled interference on the part of another – interference can involve the removal, replacement or misrepresentation of one or more options – or just by suffering domination: that is, just by being exposed to a power of uncontrolled interference on the part of the other. And to add to the complexity that this distinction introduces, there are different degrees in which a given option may be removed, replaced or misrepresented; there are different degrees in which such interference may be uncontrolled by you; and there are different degrees in which you may be exposed to a power of uncontrolled interference. Since it is unclear how exactly to measure or commensurate such variations in degree it is clearly going to be extremely difficult to measure the extent to which a hindrance may reduce your exercise-freedom in the choice.

There are similar difficulties in store on the issue of how to measure and compare degrees of opportunity-freedom, despite the fact that the issue has received a good deal of attention in recent literature (Sugden 1998; Carter 1999; Kramer 2003). Just to illustrate the sort of problems that arise here, take a set of options X, Y and Z in which you and another have the same freedom of exercise: there is no one in a position to subject either of you to their will. And imagine now that you only have the opportunity to choose X or Y and the other has the opportunity to choose any of the three options. Presumably that means that you have lesser opportunity-freedom. But what are we to say about the degree by which your freedom falls short? Do we think that the shortfall is the same, regardless of how far the new option, Z, is intuitively different from X and Y, for example, or regardless of how far it represents an option that you value or ought to value? If X and Y involve drinking one or another beer, does it matter that Z is a beer rather than a wine option, or a beer or wine option that you would particularly like to have?

Should these observations lead us to despair about the prospect of measuring freedom of choice? I think that there is reason not to expect a plausible, more or less mechanical algorithm for ordering all possible variations in people's fortunes on a common scale of freedom. But we need not despair about being able to establish some accepted standards whereby, for a given range of choices, we can compare and order the more salient differences found amongst the citizens of a given society or, perhaps, across two or more distinct societies.

This issue will be central to the next chapter, when we consider how we might pursue the goal of securing equal freedom as non-domination for the members of a society. We shall see in that context that it makes good sense to identify a range of significant choices or option-sets – the basic liberties, as I think of them – and to look for a system that safeguards against shortfalls from a culturally established, common yardstick in the extent to which people have the opportunity to make those choices and in the extent to which they avoid subjection to the will of others in how they exploit that opportunity. I take the relevant yardstick to be set by what I call the eyeball test. At the level set by this test, the safeguards should enable people, by local standards, to look one another in the eye without reason for fear or deference. The achievement of that discernible and applicable ideal would make, intuitively, for the equality of people in their status as free persons or citizens: that is, in the free status that has long been an ideal in republican thinking.

Revealed will and real will

At this point, we are positioned to discuss the different modes in which your freedom of choice may be invaded, looking at the notions of interference and domination just mentioned. But before turning to that discussion, which will be developed over the next two sections, I should mention an important issue that deserves some attention. Assume that you have the unvitiated capacity to enact a choice between X, Y and Z, having all the internal and external resources required, and that you are not subjected to anyone else's will in how you use those resources and exercise that capacity. Does it follow that whatever you choose to do, you count as enjoying freedom of choice in every possible sense of that phrase?

Not according to a certain psychological ideal of freedom or, as it is often put, autonomy. You may be subject to a malaise – a sort of heteronomy – that consists in forming a will over the relevant options that is not, as it is often put, your reflective or stable will, your true or real will. You may be the sort of person whose will-formation is distorted in such a way that the will that forms within you takes the form of an alien force and does not carry your authority. It may not reflect your highest aspiration for yourself but rather a disposition that you regard as a weakness of will or intellect. In giving into that disposition, then, you will tend to think of yourself as a slave of the passions, in the traditional image, and of the various pressures that the passions have traditionally served to exemplify (James 1997). You will not be able to think of yourself as fully present in the action. Rather you will probably think that you have been betrayed by pathologies like obsession, compulsion and low impulse-control, on the side of desire, or *idées fixes*, paranoia and credulity on the side of belief.

The topic of autonomy, understood in this sense, has generated a large literature. Isaiah Berlin (1969) had autonomy in mind when he spoke of the positive, psychological liberty that consists in being your own master, if not in the social world, at least in the citadel of the soul.[23] Harry Frankfurt (1988) argues that such autonomy requires that the desires you act on are desires that you identify with; at the least, unlike addictive yearnings, they are desires that are controlled by a higher-order desire that you should be moved by them (see too Dworkin 1988). Michael Bratman (2007) associates such autonomy or self-governance, not with the control of a higher-order desire, but rather with a form of control exercised by a longer-term plan. My own preference, following Pettit and Smith (1996), is to cast it as an ideal of orthonomy – a rule of the 'orthos' or the right rather than a rule of the 'autos' or self – arguing that it requires you to form and act on desires that answer to your evaluations, in particular to evaluations that reflect whatever count as the relevant facts (see too Watson 2003: Introduction, 2005).[24]

---

[23] Here I follow MacCallum (1967) in assuming, for simplicity, that even the notion of positive liberty can be cast as requiring the absence of an obstacle. But the notion of positive liberty is often associated with late nineteenth-century liberalism in Britain – modern liberalism, as it was then called (Gaus 1983) – and in that tradition positive liberty consisted, not in escaping internal obstacles, but in making positive use of their absence by achieving a form of self-realization (Baldwin 1984). Note that while I go along with MacCallum's schema here I break with it in the next chapter when I argue that the freedom of a person does not just require the absence of certain obstacles but, more specifically, an absence that is secured by a rule of accepted norm and law.

[24] The notion of autonomy or self-governance is employed by another set of thinkers for purposes of developing, not an ideal of personal life, but an ideal also for politics. See for example Christman (2009).

There is a perfectly good sense in which freedom of choice requires some version of autonomy or orthonomy – some kind of psychological freedom, as it might be put (Pettit 2001e) – but I will be ignoring it in the present context. Our concern is with your freedom of revealed will, not with whether the will that you reveal counts as your true or real will. This is appropriate in a book on political philosophy. All of us face a challenge as to whether the will we form in one or another domain of choice answers to standards of autonomy or orthonomy. But that is a psychological or ethical challenge, not one that can plausibly be laid to the charge of a collective, coercive agency like the state.

I mentioned early in the chapter that we are not concerned in this book with what gives you metaphysical free will: that is, with what makes you into an agent with the capacity, however that is understood, to take one or another option in a given choice. What we have just seen is that equally we are not concerned with what gives you psychological free will, enabling you to form your will autonomously, however autonomy is understood. Our concern is solely with social free will or, in effect, political freedom: that is, with what is required for it to be the case that however imperfectly formed your will may be, you are in a position to make your choice, without vitiation or invasion, according to that will.

3. NO INVASION WITHOUT DOMINATION

The upshot of the argument in the last section is that given the unvitiated capacity to make any choice – given any set of options between which you have the effective opportunity to choose – the issue of how far you are free to make the choice turns on whether you are subjected to the will of another in exercising that capacity. But what are the ways in which you can be subjected to another will, be that the will of an individual agent or the will of an organized agency or group (List and Pettit 2011)?

The canonical term for the act whereby one agent or agency intervenes in the choice of another, with a view to restricting that choice – or at least with the negligent effect of restricting the choice (Miller 1984) – is 'interference'. Interference is taken to involve the intentional restriction of the choice – or, as in the negligence case, its quasi-intentional restriction – so that someone interferes in a choice only if they themselves have a choice between interfering and not interfering. The main issue that arises in discussing what subjection to the will of another involves is whether such subjection, such invasion of your free choice, is equivalent to enduring the active interference of that other.

The republican theory of freedom as non-domination, to anticipate the position I defend, maintains that the restriction of choice constituted by active interference is not sufficient or even necessary for such subjection to the will of another and that it is only domination that fits the bill. Domination is defined by reference to interference but is distinct from it. Someone, A, will be dominated in a certain choice by another agent or agency, B, to the extent that B has a power of interfering in the choice that is not itself controlled by A. When I say that B has a power of interference I mean that B has the unvitiated and uninvaded capacity to interfere or not to interfere. And when I say that that power of interfering is not controlled by A, I mean that it is not exercised on terms imposed by A: it is not exercised in a direction or according to a pattern that A has the influence to determine. In that respect, it is unlike the interference that someone invites when they hire an agent, for example, to make certain decisions for them.

In this section I deal first of all with the issue of what interference should be taken to comprise, assuming it is a way of actively restricting your choice and so a possible way of subjecting you to my will. This discussion is important, since the notion of interference is presupposed in the definition of domination that I have just given. While the discussion involves some detailed analysis, the bottom line is fairly straightforward, and is summed up in a simple matrix. With that discussion in place, I then argue that interference without domination does not constitute subjection. In effect, as the title of the section phrases it, there is no invasion without domination: domination is necessary for the invasive reduction of freedom. In the next section I shall argue for the parallel thesis that there is no domination without invasion, so that domination is sufficient as well as necessary for the invasive reduction of freedom.

The nature of interference

If interference is to restrict your choice between X, Y and Z, then it has to affect your use of the otherwise accessible objective or cognitive resources in virtue of which we say that you have the unvitiated capacity to do X or Y or Z. It has to ensure that as a matter of objective fact, or as a matter of your cognitive perception, you no longer have access to those options.

The most obvious way in which I can restrict the use of your objective resources is by removing one or more of the options, so that it is no longer available to you. If you face a choice between X, Y and Z, having the unvitiated capacity to take one or another option, I can impose on your choice by objectively removing one or more of the options. I can transform the set, X, Y and Z, for example, into the set, X and Y. I may do this without signalling or communicating the fact, but if I am anxious to get you to choose one of the remaining options, I will inform you of the unavailability of the removed option and not have you waste your time on trying to get it.[25]

If I can impose my will on you by removing one of your options, I can presumably have the same effect by replacing one of the options in the choice by a different option. Suppose that I change the options so that you have to choose, not between X, Y and Z, but between X, Y and Z*. This intervention, too, will mean that I have changed the profile of options you face and thereby restricted your choice. As it was not possible in the earlier case for you to choose the removed option, so it is not possible in this case to choose the option replaced: Z is no longer available but only the option that replaces it, Z*. As in the other case I may not communicate the fact that I have replaced Z in this way, though I will do so if I am anxious to direct your choice towards one of the other options rather than have you waste your time on trying to get Z.

The standard way in which I might replace one or more of the options in your choice between X, Y and Z would be to attach a penalty to the option; this will change that option, say Z, into penalized-Z or, if you like, Z-minus. I may do this without telling you, though if I want you to choose X or Y, as distinct from just wanting to have a negative impact on your life, it will be a good idea to communicate what I have done, thereby threatening or coercing you. Penalizing an option in this way may not actually stop you from choosing the penalized option – that is, stop you from choosing Z-with-the-penalty. And if you do choose it, we may say that you chose it freely: chose it in a way that makes you responsible for what you did (Frankfurt 1969). But still, my intervention in penalizing and replacing the option, however slight it may be, denies you the unrestricted choice between X, Y and Z. It replaces it with a

---

[25] Perhaps because of wanting to make it easier to measure and compare the degree of freedom that people enjoy, some recent thinkers have argued for limiting the interference that can reduce freedom of choice to the removal of an option in this sense – to what is often described as prevention (Steiner 1994; Carter 1999; Kramer 2003). Representatives of this view of freedom, sometimes described as the pure negative theory (Carter 2008), have elaborated the most systematic, freedom-based alternative to republican theory. While I believe that the two theories have to be judged ultimately on the basis of a methodology of reflective equilibrium, as indicated in the Introduction, I think that this rival theory has to live with some strikingly counter-intuitive judgements on how freedom may be reduced in a given choice. On the one side, it would force us to ignore activities whereby I do not remove an option in the choice but I do replace it; for debate on the claim that still I reduce your 'overall freedom' in such a case see Kramer (2008) and Pettit (2008d). On the other, it would force us to ignore activities in which I do not interfere with how things are as a matter of actual fact but I do interfere with how they are according to your perceptions; I impose a cognitive rather than an objective restriction on you. And, on the face of it, those interventions have a capacity to impose my will on you, as argued in the text.

choice between X, Y and Z-minus. It prevents you from choosing Z, albeit not in the sense in which the actual removal of that option would do this.

Why say that penalizing an option means replacing it? The question raises some tricky issues about the individuation of options but, for the record, my own approach is as follows. I assume that for any agent there are features or properties such that their presence reliably supports the attraction or aversion felt for a given prospect or option (Pettit 1991, 2005c). I hold that a given option ceases to be the same option – it shifts identity – in the case of any alteration in such a desiderative feature. To impose a penalty or even the chance of a penalty on one of your options, then, is presumably to change its desiderative features and to replace it by a different option. But to impose a change that does not alter the desiderative features is not to replace the original option; it changes the option but does not replace it.[26]

Thus, to explain how this stipulation should be understood, I do not replace the option of your reading, as distinct from not reading, a book just by moving the book from your left side to your right. This changes the option but not in a desiderative and relevant fashion. Nor do I replace that option just by offering you a reward for not reading it. This makes for a desiderative change but not for a change in the option itself.[27] While the offer raises the opportunity cost of that option, as economists say, this just means that there is now a more attractive alternative than previously.[28] Assuming that desiderative features are not subject to much variation across people, or at least across people in a given culture, we can take the replacement of an option always to involve a change in any socially recognized

---

[26] On the approach sketched, I can change any of your options by associating it with a property that matters to you, whether it matters in a personal, self-regarding way or matters in a wholly impartial manner: it reflects your moral vision of the universe. We might vary the picture by restricting the relevant properties to ones in the self-regarding category. This would guard against the consequence, which I am prepared to live with, that I can restrict your freedom by ensuring that should you take a certain option then some bad consequence will follow for people elsewhere for whom you have a moral, though not a personal, concern.

[27] I rely here on an intuitive sense of the distinction between changes that alter a thing itself and Cambridge changes, as they are sometimes called: changes such as the change I undergo when someone emigrates from the country and I become thereby the nth oldest resident. An option changes when its character or consequences change, as we may put it, but it does not change just because there is a change somewhere else in the world. In our example it does not change – or, to anticipate the next footnote, does not necessarily change – because of a change in the alternatives.

[28] Although increasing the opportunity cost of an option does not necessarily change the identity of the option, the nature of alternatives can sometimes affect the identity of an option. Taking an apple and leaving an orange for your companion is a different option from taking the apple where the alternative is a smaller apple; in the former case it is a perfectly polite option, but in the latter it is not, and politeness is a presumptively desiderative feature. See Pettit (1991).

feature of that kind: in any established desirability characterization, to use a term of Elisabeth Anscombe's (1957).[29]

Although the replacement of an option, Z, makes it strictly impossible to choose Z, as distinct from Z-minus, it does so in a sense that allows us to distinguish between many different grades of interference. There are degrees in how far an option may be removed or replaced, since it may be removed or replaced across a smaller or larger range of possible scenarios. But there are also other, more salient differences in the degree to which an option may be replaced. The penalty attached to Z may be lesser or greater, to go back to our example, and Z-minus may vary in a lesser or greater degree from Z. It may even be so small a penalty, as we say, that it does little or nothing to stop you from ignoring the penalty and still choosing Z-minus. The removal of the option, Z, would prevent you across relevant variations of scenario from choosing any Z-like option; the replacement of the option prevents you from choosing only the narrowly individuated Z – in effect, Z unpenalized. Your freedom in the choice will be reduced by any penalty and any replacement – you will strictly be denied a choice between X, Y and Z – but it may not be reduced, intuitively, by much. This observation points us to a particularly striking respect in which the measurement of freedom is bound to be a complex project.

If a penalty or threat of a penalty can invade your freedom of choice, do we have to say that a reward or offer of a reward – an ordinary, non-mesmerizing reward – can have the same effect? Do we have to say that I restrict your choice by offering you a regular, non-mesmerizing reward for choosing X, for example, introducing the enhanced option of X-rewarded or X-plus? That depends on whether the reward is refusable or not. If it is not refusable, so that your options are now X-plus, Y and Z, then we have to say that I have replaced one option and restricted your choice between X, Y and Z. But if the reward is refusable, as rewards generally are, then I will not have had any restrictive effect. It will still be the case with each of the three original options that you can choose that option; for all I have done, you will still have all the objective resources required and, we may assume, all the cognitive resources too. I will have added a further option, X-plus, to that set of options but I will

[29] The assumption entails that we cannot easily change our attachment to one or another feature. And that is independently important in my perspective. Otherwise, you might be able to make yourself free in certain choices by adapting so that the options are individuated in a way that removes obstacles: adaptation might promise liberation. I am grateful to Hrishikesh Joshi for pressing the point.

have left each of the original options, X, Y and Z, in place.[30] Thus the offer of a reward does not serve to restrict your choice.[31]

We have seen that I may restrict a choice of yours by removing or replacing one or more of the options you face, changing the set of alternatives that is objectively available. But I can also restrict your choice by changing how the alternatives present themselves according to your perceptions: by putting apparent but merely pretend options on the table, thereby misrepresenting the actual options in place. An option will be available for your choice just insofar as you can make use, first, of the objective resources required for taking it rather than any alternative and, second, the cognitive resources needed to identify and understand the options on offer, to see that you are in a position to choose any one of them, and so to decide on what you prefer. Apart from affecting the use of your objective resources in order to change the choice you face, I can act to similar effect on the use of your cognitive resources. And that type of action should count equally as a mode of interfering with you: a potential way of restricting your exercise of choice.

There are two distinct strategies I might adopt with a view to misrepresenting your options, each of which comes, like removal and replacement, in degrees. One is deception; the other manipulation. If I deceive you about the options available in a choice, or about the consequences they are likely to trigger, I can obviously lead you to believe that the options are other than, as a matter of fact, they are. I can act on you so that the set of options you confront, according to your perceptions, is not X, Y and Z, but a set in which one or another option is removed or replaced or a further option is added. I will do this for example if I misinform you about the options on offer, or issue a bluff threat to penalize one of them, or even make an insincere offer to reward its choice. These are all means whereby I can impose cognitive, if not objective, limits on your exercise of choice.

This observation raises a natural question. It should be clear why I can restrict your choice by removing or replacing an option according to your perceptions, since removing or replacing an option as a matter of actual fact has the same effect; in either case I will deny you access to the option affected. But I do not restrict your choice by the objective addition of a

---

[30] Adding X-plus will change the opportunity costs of taking any of the other options, in particular, X. But I am assuming, as mentioned earlier in the text, that a change in the opportunity cost of an option does not entail a change of identity.

[31] What if the offer is exploitative, taking advantage of your lack of acceptable alternatives and offering an X-plus that is manifestly unfair? Strictly, the offer will not reduce your freedom in that particular choice, though you may count as taking the offered option involuntarily (Olsaretti 2004). But the offer may establish a relationship between us, as exploitation is generally taken to do, in which I dominate you. Similar remarks apply to the offer of the blackmailer.

further option, as when I make an offer and add X-plus to the set. So why do I do so when I lead you to believe falsely that another option like X-plus is available?

When I add an option objectively to your choice, allowing you to see the actual options available, then it remains up to you whether you choose X or Y or Z; it's just that you have the extra possibility of choosing X-plus instead. Thus I leave you in a position where you can act on your will or preference, whatever that should turn out to be. When I deceive you about the availability of an extra option like X-plus, however, the apparent availability of X-plus affects the presentation of X. It makes the option of choosing X, which is all that is actually available to you, look like an option that can have the reward attached. In effect, it replaces the option X, as it is cognitively registered, by a pair of options: X-and-refuse-the-reward, or X-and-accept-the-reward.

I will not succeed in deceiving you, and so not succeed in restricting your freedom, if you realize that I am deceptive and ignore what I say. But what of the case where I do successfully deceive you but do not stop you choosing as you would have done in my absence? What of the case where I issue a bluff threat to penalize an option, say Y, and this is not enough to make you change your mind: you still opt for Y? Can I be said to restrict your choice in this sort of case? I will have forced you to choose from amongst a set of apparent options that did not conform to the set actually available. Where the actual choice was between X, Y and Z, I forced you to choose as if it were a choice between X, Y-minus and Z. It may be a happy result that having formed a will to take Y-minus, you actually get something better, plain Y. But nonetheless, I forced you to form your will in the dark, not on the basis of how things actually were.

Apart from deceiving you, I may deny you the use of your cognitive resources in making a certain choice by recourse to what I call manipulation. Manipulation denies you the possibility of making a choice on the basis of a proper understanding of the options on offer. It applies pressures that affect your exercise of the capacity to think straight about the considerations for and against different choices and so about the nature of the options on offer. Manipulation may involve hypnotizing you, mesmerizing you with the prospect of extraordinary rewards, making you feel guilty about not doing what I wish, snowing you with so much information that you are putty in my hands, or exposing you, if I am capable of it, to the undermining power of my rhetoric.

Like successful deception, successful manipulation will affect the exercise of your cognitive capacity to choose between certain options, even if it leaves your objective capacity in place. By means of manipulation, I may succeed in getting you to choose as I wish, but even if I fail in that, I will still

Table 1.2 *Modes of interference*

Do I interfere in your choice between X, Y, Z	a. objectively (whether signalling the fact or not)	b. cognitively (but not objectively)
1. by removing an option?	Yes. Real obstacle.	Yes. Pretend obstacle.
2. by replacing an option?	Yes. Real penalty.	Yes. Pretend penalty.
3. by adding an option?	No. Real reward.	Yes. Pretend reward.

have restricted your choice by getting you to face what seem like different options from those that were objectively available. I rig things so that your will between X, Y and Z – the will you would form if you saw those options for what they truly are – does not dictate the action you take; rather it is dictated by your will over the distorted versions of those options that I conjure into existence.[32]

In summary of what we have argued, then, there are three ways in which I may interfere with you and restrict your choice: by removing options, by replacing options or by misrepresenting options. And misrepresentation can involve removing, replacing or adding an option in your cognitive perception of things. The different modes of interference are salient in the questions and answers mapped in the accompanying Table 1.2.

Interference is not sufficient for subjection

Interference in the sense characterized always restricts your choice, affecting the options that are actually or apparently available. But does that mean that it always subjects you to the will of the interferer? Surprisingly, it does not.

---

[32] Given that manipulation can affect free choice only insofar as it distorts the presentation of the options, it is important to recognize that not all attempts to change the way in which an agent sees certain options count as manipulative and hostile to freedom. Consider the nudge, as it has recently been described – and proposed as an acceptable resource of government (Thaler and Sunstein 2008). For example, consider the nudge involved in presenting people with an opt-out versus an opt-in choice when they sign up for driving licences and are asked about whether they are willing, in the event of a fatal accident, to donate their organs to others. The difference between these presentations has a great impact on whether people sign up for donation or not: most sign up if they have to opt out of donation, most don't sign up if they have to opt in. So does nudging in a case like this amount to manipulation? While we may not be able to provide a general algorithm for answering the question, I think it is clear in this sort of example that the answer should be negative. The opt-out system probably evokes more positive choices because it communicates the presumptively correct and non-deceptive message that there are no horrific consequences attached to the choice; if there were, the opt-in system would scarcely have survived. The nudging involved does not replace any of the options on offer with a distorted counterpart and it does not have the potential to affect a person's freedom in making the choice between signing up and not signing up for organ donation. It serves to provide further information on the options, at least on the presumption about the correctness of the message conveyed.

Suppose you wish to restrict your alcohol consumption and hand over the key of your alcohol cupboard to me, making me promise to return the key only at twenty-four hours' notice and not in response to a request for its immediate return. When I refuse a request for immediate return of the key, I interfere with your choice, removing the option of having a drink now. I deny you the possibility of choosing according to your current will. But do I subject you to my will? Do I impose my will on you, for example, in a way that might reasonably trigger resentment? Surely not.[33]

In refusing the key I act under your instructions, not on my own wishes or impulses: not at my own will or discretion. And, so we may assume, I refuse the key only because your instructions require me to do so. There is no real possibility that I might try to keep it against your wishes, refusing to hand it over at twenty-four hours' notice; such an action would jeopardize a relationship that matters to me. In these conditions it should be clear that you control what I do in refusing your request that I give you the key now; I interfere with you, but only on your terms.

The arrangement in place with the key is a means, we might say, whereby you impose your own longer-term will on yourself, not a means whereby I impose my will on you. You are the one who set up that arrangement and you are the one who decided the conditions it imposes. You use me to give effect to your own will, not relying on yourself to be able to do so. When I shut off the option that you now want to take, interfering with you and even frustrating you, I channel that will and enable it to have an impact on your behaviour. I perform like a robot that is programmed to satisfy your instructions. I act as your servant, not your master. The lesson of the example is that the interference that I or any others practise in a choice of yours will not impose an alien will, and not therefore invade your freedom of choice, to the extent that my discretion in exercising interference is subject to your control: it is shaped by your influence so as to assume a form that appeals to you; it materializes on terms that you dictate.

Interference is defined broadly enough to cover any plausible form of activity whereby others might deliberately restrict your choices. In effect it is defined broadly enough to represent the only candidate for a form of active invasion; in particular, a form of active invasion that need not require the presence of an uncontrolled power in another. And so the lesson of the

---

[33] I assume in this example, and I make analogous assumptions in the other cases where I apply the lesson of the example, that the will that you display in giving instructions can be identified as suitably stable or authoritative in comparison with the will that the instructions require me to frustrate. There are a number of ways in which this assumption might be vindicated but I do not pursue them here.

example is that there can be no active invasion of choice unless there is domination. The active, intentional restriction of your choice by any other agent or agency will be invasive only to the extent that it reflects a will that you do not control.

The republican lesson about uncontrolled interference has often been formulated in the claim that, provided it is non-arbitrary, interference does not subject you to an alien will. Arbitrary interference, on this interpretation, is interference practised in accordance with the *arbitrium*, or 'will', of another. It is precisely what I describe here as uncontrolled interference: that is, interference that is exercised at the will or discretion of the interferer; interference that is uncontrolled by the person on the receiving end (Skinner 2008a).

In what follows I shall make little or no use of the term 'arbitrary', preferring to speak of uncontrolled interference. The reason is that while I believe that in earlier republican usage the word had something close to the meaning I ascribe, it has other, misleading connotations today. In one usage, arbitrary interference is interference that is not subject to established rules. But interference that conforms to rules, and is non-arbitrary in that sense, may still be uncontrolled by you and can count as arbitrary in our sense. In another usage, arbitrary interference is interference that is wrong or objectionable, so that what is arbitrary from one evaluative standpoint may not be arbitrary from another. But while uncontrolled interference is going to count as uniformly objectionable in most moral views, even those who adopt a contrary view – even someone, for example, like Hobbes – ought to be able to agree on whether, and to what extent, an act of interference counts as uncontrolled and arbitrary in our usage. On that usage the term has a perfectly descriptive, determinable meaning and people can agree on when it applies and when it does not apply, independently of differences in the values they espouse; it is not a value-dependent or moralized term.[34]

It may be useful to add one further comment about treating licensed or controlled interference as non-invasive of free choice. This is that the concession does not allow paternalistic interference. When I am being paternalistic I interfere in your choice according to your interests, though not necessarily according to your wishes. But interests are always open to interpretation, since they consist roughly in the wishes that you would have for yourself, if you were able to view your predicament accurately and rationally

---

[34] For an understanding of 'non-arbitrary' that preserves the rule-conformity connotation, though without creating a great gulf between us, see Lovett (2010). For an evaluative understanding of the term, but again one that does not create any substantive divergence of views, see Richardson (2002). For a critique of my position that turns on related issues see McMahon (2005) – and for related discussion, Costa (2007) – and for my response to that critique see Pettit (2006a).

(Geuss 1981; Smith 1994). And to the extent that I impose my own inter-pretation on your interests, discounting yours as inferior, I act paternalistically (Shiffrin 2000). Such paternalistic intervention, in the nature of the case, involves interfering according to my own *arbitrium*, or 'will', not yours, and is an exemplar of domination. The most that might be allowed on the repub-lican view is interference according to interests that you are disposed or ready to avow, where that readiness is easily tested and established; only this could give you the control required to avoid domination (Pettit 2001e).

4. NO DOMINATION WITHOUT INVASION

The considerations presented show that I do not reduce your freedom in a choice to the extent that I actively interfere without domination: that is, to the extent that you control my interference. But the paired issue we have to consider is whether I can invade your freedom in the exercise of a choice, not by means of any activity – not by interfering with any of the options – but just by having an uncontrolled power of interfering with the choice of any option: just by dominating you.

By the argument provided so far, you are unfree in a choice to the extent that you are subject to my will – or, of course, the will of any other agent – in making that choice. I can impose my will on you in a choice between X, Y and Z by taking steps, uncontrolled by you, that change the cognitive or objective profile of the options. But it turns out that you can be subject to my will in a choice, and this subjection can change the profile of options you face, even if I do not actively impose my will in this way. You will suffer that sort of subjection to the extent that I have the uncontrolled power of interfering in the choice – the unvitiated, uninvaded capacity to interfere. You will suffer that sort of subjection, in other words, to the extent that I dominate you.

Suppose that I have such a power of uncontrolled interference in your choice between X, Y and Z. And suppose that I do not actually exercise that power, because I am favourably disposed towards you. While I am not constrained to let you choose as you will, I view you with affection or indulgence and am happy to let you choose according to your own wishes. Even in this benign case, it turns out that there is a sense in which you are subject to my will and a sense in which your options are not what they would have been in the absence of such a power on my part.

You will be subject to my will, in the sense that you depend on my will remaining a good will, for the ability to choose as you wish. Let me remain benevolent and you will be able to choose X or Y or Z, as you please. Let me become malevolent, however, and this will cease to be so: I will exercise my power of interference so as to change the profile of the options before you. This dependency on the state of my will constitutes a form of subjection to my will, even when I do not actively impose my will on you. The subjection shows up in an alteration of the options you face. You will no longer confront a free choice between X, Y and Z. Rather, the objective or cognitive profile of the options will be changed so that what you confront is a choice between X-if-it-please-me, Y-if-it-please-me and Z-if-it-please-me. The options will alter in a manner that parallels the alteration imposed by the removal, replacement or misrepresentation associated with unlicensed and uncontrolled interference.

But why should you care about subjection to me, if I am a wholly benign master? Why should you care about the possibility of my interfering with you if, as it happens, you think my benevolence runs so deep that it is vanishingly unlikely that I would ever interfere? Shouldn't your concern about the possibility of interference on my part, or on anyone else's, be scaled to the probability of such interference?

The answer is that you could think of me in this purely probabilistic way only if you adopted the sort of objective stance in which I cease to deserve reactive attitudes like gratitude or resentment and become reduced to the status of a force of nature: in this case, a wholly benign force of nature (Strawson 1962; Pettit and Smith 1996). If you treat me as a regular human being operating in regular circumstances you must be ready to feel gratitude or resentment, approval or indignation, as my choices merit: you must be ready to hold me responsible for the choice. And so you must think of me as having the capacity with any of the options I face to take one or to take another; that is a precondition of being poised to treat me reactively, holding me responsible for what I choose. From within the perspective that you are more or less bound to adopt, then, you will see me as a centre of choice for whom interference is equally available with non-interference: as someone for whom the question of whether to interfere or not is an open issue and as someone, therefore, on whose goodwill you depend. Thus my access to interference is going to be challenging, even if you think it unlikely that I will interfere. The accessibility of the interference will signal your dependence on my will quite independently of the probability of my actually interfering.

Invigilation and intimidation

There are a number of ways in which I may dominate you without any interference, as there are many ways of practising interference itself. They divide into two broad types, invigilation and intimidation. While these normally go together they can also come apart: there can be invigilation without intimidation and intimidation without invigilation.

In invigilation I stand guard over what you do, ready to interfere should my will tend that way. As things are, I may not be disposed to interfere in any way but even so I remain in a position where I can and will interfere in the event of a change in my disposition. As a result of this invigilation, and whether or not you are aware of the fact, you will be subject to my will; you will be dependent on my goodwill for retaining the capacity to exercise choice. The options you face, then, will not be X, Y and Z, just as such, but rather X-if-it-please-me, Y-if-it-please-me and Z-if-it-please-me. In other words, the objective profile of the options will be changed by my presence so that, in the old phrase, you can choose as you wish but only *cum permissu*: only 'by my leave', or 'with my permission'. Being able to choose as you wish you may be said to be at liberty to choose X, Y or Z, but to be at liberty in that sense is not to be free in the sense of escaping subjection to the will of another. Your choice may reflect your will, but it does so only because your choosing according to your will is something that accords with my will. I am in the position of a master.

If I invigilate your choice and you become aware of the fact, then the options will change their cognitive, as well as their objective, profile. In that case you are likely to suffer intimidation as well as invigilation, recognizing your dependency and vulnerability. The intimidation will boost the effect of the invigilation, giving you an incentive to be cautious and deferential, in the same way that recognizing that I will penalize a particular option will boost the effect of the penalty, giving you an incentive to avoid it. Indeed, it may lead you to behave as I would obviously prefer that you behave, even when I am willing to let you have your own way; it may ensure that my presumptive preference guides your choice without my having to lift a hand or utter a word.

Intimidation may also have this effect, however, in the absence of invigilation. In the standard case of invigilation-cum-intimidation, the resources of interference on which I rely are independent of your belief that I have them and of the intimidating effect of that belief. But even if I have no independent resources, and even if I cannot strictly practise invigilation, the fact that you believe that I have the resources, and the fact that this intimidates you, will still give me power over you. It will enable me to deceive you, say by making a credible threat – though, of course, a bluff threat – to penalize a certain option, and so it will enable me to subject you in a certain measure to my will. It will mean that the options you take to be present are not X, Y and Z but rather X-if-it-please-me, Y-if-it-please-me and Z-if-it-please-me. This observation illustrates the truth of Hobbes's (1994b: 10.5) remark that whether or not it is well founded, the 'reputation of power is power'. It gives us reason to recognize that intimidation counts, side by side with invigilation, as a way in which I may subject you to my will, even when I do not actively impose that will in interference.[35]

These observations are enough to show that I can reduce your freedom in a choice to the extent that I can expose you to the possibility of interference: to the extent that I have a power, uncontrolled by you, of interfering in your choices. One thing worth noting in particular is that I may do this even without wishing to have or exercise this power. Suppose that I have the power on such a basis that I can neither renounce it nor do anything to reduce it. I cannot help knowing how you act, so that I have the cognitive resources required for interference. And I have the objective resources on an inalienable basis – say, because of having certain legal advantages, more physical prowess or greater social clout. I may wish not to dominate you in such a case – my will may be that you are not dependent on my will – but whether I like it or not you are dependent and I exercise domination. You are dependent on my will, and subject to my will, even though it is not my will that you should suffer such domination.

It may seem quixotic to hold that I can subject you to my will without it being my will that you should be subject to me in that way. But there is nothing impossible about such unwilled domination. It is likely to be exemplified in any relationships of inalienable asymmetrical power, as with the husband over the wife in a sexist culture, the employer over employees in an unregulated economy, the professor over students in a traditional college. If I dominate you in this way, you will depend on my will in the sense that how you fare in relevant choices – whether or not, for example, you can choose between X, Y and Z – is going to vary as I vary in my will towards you; you will retain access to those options so long as I remain goodwilled, but you will lose access as soon as that goodwill decreases or disappears. But I will not relish this subjection that you suffer and, could I do something to rectify it, I would. Our relationship means that I subject you to my will, and the fact that I shrink from the domination thereby imposed means that I subject you to my will non-intentionally.

---

[35] Note that if we include the non-standard resources activated under your belief that I have a power of interference, intimidation will count as a form of invigilation; the distinction depends on requiring invigilation to depend on standard, presupposed resources of interference. Note also that while intimidation without invigilation depends on your falsely believing that I have a power of interference, it is distinct from deception, considered as a particular, intentional act of deceiving you about the options available in the relevant choice. This is to clarify how I keep the books on these questions, but not to suggest that it is a uniquely appropriate way of doing so. I am grateful to Dorothea Gadeke for discussion on this point.

Can I alienate my power of interference, and suspend the domination I practise, by persuading myself that it is wrong to interfere in your choice? Will the moral constraints that I thereby recognize act as checks on my will and serve to liberate you, whether wholly or in part? I do not think so. Even if I form the view that it is wrong to interfere with you, it remains the case that I may prefer to practise interference, whether out of weakness of will, out of malice, or out of a will for evil; the option continues to lie within my capacity. My power of interference in your choice, and my domination over you, can only be contained by external checks that remove or replace the interference option or put it cognitively off the menu. My believing in the wrongness of interfering will only introduce an external check to the extent that I am thereby exposed, as I see things, to the penalty of moral disapprobation for behaving in that way.

For those who continue to baulk at the idea that domination without interference constitutes an invasion of your freedom, subjecting you to my will, there is one last consideration worth introducing. This is that such subjection is enough in itself to trigger the resentment that, as we saw, typically characterizes the invasion, as distinct from the vitiation, of choice. You may not resent me for the power that I am given by social convention or natural prowess over you, since I am not responsible for having such power. But it would only be human of you to resent me for acquiescing in the power and, in particular, to resent the failure of the society not to rectify that imbalance and affirm your equal standing. You may burn with such resentment, as documented in oral and literary tradition, even as you recognize that I do not want to have a power of interference and even think it wrong to exercise that power against you.

These observations are interesting in themselves, but they also suggest that we should recognize an indirect or structural form of domination as well as the direct or personal kind, willed or unwilled, that we have been describing (Hayward 2011). It is usually because of the ways a society is organized, culturally, economically or legally, that some people have such power in relation to others that they dominate them directly, and dominate them without necessarily wishing for domination or even approving of it. Thus it is usually because of the way that marriage law or workplace law is structured that husbands or employers have a dominating power over their wives or workers. These modes of organization may vitiate, but not invade, choice, as when they emerge for example from customary practice, but they can indirectly facilitate the worst forms of invasion and domination in a society. The republican theory of justice, which we discuss in the next chapter, is designed in great part to target such structural domination, looking for measures whereby people can be assured on a public basis of not being dominated by others in the broad range of the basic liberties.

Three theories of freedom

Let us assume, as argued earlier, that any plausible theory of freedom should accept that free choice requires the absence of vitiating factors. With that assumption in place, we can distinguish three broadly different theories of freedom, each giving a different account of what suffices for freedom on the invasive front. One theory, Hobbesian in inspiration, would say that freedom of choice consists in the absence of invasive obstruction to your actually preferred option, thereby equating freedom with non-frustration. A second, in the style of Berlin, would hold that freedom of choice consists in the absence of invasive obstruction to any option, preferred or unpreferred, thereby equating freedom with non-interference – non-frustration, actual or counterfactual. And a third, republican in character, would hold that freedom of choice consists in the absence of a power of interference on the part of any other, thereby equating freedom with non-domination. In bringing the discussion to a close it may be helpful to see that Berlin's argument against Hobbes – in effect, the argument for freedom as non-interference and against freedom as non-frustration – suggests a parallel argument for freedom as non-domination and against freedom as non-interference (Pettit 2011b).

The argument against freedom as non-frustration is that it leads to an absurdity; it entails, contrary to powerful intuitions, that adapting your preferences can give you freedom of choice. The argument against freedom as non-interference is that it leads, by a parallel argument, to a parallel absurdity; it entails, contrary to equally powerful intuitions, that ingratiation – toadying, kowtowing and cosying up to the powerful – can give you freedom of choice. I understand ingratiation in this context as an intervention that wins the indulgence of the powerful without exposing them to any cost or penalty, not even the cost of disesteem.

I set out the argument in steps that highlight the parallel with Berlin's argument against Hobbes.

1. Suppose with Berlin that you enjoy freedom in a choice between X and Y just to the extent that you avoid interference; suppose that non-interference, with or without domination, is enough for freedom.
2. By that supposition, you do not enjoy freedom of choice in the case where I have a power of interference and, being ill-willed, am disposed to interfere with one or the other option.

3. But, by supposition, you would enjoy freedom of choice in that case if I were disposed, notwithstanding my power of interference, to interfere with neither.
4. If you know the situation, then, it appears that you can give yourself freedom of choice, without reducing my power of interference, just by ingratiating yourself with me and getting me to let you have your way.
5. But this is absurd. You cannot give yourself freedom in the choice just by accommodating yourself to my power of interference.
6. Thus the original supposition that non-interference is enough for freedom of choice must be false.

The view that non-interference is enough for freedom of choice entails that ingratiation is a possible means of liberation in the same way that Hobbes's view that non-frustration is enough entails that adaptation is a possible means of liberation. And this entailment argues against the theory of freedom as non-interference as the corresponding entailment argues against the theory of freedom as non-frustration. Let the anti-adaptation assumption be granted and the non-frustration theory must fail; let the anti-ingratiation assumption be granted and the non-interference theory must fail.

The problem is not that adaptation or ingratiation in the relevant contexts is intuitively objectionable, as it surely is, or even that it will occur very often, which it may not do. The problem, rather, is that neither adaptation nor ingratiation counts intuitively as a means of liberation in a given choice and any theory that entails that it can serve such a liberating role has to be inadequate. Adapting your preference so as to want what I let you get takes my interference as a given and tries to secure a decidedly second-best result: the avoidance of frustration. And ingratiating yourself with me in order to win my permission for you to do what you want takes my power of interference, and so your own subjection, as a given, and tries to secure a somewhat better but still second-best result: the avoidance of actual interference. In each case we want to say: this is not freedom in the most attractive sense – the sense in which it requires the availability of each option and independence from the will of any other as to what you do. There is a Pickwickian flavour to claiming that you have won your freedom in a choice by dint of adapting to my interference or in virtue of softening me up. Each is a way of sugaring a bitter pill, not a means of rejecting the need to swallow it.[36]

---

[36] The point is more easily lost in the ingratiation case, it should be noticed, than in the case of adaptation. We can readily imagine cases in which one single episode of ingratiation secures access for you to a range of undominated choices. And in such cases it is easy to forget about the question of whether the choice in which ingratiation enabled you to get your way was itself free – I say it was not – and to focus on the fact that in view of the new choices that become available, the ingratiation was

Adaptation may be a rational response to the frustration imposed by another, since it does indeed give you a second-best: if not freedom to satisfy your preference, regardless of what you prefer to do, at least the formation of a preference you can satisfy. And ingratiation may equally be a rational response to another's power of interference, since it also gives you a second-best: if not freedom to satisfy your preference, regardless of what others prefer that you do, at least enough breathing space to let you act as you will. It may not give you the benefits of a secure peace in your relations with the powerful, but it will give you the consolations of a fragile cease-fire.

The gain secured in each case allows us to say, in ordinary usage, that by contrast with the situation where you do not make such responses you can win a degree of freedom for yourself by adaptation or ingratiation. This is because in ordinary usage, as we have seen, talk of freedom is often used to mark context-sensitive contrasts, so that one and the same choice may be described as free or unfree, depending on the contexts under comparison. But no matter what the context of usage, the benefit that you win by adaptation or ingratiation is not freedom in the regimented sense that we have been developing; in this sense, freedom of choice requires that every option be accessible and that your access to any option be independent of the preference of another as to what you should do.

We can give nice expression to this sense of freedom by elaborating on Berlin's open-doors metaphor. Where the anti-adaptation assumption means that all the options in a free choice have to be open doors, the anti-ingratiation claim implies that not any mode of openness will do. Are you free just insofar as both doors are open in the choice between X and Y? Not necessarily. What freedom ideally requires is not just that the doors be open but that there be no door-keeper who has the power of closing a door; there is no door-keeper on whose goodwill you depend for one or another of the doors remaining open. If I am in the position of such a door-keeper, therefore, your access to the X and Y options is not supported in the manner that freedom of choice strictly requires.

As the plausibility of the anti-adaptation assumption argues that all the doors in a free choice must be open, then, so the plausibility of the anti-ingratiation assumption argues that there must be no dependence on the

---

liberating in a distinct sense. Suppose, to go back to our old example, that you ingratiate yourself sufficiently with the warden or parole board to have a choice between remaining in prison or living outside. The ingratiation will mean that you did not have a free choice in that instance but it will be liberating in the distinct sense that it enables you now to enjoy all the undominated choices that become available in the world outside.

good graces of a door-keeper. When you ingratiate yourself with me and I let you go by a door that I would otherwise have closed, you do not cease to be subject to my will. You have not escaped the constraint that made you unfree in the first place, nor done anything to reduce the effectiveness of the constraint. While continuing to operate under the yoke of my will, you have merely adjusted so as to make your life more comfortable.

Freedom, robustness and probability, again

In holding that all the options in a choice should be open doors, the view of freedom as non-interference implies that ideally you must be unfrustrated in the actual world where you prefer X and also in the possible world where you prefer Y. It requires that you should enjoy non-interference, not just actually, but robustly: that is, in a range of possible worlds associated with the available options, however unlikely some of those worlds may be.

In requiring that all options should be open, and in addition that there should be no door-keepers, the theory of freedom as non-domination implies that non-interference should be modally robust in a greater measure still (Pettit 2001a; List 2004).[37] It is not enough to enjoy non-interference across a range of worlds in which your preference or will changes, now seeking X, now seeking Y. For full or ideal freedom of choice, you also have to enjoy non-interference across a range of worlds in which there are also changes in the preference or will of other agents as to what you should do.

Thus you have to enjoy non-interference in X-worlds where others are friendly, but also in X-worlds where others are unfriendly. And you have to enjoy non-interference in Y-worlds where others are friendly and Y-worlds where others are unfriendly. You have to enjoy non-interference in a way that is invariant across relevant alterations both in your own will and in the will of others as to what you should do. We saw in Section 1 that in order to increase the probability of your freedom in an X–Y choice, on the theory of freedom as non-interference, we have to minimize the following sum, assuming that addition is appropriate: P(H if X) + P(H if Y). Things are going to be a bit more complex if we want to increase the probability of your freedom as non-domination, for we will have to allow for worlds where others are unfriendly (U) as well as friendly (F). Sticking with the additive

---

[37] For a somewhat variant treatment see List (2006b) and the discussion of freedom, which follows this treatment, in List and Pettit (2011: Chapter 6).

version of the approach, we will want to minimize the sum: $P(H \text{ if } X \& F)$ + $P(H \text{ if } X \& U)$ + $P(H \text{ if } Y \& F)$ + $P(H \text{ if } Y \& U)$.[38]

Minimizing this sum will mean maximizing expected non-domination. It will involve keeping or putting barriers in place against the possible interference of those who would otherwise have a power of interference in your relevant choices. And it will mean keeping or putting obstacles in place against the formation of agents or agencies that could have such power, if they did come into existence. Thus it might mean taking steps to guard against the possibility of a loose collection of individuals – say, a belligerent minority or a potentially oppressive majority – incorporating to form a dominating presence in the lives of others.

I add one final comment on the relationship between domination, interference and frustration. We noted earlier that hindrance with frustration is more harmful than hindrance without and that hindrance without frustration gets worse – it holds out the prospect of greater harm – as the probability of frustration increases. Equally, domination with interference is intuitively more harmful than domination without, so that we can associate progressively greater levels of harm with the following three conditions: domination without interference or frustration; domination with interference but without frustration; and domination with both interference and frustration. And correspondingly, we can say that domination without interference gets worse as interference becomes more probable, and that interference without frustration gets worse as the probability of frustration rises. My inclination is to cast the extra harms imposed by interference and frustration as distinct harms from the loss of freedom but, as I mentioned in

---

[38] In an earlier footnote on freedom as non-interference I suggested that in an X–Y choice it is not enough for such freedom that you enjoy the absence of hindrance in the actual world where you prefer X and in the nearest possible world in which you choose the other option, Y; it is required, plausibly, that you can get X in any of a wider range of worlds, including the actual one, in which you prefer X; and can get Y in any of a wider range of possible worlds, including the nearest possible one, in which you prefer Y. I take a similar view of the range of possible worlds in which you must avoid interference if you are to enjoy non-domination. And here as in the other case, I think that this range of worlds is discernible only on an intuitive, context-sensitive basis and, of course, that it does not include all possible worlds. The worlds where non-domination requires that you choose X without interference, for example, may vary in the precise physical movements whereby your X-ing is realized and in the degrees of friendliness or hostility that others display. But they do not extend to all possible worlds in which you choose X. Thus you are not unfree to make the choice between X and Y just because you would suffer interference with X, should those in whose presence you act not only turn hostile, but also develop super-human powers. The need to rely on contextual assumptions to determine the range of relevant possible worlds is regrettable, but from the point of view of formalizing the theory of freedom it seems inevitable. As mentioned in the earlier footnote, the indeterminacy is akin to that which arises in epistemology when we ask about the range of possible worlds in which true belief has to be present – when we ask about the extent to which true belief has to be robust – if there is to be something deserving of being called knowledge.

discussing hindrance and frustration, there is no objection in principle to seeing them as freedom-related harms.[39] We might well think that while domination is enough for the loss of freedom, interference and frustration make the loss more severe still.[40]

5. HOW CAN WE ENSURE YOUR FREEDOM OF CHOICE?

Resourcing and protecting

We have concentrated in this chapter on how you can fail to be free in a choice between options like X, Y and Z. We argued that you can fail through having any of the options hindered and that hindrance may take the form either of vitiation by impersonal factors or of invasion by another agent or agency. And we saw that invasion – subjection to the will of another – may or may not involve the interference of the other, but requires in either case that the other has a certain power of uncontrolled interference and counts in that sense as dominating the choice.

How might we ensure, then, that you are free in the exercise of a choice? Two things are required. First, we would have to resource or facilitate the choice in the sense of ensuring that any of the required resources you happen to lack – these may be personal, natural or social – are made available to you; we would have to compensate, in other words, for any vitiation of the choice. And second, we would have to protect you in the exercise of that choice; assuming that protection is needed, we would have to guard against your being subject to the will of another in how you exercise it: that is, against invasion.

Resourcing or facilitating the choice could involve many different sorts of things. Were it a choice like driving or cycling to a certain destination, for example, it might involve making sure you have a car and bicycle, that you possess the skills that driving and cycling require, that there is both a network of roads and a set of conventions governing their use, and that you know the rules of the road and the route to the destination. It might even involve helping you to make up for certain unusual physical or psychological deficiencies, providing suitable assistance or therapy. Most of the resources

---

[39] If we do take this view then, by analogy with a point made in discussing the interference-frustration case, we will have to give some weight to the probability of interference and to the probability of frustration. See the earlier footnote on the interference-frustration case.

[40] This observation shows how we may take on board the lesson emphasized by Sen (2002) – in part, against the republican view that he finds in my work – that there are many dimensions relevant to the measurement of freedom.

required for exercising the choice will be available to you independently of any help from us and these steps will usually be unnecessary. But they illustrate what resourcing the choice might come to.

I mentioned earlier that you will not be suitably resourced – you will not be resourced in a way that gives you the capacity presupposed to freedom – if you have to depend on the goodwill of another for getting the resources. The rationale for that stipulation should now be clear: if you depended on me for the resources needed to choose an option, then I would have a power of uncontrolled interference in the choice and would dominate you. This stipulation means that any resourcing we provide for you will be suitable only if we can provide it in a way that does not introduce dependence on any particular agent or agency. We would avoid introducing dependence by resourcing you on the same grounds that we resource each one of us, as in the case of providing for shared roads and shared rules of the road. And with resources that you in particular need, we might avoid introducing dependence by giving you claims under general rules to the resources needed.

Protecting, as distinct from resourcing, the choice involves guarding you, where that is necessary, against subjection to the will of any other person or group in how you exercise the choice. Such protection will be focused on the potential interference of any other and will put blocks or burdens in place which ensure, so far as possible, that no one has a power of interfering in the choice – or at least that no one has a power of interfering that is not controlled by you.

The most important point to register about protecting against such interference – strictly, against such a power of interference – is that it is quite distinct from promoting non-interference: that is, taking steps that make non-interference as likely as possible. We might make interference very unlikely, even more unlikely than under a protective regime, by buying off potential interferers: that is, by offering them rewards for not interfering with you. The fact that someone was persuaded on that basis not to interfere in your choice, however, would not release you from subjection to their will. They would still have access to the option of interfering, for all that our rewards ensured; the rewards would just mean that apart from not interfering, period, they would have the further option of not interfering and accepting our reward. The point in protection is not to maximize expected non-interference but to maximize expected non-domination. It means taking steps to ensure that you enjoy safeguards against interference that remain in place across variations both in what you prefer to choose and in what others prefer that you choose.

The requirements of protection

How are we to protect you against someone's interference in one or another choice? It might seem that we should just reduce the person's freedom of choice between interfering and not interfering. But that is not right, for two important reasons.

The first is that the person may be denied the freedom to interfere or not interfere because of facing a check against non-interference rather than against interference. We will not protect you if we check someone's option of not interfering, thereby reducing their freedom to interfere or not to interfere. If the check is serious enough – if it involves removing the option of non-interference, for example – it will mean that strictly the person does not interfere with your choice, not intentionally restricting it, but in that case we will ourselves interfere insofar as we use them to restrict the choice. And if the check is not so serious, it will allow the person to continue to interfere, intentionally restricting the choice, and give us a role or a share in that interference. In order to protect you against another person or party, we must try to reduce their capacity to interfere, not their freedom to choose between interference and non-interference.

The second reason why protecting you against someone's interference must do more than reduce the person's freedom of choice between interfering and not interfering is that we can replace the interference option in that choice, and reduce the person's freedom, just by imposing an actual or apparent obstacle or penalty – or an actual or apparent probability of obstacle or penalty – that has little defensive or deterrent value. To protect against interference is not just to interfere in any old way with the agent's interference option. In the limit case it is to prevent interference: to impose an indubitable, insurmountable obstacle. And short of that limit it is to impose such a probability of such an obstructive obstacle or such a deterrent penalty – in either case actual or apparent – that the person's power of interference in your choices gets to be reduced to a point where, by local standards, you have no good reason to be anxious. Interference may not be impossible for the other but it will incur such difficulty or such danger for the interferer that it is relatively unacceptable or ineligible.

We said earlier that someone will dominate you and compromise your freedom in a choice to the extent that they have a power of uncontrolled interference with one or another option. While preventive protection may be preventive under a smaller or larger range of variations in the attitudes of others – and while in that sense it can come in degrees – it removes that power in a radical way. Other forms of protection do not have the same sort of impact but they can reduce the person's power of interference to the point where interference is effectively ineligible and not interfering is a forced or involuntary choice (Olsaretti 2004).

We need not worry about the subjectivity of this benchmark for determining whether protection is adequate, if in the local culture there is an accepted sense of where the benchmark lies. In the next chapter, as already advertised, I will be introducing the eyeball test to determine what level of freedom you must enjoy in the exercise of the basic liberties, as I call them, in order to count as a free person or citizen. The test suggests that you should have access to a level of resources and protections for those choices that enables you, by local standards, to look others in the eye without a reason for fear or deference. It will provide the required benchmark for adequacy in protection.

We know that some forms of interference are going to be less serious than others, say because of involving the replacement of an option, X, by an option that is just barely different from it: the option of doing X with a little discomfort, or at a little extra cost. The effect of the eyeball test will be to require a degree of protection against others that makes the interference option ineligible, if not actually impossible, and that does this more and more effectively with progressively more serious forms of interference.[41]

While protection against interference comes in degrees for these reasons, it is worth stressing that this in no way softens the contrast between enjoying a low prospect of interference that is induced by protective measures and enjoying a low probability of interference that is just based on the unlikelihood of potential interferers turning nasty. It is only when you are protected, however probabilistic the protection may be, that you can achieve a degree of independence from the goodwill of others for being able to choose as you wish. The decreasing probability of (uncontrolled) interference is a good, as we saw earlier, even if it comes of an increasing goodwill, perhaps induced by your ingratiation, on the part of the powerful. The decreasing probability of (uncontrolled) interference that is induced by protection is good in the same way and also good in a second: not only does it make

---

[41] This line of thought is connected with the old slogan, according to which you are unfree in a choice when you are exposed to forms of interference, presumptively serious, that others can impose at will and with impunity. Others will be able to interfere at will insofar as they are not prevented or not likely to be prevented from interfering. And others will be able to interfere with impunity insofar as they are not subject to a penalty that inhibits and deters interference, making it effectively ineligible. We can make you free, so the idea goes, to the extent that we can prevent or inhibit interferers in a suitable degree: we can deny them interference-at-an-acceptable-cost.

(uncontrolled) interference less likely, it also reduces the power of interference on the part of the powerful.[42]

Actions and omissions

When we are in a position to resource and protect your freedom, there is going to be a question about whether the failure to provide resourcing and protection counts as inimical to freedom in the same way as the invasion of that choice. Is the failure or omission that materializes here as serious in freedom terms as the more active harm? And is the power of omission as serious therefore as the power of interference that constitutes domination? In some circumstances omission or failure of the kind envisaged may be as morally, politically or even legally culpable as invasion. But a failure to resource or protect is not itself a way of invading that capacity, nor is having the power to fail a mode of domination. If such failure is an offence, as it will often surely be, it is a distinct offence from invasion.

That said, however, there is a very fuzzy line between certain failures of resourcing and protection and actual invasion. Suppose that I provide for your resourcing and protection in a certain range of choice and that, as time goes on, this comes to represent the default expectation, shared between us, as to what is going to transpire. In the context of these expectations, and the pattern of one-sided reliance it sets up, the negative action of refusing further help can be indistinguishable from an invasion of your free choice. Indeed, my assumption of such a routine resourcing or protective role may place me in a position where I dominate you. You will depend on my goodwill for my continuing to provide for you, and, as it will appear in the new context, for not invading your relevant choices. Or at least this will be the case insofar as I am the only one able to help – there is not a queue of people lined up to take my place – and there are no pressures that more or less constrain me to do so.

Our discussion of the nature of resourcing and protection leads us naturally into the project pursued in this book. I shall argue in the coming chapters that the freedom as non-domination of its citizens is of paramount importance for the state insofar as it is interested in justice or legitimacy and that its first duty in both justice and legitimacy is to try to make its people

---

[42] The point of this paragraph might be nicely illustrated with the help of a graph in which the vertical axis represents increasing opportunity costs on the interference of others in your affairs and the horizontal represents increasing protective costs. The indifference curves that represent equally valuable bundles from your point of view will be skewed in a way that reveals the greater value at any level of interference of being shielded by protective rather than opportunity costs.

free. Subject to the constraint of treating its citizens as equals, the state ought to be guided by the idea of promoting such freedom, putting in place the resources and protections that can guard people against domination.

In arguing that the state ought to promote freedom in this manner, I endorse a broadly teleological or consequentialist view of the state's task (Pettit 1997a, 2001d, 2012a). The grounds for taking the consequentialist approach are that it delivers satisfactory theories of justice and legitimacy: that is, theories that fit well with our considered judgements and satisfy reflective equilibrium. We shall see how the promotion of freedom as non-domination is to be interpreted, under the guidance of republican tradition, in our discussion of justice and legitimacy. And we shall see that a state that promotes freedom under that interpretation of the project is going to provide us with theories of legitimacy and justice that have a powerful, independent appeal.[43]

---

[43] As we shall see, I think that the state should pursue people's enjoyment of freedom as non-domination under the normative constraint that it treats all its citizens as equal. But this does not involve giving up on consequentialism. It merely implies that the state's treating people as equals is a good in its own right and has to be built into the strategy that the state adopts. Consequentialism does not put any restriction on the goods that may be given countenance; it merely stipulates that the strategies it is right for any agent or agency to adopt are a function of the goods that it can thereby expect to promote.

CHAPTER 2

Social justice

Assuming for the moment that state and government are required in order to organize life in a society on a coercive basis, there are two large questions that any political philosophy must address in the context of that society. First question: what decisions or policies should the state impose in order to establish social justice in the relationships between its citizens? Second question: what processes of decision-making should it follow, if it is to count as a politically legitimate decision-maker for its citizens on questions of justice, and indeed on related matters too? Both questions might be treated as questions of justice in an encompassing sense of the term, but since I think they are importantly distinct, I shall cast the first as a question of social justice, the second as a question of political legitimacy.

I take citizens in this discussion to comprise, not just citizens in the official sense, but all the more or less settled residents of a state who, being adult and able-minded, can play an informed role at any time in conceptualizing shared concerns and in shaping how the state acts in furthering those concerns (compare Tully 2009: 1, 3). Special issues of justice and legitimacy arise with those who are not adult or not able-minded, with those who are not permanent residents, and indeed with those who are not yet born, as related issues arise, of course, with the treatment of other animals. But I shall almost exclusively concentrate on the general issues that arise for how the state should treat current citizens in my broad sense.

I shall take the state and the government to be corporate entities related in such a way that the state acts through government agents or agencies – legislative, executive or judicial – and whenever those agencies act, the state acts through them: they act, as it is said, in the state's name. The issues of social justice and political legitimacy that I discuss can be equally well cast either as issues involving the state or as issues involving government and I shall make use of both formulations. In each formulation, the issues raised presuppose that the relevant entity, state or government, is an agent. While it may involve the participation of many different individuals, it is disposed and expected to form and avow a coherent set of purposes and judgements and to live up to them in how it behaves; it counts in that sense as a corporate agent (List and Pettit 2011).

The state or government in every society imposes an order of law, however we choose to define law, and the questions of social justice and political legitimacy involve two different aspects of that order. The social justice question is: does the state treat its citizens well and equally in selecting the order that it imposes? The political legitimacy question is: does the state treat its citizens well and equally in the way it imposes that order? Each question can be taken as the universal form of a question that every citizen is in a position to raise in his or her own case: does the state treat me well in the nature of the order imposed and in the manner of its imposition? The universal form is generated on the assumption that there is no reason to privilege any one citizen over others and that the particular question arises with the same force in everyone's case.

The order of law that a state imposes will generally include substantive provisions on how citizens should relate to one another and procedural provisions on how they should relate to the state: provisions, for example, on the rights of voting and of standing for office that they should have. Such procedural provisions are relevant, particularly on the approach taken here, to the issue of political legitimacy. And so, for reasons of convenience, I shall take the social justice question to bear only on the nature of the order imposed by the state as the determinant of people's relationships with one another, whether as individuals or as members of various groups. In asking the social justice question as to whether the state imposes a suitable order, then, the focus will be on how satisfactory the order is as a social order: as an order that shapes people's relationships with one another. In asking the political legitimacy question as to whether the state imposes the order in an appropriate manner, the focus will be – at least in part – on how satisfactory the order is as a procedural order: as an order that shapes people's relationships with the state itself.

The issue of political legitimacy, which will lead us into democratic theory, I postpone until the next chapter. The issue of social justice I address in this.[1] I have no quarrel with those who see the questions as each bearing on a different aspect of justice in the more comprehensive, social-cum-procedural sense – justice, for example, in the sense of John

---

[1] A concern with social justice, as distinct from political legitimacy, is the sort of concern that Madison had in mind in *Federalist Papers*, no. 51, when he said that it 'is of great importance in a republic . . . to guard one part of the society against the injustice of the other part' (Madison, Hamilton and Jay 1987).

Rawls (1971, 1993) – but I shall continue to describe them in separate terms. As will appear in the next chapter, I believe that treating the questions together within a theory of comprehensive justice has led to a misconstrual of the second question.

The position for which I will be arguing in this chapter is, roughly, that the republican theory of social justice – depending on context, I shall often say simply, justice – requires that people should enjoy freedom as non-domination in their relationships with one another, whether as individuals to individuals, as groups to groups, or as groups to individuals. And the position for which I will be arguing in the next is that the republican theory of political legitimacy – again, I shall often say simply, legitimacy – requires that people should enjoy freedom as non-domination in their relationships to their state or government. Republican justice is primarily opposed, on this approach, to private domination; republican legitimacy to public. In introducing the approach in the present chapter I shall assume, as mentioned, that a state is necessary and has a corporate character. I will try to vindicate those assumptions in the next.

This chapter falls into four sections. In Section 1, I introduce the republican ideal of justice as the enjoyment of equal freedom as non-domination amongst citizens, arguing that this can only mean equality in the enjoyment of certain fundamental choices, the basic liberties, on the basis of a guarantee of public resources and protections. When choices are safeguarded by public resourcing and protection in this way I will often describe them for convenience as being secured or safeguarded or entrenched, though entrenchment in this sense does not necessarily connote constitutional embedding. In Section 2, I use two plausible constraints to identify the basic liberties that ought to be publicly entrenched in that sense. In Section 3, I give an illustrative sketch of the policies that the republican theory of justice would require; this is to gesture at an institutional model of republican justice on a par with the institutional model of republican legitimacy – in effect, republican democracy – that I seek to provide in the final two chapters. And then in Section 4, I offer some comments on the distinctive features of the emerging theory.

I. SOCIAL JUSTICE AND EQUALITY

The connection

Almost everyone will agree that the challenge in a theory of justice, social or indeed comprehensive, is to identify in any context the 'proper balance between competing claims' that arise there (Rawls 1971: 9). In the domestic context of a particular state I take the citizens to be the relevant claimants, where the citizenry includes all adult, able-minded, more or less permanent residents. And I take the state or the government – that is, the agency whereby the state enacts its business – to be the addressee of their claims and so the entity that has the job of identifying and enforcing the demands of justice. So what are the claims that citizens have within the state and what would constitute a proper balance between those claims?

Almost everyone will agree, not just that this is the central question in a theory of domestic justice, social or comprehensive, but also that any plausible answer to the question has to satisfy a certain egalitarian constraint. In order to establish a proper balance between the claims of its citizens, the state must treat them as equals in determining that balance: it must express or manifest an equal degree of concern for each of them (Dworkin 1978). And so, whatever benefits the state makes available as a matter of justice to its citizens, it is subject to the constraint of making them available in an expressively egalitarian way. This constraint does not necessarily argue that the state should adopt a policy that imposes a certain substantive equality amongst citizens. In itself it requires only that in selecting policies, the state should recognize that people count equally: it should act on the principle that 'all are entitled to respect' (Raz 1986: 219).

The connection between social justice and expressive equality is scarcely surprising, for the very paradigm of injustice is the scenario where those of a certain caste or colour, religion, gender or ethnicity suffer discrimination under the institutions established by the state. The just system, so the lesson goes, cannot be a system that discriminates on any such basis between its members; it is inherently impartial.

My discussion of social justice in this chapter, and my discussion of political legitimacy in the next – my discussion, in other words, of each aspect of comprehensive justice – starts from the normative assumption that the state ought to be expressively egalitarian in this sense. The assumption that the state ought to treat people as equals, satisfying expressive egalitarianism, implies on the side of the citizenry that they ought to be willing to live in society under an arrangement where they are treated as equals: they ought to be prepared, as we may put it, to live on equal terms with others and not claim a special position for themselves. This means that any complaints about their treatment that citizens can expect to command a hearing must be consistent with a willingness to live on equal terms with their fellow citizens: in effect, they must be publicly avowable in the context of reciprocal exchange.

Why commit to expressive egalitarianism in this sense? The reason goes back to a point registered in the introduction to the chapter. Each of us can reasonably ask about how well the state treats us both in the nature of the order it imposes and in the mode of its imposition. And the assumption that we are each in a position to raise those questions with equal validity – an assumption encoded in our being willing to discuss them with one another – generates the universal counterparts. Thus a theory of social justice will address the question as to what order the state must impose if in that respect it is to treat its citizens well and equally. And a theory of political legitimacy will address the question of how it must impose that order if in that distinct respect it is also to treat them well and equally.

The two points of general agreement that we have registered take us only a limited distance in thinking about the demands of social justice. Particular theories of justice diverge on the good or goods in respect of which the state should treat its citizens as equals: that is, on what it is to treat them well. And they diverge also on what it is for the state to satisfy the equality constraint in delivering that treatment: that is, on what it is to treat them equally. They go different ways both on the substantive matter of what should be pursued in an expressively egalitarian fashion, and on the methodological issue of what expressive equalization entails.

Take the substantive issue, first of all. Libertarian theory holds that the state ought to treat people as equals in protecting their purportedly natural rights; depending on how rights are interpreted, this comes in two versions, respectively right-wing (Nozick 1974) and left-wing (Vallentyne and Steiner 2000a, 2000b). Luck-egalitarian theory holds that the state ought to treat people as equals in distributing resources, except when people can only blame themselves for their misfortune: the inequality they suffer, as it is sometimes put, is a result of 'option-luck' rather than 'brute luck' (Dworkin 2000; Fleurbaey 2008). Utilitarian theory holds that the state ought to treat people as equals in a concern for their utility or perhaps their opportunity for utility (Arneson 1989; Roemer 1998). Capability theory maintains that it ought to treat them as equals, rather, in providing for their basic capacity to function in the local society (Sen 1985; Nussbaum 2006; Alexander 2008). And mixed theories look for the treatment of people as equals in respect of different goods in different spheres (Walzer 1983) or in respect of any of the goods that confer a presumptive advantage (Cohen 1993).

Rawls's (1971) theory, to which we will return later, belongs in this mixed category, for it requires the state to treat its citizens as equals in providing for each the mix of primary or omni-functional goods – goods that are indispensable for people, regardless of their particular goals or wishes – that are prescribed under his two principles of justice. These goods include liberty and opportunity, income and wealth and a basis for self-respect. Rawls formulates the principles of justice that are meant to deliver primary goods as follows, with the first principle having lexical priority: that is, it cannot be violated for any gain in the second.

a. Each person has an equal right to a fully adequate scheme of equal basic liberties which is compatible with a similar scheme of liberties for all.
b. Social and economic inequalities are to satisfy two conditions. First, they must be attached to offices and positions open to all under conditions of fair equality of opportunity; and second, they must be to the greatest benefit of the least advantaged members of society. (Rawls 1993: 291)

Whatever good or mix of goods they favour, theories of justice differ also on the methodological issue of what it is for the state to treat people as equals with respect to that good. In order to understand this point of divergence it may be useful to think of the different ways in which parents might think of treating their children as equals in providing from a fixed set of funds for a good like education. Assuming that none of the children suffers from cognitive or related problems, parents might follow any of five salient, though not necessarily exhaustive, strategies.

- Equal investments. The parents might take expressive equality to require providing exactly the same funds for the education of each child; this would give the children equal opportunities for success.
- Equal direct returns. They might take it to require providing or refusing such funds for each as ensure that, regardless of their different capacities, the children all end up at the same educational level or position; this would give the children equal educational outcomes.
- Equal derived returns. They might take expressive equality to require providing funds for each that will enable the children to develop their educational potential and thereby to achieve the same level of fulfilment in their work and life; this would give the children equal outcomes in a different currency.
- Equal rates of return. They might take it to require providing funds in proportion to the children's different capacities to gain educational returns from the funds invested in them.
- Equal threshold benefits. Or they might take it to require providing funds that enable the children each to enjoy a certain threshold benefit, where this provision may allow some of the children to do better than the threshold while others barely reach it.

As the parents in our little example might treat their children as equals under any of these five strategies, so a theory of justice might require the state to treat its citizens as equals in any of the corresponding ways. Each strategy is expressively egalitarian insofar as it can be taken to reflect an equal concern for members of the relevant constituency, children or citizens. But only the first three can be cast as strategies that reflect a concern that equality should prevail amongst those individuals (Temkin 1996). Those three strategies are substantively as well as expressively egalitarian.[2]

The substantively inegalitarian character of the fourth, rates-of-return strategy appears in the fact that the utilitarian project of maximizing overall happiness in a society, however unequal the distribution amongst individuals, exemplifies this approach. It involves investing resources at any time wherever the rate of return is highest and doing so to the point where resources are exhausted and the marginal rate of return from investment in any one person is the same as the marginal rate of return from investment in any other. The substantively inegalitarian character of the fifth threshold-benefits strategy appears in the fact that it would allow some individuals to do significantly better than others in relevant benefits, provided they all reach the appropriate level. One example is Harry Frankfurt's (1987) sufficientarianism, which argues that all should be provided with what by suitable standards is a sufficient level of resources for social flourishing. The capability approach adopted by Amartya Sen (1985) and Martha Nussbaum (2006) is also sufficientarian, on the face of it, since it argues that all should be provided only with a basic capability for functioning in the local society.[3]

These observations give us a useful lead on what form we might expect a republican theory of justice to assume. On the substantive question, they suggest that it ought to make some version of freedom as non-domination into the good with respect to which the state is required in justice to treat its citizens as equals; otherwise it can hardly count as a distinctively republican theory. And on the methodological question, they suggest that while the theory has to be expressively egalitarian, it may take any of a variety of forms, some of them substantively egalitarian, some of them not. I look now at how best to interpret the goal of republican justice and then at what this interpretation implies for the equality strategy that the theory ought to endorse.

[2] Another strategy that might be taken to reflect an equal concern for the children, while not being substantively egalitarian, is prioritarianism (Parfit 2000). I discuss it briefly later in the text.
[3] For discussions on how far the approach is sufficientarian see Part 1 of Kaufman (2006).

The freedom goal of republican justice

In order to build further on these observations we need to identify in greater detail the ideal of freedom as non-domination that the state should be required to foster. In principle, the state ought to promote the enjoyment of free or undominated choice amongst its citizens, under the expressively egalitarian constraint of treating those citizens as equals. But what does this prescription entail in practice?

In seeking a more concrete version of the prescription I propose that we should take as a guiding heuristic the image of the *liber*, or 'free person', in the republican tradition. That picture claims to represent a status in which people can all enjoy freedom of choice fully, and yet also enjoy it equally. Using this heuristic as a guide to what republican justice would require presupposes that the circumstances of the society are not so dire, nor the disparities between people so severe, that it is impossible for people generally to achieve the status of a free person. This is just to require that the circumstances of justice obtain, in John Rawls's (1971: 126–30) phrase: that is, that the society is operating within a more or less normal range of material scarcity and individual capacity.

In the received republican image, free persons can walk tall, and look others in the eye. They do not depend on anyone's grace or favour for being able to choose their mode of life. And they relate to one another in a shared, mutually reinforcing consciousness of enjoying this independence. Thus, in the established terms of republican denigration, they do not have to bow or scrape, toady or kowtow, fawn or flatter; they do not have to placate any others with beguiling smiles or mincing steps. In short, they do not have to live on their wits, whether out of fear or deference. They are their own men and women, and however deeply they bind themselves to one another, as in love or friendship or trust, they do so freely, reaching out to one another from positions of relatively equal strength.[4]

There are three important lessons that the traditional image of the free person teaches us about how we might concretize the ideal of freedom as non-domination as a target of justice. The first offers direction on the range of free choices that free persons ought to enjoy, the second provides an indication of the basis on which those choices ought to be secured or

---

[4] Presented in this way, the image of free persons may seem to be silent on the political front, implying nothing about people's political rights or responsibilities. But the presentation is adequate for our purposes, since we are abstracting in our discussion of justice – that is, social justice – from the relation between citizens and government. I reintroduce that relation in the following chapters when I go on to discuss legitimacy and democracy.

entrenched, and the third gives us guidance on when such entrenchment is enough to give people the status of free persons.

The first lesson is that free persons are free in virtue of being secured in the exercise of a specific class of choices, not in making just any old choices. They are not to be entrenched in acting violently towards others, for example, in appropriating as much land as they want, or in pursuing spectacular adventures. They are to enjoy access to needed resources and protections in a range of choice where all can operate at once – perhaps with special assistance for some individuals – without getting in one another's way. This is the domain of the fundamental liberties, as they were described by the seventeenth-century radical, John Libourne (1646). While these liberties were often cast in his time and place as the ancient, historically sacred rights of Englishmen, they gave institutional expression for Libourne to 'the freeman's freedom'; they reflected the fact that men and indeed women 'are, and were by nature all equal and alike in power, dignity, authority, and majesty – none of them having (by nature) any authority, dominion or magisterial power, one over or above another' (Sharp 1998).[5]

The second lesson of the free-person image is that in order to enjoy freedom in the exercise of the basic liberties, people should have a publicly established and acknowledged status in relation to others; only this could enable them to walk tall and look others in the eye. Within the sphere of those liberties people should be entrenched on a public basis against the incursions of others. They ought to enjoy objective safeguards that apply regardless of the will of others as to how they should choose in that domain. And it ought to be a matter of shared awareness in the society that they are so guarded. They should have an undominated status both in the objective and the subjective or inter-subjective sense of status.

The public safeguards required for the enjoyment of such status are traditionally taken to include the laws that provide in a saliently equal manner for the entrenchment of people's liberties. But given that universally beneficial laws are likely to be supported by attitudes of approval for compliance and disapproval for non-compliance, the safeguards are also bound to include associated norms or morals. Norms in this sense are regularities of behaviour such that, as a matter of public awareness, most members conform to them, most expect others to approve of conformity or

---

[5] The abstraction from issues of legitimacy means that the basic liberties envisaged here do not include the political rights that Rawls counts as basic liberties in his first principle of justice.

disapprove of non-conformity, and most are policed into conformity by this expectation about what will attract approval and disapproval.[6]

Corresponding to the coercive effect of laws against fraud or violence or murder, we might expect to find norms that occasion a complementary, approbative effect, deterring potential offenders by holding out the prospect of communal disapproval. Machiavelli (1965) remarks in *Discourses* (1.18) on the importance of having norms available to support the laws in this way: 'just as good morals, if they are to be maintained, have need of the laws, so the laws, if they are to be observed, have need of good morals'.[7] We shall be exploring the connection more deeply towards the end of the chapter.

The first lesson that I drew from the free-person heuristic bears on what should be safeguarded – the fundamental or basic liberties – and the second on how they should be safeguarded: by reliance on public laws and norms. The third lesson identifies the criterion for determining what is enough by way of safeguarding them – what level of support is sufficient to let us think that for practical purposes people all enjoy freedom as non-domination in the relevant choices. The lesson suggests that people should securely enjoy resources and protections to the point where they satisfy what we might call the eyeball test. They can look others in the eye without reason for the fear or deference that a power of interference might inspire; they can walk tall and assume the public status, objective and subjective, of being equal in this regard with the best. This eyeball test fits with our discussion at the end of the previous chapter of the level of prevention and inhibition that might effectively counter domination. The satisfaction of the test would mean for each person that others were unable, in the received phrase, to interfere at will and with impunity in their affairs.

The eyeball test does not require that people should be able to look one another in the eye, regardless of their personal lack of nerve. It requires that they have this capacity in the absence of what would count, even by the most demanding standards of their society, as mere timidity or cowardice. The reference to timidity is essential, since no public safeguards can

---

[6] The definition follows Pettit (1990) and Brennan and Pettit (2004: Part III) with one amendment: it says that a norm is a regularity such that almost everyone expects others to approve of conformity rather than, in the older formulation, that it is a regularity such that almost everyone approves of conformity. The change allows us to recognize as norms regularities that, unbeknownst to people, do not actually attract general approval (Prentice and Miller 1993); for a fuller discussion of this possibility see Pettit (2008e). While I do not offer a defence for defining norms in this way, it should be noted that it fits extremely well, particularly in the way it connects norms and approval, with the understanding of norms in the larger literature (Hart 1961; Winch 1963; Coleman 1990; Sober and Wilson 1998; Elster 1999; Shapiro 2011).

[7] See too Tyler (1990).

compensate for differences between individual personalities and for variations in people's capacity to deal with the overbearing assumptions of
others. The reference to the standards of their society is necessary since
there is likely to be cultural variation in what counts as mere timidity rather
than rational fear or deference. People are liable to vary across societies in
the different levels of vulnerability to which they have become inured, in the
probability that they assign to others becoming hostile, and in the levels of
trust that they invest in one another. If there is cultural variation on this
front, then it is clearly local standards that should provide the relevant
benchmark for determining when fear or deference is irrational and when
prudent; there is not going to be any universally valid alternative that might
be invoked in their stead.

The effect of the eyeball test is to require a certain threshold of
resourcing and protection that should be secured for all in the domain
of the basic liberties. We know from the last chapter that other people's
capacity to interfere may vary in two ways. They may be capable of any
form of interference in a lesser or greater degree, facing lesser or greater
difficulty and lesser or greater danger. And they may be capable in
whatever degree of a more or less serious form of interference: they
may be capable of preventing the choice of an option at one extreme
or, at the other, capable just of imposing a more or less trivial cost. This
variation teaches an important lesson for how the eyeball test should be
understood and applied. Since both dimensions of variation are important, the test requires that the level of protection provided in any area of
choice should increase with the seriousness of the interference against
which protection is needed and with the ease of access to that level of
interference.

The third lesson of the free-person heuristic makes the goal of a republican theory of justice more accessible than it might otherwise be. It means,
as we saw, that you cannot rely on the state to compensate for your timidity
or other failures and that you can enjoy the full benefits of public resourcing
and protection only if you display a certain degree of personal affirmation
and courage. And it also means that having resources and protections
over and beyond what is required to satisfy the eyeball test – say, as a result
of enjoying above-average wealth – is excess to the requirements of your
status as a free citizen. Certain differences of wealth and power may
jeopardize the freedom as non-domination of the less well off, as we shall
see, and be objectionable on that count. But, assuming that they are not
allowed to have this effect, they are consistent with the status of a free citizen
being available to all, richer and poorer alike.

My characterization of the three lessons of the free-person heuristic suggests that they apply independently of one another, and for simplicity of presentation I shall generally continue to write as if they do. But the third lesson about the eyeball test has an important priority and is bound to impact on the application of the first two. That test plays a part in determining, not just the level of resourcing and protection that ought to be secured for given choices, but also the range of choices that ought to be entrenched in that way and the nature of the public entrenchment that ought to be provided.

Take the first lesson, which teaches that free persons should enjoy resources and protections in an area of choice where all can operate at once, at least with special assistance for some individuals, without getting in one another's way. When is special assistance to be provided for those in particular need, presumably by the state? Suppose that some people are impaired or disabled in a way that makes them incapable, without state assistance, of operating in a certain area of choice; perhaps they need some prosthetic aid in order to be able to function there and are incapable of purchasing it for themselves. How are we to determine whether they should be given that aid and whether the relevant choice should be entrenched as a basic liberty for all? The answer can only be determined by the eyeball test. That a choice is such that those who lack access to it will not be able to pass the eyeball test in the local society makes the canonical case for why the state ought to resource the needy in a special way and ought to entrench the choice as a basic liberty for all. Thus, to take a salient example, it may argue for providing wheelchairs for those who cannot afford them and for building wheelchair ramps in public buildings.

Or consider the second lesson, according to which free persons should be entrenched on a public basis in the exercise of the basic liberties. What exact sort of public entrenchment ought to be provided? Take the presumptively basic liberty of moving wherever you will within a society. Does that require just the protection of travellers, without any particular resourcing? Or does it also require the provision of a public network of road or rail or air travel, as distinct from some privately provided routes? Or the provision of a public means of travel, as in a publicly subsidized rail or bus or plane network? Or even the provision of subsidies for those who cannot afford to use a public or private network? Here, as elsewhere, such questions teem, and the eyeball test provides the only compelling basis for an answer. Thus when I speak in what follows of the need to entrench or secure or safeguard various basic liberties I shall abstract from the question of whether this means just protecting them, or protecting them and providing general resources that everyone needs, or doing those things and, in addition, providing special resources for some who are particularly needy, whether financially or by reason of requiring a mechanical aid like a wheelchair. In every case the question can only be answered on the basis of the eyeball test but I shall not explore the precise answers that are appropriate in different cases.

In giving a central role to the eyeball test, I follow an approach opened up by Amartya Sen (1983b) in the development of his criterion of functioning capability. He suggests that to be poor – to lack a basic functioning capability in your society – is closely related, as Adam Smith (1976: 351–2) argued, to being unable to live without shame amongst your fellows: to failing to meet material standards that others in the society expect all 'creditable people' to attain. Smith's criterion is less demanding than that employed here but it is in the same spirit and may even reflect his own allegiance to republican ways of thinking (Winch 1978). Smith suggests that poverty entails not being able to look others in the eye without reason for fear or deference: that's where the shame lies. The line taken here is that while that is certainly true, satisfying the test requires full freedom as non-domination and not just the absence of poverty. Escaping the shame of poverty is only a first step towards the enjoyment of interpersonal status and the achievement of freedom.

The equality strategy of republican justice

The lessons supported by the free-person heuristic give us helpful pointers to what a republican theory of justice would require the state to seek, under the circumstances of justice, in the relations amongst its citizens: that is, in my usage, amongst the adult, able-minded, more or less permanent residents of the society. It suggests that the state should be required to treat its citizens as equals in promoting their freedom as persons, where freedom in any choice is taken to require non-domination. To the greatest extent possible, the state should entrench people's fundamental liberties, on the basis of public laws and norms, to the point where each is able to pass the eyeball test in relation to others.[8]

---

[8] I observed in the last chapter that domination with interference and frustration plausibly counts as worse than domination with interference but without frustration, and that in turn as worse than domination without interference or frustration. But that observation will not play any role in this chapter, or indeed in the next. In guarding against unfreedom in the enjoyment of fully resourced choices, it is essential to guard against domination, since domination is sufficient, as well as necessary, for unfreedom. And if we eliminate domination then that will be enough to eliminate forms of interference and frustration that are hostile to freedom. The observation from the last chapter will

With these observations in place, we can see that what it means for the state to treat citizens as equals in this way, satisfying the expressively egalitarian constraint, is to provide them each with a certain threshold benefit in the currency of free or undominated choice, as required under the sufficientarian strategy described earlier. It means providing for such a level and kind of entrenchment, in such a range of choice, that people each have the status, traditionally understood, of the free person or citizen. The choices to be entrenched are the basic liberties; the kind of entrenchment to be provided is the public sort that enlists laws and norms; and the level of entrenchment to be secured is whatever is necessary for passing the eyeball test in the local society. That each is required to enjoy this threshold of free undominated choice is consistent with some people having such private sources of power and wealth that they enjoy free undominated choice in a yet greater range and with yet greater security. That is why the approach can be cast as sufficientarian.

Since the enjoyment of such a sufficiency of free or undominated choice means enjoying the status of the free person or citizen, however, we can describe the strategy in other terms too. We can cast it as an approach that argues for equalizing derived returns, as in the third strategy mentioned earlier, where free-person status is a return derived from the required pattern of resourcing and protecting choice. Although it constitutes a sufficientarianism in the currency of free or undominated choice, the republican theory of justice supports a substantive egalitarianism in the currency of free or undominated status. Depending on what the relevant currency is taken to be, it assumes one or the other profile.

In the remainder of the book I shall generally speak of the republican theory of justice as substantively, as well as expressively, egalitarian, taking it to argue for promoting people's equality in freedom as non-domination, where this is now understood as freedom of undominated status, not freedom of undominated choice. It may have been the substantively egalitarian aspect of republicanism that Cicero (1998: 21) had in mind when he made his much-quoted comment on the nature of the *libertas* enjoyed by the *liber*. 'Nothing can be sweeter than liberty. Yet if it isn't equal throughout, it isn't liberty at all.'

As a substantively egalitarian theory, the republican approach to justice may seem to be exposed to the now well-known complaint that like any such theory it would argue for reducing the level of the better off in order to

assume relevance only in ranking imperfectly just or imperfectly legitimate regimes. Thus it will count in favour of one imperfect regime over another that the domination it allows, unlike the domination allowed in the other, does not promise actual interference or frustration.

achieve equality with the worse off, even when that reduction has no other beneficial effects; it would support levelling-down (Parfit 2000). This objection will be irrelevant so long as all actually achieve an undominated status. While some may have greater wealth or power in such a scenario this will not give them a greater status freedom, as we saw, and so will not provide a reason for levelling down. Nor will the objection be relevant where all can in principle be brought to achieve an undominated status but not all actually attain it. In such a situation there will be transfers possible that lift all to that undominated level. But what of the case where it is impossible for everyone to enjoy an undominated status? What of the case where some are deprived of status freedom, and deprived in such a way that their position cannot be remedied by redistribution from the better off? Would the approach argue that in this scenario the state should worsen the position of the better off just for the sake of establishing equality: just for the sake of depriving everyone in the society of an undominated status and setting up a beggar-thy-neighbour form of equality?

No, it would not. The primary commitment in the republican approach is to expressive egalitarianism and the first injunction is that the state should promote people's enjoyment of undominated choice under the constraint that it treats them as equals, displaying an equal concern for each. We argued that this commitment would support an equal free status for all, invoking the traditional image of the free citizen, on the supposition that the circumstances of justice prevail and that such a status can in principle be achieved for all. If that assumption fails, as it is taken to fail here, then the only commitment remaining in place will be the original, expressive one. It may be reasonable to assume that short of emergency situations, or grave disparities in the capacities of different people, there will be an applicable ideal of free citizenship that all can in principle achieve; this is because the ideal is differently interpreted in different societies and can allow for variations in background fortune or misfortune. But if things were so bad that no such ideal could be satisfied for all, then the only commitment would be to expressive, not substantive, equalization.

What might expressive equalization in the sphere of free choice support under such hard circumstances? What might it mean for the state to promote free or undominated choice amongst its citizens, under the constraint of treating all as equals? There are a number of possibilities, one of which is a version of the prioritarianism that Derek Parfit (2000) supports. This holds that in the circumstances imagined the state's equal concern for each would argue for giving a greater weight – of whatever magnitude – to bettering the lot of the worse off. The idea is not to prioritize the worse off as a way of reducing the relativity between them and others – it is not driven by a concern with furthering substantive equality – but to prioritize the worse off because of the poorer absolute level at which they exist and function. If the state is to care equally for each of its citizens, then such a weighting of the worse off would make very good sense.

The possibility envisaged in the objection just raised is that the republican theory of justice might be over-demanding, assuming as it does that people within a society can all be positioned to achieve the status of the free person or citizen. But another objection to the theory might be that it is likely to be intuitively under-demanding, looking for an ideal of equal status freedom that allows for differences in people's private wealth and power. The objection is that the theory may permit such differences in private resources that it ceases to be intuitively appealing: to recall John Rawls's (1971) test, it fails to deliver a reflective equilibrium with our considered judgements as to how far differences in private resources are allowable.

This objection also misfires. The level of resources and protections required for undominated status – the threshold of provision necessary – is determined on a basis that takes into account the resources and protections available to others. If the state allows excessive disparities between the endowments of different people, then the less well off are unlikely to be able to attain that threshold. It is true that equality in status freedom – equality, as we may say, in freedom as non-domination – is consistent with differences of private wealth and power and with corresponding differences in resources and protections. But still the ideal imposes severe constraints on how large or pervasive those differences can be allowed to be.

The constraining aspect of the ideal comes out in a pair of related effects that are going to be present in many, although perhaps not all, contexts (Pettit 1997c; Lovett 2001). Suppose that you have fewer resources and protections than your neighbour and that we, acting for the state, have a choice between conferring more on you or conferring more on the neighbour; the choice may arise with providing services, delivering subsidies or imposing taxes. If we invest in the neighbour rather than investing in you, then we are likely to do relatively less well in guarding against domination, since you are in more danger of domination and so more likely to be in a position to benefit from the extra investment. And if we invest in the neighbour rather than investing in you, then we are likely to worsen the danger of domination in absolute terms, since the neighbour is more likely to be enabled by the extra investment to dominate you or others.

The first of these effects means that investing resources or protections in the better off has diminishing marginal productivity; as it targets the better and better off, it is less and less likely to be productive – that is, less and less likely to increase non-domination. And the second of the effects means that such investment also has increasing marginal counter-productivity; as it targets the better and better off, it is more and more likely to be counter-productive – that is, more and more likely to reduce non-domination. The effects combine to give us reason for thinking that if the state seeks to promote equal freedom as non-domination – that is, to make the status of free citizenship available to all – then it will be systematically programmed to reduce material inequalities in people's resources and protections.

The reason why the ideal of equal status freedom supports an antipathy to material inequality is that it is essentially social in character. You would not enjoy freedom as non-domination in a universe where there were no others, as by traditional accounts you might enjoy freedom as non-interference. To enjoy this freedom presupposes relationships with others and consists in relating to them on a pattern that rules out domination. It requires the absence of domination, not as such, but in the presence of relationships that make domination saliently possible and non-domination correspondingly desirable. To enjoy the relevant freedom of non-domination is to be someone who commands a certain standing amongst your fellows.

The social nature of the ideal of equal freedom as non-domination means that it has an interactional character of a kind that some recent theorists of equality have celebrated (Anderson 1999; Scheffler 2005; O'Neill 2008). What matters is not that individuals are allotted the same good in a certain dimension, independently of how this affects their relations with one another. What matters is that they have the same good in a dimension that impacts on how they can interact with one another and on what standing they can command in one another's eyes. Thus it is entirely intelligible that how far you enjoy undominated status depends, not just on the resources and protections at your disposal, but on how they compare with the resources and protections at the disposal of others. Let them compare too unfavourably and you are very unlikely to enjoy an undominated status.[9]

---

[9] A nice test that emphasizes the importance of interactional equality, built on an idea taken from Derek Parfit (2000), is this. Imagine a world of mutually insulated societies and suppose we have a choice between two egalitarian policies, A and B. The policies would produce the same average equality score, measured by whatever index we favour, but policy A would do so while achieving a high degree of equality within each society and policy B would leave as much inequality within societies as between them. From the point of view of equality which policy should we prefer? If we prefer A, which seems like the obvious choice, then that shows just how far we value equality for its impact on interactions between people.

The discussion in this section gives us a good idea of how to go about elaborating a republican theory of justice and I try to provide a model of its institutional implications in Section 3 of the chapter. But before coming to that sketch we need to devote some time to a preliminary task. This is to try to work out a conception of the fundamental or basic liberties that, as we have seen, are going to require safeguarding under a republican theory.

2. THE BASIC LIBERTIES

Two criteria

One approach to promoting people's equal freedom as non-domination might be to look for a system under which people have the same level of freedom in different sets of choices, where the set of choices available to each gives no one reason to envy the position of another. I might be free in a domain of choice where it really matters to me that I have freedom and you might be free in a distinct domain that answers better to your concerns.[10] But even if we could find customized domains of choice that satisfied the envy test at any moment, they would not continue to satisfy it as the membership of the society changed or as the preferences of members altered. And in any case it is extremely hard to see how the system imagined could be implemented. In seeking to equalize freedom as non-domination, the only feasible project is to look for a system under which people approximate the same level of freedom in the same choices.

But what choices should people be put in a position to enjoy equally? They must be choices that people can each have the wherewithal to make, at least when some are given special assistance by the state; whether special assistance is appropriate, as we saw earlier, will be determined by the eyeball test. And they must be choices, of course, that the state can protect, shielding people from the domination of others. So what choices should the state safeguard if it is to provide people with the equal freedom that justice would seem to require? What are the choices that people ought to be enabled to make, and to make without the domination of others – without dependency on their goodwill and forbearance?

---

[10] We might take this to be what Hobbes recommends when, as we saw, he thinks that free-men will each be unhindered in doing the things that by their strength and wit they are able to do; we might take him to suggest that native wit and strength determine the choices in which each will want to avoid hindrance.

The free-person heuristic provides us with useful guidance in dealing with this question (Pettit 2008a).[11] Since freedom on that heuristic is an ideal that all the citizens in a society ought to be able to enjoy under the law, the basic liberties ought to be construed so as to make such universal enjoyment possible. The exercise of the basic liberties ought not to be an impossible ideal that is accessible to none; an elite ideal that only some can access; or a competitive ideal such that if some access it, that reduces the chances of others doing so. John Locke (1960: 11.57), who remained faithful in this respect to republican thinking, spells out the message clearly. Arguing that 'where there is no law, there is no freedom', he says that everyone should be provided only with a liberty to act 'within the allowance of those laws under which he is, and therein not to be subject to the arbitrary will of another, but freely follow his own'.

This observation argues in favour of two basic criteria that candidates for entrenchment as basic liberties ought to meet. First, the choices to be entrenched ought to be capable of being exercised by each, consistently with being exercised by all. And second, they ought to be capable of satisfying or fulfilling each, consistently with satisfying all (see Anderson 1999). I call the first the criterion of co-exercisability and the second the criterion of co-satisfaction. If co-exercisability were breached, then people would have to compete for being able to exercise the basic liberties, so that the status of the free person would not be equally accessible to all. If co-satisfaction were breached, then the basic liberties would not enable people to achieve the level of fulfilment we naturally associate with having the status of a free person.

The basic liberties ought to include only choices that meet these two criteria. And they ought to include all of the possible choices that do so. Any shortfall in the choices that the state safeguards would be an unnecessary restriction on the freedom that can be enjoyed by citizens and would not fit well with the traditional image of the free person. Thus we may identify the basic liberties with all, and only, those choices that are co-exercisable and co-satisfying in a society.[12] I now proceed to look in greater detail at the choices that are likely to qualify for being basic liberties in that sense.

[11] While I follow the lines developed in Pettit (2008a), I make some small amendments and abstract from much detail.
[12] The extension of a set of choices in this manner will be uncontentious in the case where there is no impact on the existing choices by the addition of more. But there will certainly be issues of how to measure and compare liberties when two or more extended sets differ in the precise choices entrenched. I ignore those questions here, however, as I think that there is no easy answer in the abstract, no algorithm for determining the relative merits of contending sets; the comparison between such sets can only be carried forward in context-bound judgements about their relative attractions.

The two criteria that I employ in identifying basic liberties, it should be noted, are not value-laden and should be capable of being applied in common by thinkers with very different commitments. The assumption that the basic liberties should be as large a class as possible makes almost all potentially free choices into candidates for consideration and then the co-exercisability and co-satisfaction constraints act as filters to narrow down that class. The approach breaks with two more standard lines. One offers a few examples and directs us to the class of basic liberties without the help of any criteria, only a gestural 'and so on'. The other identifies the basic liberties by a value-laden criterion: say, as liberties that are essential for the development of the moral personality (Rawls 1993). Our approach is more directive in the guidance it provides than the first alternative and it is less dependent on a particular moral vision than the second.[13]

Co-exercisable choices

The first criterion holds that any choice that deserves to be safeguarded should be the sort of choice that all the citizens of a society – roughly, all adult, able-minded, relatively permanent residents – can exercise, and exercise at more or less the same time. This criterion can be taken to outlaw two categories of choice. As a constraint of individual exercisability, it outlaws choices that are inaccessible to particular people, even with special state provision. And as a constraint of collective exercisability, it rules out choices that people cannot exercise together – roughly, at one and the same time – even with suitable state resourcing.

Taking up the first constraint, it should be clear that there are many choices that not everyone is able to enact or exercise. Not everyone can decide what you think or say or wish for; only you can do that. So by this requirement there is no possibility of entrenching for all a basic liberty of making up your mind on such matters. All that might be entrenched is the liberty for each to make up his or her own mind on the issues: your liberty to make up your mind, my liberty to make up my mind, and so on. What goes for making up your mind goes for any action that involves you, or any particular individual, in the position of agent, and this suggests that the basic liberties must all have a self-referential or agent-relative character. They must be restricted to liberties on the part of A to determine how A acts, liberties on the part of B to determine how B acts, and so on. They cannot extend to liberties on the part of anyone to determine how others act.

---

[13] My thanks to Annie Stilz for forcing me to see this point.

The individual exercisability constraint imposes this restriction on the basic liberties as a matter of logical or metaphysical necessity. But it imposes other restrictions as a result of contingent facts about what most of us can and cannot do. It is a contingent fact that not everyone can climb Mt Everest and that not everyone – perhaps not anyone – can jump ten feet. Since these limitations are not ones that the state could plausibly enable people to overcome, the basic liberties must operate within the boundaries of exercisability that they establish. They must be limited to choices that fall within everyone's competence, at least when that competence is enhanced by the state. Everyone might have a basic liberty of movement within the public territory of the state – and a basic liberty of leaving that territory if another state allows this – even though such movement might require the state provision of transport facilities for those who cannot walk or cannot afford the cost of transport. And while that basic liberty would enable some individuals to exercise their special capacity to climb mountains, climbing mountains is still not a basic liberty. At most it is a derived liberty that is available, in virtue of their having the basic liberty of travel, to those with mountain-climbing skills.

The individual exercisability constraint does not only restrict basic liberties to choices we are individually capable of exercising, at least with public support. It also restricts them to choices in the exercise of which we do not depend on the voluntary cooperation of others. None of us can be sure of being able to tango or to sing in a choir or to incorporate with others in a group agent, since such actions require others to be willing to join with us in their performance. And so choices involving those activities cannot count as basic liberties that ought to be secured by state resourcing and protection. The only choices that might call here for entrenchment as basic liberties are the choices of tangoing, or associating in other ways, with those who are willing to tango or associate with you.[14]

The collective, as distinct from individual, exercisability constraint imposes further restrictions on candidates for the choices that the state ought to secure.[15] Clearly, it would rule out entrenching options that as a matter of necessity not everyone can adopt at once. Thus no option that requires achieving a superior position to others could be a basic liberty. You cannot have a basic liberty to achieve an above-average score in a test, or to win a

[14] Nor, it may be added, should the state secure the choices of existing groups, since this would favour those who already happen to have formed such groups and would fail to treat people equally.
[15] This constraint is close to the compossibility constraint that Hillel Steiner (1994) imposes on basic rights.

citizen-of-the-year award, though, of course, you may have the liberty to try to attain such a distinction (O'Neill 1979–80). Apart from ruling out such positional options, the constraint would also rule out options that are available only conditionally on others not availing themselves of that option. As things now stand, you may have a choice between selling your house at current market value or continuing to own it. But not everyone who owns a house can exercise that choice at once. Let all house-owners try to sell their houses at current market value and the inevitable consequence will be that the market value will fall well below its current level.

The collective exercisability constraint imposes these particular restrictions as a matter of logical necessity. But it imposes even more interesting restrictions on the basis of contingent fact. Thus the fact that many of the resources required for certain choices are scarce rules out making those choices into basic liberties. In these cases, as Herbert Hart (1955: 175) puts it, 'owing to scarcity one man's satisfaction causes another's frustration'. The farmer and the cowboy may be friends if there is country enough for them each to find land that they can use as they wish; the farmer will fence in one region, the cowboy let cattle roam in another. But if there is only so much land to go around, then under that condition of scarcity it will be impossible for them each to use the land as they wish. Thus the collective exercisability condition implies that the freedom to use land to your personal taste cannot be a basic liberty.[16]

Hart himself invokes the unrestricted use of land to illustrate the fact that there are some liberties that cannot be simultaneously enjoyed by all; there would be physically inevitable conflicts amongst people who sought to exercise that liberty at once (Hart 1973: 546–7). Another example, as he suggests, would be the action of travelling by one's preferred mode of transport, since there would be a similar 'conflict between pedestrians' freedom of movement and the rights of automobiles' (Hart 1973: 546, n. 49). And another might be the action of withdrawing one's money from a bank; let everyone try to do that and the institution will break down. Further examples can readily be imagined. The principle generating them is captured nicely in G. A. Cohen's (1979) observation that while everyone in a room might be individually able to leave by the doorway, they need not be able to do so together: the door may be just too narrow.

---

[16] The farmer and the cowboy will be familiar from Rogers and Hammerstein's musical, *Oklahoma*, but the predicament they exemplify was already a matter of human experience in clashes between farming and foraging peoples, some as early as the fifth millennium BCE; see Morris (2010: 112–14, 127–8, 271).

No plausible sort of state resourcing could overcome problems of collective exercisability that are based in logical necessity.[17] But is there anything that the state might do to overcome the problems raised by contingent facts of scarcity? Are there any legal or political measures that might enable people to co-exercise options otherwise precluded by scarcity, or at least to enable people to co-exercise options that are closely related to the precluded options? If there is nothing the state can do on these fronts, then the alternatives are bleak. We will have to give up on the idea of establishing basic, co-exercisable options in the use of land or transport, for example. We might then have to acquiesce in an anarchic free-for-all where the spoils go to the victor. Or we might have to adopt a system of central rationing under which people live with whatever they are centrally allocated in the way of permits for land-use or transport. Neither sort of alternative is appealing.

Fortunately, however, there are measures that the state can take to resource collectively exercisable choices in such areas. It can introduce rules of coordination that would eliminate the problem of competition in the use of land and transport and under those rules it can define or identify choices that all can exercise at one and the same time. Let the state set up common rules of ownership, for example, and it will be possible for everyone at once to own and use land – or any other commodity – according to those rules. Thus there can be a basic, rule-dependent liberty of owning and using property. Let the state set up rules of the road and it will be possible for everyone at once to use his or her preferred mode of transport; drivers will take one route, pedestrians another. And so, again, there can be a basic, rule-dependent liberty of travelling under the rules of the road by whatever means you prefer.

Regulatory or coordinating initiatives of this kind would enable a society to resource choices in ownership or travel that can then be candidates for protection as basic liberties. And parallel initiatives could allay a vast array of similar problems. The rules that govern banking can make it possible for people to have regulated or coordinated access to their funds. And any rules that coordinate access to something that cannot be accessed at once by all – this, on the model of exit from a crowded room – can make it possible for people to have a basic liberty in the exercise of the corresponding rule-dependent choice.

---

[17] I ignore rather implausible measures whereby, for example, everyone might have a choice of being top dog for a day.

Co-satisfying choices

If certain choices are worthy of being entrenched as basic liberties then not only should they be individually and collectively exercisable – not only should they be capable of being exercised by each, consistently with being exercised by all – they should also meet a further condition. This is that they should be sufficient to satisfy each consistently with satisfying all. As the criterion of co-exercisability imposes a constraint of individual exercisability and a constraint of collective exercisability, so this criterion imposes two constraints also, one of which requires individual satisfaction, the other collective satisfaction.

The criterion of individual satisfaction argues that the choices we entrench as basic liberties should be ones that by received social criteria promote the enjoyment and welfare, over the long term, of those who make them. In principle this criterion leaves room for denying protection for certain choices that are judged to be harmful for the individuals exercising them, even for criminalizing them as victimless offences. In practice, however, the republican approach is unlikely to argue for establishing such intrusive criminalization, as we shall see later. Doing so would impose collective judgement and preference on any individual in choices that are, by hypothesis, co-exercisable. To treat such choices as victimless crimes, or just to leave them unprotected, would be to impose society's interpretation of their interests on people and would represent a sort of paternalism that is inconsistent with freedom as non-domination, as we saw in the last chapter (Shiffrin 2000).

This is a point at which the eyeball test serves an important role, as foreshadowed earlier, in determining how choices ought to be publicly entrenched. When choices have the potential for harming the adult, able-minded agents who exercise them, the eyeball test argues against criminalizing them or leaving them unprotected but does not support any more active provision in their support. Take the choices associated with the use of recreational drugs or with certain forms of gambling. The eyeball test suggests that such choices do not call for any active form of resourcing, and may even deserve to be subjected to heavy taxes.[18] But it strongly supports the view that since any other approach would be paternalistic, failing to acknowledge the status of the agents, still the choices ought to be protected. They ought to be given at least that minimal form of entrenchment.

---

[18] Even John Stuart Mill (1978) argued that such a line would be perfectly defensible, suggesting in some cases that a society should seek to reduce the attractions of choices that can threaten long-term damage to the chooser by imposing relatively higher taxes on the resources that they require.

Turning to the other aspect of the co-satisfaction criterion, the constraint of collective, as distinct from individual, satisfaction implies that in order to count as entrenchable basic liberties, choices should not be such that if some or all individuals exercise them then many people, perhaps including those individuals themselves, will cease to enjoy the choices. Candidates for entrenchment as basic liberties should be choices of such a kind that even if everyone takes them, everyone can be more or less fully satisfied. This constraint rules out choices in three broad categories: counter-productive choices, over-empowering choices and harmful choices.

Taking harmful choices first, it is worth noting that there are many choices that include the option of intentionally harming another person and yet pass the constraint of co-exercisability. There is nothing in the constraint of co-exercisability to stop people being able to lie and to steal and even be violent to one another. But clearly establishing the choices of inflicting such harms as basic liberties would in no way contribute to the satisfaction of people overall. And so, unsurprisingly, the constraint of collective satisfaction would argue against giving such choices an entrenched status. The choices to be established as basic liberties should all be innocent choices, as we might put it.

Over-empowering choices, to move onto a second category, are choices whose entrenchment might allow the emergence of serious asymmetries in the relative balance of resources and power amongst people. We saw earlier that there is good reason to establish rules governing the use of land and, by extension, property in general. Such rules would introduce rule-dependent choices in the domain of ownership, exchange and bequest that people can each exercise without coming to blows in the manner of the cowboy and the farmer who struggle for possession of the same land. But it should be clear that the rules of property may enable some individuals to gain such economic power that they are bound to dominate others in certain contexts – for example, in employment or legal action or competition over access to health resources. The constraint of collective satisfaction would argue against introducing a system of choices that is liable to have such an over-empowering effect. It would support any less dangerous alternative that may be available.[19]

---

[19] How might we cope with this problem, giving effect to the requirement of collective satisfaction? There are a variety of measures that might be explored. Introducing progressive taxation as part of the property system would be one possibility (Murphy and Nagel 2004). Another might be a system of support or subsidy, in relevant contexts, for the economically weaker. Or yet another might be a restriction on the comparative advantages that money can buy.

The problem illustrated by harmful and over-empowering choices derives from the fact, as Herbert Hart (1973: 550) observes, that entrenching a choice as a basic liberty 'necessarily does two things: first, it confers on individuals the advantage of that liberty, but secondly, it exposes them to whatever disadvantages the practice of that liberty by others may entail for them' (550). But this observation also explains why choices in a third, counter-productive, category should be ruled out by the constraint of collective satisfaction. These are choices whose exercise by a number of people – at the limit by all – undermines the benefit that gives the choice its characteristic rationale and appeal for some or for all (see Parfit 1984: Part 1).

Hart (1973: 543) illustrates the case where the exercise of a choice by any number of people undermines the benefit that it promises for each. Let people all have a choice of addressing a group at will: say, a group comprising their fellow citizens. It will clearly be possible for them each to address the group and to do so at the same time, so that the earlier constraints raise no problem here. But still we might pause over thinking that this choice should be established as a basic liberty. For if a number of members try to speak to the assembly at one and the same time, no one will be heard. And so no one will be able to enjoy the characteristic benefit of speaking to the group. Other examples of this sort of case arise wherever the individual choice of a certain option promises a certain reward for each but the aggregate result of a number of people taking that choice is that that reward is not delivered. People may each wish to own a gun for their own defence but if everyone owns a gun then, plausibly, no one is defensively better off. People may each wish to drive into the city centre, but if everyone does so then the point of driving there may be undermined for all.[20]

Another sort of case that fits in the counter-productive category arises with choices that impose external costs on others, often triggering claims in tort law. Let people have the liberty of making whatever use they wish of a river that runs through their land and there is bound to be trouble in prospect. The use which those upstream make of the river may severely limit the use to which those downstream wish to put it; for example, the

[20] In these cases, as in the case of speaking to the group, it is generally true, first, that everyone has a reason to pursue the activity if no one else does; and second, that everyone prefers that no one pursues it than that everyone pursues it. But it is worth noting that in some of the cases, unlike the group case, a third clause is satisfied too: everyone may have a reason – a new reason – to pursue the activity if others all do so. Setting virtue aside, no one will relish being the only person without a gun in a gun-toting society. This makes these particular examples into cases of a broadly free-riding character (Pettit 1986). In these cases, people each have a reason for pursuing the activity even if all others do – they will not want to be made a sucker, as it is sometimes said – but that reason is not the consideration that originally gave the choice its appeal.

upstream factory can make it dangerous to allow downstream cattle to drink the water. If any choice that is to be established as a basic liberty has to be co-satisfying for all, not just co-exercisable by all, then this sort of choice cannot be entrenched in that way.

Can the state help to overcome the sort of problem raised in our three sorts of harmful, over-powering and counter-productive choices? Yes, clearly it can. As with some of the problems raised by the constraint of collective exercisability, it can introduce rules under which people are given options that are close to the original, problematic options but are capable, unlike them, of meeting the constraint of collective satisfaction. Thus the problem illustrated by the case of speaking to a large group can be solved under rules such as *Robert's Rules of Order* (Robert 2011). These allow people to take turns in speaking, dictating a pattern under which they can each make proposals, suggest amendments to the proposals of others, and debate and vote on the various issues that arise in their discussion. As such rules might resolve the debating predicament, similar rules might resolve the problems illustrated with gun ownership and car use. People can be given the rule-dependent option of owning guns on condition of passing certain tests or of using free or cheap parking facilities and taking public transport into city centres.

The case illustrated with the upstream and downstream use of a river is typically resolved in a different manner. The law of torts allows plaintiffs to appeal to the courts for case-by-case judgements on whether someone should be allowed to exercise such a choice and, if allowed, whether they should be required to adopt precautions against damage to others. The Hand test, named after the US Judge, Learned Hand, offers useful guidance in the area. The idea, roughly, is that if the expected cost of effective precautions to an agent in the exercise of some choice is less than the expected cost to others of the harm associated with the choice taken without precautions, then the choice should only be allowed when relevant precautions are in place. Applied to the river case, it would require those upstream to make use of the river only under limitations or precautions that involve a lower expected cost for them than the expected cost to others of the upstream activity taken in the absence of limitations or precautions.

Towards a meaningful life

Consider the range of choices that present themselves at this point as candidates for entrenchment as basic liberties. They are all individually exercisable, at least with the help of state resourcing, and all individually satisfying. And equally they are all collectively exercisable and satisfying. Perhaps as a result of suitable coordinating rules, they are designed so that any number of individuals may adopt them without this affecting their exercisability as choices or the satisfaction that they deliver across the community. Would the availability of those choices – of all the choices that satisfy such conditions – make a full and meaningful life available for the free citizen (Wolf 2010)? Or would the range of choices entrenched still fall short in some way of what is needed?

The question is hard to address without a good sense of the sorts of choices that the criteria would require us to entrench. And, on the face of it, this raises a problem, for there is no obvious end to the choices that satisfy our constraints. Happily, however, there is a way around this problem, for it transpires that amongst the choices that meet the criteria we need only concern ourselves with a small sub-set. The choices that prove co-exercisable and co-satisfying may vary in two dimensions: in the distality and generality of the options involved. And it turns out that it will be enough to entrench only the more distal and general choices. Let the state entrench them and it will automatically entrench all the other choices too.

One option will be more distal than another when, despite the fact that it can be realized by one and the same action, it involves effects at a greater distance from the agent: effects, in other words, that reach out further into the world. I realize progressively more distal options as I open and close my mouth, make sounds that you hear, and let you know my holiday plans. But options that are relatively distal in this sense may vary in the separate dimension of generality, even when they can also be realized by one and the same action. Telling you about my holiday plans is distinct from the progressively more general options of giving you information about my private life, giving you any information whatsoever, and speaking to you in any modality, whether of information-giving or not.

Given this account of distality and generality, it should be clear that if we secure the more distal and general choices, then we will automatically secure the less distal and less general counterparts as well. If I am free to tell you about my holiday plans, I will be free to make certain sounds – maybe these, maybe those, depending on the words I employ – in your presence. And if I become free to communicate with you in any modality, then I will be free to tell you about my holiday plans or to talk to you about any topic what-soever. If we entrench freedom of speech as such, in other words, then we will have entrenched the freedom to make the various sounds associated with speech, to discuss the various topics that speech can engage, and to exercise speech in addressing one or another audience.

Generalizing from this observation, the lesson is clear: if we entrench the most distal and general of the choices that pass the constraints on basic liberties, we will have entrenched all the related choices that pass those constraints. That proper subset of distal and general choices is all we need think about, then, and all we need to entrench. Indeed, it makes good sense to count only members of that set as the basic liberties proper and in what follows I shall stick to that convention.

What are the general, distal choices that are likely to require entrenchment, on the proposal we have been exploring? The following list may not be exhaustive but it is surely indicative:

- The freedom to think what you like.
- The freedom to express what you think.
- The freedom to practise the religion of your choice.
- The freedom to associate with those willing to associate with you.
- The freedom to own certain goods and to trade in their exchange.
- The freedom to change occupation and employment.
- The freedom to travel within the society and settle where you will.

Back now to the crucial question. Suppose that the largest possible set of such basic liberties is secured by public resourcing and protection in a society. Does the entrenchment of liberties like these suffice on its own for making a full and meaningful life possible for individuals? Suppose you have the resources for making such choices and are not dominated in any of these broad areas: you are able to exercise your own discretion, by intuitive criteria, without worrying about the goodwill of others. Would the enjoyment of the unvitiated, uninvaded capacity to exercise choice across that range of opportunities suffice to give you access to the life that we would expect a free person to be able to achieve?

The enjoyment of such liberty might not suffice for a meaningful life under a Romantic or post-Romantic image of the fulfilment required – for example, the Nietzschean image of life as an *Übermensch*. But the assumption in the republican tradition is that it certainly can. It is possible to be as free as a full and meaningful life requires, so the idea goes, and yet only to be as free as other people: only to enjoy the same freedom across the same choices and on the same public basis. It is possible to be personally fulfilled without being socially privileged.

I go along, unhesitatingly, with this traditional view. Looking at the list of entrenched liberties, I am inclined to ask a rhetorical question. If the availability of these choices is not enough to make a meaningful, independent life possible, what else is needed? If not this, what? Perhaps the best way of defending an affirmative attitude, however, is to look at what individuals would have to enjoy in the way of resources and protections if they really had access to a maximal set of entrenched basic liberties. That takes us to the topic of the next section. I sketch a model there of the institutions and policies that the republican theory of justice would require – a model of how we might safeguard the basic liberties equally for all – and suggest that the model fits well, as reflective equilibrium requires, with our considered judgements of justice.

Variations in basic liberties

Before moving onto that model, however, it may be useful to make a general observation on the nature of the basic liberties, as that has emerged in our discussion. This is that while the basic liberties may seem to have a universal cast, at least when they are formulated abstractly, they can vary in more concrete interpretation and practice across different regimes; they are not a natural kind. They can vary, broadly speaking, in either of two ways: in a radical fashion that divides off past from present cultures, for example, and agricultural from industrial societies; and in a less radical manner that appears in differences between otherwise quite similar dispensations, even between contemporary advanced democracies.

The more radical divide shows up in the fact that the choices that it would have seemed important to entrench as basic liberties in classical Rome or medieval Italy or seventeenth-century England – and the choices that are judged important to secure in extremely poor countries today – are very different from the choices that we would expect to be established in a contemporary liberal and democratic regime. The technology and affluence of advanced societies makes it possible for people to be able to co-exercise with satisfaction a much richer range of choices than those that would be available elsewhere. This is true for two reasons. First, everyone in such a society can do things, and can be secured in the choice of doing them, that would be unavailable elsewhere; think of how we can travel in an advanced society, or express ourselves, or win employment. And second, those who are limited in their capacities can be enabled in an advanced society to exercise choices that would be unavailable elsewhere: think of the impact of eyeglasses or hearing aids or wheelchairs or various prosthetic devices.

It may be useful in this connection to go back to how Amartya Sen (1983b, 1985) has suggested we should conceive of what it is to count as poor, or as non-poor (see too Nussbaum 1992, 2006). Poverty should not be conceptualized on a relative basis, he says, so that by definition a certain percentage of the population in any society are bound to be poor. Nor should it be conceptualized on an absolute basis, so that the resources that would put someone amongst the poor of an advanced democracy would also put that person amongst the poor of an undeveloped, agricultural society. To be poor is to be lacking in the resources required for being able to function at a basic level in your local society and to be able, in Adam Smith's terms, to live without shame amongst your fellows. And to avoid poverty is to enjoy a basic functioning capability under the local conditions of that society. While functioning capability is a universally intelligible ideal, on this approach, it may require quite different resources in the context of different cultures, economies and societies.

What goes for functioning capability goes for freedom as a person and for the basic liberties with which it is associated. The idea of having such freedom is a universally intelligible ideal, directing us to the standing someone enjoys when they satisfy the eyeball test and can look their compatriots in the eye without reason for fear or deference. But freedom as a person in this unchanging sense may require the safeguarding of different ranges of choices in different societies. The Roman commoner, the medieval burgher, the modern yeoman and a contemporary professional might each well pass in their own society as enjoying the freedom of a person. But the choices we should expect to be secured for each may differ quite deeply across the historical divides.

Not only may the basic liberties vary radically insofar as different cultures offer different possibilities of action and impose different conditions for passing the eyeball test; they may also vary less radically across quite similar societies, even societies as similar as contemporary advanced democracies. There are three sources of this less radical variation, all of which turn on the fact that basic liberties have no natural interpretation; they depend for their articulation on the introduction of conventions that are bound to vary across political divides.

The first of our three sources of variation is the fact that co-exercisability requires many basic liberties to be rule-dependent in the fashion of the liberties of ownership and movement. There are many different sets of property conventions, varying in how far they recognize collective or communal property and in the different titles and rights and tax liabilities they associate with private ownership. And as there are differences in the conventions governing property rights, so there are great differences across societies in conventions bearing on rights of way and rights of residence. There may be considerations that argue against some such conventions on the basis of the demands of non-domination, as we saw – some may allow over-empowering choices, for example – but it is very likely that certain variations are not determinately better or worse than others. Thus we may expect to find differences in the conventions adopted, and the liberties entrenched, even between quite similar and equally commendable societies.

The second source of variation in the basic liberties, even across similar societies, is that culturally variable rules are needed, not just to make certain choices co-exercisable, but also to make them co-satisfying. These rules are required to make it possible for people to enjoy certain liberties, even when all or many exercise them at once. Thus regulations like *Robert's Rules of Order* (Robert 2011) are required to create the basic liberty of addressing your compatriots in any group. And parallel sets of rules are required to solve problems such as those with the use of cars or the use of guns. While some such rules may be better than others in republican terms it is likely that many different sets can serve the promotion of freedom as non-domination equally well. Thus this factor, too, explains why we may expect to find variation in the basic liberties established in similar, equally attractive societies.

A third reason for expecting such variation derives from the difficulty of identifying a suitable set of basic liberties. The constraints on basic liberties cannot always be identified in advance, as indeed the case of the upstream and downstream use of a river already illustrates. There is bound to be a problem in definitively establishing, in the abstract, liberties such that their exercise by some is not going to impact on their exercisability by others or on the satisfaction available to others; there is bound to be a problem in finding a set that precludes all such negative interactions (Sen 1970; Dietrich and List 2008). The only feasible solution is to establish in law – not just in the law of torts but also in criminal law, contract law and constitutional law – a way of handling different problems as they arise, leaving room for the sort of judicial intervention, or even legislative or constitutional amendment, that would interpret and revise the basic liberties so as to reduce unwanted interactions (Zucca 2007). As we recognize the necessity of subjecting any system of basic liberties to such dynamic adjustment, we can see that two similar societies, even societies that begin from the same specification of basic liberties, are likely to come apart in the course of their development.

The three factors invoked explain why there should be acceptable variations in the interpretation of the basic liberties across societies as close as contemporary advanced democracies. Such variation is very likely to materialize in view of the fact that such societies often come apart in the cultural expectations that people bring to bear on public matters. In one society, there may be a very lax view of the background tests that gun owners should pass; in the other, the tests may be so strict that most citizens are given no access to guns. Or in one society people may take a very tolerant view, and in the other a very strict view, of how far offensive speech is damaging and should be restricted. The possibilities are legion.

The three sources of variation just reviewed show that the basic liberties, as we understand them here, are deeply dependent on interpretative rules. This rule-dependence does not get in the way of our identifying in the abstract the set of basic liberties that ought to be entrenched in any contemporary society. But it does mark an important complexity. The promotion of equal freedom as non-domination is bound to mean subtly different things in different social contexts, even in contexts that differ in the relatively small ways that distinguish contemporary, advanced societies from one another. Not only do the basic liberties have to be secured by the resourcing and protection of the law, then. The precise choices that are to be entrenched as basic liberties depend on the laws even for being identified.

3. SKETCH FOR A MODEL OF JUSTICE

Beyond Rawls

How plausible is it to claim that what justice requires amongst citizens is equal freedom as non-domination, as we have articulated that ideal, and nothing more? The claim may seem downright incredible in virtue of the fact that whereas John Rawls's (1971, 1993, 2001) theory of justice imposes two principles, one prescribing equal freedom and the other a close cousin of material equality, this theory imposes the first alone. Rawls's theory, after all, is the very paradigm of what we ought to expect of a theory of justice, and if ours departs significantly from it, then that may seem to raise a question about its plausibility.

It turns out, however, that the republican account cannot be cast as an attempt to espouse Rawls's first principle and to dispense with his second. There are two reasons for this, even assuming that the same basic liberties are targeted by each.[21] First, unlike the republican approach, Rawls's first principle does not require full resourcing for the basic liberties; and, second, it does not require their protection against domination, only their protection in a weaker sense.

---

[21] Rawls's basic liberties are not derived on a systematic basis, unlike those we target. In any case they include certain liberties associated with political rights, such as the freedom to vote, since Rawls does not distinguish the issue of legitimacy, as I understand it here, from the issue of justice.

In Rawls's usage people are free to do or not do something just insofar as it is legally permissible for them to do it or not do it: they have a legally protected right in respect of the choice or, equivalently, 'government and other persons . . . have a legal duty not to obstruct' (1971: 203). 'Liberty', as he says, 'is a complex of rights and duties defined by institutions' (Rawls 1971: 230). But the liberty to choose in this sense between two options is quite consistent with an inability to make the choice: having that ability is not required for the liberty as such, only for its worth or value (Rawls 1971: 204–5). Thus, for all that Rawls's first principle requires, the choices that are established as basic liberties need not be secured for all by public resourcing. There is a direct contrast with the republican approach.

The second way in which the principle falls short of the republican requirement is that it does not support an equally high level of protection for the basic liberties. Rawls assumes, in line with standard practice, that insofar as others are meant to have a legal duty not to interfere with one of his basic liberties, they are subject to penalties. But he thinks that such penalties may be scaled to the probability that others will indeed interfere. Thus he says that while penalties may always be necessary for purposes of giving people confidence that others will respect their legal duties, in the sort of regime where there is general compliance – the regime that he seeks to characterize in his 'ideal theory' – they will not be required for any other reason: 'in a well-ordered society sanctions are not severe and may never need to be imposed' (Rawls 1971: 240).[22]

This makes clear that for Rawls domination is not a problem as such. The society envisaged in his ideal theory may be well ordered just because the powerful generally display goodwill towards others. And so protecting people against them only by such penalties as are required to create confidence that they will not interfere – a confidence that is easily achieved, given the evidence of goodwill – may leave the powerful effectively

---

[22] Rawls's views on freedom are quite complex. He begins with the idea that any form of freedom is a freedom from constraint: 'this or that person (or persons) is free (or not free) from this or that constraint (or set of constraints) to do (or not do) so and so'. On this account, 'many kinds of conditions' may serve a constraining role, including 'duties and prohibitions defined by law' and 'coercive influences arising from public opinion and social pressure', so that freedom presumably consists in the absence of such constraints (Rawls 1971: 202). But he quickly goes on to give freedom an institutional cast, as in my presentation here, holding that you are free to do something just insofar as you have the legal right to do it or, equivalently, just insofar as 'government and other persons . . . have a legal duty not to obstruct' (Rawls 1971: 203). 'Liberty, as I have said, is a complex of rights and duties defined by institutions' (Rawls 1971: 230). On this institutional account to be free to do something is not necessarily to avoid vitiating factors, for you may not avoid natural limitations, which are now said just to deprive your liberty of its worth or value (Rawls 1971: 204–5); and presumably you may not avoid the 'influences arising from public opinion and social pressure'.

unbound; it may leave them able to interfere at a relatively low cost. Were domination taken to be a problem by Rawls, then he could not adopt this line. He would have to recognize that even in a well-ordered society, it is essential to have suitably protective blocks and burdens in place in order to establish that no one depends on the goodwill of others for avoiding interference.

What would make for a suitable level of protection – and, more generally, entrenchment – against others? Some protection will come about via the denial of resources or opportunity to the powerful – this amounts to disarming those individuals or groups – and some via the defence of individuals against them, whether at the time of the attempted offence or by means of later requital. But no matter what form it takes, it is likely to come in degrees. So what level of protection is going to be adequate to deal with the danger of domination? The republican answer, of course, is that protection ought to extend to the baseline dictated by the eyeball test: a threshold, recognized in public awareness, such that for those at or above it, a tendency to worry about the power of others – and so a tendency, for example, to try to keep the powerful sweet – will be taken to express an unwarranted, perhaps even irrational, degree of timidity or cravenness. Whatever the level of protection that all should enjoy under such a test, it is certainly higher than anything envisaged by Rawls in his vision of a society that satisfies only his first principle of justice.

Because it does not guarantee the resourcing of the relevant choices, or provide for their protection against domination, Rawls's first principle leaves many intuitively unjust inequalities in place. Not guaranteeing resources required for exercising the relevant basic liberties, it may leave some people in a position where they are unable to exercise those choices. And failing to protect the liberties against domination, it may not register the same degree of vulnerability, or the same need for safeguards, that would appear in the republican project. It is because of the inequalities that this principle would leave in place that Rawls introduces the second principle of justice, seeking a fit – perhaps after some adjustment on the two sides – with his considered judgements of justice; such a fit would help to establish the reflective equilibrium with the judgements that his methodology requires.[23]

I argue that things look very different if we articulate the freedom-centred concern in the republican way, relying on the eyeball test for interpreting it. Let the resourcing of basic liberties, not just their protection, be important

---

[23] For an explicit comment on how fulfilment of the second principle is required to provide in this way for the basic liberties – in Rawls's terms, to give them value. See Rawls (2001: 177).

for freedom as non-domination, as the first chapter showed. And let the protection required be sufficient to guard against domination under the eyeball test. My claim is that in that case, the cause of entrenching the basic liberties will come intuitively close to providing for what most of us will be happy to think of as justice. It will not leave in place the shortfall that prompts Rawls's recourse to his second principle.

In order to see that this is so, it will be useful to look briefly at a model of the policies that the equal entrenchment of the basic liberties is likely to require. This is a slightly hazardous enterprise, for two reasons. Policies have to be guided as much by empirical assumptions as by philosophical principles, so that principles alone will not lead us firmly to policies. And in a real-world scenario of limited resources any policy programme is going to have to require a variety of trade-offs, some of which are hard to track in advance. The following sketch of the sorts of policies that a republican theory of justice would support is bound, therefore, to have only a tentative and illustrative status. For reasons of simplicity I set it out without much argument over detail, though at almost every point I rely on the intuitive guidance provided by the eyeball test.[24]

There are three main areas of policy-making that any plausible project of entrenching the basic liberties would have to address. To describe them alliteratively, the first of these has to do with public infrastructure, the second with public insurance and the third with the public insulation of people against danger from others. Infrastructural programmes would establish a framework for the enjoyment of freedom as non-domination amongst all citizens, insurance programmes would guard each against some of the misfortunes that can undermine the achievement of equal freedom as non-domination and insulation programmes would provide for their protection against the dangers that others can represent within specific relationships and on a more general front.

Infrastructural programmes

There are three kinds of infrastructural programmes that will be required in a republican theory of justice. These are necessary to establish a suitably

---

[24] Notice, however, that republican policies will not have to alter with every change in actual circumstances. No matter what the actual circumstances, they are required to promote non-interference across a range of possible circumstances; they have to make non-interference robustly available over variations both in people's own preferences for what they should do and in other people's preferences for what they should do. I return to this point in the concluding section of the chapter.

broad range of choices in which people can hope to enjoy equal freedom as non-domination in relation to one another.

The first requirement is that children in the society each have access to the sort of education necessary to provide them with essential skills, to bring their particular talents to fruition, to give them a full sense of the rights and responsibilities of citizenship and indeed to let them see how bad it is for anyone to suffer domination in the sphere of the basic liberties. Let people be lacking in such developmental ways, and they will be incapable of asserting themselves with others, or assuming the status of free persons; indeed they may even be a danger to others, not recognizing the reciprocal, freedom-based claims that are made upon them.

The second and third programmes required by way of infrastructure are environmental in character, not developmental. One bears on the institutional environment in which people operate, the other on the physical environment, natural and constructed, in which they live.

In order for people to be able to enjoy the basic liberties equally, there has to be a legal dispensation in place that provides a suitable institutional environment for people's lives together. That dispensation would establish the property conventions and other arrangements required for the availability of certain co-exercisable, co-satisfying choices; provide rules for the definition and redress of torts or wrongs that people may suffer as a result of the negligence, if not the intrusive ill will, of others (Goldberg 2005: 6); enable people to associate and incorporate with one another on a suitable contractual basis, whether commercially, in employment, or in marriage (Cohen 1933); and allow them to argue through the courts or other channels for adjustments to the basic liberties that are protected. Beyond that, it would enable people to enjoy the extra choices that may be made available for entrenchment as a result of stable economic and financial institutions (McGilvray 2011; Tomasi 2012). And at the same time it would establish restrictions and regulations that guard against financial crisis, economic recession, uncoordinated competition, commercial monopoly and uncosted externalities, as well as the inequalities of power and influence that allow some to lord it over others. All of these ills are likely to limit or frustrate people's equal access to basic liberties.

The third domain of policy-making that the state must address, if it is to promote the widespread enjoyment of freedom as non-domination, involves the material rather than the institutional environment. There will be fewer basic liberties available for people, at least in the long run, the less sustainable the natural environment, the less efficient the energy network, the less reliable the organization of transport and information, the less

effective the public health system and, indeed, the less secure the territory of
the state. Thus it will follow under the republican programme, as it will
follow under any plausible agenda for the state, that there have to be policies
in place to promote corresponding, broadly ecological goals.

Catering for the development of citizens, and for the maintenance of a
suitable environment, institutional and material, is one basic part of what is
going to be domestically required of a state if it is to promote equal freedom
as non-domination, establishing a suitably broad range of choices that can
be entrenched as basic liberties. The other two parts require arrangements
for the public insurance of individuals against certain ills, and for their
public insulation against the power and ill will of others.

Insurance programmes

There are a variety of conditions in which people are going to be unable to
exercise some of their basic liberties or are going to be exposed to the
domination of others. People will suffer such vulnerabilities if they do not
have sure access to shelter and nourishment; to treatment for medical need
or support for disability; or to representation in appearing as plaintiffs or
defendants in the courts. It is going to follow straightforwardly, on the
republican approach, that they should therefore be publicly insured – or
publicly required and enabled to have private insurance – against such
possibilities. They should be provided with social security, medical security
and judicial security, whether by means of a system of social insurance,
national health and legal assistance, or by any of a number of alternatives:
say, the provision of a basic income for each citizen (Raventos 2007). They
should be provided in these domains with Sen's (1985) basic capabilities for
local functioning (Nussbaum 2006).[25]

Why require insurance against the ills listed rather than just putting
arrangements in place that make it likely that those in need will be helped
out? Why not just provide incentives – for example, tax concessions – that
will motivate the wealthy and powerful to help the needy? Or why not just
rely on people's natural philanthropy to cater for the needs of others?
Perhaps those in physical need will be better off if they can have recourse
to privately funded kitchens and shelters, and perhaps those in medical and

[25] This policy recommendation presupposes certain empirical assumptions, as I said that almost all such
recommendations do: in this case, the assumption that markets will typically leave people in need of
such insurance. For a defence of that assumption, and a critique of the 'great risk shift' whereby
markets were supposed to be capable of providing suitably, see Quiggin (2011).

legal need will be better off if they can enjoy the pro bono services of philanthropic professionals.

Republican theory is bound to reject the idea of forcing the less well off to have to rely in this way on voluntary forms of philanthropy. The needy will depend on the goodwill of voluntary benefactors for not being exposed to the interference of those who are in a position to interfere in their lives, which already comes dangerously close to being dependent on their goodwill in a dominating way.[26] And once the needy are incorporated into relations of such dependency, the baseline of expectation is bound to shift so that any withdrawal of philanthropic assistance will count as the denial of an established option: that is, as a form of interference. At that point the needy will be exposed to a salient power of interference on the part of their benefactors – an unvitiated, uninvaded capacity to interfere – and they will be straightforwardly dominated. Or at least that will be so in the event, surely quite likely, that benefactors are not pressurised to provide their services or there are not so many benefactors lined up to provide help that the needy depend on the goodwill of none in particular.

Not only should the needy be insured against the sorts of misfortune we have been considering, they should be publicly insured in this way or, at the least, publicly required and enabled to have private insurance. The need for public insurance derives from the republican requirement that people should be guarded against private domination by their enjoyment of a public status as citizens who can access needed resources and protections. If people enjoyed only publicly unmarked safeguards against private domination then they could not hope to live up to the traditional image of free persons. Public insurance does not require universal provision for social, medical and legal security but it does require that if people are unable to provide for themselves in that manner, the public purse is available for their support.

Many advanced societies fail to provide properly for the insurance of their members on the social, medical and legal fronts, but it is worth noting that almost all admit the desirability of public insurance on other fronts, so that they can hardly object in principle to the argument here. No advanced society is ready, for example, to deny help to those in a particular area who are exposed to a natural catastrophe such as an earthquake, a hurricane or a

---

[26] This goes back to the issue at the end of Chapter 1 as to whether failing to guard against the invasion of freedom is as bad as invasion and whether the power of so failing is as bad as the power of invading. I am assuming here that any philanthropic agency is going to be in a position, should it suit its purposes, to withdraw benefits from a particular individual or at least from a particular area, whether of geography or activity.

tsunami. Very few are willing to deny special assistance to those unlucky enough to be born with certain disabilities, or to develop them in later life. And few are ready to allow depositors to lose all their savings when a major bank is in difficulty. Such catastrophes expose people to the possibility of domination in just the way that more personal crises can do. If it seems reasonable for government to guard against their effects, then it should seem equally reasonable for it to guard against the effects of personal crises as well.

But what if the personal crises are self-induced, as we might say? What if the people who suffer them are to blame for falling on such bad times; they gambled their money away, they smoked excessively or drove recklessly, or they engaged in legally risky ventures? What, in short, if their problems are due to bad option-luck rather than brute, bad luck? Does that imply that there is no ground for state provision?

This implication is not supported by a republican approach to these issues. For whatever the origin of the problem in any such case, the crisis still exposes people to domination and still calls for remedy (Scheffler 2005). But isn't there a certain moral hazard in providing the benefits of a public insurance for the bad results of an event for which a person holds a certain responsibility? Might it not lead to reckless risk-taking on the part of some? It might but it probably wouldn't, for two reasons. First of all, the crises involved are such that few would willingly run a salient risk of suffering such a problem. And second, the insurance benefits available are not likely to be such as to compensate fully for the loss endured in such a crisis. In any case, it would seem perfectly reasonable for a community or state that is prepared to insure its citizens in certain ways to take measures that guard against reckless risk-taking. Such measures might take the form of obliging people to wear seat belts while driving or of imposing restrictions on their opportunities to gamble or to incur excessive contractual obligations.

Insulation programmes: special protection

The third area where the republican agenda of entrenching basic liberties would prescribe a distinctive pattern of policy-making is in protecting or insulating people against specific and generic dangers from others. I look first at issues of special insulation and then at the questions raised by general cases.

Special insulation is the sort of protection that is required in relationships like those of wife and husband, employee and employer, debtor and creditor, where there are often asymmetries of power. A standard approach in such areas is to legislate for equality, imposing legal duties on the presumptively stronger party – typically, the husband, the employer and the creditor – and thereby establishing the corresponding rights of the weaker. But often such rights, however well supported, are frail reeds, for they have to be triggered by the weaker party and the act of triggering them can have costs of its own. The wife who calls in the police against an abusive husband may find herself exposed to anger and further abuse as a result. The employees who complain to an inspector about working conditions may find that they consequently get all the rougher jobs. And so on.

The measures that have to be put in place to give even a modicum of protection within relationships of this sort have to go beyond formal, legal rights. They may include screening in various options for the weaker, as in making provision for the abused wife to take refuge in a women's home, or as in legalizing the unionization of employees and recourse to strike action. They may include screening out various options for the stronger, as in imposing a court order against an abusive husband or in restricting or regulating the right of an employer to fire at will.[27] And they may include creating new opportunities for the weaker, as in allowing a spouse to sue for no-fault divorce, or in establishing the possibility for the unemployed to be able to rely on public support.

No such measures are likely to be effective, it should be said, unless the actions of the state are complemented by supportive norms of civil society. If women are to be rid of the domination of abusive husbands, then there must be a women's movement that provides them with the support and solidarity of fellow spirits, should they fall on bad times. And if employees are to be rid of domination at the hands of employers, then there must be a willingness to organize and stand up for one another amongst the employees. There is only so much the state can do on its own.

The relationships within which people need special protection are not limited to person-to-person relationships. One of the most dramatic developments of recent times is the proliferation of corporate entities, commercial and otherwise, and these group agents pose a great danger of domination in how they relate with individuals and with collections of individuals (Coleman 1974). They act only via their own individual members but usually those members play different parts, take turns – on office hours, as it were – in playing their parts, are shielded from scrutiny in the

---

[27] The policy likely to be supported would run directly counter to 'the traditional negative libertarian "at-will" doctrine that, consistent with contractual obligations, an employer may fire an employee for "good cause, no cause or even for cause morally wrong"' (Levin 1984: 97). For historical background see Cornish and Clark (1989: 294–5).

parts they play, and act to an aggregate effect that may not be clearly visible to any one of them (List and Pettit 2011). Consequently, the corporate agents they bring to life lack the vulnerability and the capacity for empathy that individuals generally display (Bakan 2004). Compared with individual human beings, such organizations will generally have an indefinite time-horizon, a systematic indifference to life's anxieties, and a more or less bottomless purse.

Given the rights that they now enjoy in most societies, corporate agents represent salient sources of domination. Think of how a multinational corporation can treat its workforce – say, in its determination of working hours or conditions – when it can move base without excessive cost and the workforce are heavily dependent on it for employment and welfare. Or think about how it may treat the local population or the local environment when the community would be put in serious economic jeopardy by the corporation's departure. Or think, finally, about how it may treat those who suffer as a result of its negligence, whether as individual customers or as the victims of an explosion or oil-spill, when it has access to better legal counsel, can drag out court cases for years, and is subject to none of the pressures that shape individual mentalities, not even the pressure of prospective death.

This rehearsal of problems is confined to the commercial sphere, ignoring the issues raised when the victims of child abuse try to take on a church, for example, or disaffected students or their parents attempt to achieve redress from a school or university, or indeed a small business tries to negotiate terms with a powerful union. But the problems should be more than enough to illustrate the difficulties that have to be overcome if domination is to be reduced within relationships between individuals and corporate bodies.

I do not mention the problems now in order to list some pat solutions. What I mainly want to do is to stress the depth of specific safeguards that the republican programme would call for and the challenge that it raises for the design of suitably protective institutions (Lovett and Pettit 2009). But I cannot resist making one suggestion. This is that corporate bodies of the kind reviewed might be subjected in their own right, and on various fronts, not just to the tort law that is universally allowed, but also to the discipline of the criminal law that I shall be discussing shortly (Pettit 2007d, 2009a; List and Pettit 2011).

The criminal law presupposes a capacity for understanding the merits of the options presented in any choice, in particular the prohibition to which relevant options are subject, and a capacity to respond appropriately to a judgement of those merits. But there is every reason to think that a suitably organized corporate entity will have, or can come to have, such capacities.

And equally there is every reason to think that it makes sense to hold such an entity responsible for any acts that it sponsors, organizing things in a way that allows members to perform the acts in its name. Holding such an entity responsible in its own right is consistent with holding those members responsible at the same time for playing the parts required of them.

If we do expose corporate entities to criminal liability, then we can impose penalties that ought in the longer term to deter offenders. While the penalties may have to be mainly financial – we can't put corporate entities in prison, though we can disband them – they will inevitably carry associated reputational costs: punishments in the currency of esteem (Brennan and Pettit 2004). Such costs are bound to be particularly problematic for any corporate agent. They will affect the capacity of the commercial corporation to attract or retain customers and the capacity of non-commercial corporations like a church to attract or retain members. They can chasten and discipline the most powerful organization and they direct us to a way of establishing significant political control over corporate behaviour.

Insulation programmes: general protection

Let me turn, finally, to the measures of general protection that the entrenchment of basic liberties, as understood in republican terms, would require. I focus on general protection within the state, not internationally, and will be looking only at issues of criminal justice, therefore, not global security. I will address four questions in particular that arise within the theory of criminal justice. What is it for the state to criminalize an act? Why should it criminalize any acts? What acts should it criminalize? And how should it criminalize them?[28]

Q. 1. What is criminalization?

To criminalize certain types of act is to introduce a system of law that is designed to regulate – in particular to minimize – their occurrence by the imposition of penal costs. Regulation by such penal costs is a distinctive form of regulation. It contrasts in particular with opportunity-cost regulation, on the one side, and admission-cost regulation on the other. Opportunity-cost regulation would rely on regulating a particular sort of action by rewarding the alternatives to such action. Admission-cost

---

[28] I draw freely in the following discussion on Braithwaite and Pettit (1990) and Pettit (1997b). I have been deeply influenced by Braithwaite's work in this area.

regulation would regulate the action by permitting people to perform it, but only on condition that they pay a certain absolute cost: in effect, it charges them for the right to perform the action.

By contrast with opportunity-cost regulation, criminalization imposes absolute rather than relative costs: it makes threats against those who perform a criminalized act rather than offering rewards for those who avoid it. And by contrast with admission-cost regulation, it does not exonerate criminal offenders who are willing to accept the penalties attached to their behaviour and pay the cost; it continues to condemn the acts performed, communicating a presumptive disapproval on the part of the community in general of anyone who would perform them (Duff 2001). In making these points, I draw on what I consider as a more or less commonly shared understanding of what criminalization involves. I take myself to be explicating the meaning of criminalization rather than prescribing anything about the form that it should assume.

Q. 2. *Why should the state criminalize any acts?*

It goes without saying that the state will have to regulate against certain hostile types of act that citizens may perpetrate against one another. But why should it regulate in the penal, condemnatory fashion of criminalization? The answer from a republican perspective is straightforward. While opportunity-cost or admission-cost regulation might reduce the probability of interference with people's basic liberties, it would not indict or reduce domination in itself. Opportunity costs – in effect, refusable rewards – would allow potential offenders to retain a power of interference. And admission costs would allow them to interfere without shame on condition that they are prepared to pay those costs.

Severe admission costs might work reasonably well in inhibiting potential offenders, of course. But lacking the element of condemnation, even extremely severe admission costs would be unlikely to do as well as costs that have a condemnatory aspect. They would not serve in the same way to indict offences and to affirm the protected status of victims against such offences. And they might well fail to have the same deterrent impact. Criminological evidence suggests that what keeps most people on the right side of the criminal law is the fact that that law communicates public disapproval of offenders and leads most people to put most offences off the menu of possibilities that they consider as genuine options (Tyler 1990).

Q. 3. *What acts should the state criminalize?*

Criminalization involves the state in an oppressive role in which it can use force to prevent criminalized acts and impose punitive retaliation for the performance of such acts. The danger of allowing a state to become too powerful, constituting a threat to domination, argues for restricting the criminal law to acts of unlicensed interference with people's basic liberties, as those liberties are defined in the society, and to acts that make such acts of interference more likely in various ways. Acts may make incidents of interference more likely by undermining measures for their criminalization, as in contempt for judicial proceedings; by putting preparatory steps in place, as in purchasing materials required for crime; by inciting others to such acts, as in offences against public order; by creating a slippery slope, as in minor environmental offences that can spread to devastating effect; and so on.

The restriction of the criminal law to acts in these categories does not mean that all such acts should be criminalized; only those whose criminal-ization promises a net benefit should be dealt with in this way.[29] There would be no useful point, for example, in criminalizing deception in general, only deception perpetrated under well-defined circumstances, as in the case of perjury. The restriction of the criminal law to acts in the specified categories argues that many of the acts that count as criminal offences in current legal systems, particularly in America and other common-law regimes, ought to be designated as breaches of a non-criminal sort; they ought not to attract the full condemnation of the criminal law (Husak 2008). Crimes ought to be confined to the paradigms of violence, fraudulence and theft that are recognized everywhere as offensive and to acts that clearly open the way to such offences.

Q. 4. How should the state practise criminalization?
This is a large and difficult issue, bearing on arrangements for the pursuit, prosecution, judgement and sentencing of offenders. But there are three plausible principles that should guide policy in this area on the republican approach (Braithwaite and Pettit 1990; Pettit 1997b). The first principle is that people should be liable to conviction or sentence only to the extent that they are culpable: only to the extent that they are fit to be held responsible for an offence. Were the state entitled to impose sanctions independently of culpability then it would be given an extraordinary degree of dominating power. This principle requires departures from normal penal practice when

---

[29] In taking this restrictive line I adhere to an implication of John Stuart Mill's (1978) harm principle: 'the only purpose for which power can be rightfully exercised over any member of a civilized community, against his will, is to prevent harm to others'. That this is the only purpose for which power can be rightfully exercised is consistent with its not being a purpose for which power is always rightfully exercised.

duly convicted offenders are deemed to be less than fully culpable.[30] And it supports a tough standard of due process, arguing that no one should be convicted of an offence unless there is evidence of culpability that stands up under arrangements that put the onus of proof on the prosecution.[31] This standard should reduce the capacity of authorities to scapegoat an innocent party, thereby protecting against a salient possibility of domination. If a police force or a court system can scapegoat opportunistically, then no one, however innocent, will be guarded against such domination. And if this is a matter of common awareness, then everyone will be likely to be intimidated by the presence of such a capricious power in the criminal justice system.

But while the republican approach guards in this way against the punishment of the innocent, or the punishment of the less than fully culpable, how does it say that those convicted as guilty should be punished? Here a second, obvious principle applies: that the penalty imposed should seek to rectify the crime, vindicating the status of victims and potential victims, and yet at the same time that it should keep open the prospect of reintegrating the offender into the community of citizens. There are a number of requirements built into the rectificatory goal. First, to reassert the victim's status as a free person, condemning the offender's assumption of power and, ideally, eliciting a credible apology. Second, to compensate to the greatest extent possible the victim – or in the case of a capital offence, the victim's family – for any material or related loss. And third, to reassure the community – in particular, those for whom the victim's status is indicative of their own status – that they are no worse off as a result of the offence: the probability of suffering such an offence has not increased.

The third principle supported by the republican approach is that while the threat of domination argues against giving the criminal justice authorities a right to impose an exemplary punishment – this right could easily be

---

[30] Where there is a shortfall from full culpability, different cases may require different departures from normal procedure. Many forms of shortfall mean that the offence will not involve the first of the three elements of harm that the text goes on to discuss, or at least not in the full degree; it will not impose the will of a fully conversable agent. That argues that the departure from normal procedure should be towards greater leniency. But the case of the highly dangerous, if not fully culpable, offender – say, a certain sort of psychopath – suggests that this need not always be so. While such an offender ought not to attract the condemnation attached to the criminal law, it may be necessary to impose severe restraints for the sake of public protection. There is a difficult issue as to how such offenders ought to be treated under a republican dispensation but I cannot explore it further here. I am grateful to Ben Ewing for discussion of these issues.

[31] For reasons advanced elsewhere, I believe that corporate bodies may be fit subjects for the criminal law and that in their case it may make good sense to require, not actual guilt or *mens rea* – not full culpability – but the capacity to develop procedures for guarding against the offence in question (Pettit 2007d, 2009a; List and Pettit 2011).

abused – there is no parallel argument against giving them a right to exercise mercy under specified circumstances. Thus if an offender becomes disabled in the course of committing an offence, there may be no pressing need to reassure the community, and independent considerations may argue for clemency. The right to exercise mercy would occasion domination only if it were used at the unchecked discretion of authorities to treat like cases differently, or used in such a widespread fashion that offenders can generally expect to escape the advertised rigours of the law.

Any sentence that incorporates rectificatory features will have a deterrent quality, since it is bound to impose costs on the offender. These include the reputational costs of condemnation and the material costs of compensation. But they include in particular the costs that must be paid for communal reassurance, since these are determined precisely by the requirements of effective deterrence. A criminal justice system is designed in the first place to provide people with a suitable level of public protection against crime, and hence assurance that they are not likely to be subject to the will of criminal offenders (Kelly 2009).[32] The threatened penalty required by such protection and assurance is designed to deter potential offenders and it is the imposition of such a deterrent penalty – the implementation of the threat – that provides the reassurance that rectification of the crime may require. Since reassurance will be less readily forthcoming with chronic offenders, this consideration also allows for the possibility of increasing penalties for repeat offenders (Braithwaite 2002).

This connection with deterrence does not mean in itself that the approach taken here has a consequentialist character, since retributivists can also argue that while penalties should be scaled with offences on independent, non-consequential grounds, the nature of the penalties employed at different levels should be determined by deterrent considerations.[33] But the approach sketched, like the approach adopted throughout

---

[32] This means that the severity of sanction will often have to be designed to compensate for the difficulty and unlikelihood of detecting a relevant offence and not just a function of the degree of harm caused by the offender and their degree of culpability.

[33] Retributivism, as I understand it, is defined by commitments like the following.
 1. There are certain constraints, which are not fully sensitive to consequences, that apply to criminal punishment.
 2. These include a ceiling constraint and perhaps also a floor constraint; the first argues against exemplary punishment, the second against mercy.
 3. Punishment should involve hard treatment, and not just because hard treatment has a deterrent effect or is required if criminal penalties are to have a protective purpose.
 4. Penalties should be proportional, ordinally or otherwise, to the degree of severity of the harm combined with the culpability of the act, and not to anything else (with a possible exception if mercy is allowed; see commitment 2 above).

this book, is indeed teleological or consequentialist in character. The argument is that judicial and penal practice in the state ought to be designed on such a rectificatory pattern that overall it makes for the promotion of equal freedom as non-domination. This sort of practice-wide consequentialism is consistent, of course, with requiring individual judges and courts to abide more or less rigidly by the requirements of the practice, treating those requirements as unconditionally binding (Rawls 1955). Thus, while the practice described would allow judges and courts to be merciful in certain cases, provided they can justify the exercise of such discretion, it would not allow them ever to impose an exemplary punishment, making a generically deterrent example of a particular offender.

4. THE CHARACTER OF REPUBLICAN JUSTICE

Our observations in the preceding section are broad-brush strokes but they should provide at least a rough picture of where republicanism leads in the theory of justice. It is important to have a sense of the republican requirements of justice before we approach the discussion of legitimacy. The theory of justice is meant to provide an image of how people's social relations ought to be organized, if they are each to enjoy equal freedom as non-domination: if they are each to avoid private domination. The theory of legitimacy, to anticipate later discussion, is meant to provide an image of how the state ought to make its decisions about justice and other matters, if citizens are to enjoy equal freedom as non-domination in relation to government: if they are each to avoid public domination. Unless we have a sense of what private non-domination requires, we will be ill positioned to make a judgement on the requirements of public.

In concluding this discussion, I would like to draw attention to some characteristic features of the republican theory of justice, as it has been outlined here. The theory is distinctive on three broad fronts: one, in the principle or standard of justice that it deploys; two, in the demands of justice that it licenses; and three, in the importance that it accords to the public recognition of the laws – and the corresponding norms – that secure the basic liberties.

---

5. Merely ordinal proportionality would require that penalties and crimes should be ordered from toughest/worst to least tough/least bad and then paired off appropriately, with the toughest applied to the worst crime, the next toughest to the next worst, and so on. Non-ordinal proportionality would require that something more is possible in either or both of the two scales; the limit case would be a belief in the lex talionis: an eye-for-an-eye, a tooth-for-a-tooth, and so on.

The principle of republican justice

The principle or standard that the theory deploys, as we have seen, is simply that arrangements between citizens should be designed to promote people's equal enjoyment of freedom as non-domination: that is, the equal entrenchment of their basic liberties on the basis of public laws and norms. This principle is modest in its suppositions, goal-oriented in form, and general in scope – in particular, general enough to be able to serve in either ideal or non-ideal theory. Corresponding points apply to the principle of republican legitimacy, as that emerges in the next chapter, but it will suffice to show how they apply in the case of justice.

The republican principle is extremely modest in characterizing justice by the requirements of equal freedom alone, without reference to any of the richer and more controversial values invoked in many other theories of justice; it is minimalist in the terms required to justify the policies supported (Cohen 2004). What enables it to achieve this modesty is the independently plausible argument that for relevant, unvitiated choices freedom requires non-exposure to the interference of others, not just the absence – the fortuitous absence, as it might be – of that interference. This construal of freedom is plausible and also, as we saw in the Introduction, one with a long historical pedigree. It was only in the eighteenth century, in the work of figures like Jeremy Bentham and William Paley, that freedom came to be routinely characterized as requiring non-interference rather than non-domination. Contemporary theories of justice all give importance to freedom but take equal freedom to require so little that its requirements have to be supplemented from other sources – as, for example, Rawls's second principle – in order to fix the demands of justice.

The principle of justice deployed in the republican theory, to move to a second characteristic, offers a goal-oriented or consequentialist criterion of evaluation. It says that a socio-political arrangement – a basic structure, as Rawls calls it – will be just to the extent that it promotes free or undominated choice amongst its citizens, under the expressively egalitarian constraint of treating them as equals. More concretely, assuming that the circumstances of justice obtain, it prescribes the promotion of the substantively egalitarian goal of equal status freedom for all. This does not mean that agents within the socio-political system are generally licensed to behave opportunistically or strategically, as already mentioned, adjusting their responses according to what they happen to think is best for promoting that goal. It is the structure itself that is designed to promote the goal and it is only likely to do this if the agents acting under the institutions established, be they officials or citizens, are generally required to act in accordance with the duties and rights that they have under that structure (Rawls 1955).

Not only is it a practice-wide form of consequentialism; it is also a constitutive, as distinct from a causal, variety of the approach (Pettit 1997c: Chapter 3). The goal of equal freedom as non-domination is modally demanding, as we saw at the end of the last chapter, requiring a pattern of non-interference that is robust across scenarios in which there are variations both in what people prefer to do and in what others prefer that they do. But people will enjoy the robust non-interference associated with justice – the status of a free person – as soon as there are institutions of resourcing and protection in place to safeguard them. The existence of those institutions will not provide for people's free status by way of a downstream causal effect that takes some time to materialize. It will establish them in that status without waiting on the result of any contingent causal process. The institutions will relate to the free status they establish in the way that the antibodies in your bloodstream relate to the immunity against a certain disease that they constitute. We can understand what such freedom requires without knowing which institutions are required to support it – thus freedom is not defined in terms of those institutions – as we can understand immunity without knowing anything about antibodies. But still the connection between the institutions and the freedom, or the antibodies and the immunity, is not of a causal character. As the antibodies promote the immunity by constituting it, so we can say that the institutions promote freedom and justice in a parallel, constitutive fashion.

We have seen that the principle of republican justice is modest and goal-oriented. A third feature worth mentioning is that it is available for the applied exercise of measuring and comparing regimes for how just they are, not merely for the theoretical exercise of identifying the perfectly just society. It is a general theory of justice, as we might say, not the sort of transcendental theory, as Amartya Sen (2009) describes it, which can rule only on matters of perfect justice. While we can use the principle for identifying an ideally just society – say, a society that is just enough to pass the eyeball test – we can also use it to evaluate and rank the rather less than ideal systems with which the real world presents us and to track piecemeal progress within them (Marti and Pettit 2010: Chapter 5).

There are two reasons why the theory can serve us in the exercise of measuring and comparing actual, imperfect regimes for how just they are. The first is that it is a consequentialist theory that associates justice with approximation to a certain goal. And the second is that it does not – or does not necessarily – make any idealizing assumptions about human nature or compliance with the law that would render it difficult to apply in the ordinary world. These two features combine to ensure that in principle we can measure and compare actual regimes for how just they are by seeing how close they get to the relevant goal. In both respects the approach contrasts with Rawls's theory of justice. This insists in a non-consequentialist spirit that justice is associated with instantiating a certain pattern – the two principles – not with promoting it. And, perhaps even more restrictively, it operates with the idealizing assumption that in ranking regimes by reference to this pattern, we should assume that there is full compliance in each with whatever laws are established there.[34]

But to say that the republican theory of justice allows for the applied exercise of measuring and comparing justice in actual regimes is not to say that our discussion has done enough to equip it for such application. There are different dimensions on which a society's degree of approximation to establishing equal freedom as non-domination might be charted and a fully applicable theory would have to provide weightings for these. As between two different societies, for example, people might differ in enjoying freedom in different sets of choices or in enjoying it with different degrees of entrenchment. And where they enjoyed the same low degree of entrenchment for the same choices, they might differ in the likelihood of achieving preference-satisfaction: they might differ in enjoying entrenchment, here for exercising options they are likely to prefer, there for exercising options they are unlikely to prefer. The republican theory can be used in practice for measuring and comparing justice only under stipulations as to the relative importance of these and other dimensions of variation in the measurement of freedom and other values. And if no plausible stipulations are available on the relative importance of two dimensions, that will mean that societies that differ insofar as one does better in the one dimension, the second in the other, may have to count – perhaps quite intuitively – as displaying justice in the same degree.[35]

---

[34] Rawls (1971: Part III) argues that his two principles will tend to be internalized by those living under them and to constitute a stable structure. But it would seem to be more satisfactory to consider different principles, without assuming universal compliance, and then to rank them by reference, among other standards, to how far they are likely to attract general compliance and display stability.

[35] A full and applicable political theory would not only have to allow for variations in different dimensions of social justice but also for variations in the relative degree of political legitimacy or international sovereignty that societies enjoy. While there are reasons for giving political legitimacy a basic importance, as mentioned briefly in the Introduction, the issue of weighting between these different aspects of performance is too complex to be addressed fully here.

The demands of republican justice

The republican theory of justice displays characteristic features, not just in the principle that it deploys, but also in the demands that it supports. The demands of the theory are quite substantive, despite the modesty of the principle from which they are derived, as our institutional model of republican justice indicates. They are designed to put resourcing and protective measures in place that guard against personal domination in the sphere of the basic liberties to the extent of enabling people to pass the eyeball test. They are meant to reduce the incidence of domination between people and to nullify the institutional or structural factors that facilitate it (Hayward 2011).

The demands made by republican theory are certainly not as extensive as those of egalitarian theories that seek the elimination, for example, of all the effects of brute luck on people's fortunes.[36] Nor are they even as extensive as Rawls's requirements. His second principle of justice would look for material equality, after all, except when the second principle of justice moderates it, allowing a degree of relative inequality on condition that it improves the absolute returns to the worst-off position. But those theories often seem like moral fantasies: manuals for how God ought to have ordained the order of things – or manuals for how we ought to rectify God's failures – rather than real-world manifestos for what the state should do in regulating the affairs of its citizens.[37]

Such comparators aside, the republican theory of justice would still look for quite extensive, even radical measures; while minimalist in its justificatory base, it is not minimalist in substance (Cohen 2004). Beyond the infrastructural requirements on which all sensible theories ought to converge, as we have seen, it would seek a high level of social insurance, a firm basis for the insulation of people in vulnerable relationships and a suitable basis for the general insulation provided by the criminal justice system. It would provide for the basic functioning capabilities of all citizens, as Sen (1985) and Nussbaum (2006) describe them, and would enable people to look others in the eye, without reason for fear or deference – or at least without any reason related to the danger of interference.

[36] For a recent interpretation and defence of luck egalitarianism see Tan (2008) and for a response that I find congenial see Sanyal (forthcoming).
[37] Hegel (1991: 80) has a salutary remark on the topic: 'One cannot speak of the injustice of nature in the unequal distribution of possessions and resources, for nature is not free and is therefore neither just nor unjust.'

In arguing that the just state ought to promote equal freedom as non-domination amongst its citizens, the republican theory of justice does not suggest that freedom as non-domination is the only value that matters, as a utilitarian theory might argue that utility is the only relevant value. What it holds, however, is that if we look after the requirements of equal freedom as non-domination, then we will have looked after the requirements of many other values as well: for example, the value of enjoying functioning capabilities. Look after equal freedom as non-domination in the relations between citizens and you will have looked after an intuitive, left-of-centre, account of the demands of justice. And, to anticipate the argument of the next chapter, look after equal freedom as non-domination in the relations between citizens and state and you will have looked after an intuitive, democratic account of the demands of legitimacy. Freedom as non-domination is not the only value in politics but in the account defended here it serves a gateway role: if we pay the price of securing freedom as non-domination in a suitable measure, we will have paid enough to secure social justice and political legitimacy (Pettit 2005a; for a dissenting view see Markell 2008).

The role of law and norm in republican justice

How far are the demands of republican justice likely to be met without establishing a high degree – perhaps an unattainably high degree – of material equality? Their extra material resources may enable the richer to give themselves extra protection, and the protection provided publicly will have to be good enough to make any such private measures seem redundant. Again, their extra resources may enable the richer to breach the defences of the poorer, and the protection provided publicly will have to be good enough to protect against such private assaults. Can the public entrenchment of the basic liberties guard against such dangers?

One reply to this question might be that the state may regulate the uses of wealth so that there is a limit to the extra protections or powers that the rich can enjoy. That is certainly true, but what I want to emphasize here is something distinct: that there is a quality to the public resourcing and protection that law can provide, at least when things go well, which provisions of private wealth can do little or nothing to match. Insofar as the law is the work of a legitimate state, it will connect with public habits of mind and find support in communally endorsed norms. And in doing this it can establish for citizens an entrenched status – their public status as free persons – that suffices as a bulwark against the advantages on which the rich can draw.

Norms, by our earlier account, are regularities of behaviour in a society such that, as a matter of shared awareness, most members conform to them, most expect others to approve of conformity or disapprove of non-conformity, and most are reinforced in this pattern of behaviour by that expectation. Not every regularity will be a norm, then: like the regularity whereby people eat so many times a day, it may not be taken to attract approval or disapproval. And not even every regularity that is taken to attract approval will be a norm: like the regularity whereby people wash themselves regularly, the expectation of such approval may play little or no role in supporting it. In order to count as norms, behavioural, presumptively approved, regularities have to obtain as a result, at least in part, of being expected to attract approval. And for full measure, all of this has to be a matter of shared awareness: each is in a position to recognize that the conditions are fulfilled, to recognize that others recognize this, and so on.

By this definition, any society is going to abound in norms, since human beings everywhere are disposed to approve and disapprove of the behaviour of others and are equally disposed to cherish approval and shrink from disapproval (Brennan and Pettit 2004: Part 1; Appiah 2010). Adam Smith was particularly emphatic on the point. 'Nature, when she formed man for society, endowed him with an original desire to please, and an original aversion to offend his brethren. She taught him to feel pleasure in their favourable, and pain in their unfavourable regard. She rendered their approbation most flattering and most agreeable to him for its own sake; and their disapprobation most mortifying and most offensive' (Smith 1982: 116).

The norms that we might expect to emerge in any society will include some that apply, perhaps with an unsavoury, self-seeking effect, to specific groups: those in a particular business or political party or criminal gang. But they are also likely to include norms of a socially beneficial kind that serve, on the one side, to govern the behaviour of individuals in particular positions – say, parents and children, teachers and pupils, the governing and the governed – and on the other to indict activities that are damaging to people in general such as deception and violence, infidelity, fraud and free-riding.

The secret strength of law is that if it is well shaped and well supported – if it is relatively just and legitimate – then it can recruit such beneficial, communal norms to the cause of its enforcement (Richardson 2002; Bohman 2007). Properly promulgated and defended, indeed, it can also reshape any existing norms that do not serve the cause of justice. Once law gains normative reinforcement it no longer has to rely on the strength of the public sword, in the old metaphor, for winning compliance amongst the citizenry. Being disposed to approve of compliance and to disapprove of deviance, citizens can become non-intentional sources of enforcement, as they observe one another's behaviour, and form attitudes of approval and disapproval in response (Pettit 1997c: Chapter 7). And of course that enforcement will be further strengthened by people's disposition to talk to one another about the behaviour of offenders and perhaps to talk to the offenders themselves about their misdeeds.

The fact that law can enjoy this sort of support means that when it secures the resourcing and protection of individuals then it can be powerful enough, in principle, to achieve a balance in people's relative positions, even when those individuals vary considerably in the private resources at their disposal. Thus, despite continuing variations in such resources, it can do much for the equal enjoyment of freedom as non-domination across the society. It is for this reason indeed that we can expect that, short of material equality, people may still be able to pass the eyeball test. They may still be able to live up to the image of the free person – the *liber*, or 'free-man' – that is central to republican thought.

CHAPTER 3

Political legitimacy

In the last chapter we focused on issues of social justice: that is, justice in the relations between people within a state, including relations mediated by their belonging to groups and bodies of various kinds. According to the theory developed, justice requires the state to promote the freedom as non-domination of all its citizens – broadly, all adult, able-minded and more or less permanent residents – safeguarding their fundamental liberties on the basis of public laws and norms. This focus on relations amongst citizens leaves out of consideration the relations between citizens as a whole and the state itself. It ignores the question of whether the state operates with political legitimacy in imposing a social order, however just that order might turn out to be. It is one thing to argue that the social order imposed by a state is just, it is quite another to argue that the political imposition of that order is legitimate.

Social justice does not entail political legitimacy, by this account, nor does political legitimacy entail social justice. Thus, to take the second dissociation first, a state might be fully legitimate, by whatever criterion, and yet not succeed in furthering the cause of social justice very well; it might support misconceived, if not ill-willed, policies. It is a failure of this kind that Rousseau had in mind when he acknowledged the possibility that the perfectly legitimate regime – in his terms, the regime that seeks to enact the general will – may still go astray: 'By itself, the people always wills the good, but by itself it does not always see it' (1997: II.6.10).

Turning now to the other dissociation, it also seems that the just society might fall well short of being fully legitimate. The traditional paradigm of the illegitimate regime is that which is controlled by a despot or by a foreign power. But we can imagine a benevolent despotism, or an enlightened colonialism, under which people's relations with one another are ordered in a socially just manner. That order might not have the robust entrench-ment that we would associate with justice, especially from a republican viewpoint. The will at its source might not have the reliability – the resistance to despotic or colonial discretion – that the Roman Digest of law requires when, quoting Ulpian, it says that 'Justice is the steady and enduring will to render unto everyone his right' (Watson 1985: Book 1, Part 1, para. 10).[1] But in other respects, it could be beyond reproach.

These remarks are meant to underline the conceptual divergence between the demands of social justice and the demands of political legitimacy, not to suggest that in practice they can come apart very deeply. It is unlikely that people who fared badly in justice terms could do much about constraining the state to satisfy legitimacy. And it is unlikely that the unconstrained state would do much to establish justice amongst its citizenry. But the fact that political legitimacy can come apart in any measure from social justice means that it makes a distinct demand and that we have to begin afresh in thinking about what it requires.

Not only does political legitimacy make a distinct demand, it makes a demand that we cannot ignore. In any society there are going to be different views as to what social justice requires in the organization of people's relationships. Thus there is going to be a question as to whether it is appropriate for people, recognizing their differences with one another, to accept the decisions of the state as binding on them all and to submit to the coercive application of those decisions by the state. And it will be appropriate for them to do this, presumably, only insofar as there is something about the standing of the state in relation to them as a whole – something about the relations between the state and its citizens – that makes it into the legitimate arbiter and decider in their lives. The question for a theory of legitimacy is to identify the factor that can give such a standing to the state (Nagel 1987).

My discussion in this chapter falls into five sections. In Section 1, I look at the legitimacy issue itself, asking after the precise source and nature of the problem, and seeking to combat the tendency to let it drop from sight. In Section 2, I argue for a tight linkage between legitimacy and freedom and show that under freedom as non-domination legitimacy has a straightforward requirement: a form of popular or civic control over the state. In Section 3, as in an intermission, I analyse the notion of control in general, contrasting it with consent. In Section 4, I argue that if it is to support

---

[1] The Latin is: *Justitia est constans et perpetua voluntas ius suum cuique tribuendi*. The view that justice does not require such constancy of will is expressed in Leo Strauss's (2000: 75) reading of the Greek tradition, which he may or may not endorse himself (see Vatter 2011): 'The just man does not hurt anyone, but helps everyone who has dealings with him. To be just, in other words, simply means to be beneficent. If justice is then essentially translegal, rule without laws may very well be just: beneficent absolute rule is just.'

legitimacy, then popular control must be individualized, unconditioned and efficacious in character, satisfying a rich version of the democratic ideal. And then in a short Section 5, I make some observations on the desirability of such a democratically controlled state, drawing attention to differences between the perspective adopted here and other approaches.

The chapter provides a theory of democracy, arguing that the job of democratic institutions is to ensure the form of popular control required for political legitimacy. But the discussion does nothing to identify the sorts of institutions that might actually do this job. That task is taken up in chapters 4 and 5, which provide an institutional model of democracy that is meant to illustrate what the republican theory requires.

We argued in the last chapter about the requirements of republican justice, starting from the expressively egalitarian assumption that the state ought to treat its citizens as equals. As explained in that earlier argument, the same egalitarian assumption will direct the argument in this chapter, when we look for what is required by republican legitimacy. The normative assumption is, on the one side, that the state ought to treat its citizens as equals and, on the other, that citizens ought to be willing to accept this and to live on equal terms with one another. This assumption is intuitively compelling and is not specific to the republican approach; it is endorsed in every plausible political philosophy.[2]

I. THE LEGITIMACY QUESTION

The source of the problem

We assumed in our discussion of social justice that the state is required for promoting justice and it is this assumption that raises the question as to whether the state that imposes a social order – ideally, a just social order – imposes it in a legitimate manner. But is the state necessary for the promotion of social justice? Is it required for entrenching a suitable range of basic liberties, as republican justice prescribes? There are a number of considerations, rehearsed in Section 4 of this chapter, which suggest that the state is a more or less inescapable institution, not something we might choose to have or not to have. But suppose for the moment that the state

---

[2] The egalitarian aspect of the theory pursued in this book is emphasized by the extent to which it coincides with the democratic egalitarianism advocated by Sanyal (forthcoming). He looks broadly for equality of non-domination in relations between citizens and for what he calls equality of autonomy in relations with the state; but the latter is close to equality of non-domination in relations with government.

were not inescapable. Would the cause of republican justice – or indeed the cause of any plausible view of social justice – still require us to invent it? I argue that it would.

The state, as I conceive of it here and throughout this book, is not just an impersonal apparatus of rules and routines, dictating how officials operate within its domain; in this respect it is unlike the market, for example. The state is an agent or agency that espouses any of a variety of purposes and pursues those purposes according to reliably maintained representations of the opportunities and means at its disposal. And, most important of all, it is an agent that presents itself to other agents – its own citizens, the organizations that operate within its boundaries, as well as other states and international bodies (McLean 2004) – as an entity with which it is possible to do business: an entity that is conversable in the manner of an individual human being. In this self-presentation it operates like a legal person, making avowals of attitude and promises of action to which, on pain of failing as a state, it allows itself to be held (List and Pettit 2011). While the state cannot speak or act except on the basis of the words or actions of different government agencies and officials, those agencies have to be coordinated with one another so that the state speaks with a single voice and acts to a coherent set of ends. If certain agencies or officials do come apart on either front, making inconsistent avowals or promises, or acting in ways that undercut one another, then they have to be sensitive to the need to restore harmony and they have to be able to mobilize certain procedures for doing so.

The state is necessary for implementing a conception of justice like the one outlined in the last chapter, because only an agency of that kind would be capable of discharging the many varied and demanding tasks involved: maintaining the developmental, institutional and material infrastructure that justice requires; establishing and adjusting the laws required to identify substantive and coherent basic liberties; ensuring that those liberties are resourced on the basis of any needed conventions and subsidies; and protecting people against the invasion of those liberties, whether in particular relationships or on a more general front. The tasks involved here are so complex, interconnected and dynamic that no abstract apparatus of rules could plausibly ensure their fulfilment. There can be no effective system of justice, so it appears, in the absence of a state.

The fact that a corporate, conversable entity is required for establishing a system of justice not only means that there has to be a state. It also means, more specifically, that the state has to have two characteristic features. The state must have the power of coercively imposing the order it establishes, threatening and implementing penalties for those who disobey, without competition from rival bodies. And, given that this is going to be manifest to all, the state must as a matter of its practice make an explicit or implicit claim to having the exclusive authority to use coercion in that manner.

But isn't this argument for the necessity of a corporate, coercive state too quick? Might a just order not be capable of emerging, under suitable conditions, as the by-product of a system of communal norms – a network of rules that no single agency like the state is needed to create or trigger, monitor or shape? Communal norms, as we saw in the last chapter, are regularities of behaviour that are maintained in part as a result of the fact, registered in common awareness, that people generally expect the approval of others for conforming to the regularities and/or the disapproval of others for not conforming; the background assumption is that, for intrinsic or instrumental reasons, people will generally seek the approval of others and shun their disapproval. Suppose then that, independently of state or law, communal norms emerged that had the effect of exposing all forms of deception, fraud, manipulation, intrusiveness and violence to the condemnation of the community. Might such a system of norms not prove sufficient for establishing a regime of justice?

The possibility of a rule of impersonal norm is intriguing from a republican point of view. The norms envisaged would be established by individual people, and the associated penalties would be imposed by individual people. But they would emerge and stabilize as by an invisible hand, since neither the introduction of the norms nor the imposition of costs would require a state. An effective regime of such non-intentionally policed norms should be very appealing for anyone concerned with freedom as non-domination. By hypothesis it would serve to protect people from the domination of others, imposing costs that undermine the power that the powerful might have had to interfere. And yet it would protect them without imposing the potentially dominating will of a protective agency; it would protect them in the benign manner of a will-independent force for good.[3]

---

[3] The ideal of a rule of impersonal, will-independent norms may have had a certain presence in the history of republican thought. It often seems to lurk in the background when writers emphasize that the great protection against the tyrannical and, more generally, the illegitimate regime is an 'empire of laws and not of men', as James Harrington (1992: 8) described it, invoking Aristotle and Livy in his support. The tradition led John Adams (1776) to write that 'the very definition of a republic is "an empire of laws, and not of men"'. This line of thought is also present in many authors who enthuse about the common law, on the grounds that it emerges without a concerted, potentially dominating will from decisions over particular cases. See for example Hayek (1988), who may have been influenced by Kant's (1996: 294) belief that 'the sovereign, which gives laws, is, as it were, invisible; it is the personified law itself, not its agent'. For a commentary on the Kantian influence on Hayek, see

But however attractive the idea of an impersonal, will-independent regime of protection, there is little hope that it could operate effectively in the absence of a state. There are three salient problems that it would confront. A first is that spontaneous norms would be unlikely to identify basic liberties of an appropriate kind, particularly in view of the differences between people on relevant matters and the difficulties of sorting out a suitable set of liberties. As we saw in the last chapter, a variety of more or less conventional rules, and provisions for the continuing adjustment of those rules, are required in order to define suitably co-exercisable and co-satisfying liberties.

A second problem with the proposal is that even if spontaneous norms were satisfactory in other respects, they would be unlikely to mandate and support full resourcing of basic liberties, especially when such resourcing requires a degree of redistribution. Unregulated by the agency of a state, wealth and power tend to accumulate in fewer and fewer hands. As by an 'iron law', to quote a recent history of political order, 'the rich tend to get richer, in the absence of state intervention' (Fukuyama 2011: 368). It is extremely unlikely that any spontaneous norms could resist the effects of growing economic accumulation and ensure the resourcing of basic liberties for the poor as well as the rich.

An order of spontaneous norms would be unlikely, then, either to identify or to resource a suitable set of basic liberties. A third problem is that it would also be unlikely to provide suitable protection for all. Communal norms may assume any of a variety of objectionable profiles, as they reflect divisions within society and impose patterns that are highly injurious to those on the weaker side of gender or religious or ethnic or other divides. It was for this reason that John Stuart Mill (1978) railed against the despotism of custom. Norms of the kind envisaged may not impose the will of a potentially dominating agency; after all, they are sourced and supported by non-intentional attitudes. But they will almost certainly fail to protect the members of certain groups against the most rampant domination on the part of others.[4]

Kukathas (1989). A more plausible view of the laws is found in Demosthenes (1939: Section 224) in *Against Meidias*: 'And what is the strength of the laws? If one of you is wronged and cries aloud, will the laws run up and be at his side to assist him? No; they are only written texts and incapable of such action. Wherein then resides their power? In yourselves, if only you support them and make them all-powerful to help him who needs them. So the laws are strong through you and you through the laws.'
[4] See Fukuyama (2011: Chapter 17) for a related, salutary discussion of how the emergence of the rule of law typically depends on the support of a state; it does not appear as by an invisible, non-intentional hand.

I conclude that the cause of social justice requires the corporate agency of a coercive state and that no apolitical order could serve in that role. To assume that the state is essential for the promotion of social justice, of course, is not to assume that any particular sort of state is essential, and certainly not to assume that the existing pattern of states is ideal. But the assumption that any sort of state is necessary generates the problem that is now at the centre of our concern. Given that a state is necessary for justice, there is an issue about how it ought to relate to its citizens, as distinct from the issue of how the citizens ought to relate to one another. And that, as I conceive of it, is the issue of legitimacy. Where the issue of social justice is a matter of the horizontal relations of citizens to one another, political legitimacy is a matter of their vertical relations to the state that rules over them.

What turns on legitimacy?

Where the issue of social justice bears on the nature or character or content of the social order established amongst people in the state, then, the issue of social legitimacy bears on its source or origin: that is, on how far the state that coercively imposes that order relates appropriately to the people on whom it is imposed. Does it relate to people in such a way that however well or badly it does by anyone's view of social justice – and people's views of justice may differ considerably – they each have to admit that it operates with a suitable licence or pedigree and that its presumptive authority to identify and impose the social order is unobjectionable? To give a positive answer to that question is to affirm the legitimacy of the state; to give a negative answer is to deny it.

What turns on whether a state is legitimate or not? What implications does its legitimacy have for how the citizens of the state ought to behave? And in what way do they differ from the implications of justice? As I understand the two ideals, they each impose a different set of moral obligations on citizens. The obligations imposed are *pro tanto* obligations that may not apply in special, emergency circumstances, as when the life of an innocent party is at stake. But they are none the less important for that.[5]

---

[5] That the reasons are *pro tanto* in character means that they can be overridden by countervailing considerations, as when the red lights go on. But consistently with having this pro tanto status, the reasons might function under normal conditions – that is, in the absence of red lights – in an exclusionary manner that precludes exercises in the weighing of pros and cons (Raz 1986). I am grateful to Caleb Yong for a discussion on related matters.

Suppose that the social order imposed by a state is just and that the state itself, by whatever criteria, is legitimate. In that case we will naturally say that in view of its legitimacy people are morally obliged to accept the regime, in some sense of acceptance, and that in view of its justice they are obliged to endorse and comply with the laws. But what does it mean to accept a regime? And how does such acceptance come apart, if at all, from endorsing and complying with its laws?

The answer appears once we consider a case where the regime continues to count as legitimate but certain of its laws are unjust. The injustice of those laws will mean that people are not subject to the same content-dependent obligation to endorse and comply with them, although they will certainly be subject to a fall-back, *pro tanto* obligation that applies in all half-reasonable systems of laws, just and unjust. This is the content-independent obligation to comply that derives from the fact that once social regularities are established by law people generally coordinate their activities around the expectation of mutual compliance (Raz 1986). But the injustice of certain laws will also mean, plausibly, that people are morally permitted, perhaps even obliged, to try to change those laws. That raises the question as to what is allowed to people in their attempts to change unjust laws. And it is here that legitimacy, and the acceptance that I have associated with legitimacy, are relevant.

The acceptance of the regime means, I propose, that attempts to change unjust laws should be restricted to measures that are consistent with the regime's remaining in place. It requires you to acknowledge the state as the appropriate arbiter and decider of legal issues, rather than taking the law into your own hands, and to campaign for change on the assumption that the state is to retain that role. Legitimacy imposes a *pro tanto* moral obligation, then, if you oppose certain laws or measures – and given differ-ent conceptions of justice, everyone will be disposed to challenge some – to oppose them in ways allowed by the system: to stop short of revolution or rebellion or, in an older word, resistance. It makes it permissible, invoking justice or some other virtue, to oppose certain laws within the system: in a word, to contest them. But it makes it impermissible to reject or resist the regime itself.

Most regimes will offer some ways of opposing its laws that are clearly within the system: appealing to the legislature, taking the government to court, speaking out in the media, demonstrating in the streets and, of course, challenging the governing party at election time. But the act of breaking the law – notwithstanding coordination-based reasons to comply – may also count as a mode of contestation, a way of opposing laws within the system.[6] This is exemplified in campaigns of civil disobedience where, for example, campaigners break the laws – perhaps the laws they oppose, perhaps other laws – in order to display opposition. When brought before the courts, campaigners typically acknowledge the authority of the courts to penalize them, thereby displaying their acceptance of the regime itself and disavowing revolution or resistance. They invoke their willingness to accept the authorized penalty for whatever abuse they have committed to draw attention to the injustice of those laws.[7]

The legitimacy of a social order is often thought to correlate with the political obligation of citizens. Such political obligation, on the proposal I am making, is not the *pro tanto* obligation to obey the laws but the *pro tanto* conditional obligation, if you oppose the laws, to oppose them within the system.[8] This conception of political obligation is independently plausible, since political obligation is traditionally taken to bind people insofar as they are citizens proper, not merely temporary or transient inhabitants. Even those passing through a society have a *pro tanto* obligation to obey the law; like others, they will have a content-dependent obligation to obey just laws, and may have a content-independent obligation to obey any law, just or unjust. But only citizens are likely to have substantive rights to oppose the law within the system and only they can be meaningfully bound to limit their opposition to intra-systemic contestation.

This comment squares with the broad conception of citizenship with which I have been working. All adult, able-minded, more or less permanent residents count as citizens, on this conception, not just those with the right to vote and stand for office. While not all citizens in my broad sense will have electoral rights, they will all have formal and informal rights to oppose the law of a kind not readily given to those merely passing through. And in effect most will have the right to seek electoral rights – and to expect to gain them – by applying for formal citizenship. They will be in a position akin to those enfranchised citizens who choose not to enrol on the voting lists, or not to take part in voting, and who thereby deny themselves the opportunity to exercise their electoral rights.

---

[6] The fewer the means of opposing a regime within the system, of course, the less likely it is that the regime will count as legitimate: that is, the more likely it is that there are going to be some unjust laws such that the available ways of opposing them within the system are so few that people are no longer obliged to confine themselves to such opposition. But the availability of civil disobedience means, at least in theory, that there is always at least one way in which a regime can be opposed within the system.

[7] For a broadly congenial – purportedly 'republican' – account of the sort of civil disobedience that might be warranted see Markovits (2005).

[8] For an intriguing but rather different view of political obligation, see Gilbert (2006).

The discussion so far speaks as if it is only the state, or the social order it imposes, that counts as illegitimate. But this is for convenience only. When a state or regime is illegitimate then the laws it upholds are individually illegitimate and the branches of government that run the state are illegitimate too: they are tainted by the illegitimate routines of appointment employed. But there is also room for claiming in the same sense of the term that while a regime is generally legitimate, certain laws or appointments – including the appointment of an executive or other branch – are illegitimate: they happen to breach conditions of legitimacy that the regime generally respects. While I shall continue to concentrate on the legitimacy or illegitimacy of regimes, I do not mean to deny that there is room for invoking the concept in more local complaints as well. And of course I allow that illegitimate laws, being objectionable like unjust laws, may be suitable targets for contestation within a legitimate regime.

Is it appropriate, however, to treat the legitimacy of a regime as an on–off matter, as in effect I have been doing? I believe that the factors that make for political legitimacy, like the factors that make for social justice, come in different degrees. But as I am happy to treat social justice as an on–off matter, given the eyeball test for determining where the justice threshold lies, so for similar reasons I am happy to treat political legitimacy as an on–off matter. As we shall see, there is an intuitive tough-luck test for determining in a parallel way where the legitimacy threshold falls.

I said earlier that while the justice of the laws gives people a content-dependent if *pro tanto* reason to conform, there will almost always be a content-independent reason to conform to any reasonable system of laws, just or unjust, viz., that they serve as coordinating devices around which people build mutual expectations. Given that the laws of a legitimate regime may not themselves be legitimate, and given in particular that the regime itself may fall short of legitimacy, it is natural to ask whether there is any corresponding fall-back reason why people should still not resist the regime: any reason why they should restrict themselves to opposing it within the system.

The issue is not central to our concerns but, for the record, I think that there may be a very good reason – and not just a reason of personal prudence – to stop short of resistance to a certain sort of illegitimate regime. This is that however illegitimate it may be, the regime is still capable of being made legitimate by being treated as if it were legitimate: that is, by being opposed only within the system. Without being fully legitimate, the system may in that sense be legitimizable. And my proposal is that legitimizability can plausibly count as a fall-back reason to avoid outright resistance and oppose a state only from within the system.[9]

The virtue of patriotism, traditionally associated with taking sides with your existing state in international conflicts, might be taken in the domestic context to argue for this sort of fidelity to an existing state and constitution, even in the face of the state's failure to be legitimate (Mueller 2007). I shall not have much to say about legitimizability or patriotism in the remainder of this book. But it should be clear that the issue is of immense importance when it comes to drawing practical implications for how far people are politically obligated to the states they live under. Few actual states may count as legitimate, even by the realistic, tough-luck test of legitimacy introduced later, but many are likely to count as at least legitimizable.

We have seen that according to any theory, the legitimate and just order imposes a moral obligation to accept the regime and to comply with the law – as always, in a *pro tanto* sense – and that the legitimate but unjust order imposes an obligation to accept the regime, opposing unjust laws – and, of course, illegitimate laws – only within the system: that is, contesting those laws but not resisting the regime. The illegitimate and unjust order will not require acceptance or compliance on the same basis; putting aside fall-back reasons, it will permit citizens to resist the regime and, using whatever means are available within, or presumably without, the system, to try to alter the law. What of the fourth, unlikely case, where there is an illegitimate, yet just order? That will allow resistance to the regime but offer reasons of both a content-dependent and content-independent kind for compliance with the law; it will authorize a mix of challenging the authority of the state to impose the laws combined with recognizing that the laws imposed are themselves unobjectionable. The possibilities are charted, however roughly, in Table 3.1.

Table 3.1 *The demands of justice and legitimacy*

	Just social order	Unjust social order
Legitimate social order	Should accept, should comply	Should accept, may contest
Illegitimate social order	May resist, should comply	May resist, may contest

[9] As legitimizability offers a reason for treating a state as if it were legitimate, so I have argued elsewhere that a corresponding form of responsibilizability offers a reason for treating someone as if they were responsible: that is, for holding them responsible. See Pettit (2001e, 2007d). The responsibilizable agent will be capable of being made responsible – fit to be held responsible – by being treated as if they were responsible – that is, by being held responsible. The legitimizable state will be capable of being made legitimate – fit to be opposed only within the system – by being treated as if it were legitimate – that is, by being opposed only within the system.

Legitimacy in its heyday

One reason for speaking of political legitimacy and social justice, rather than of justice in a comprehensive sense, is that it may help to guard against the danger of not recognizing how distinct these questions are.[10] The social justice question bears, as we know, on the character of the rules that determine the claims that citizens have, relative to one another, within the state. The legitimacy question bears on the way in which that set of rules – and any other associated rules – is imposed on citizens. It concerns the actual world and the contingent relationship between the people in a regime and the social order that obtains amongst them; in particular, the relationship whereby that order is sustained under the regime. By all accounts the social order will be legitimate insofar as it is sustained in an appropriate way, illegitimate insofar as it is sustained inappropriately: say, to invoke paradigm cases, sustained independently of what citizens think, by the will of a local despot or a foreign power.

Theories of the requirements of legitimacy assumed a remarkably strong form in seventeenth- and eighteenth-century political thought, though always against a background assumption that limited the people or citizenry to mainstream, usually propertied males. The theory of the divine right of kings had suggested that only the actual, if presumptive, blessing of God could establish the legitimacy of a sovereign and of the order that that sovereign chose to impose. Thomas Hobbes (1994b) directly challenged that theory in arguing that it was the implicit, continuing consent of subjects – albeit a form of consent that could be extracted under fear or pressure – that made the rule of a particular sovereign legitimate; postulating the harsh alternative of a lawless state of nature, he thought that rationality required individuals to give their consent to whatever individual or body had the power to keep the peace. John Locke (1960) argued that two conditions gave legitimacy to a commonwealth: first, the unanimous, historical consent of individuals, guided by a desire to establish a fair arbiter of disputes, to exit the state of nature and set up a state; and two, the support of the existing government by majority will, as evident in the failure of a majority to be moved to rebellion by any alleged abuses of the arbiter role. Finally, Jean-Jacques Rousseau (1997) held that legitimacy required that the majority voice of the assembled citizens should rule on issues of general law, where once

---

[10] The person who has done most to underline the distinctness of these questions in the recent literature is A. J. Simmons (1976, 1979, 1999).

again such majoritarian decision-making had been unanimously and freely accepted, in exiting the state of nature and forming a state.

Thinkers like Hobbes, Locke and Rousseau certainly had ideas about the social order that they thought government should establish, but their works were primarily addressed to the issue of legitimacy, which they made vivid with the theatrics of an imagined state of nature. Each was intent on identifying those conditions under which they thought people were obliged to accept a regime and conditions under which they were entitled to rebel: that is, to reject the state or sovereign whereby the existing order is sustained. The Hobbesian and even Lockean theories offered very limited grounds for rebellion, although it is worth recalling that Bishop Bramhall (1658: 515), his opponent in debates about freedom, thought that Hobbes's *Leviathan* was 'a rebel's catechism'. Rousseau's *Social Contract* was more radical in intent, suggesting that many existing states were not involved in a legitimate exercise but merely in 'subjugating a multitude' (Rousseau 1997: 1.5.1). It is no wonder that he attracted the hostile attention of the French and other authorities, although he was prudent enough not to call explicitly for rebellion against their regimes.

The eclipse of the legitimacy issue

These earlier figures provide vivid examples of a concern with political legitimacy rather than social justice, but this concern was eclipsed in the later development of political thought. This is clearly true of the utilitarian tradition that derives from Bentham, which dominated political theory down to the mid-twentieth century in the English-speaking world and continues to have a commanding presence. Looking for the sort of regime that maximizes expected happiness, utilitarianism focuses on the issue of how far the social order treats citizens well and equally in this dimension and it pays little attention to the issue of whether the order is suitably supported by those who live under it. Utilitarianism has been effectively challenged over the past half century or more by a variety of broadly Kantian approaches. But while these often seem favourable to the legitimacy concern, they all endorse a move that banishes it from consideration.

Kant himself exemplifies the pattern. He begins from the thought that the will imposed in the enactment of law – and so the will that sustains the social order created by law – should be 'the general (united) will of the people' (Kant 1996: 295): the will associated with the 'original contract' (480). This looks favourable to the Rousseauvian approach from which Kant begins. But the appearance is misleading, for he insists that the original contract is 'only an idea of reason', not something 'presupposed as a fact', and argues not that the state should actually be grounded in such a will but that 'every legislator' – in effect every state – should establish laws that '*could* have arisen from the united will of a whole people' (Kant 1996: 296). That the laws could have arisen in that way is 'the touchstone of any public law's conformity to right', he says; 'a rational principle for appraising any public rightful constitution' (Kant 1996: 297, 301).

With this shift, the issue of the legitimacy of a social order, on which Rousseau was primarily focused, is put aside in favour of the issue of the nature or quality of that social order: its comprehensive, social-cum-procedural justice. The fact that the laws could have been chosen in an original contract – their contractual eligibility – is now a sign of their having a certain intrinsic character, not an indication of their being sustained in a legitimate manner. It may not be surprising, then, that Kant shows scant regard for questions of legitimacy. While he favours a representative regime in which there is a separation of powers (Kant 1996: 324, 481) – a republic, as he calls it – he holds that even if a government should 'proceed quite violently (tyrannically), a subject is still not permitted any resistance by way of counteracting force' (298). No established state can be illegitimate in our sense, then, since this 'prohibition' against 'resistance to the supreme legislative power' is 'unconditional': it applies even under the most appalling regimes.

No contemporary theories follow Kant in prohibiting resistance to any established regimes, but many take his lead in making some version of contractual eligibility the criterion of whether a social order ought to be accepted, thereby downplaying the distinctness of the legitimacy concern. John Rawls (1971) does this in arguing that his two principles would have been chosen in an original position of contract where people operate under a veil of ignorance as to their own particular prospects in this or that social order. And he remains faithful to that same, broadly Kantian, approach when he later replaces the test of contractual eligibility under a veil of ignorance with a looser, associated test of civic justifiability: the justifiability of a legal order, on the basis of reasons that ought to be publicly acceptable to the citizens who live under it (Rawls 1993, 2001).[11] A concern with

---

[11] The approach that he exemplifies in this later turn is shared loosely among a large range of contemporary political and moral thinkers, including Charles Beitz (1989), Thomas Pogge (1990), Thomas Nagel (1991), Brian Barry (1995), T. M. Scanlon (1998) and Rainer Forst (2002). For a radical critique see Simmons (1999) and for a critique more closely related to the Rawlsian starting point see Reidy (2007). Anna Stilz (2009) represents a rather different approach that also starts with Kant – in particular, with his observation that the right to external freedom presupposes membership in a

justifiability in this sense is a concern that that order should have a certain intrinsic character – in particular that it should be comprehensively just – and is distinct from the concern for whether it is appropriately supported that we find in Hobbes, Locke and Rousseau (Simmons 1979, 1999).

The elision of the problem of legitimacy under the contractualist way of thinking may be due to a confusion that is easily made. Legitimacy is the ideal, under a natural formulation, of having a social order that is imposed only insofar as it satisfies terms that people actually endorse. Under this ideal people effectively dictate the terms on which a social order will be accepted and, on any interpretation of that claim, they can be said to support the order imposed. Justice, in the new contractualist formulation, is easily confounded with this. It is the ideal of having a social order that is imposed only insofar as it satisfies terms that people could have rationally endorsed, even if they didn't: in Rawls's (1995: 148) way of thinking, 'terms that all reasonable parties may reasonably be expected to endorse'. The difference in formulation is subtle but it may mark a deep divide. Even an order that is not suitably supported by its people, as they are actually disposed, might satisfy terms that they would endorse if they were properly rational or reasonable.

As I mentioned, contractualist theory focuses not only on social justice but on comprehensive or social-cum-procedural justice, so that Rawls (1971: 2003) includes procedural or political rights amongst the basic liberties required by justice. Does the wider focus of contractualist and similar theories mean that the criticism offered here is unfair? I do not think it does mean this, but postpone an account of why not until the end of this chapter. At that point we will be in a better position to see both the strength and the weakness of the approach that contractualism typifies.[12]

I have been arguing that perhaps the two major strands of political thinking, respectively utilitarian and contractualist, tend to neglect the issue of legitimacy, ignoring the importance of how people actually relate

political society: this, because there can be no property, for example, without a coercive state (Kant 1996: 409). She argues that given our joint engagement in creating our local political society, it will have a distinctive claim on us – in our terms, a claim of legitimacy – and we will have a correlative obligation of loyalty to it; or at least this will be so insofar as the society does actually provide for our enjoyment of external freedom.

[12] If the procedural rights that count for Rawls among the basic liberties were required to ensure people's control over the social order, then on the view to be defended here, Rawlsian justice – that is, his two principles – would require legitimacy in our sense. But as a matter of fact Rawls (1971: 233) himself downplays the political liberties, as we shall see, casting them as 'subordinate to the other freedoms', and does not suggest that they ought to ensure control in that sense. His focus on justice is mainly a focus on social justice, as we have been describing it, and it does not bring issues of legitimacy into prominence.

to the regime under which they live. But the oversight is not confined to these two approaches. Egalitarians of various stripes also tend to ignore the question, concentrating on the extent to which a social and perhaps procedural order displays the particular sort of equality they favour, be that equality in resources, utility, capability, or whatever. Other very different writers like David Gauthier (1986) and Robert Nozick (1974) also overlook legitimacy in favour of something else. Gauthier looks for an order that self-interested subjects would have rationally agreed on, starting from a bargaining standpoint that it would have been rational to accept. And Nozick looks in a legal order for the satisfaction of a parallel counterfactual: if people were situated in a morally acceptable world – as he thinks of it, a Lockean state of nature – then they could plausibly have generated that order as the byproduct of morally acceptable, self-interested adjustments.

But there are some contemporary figures who may be keyed, however implicitly, to the legitimacy problem. They generally start with democratic decision-making, however understood, and argue for the importance of having a social order that is sustained by suitable democratic mechanisms. This group will include deliberative democrats who insist on the importance of having an order that is actually sustained by processes of democratic deliberation; it will not include those, however, who insist merely on the importance of having an order that could have been sustained in that way.[13] More generally, the group will include those who see importance as such in the fact that a social order is grounded in a pattern of democratic decision-making, whether canonically deliberative or not.[14] The republican theory of legitimacy, as we shall see in later chapters, connects with these democratic traditions of thought.

Legitimacy in other senses

In concluding this discussion of legitimacy we should note that my use of the term should not be confused with three other uses that figure in the literature of political theory and political science. One is the common

---

[13] Juergen Habermas (1995), Amy Gutmann and Dennis Thompson (1996), Joshua Cohen (2009) and, in a different key, John Dryzek (2003) are salient figures in this category. David Estlund (2007: 87–93) argues that deliberative democrats often slip into endorsing the hypothetical test mentioned in the text and thereby move closer to Rawls. Thus Habermas (1995: 458) appears to go hypothetical in formulating his discourse principle of legitimacy: 'The only regulations and ways of acting that can claim legitimacy are those to which all who are possibly affected could assent as participants in rational discourse.'

[14] This group includes Jeremy Waldron (1999b), David Estlund (2007), Thomas Christiano (2008) and Amartya Sen (2009).

sociological use, deriving from Max Weber (1947), in which to say that a
social order is legitimate is just to say that it is widely accepted amongst
the people: accepted, perhaps, as a result of being believed in our sense to be
legitimate. According to Charles Taylor (1985b: Essay 10) this is the sense
of legitimacy in play when people speak of the legitimacy crisis of contemporary states.

A second sense of legitimacy that figures in common usage refers us to
international, as distinct from domestic, legitimacy (Buchanan 2004). A
regime might not be legitimate in the way in which it relates to its citizens
but might still count as a legitimate member of the international community: it may be a state that satisfies human rights in such a measure, for
example, that it is not exposed to certain sorts of complaints in international
forums (Beitz 2009). Such a state might not be democratic or liberal, in any
standard sense, but in a phrase used in this context by John Rawls (1999) it
might count as a decent regime that merits full respect and incorporation on
the international scene.

There is also a third sense of 'legitimacy' now often invoked within
contractualist circles, which equates legitimacy with civic justifiability
(Simmons 1999: 756–7). Rawls (1993: 224) illustrates this when he says
that 'the principle of political legitimacy' requires that the 'basic structure
and its public policies are to be justifiable to all citizens'.[15] By this account,
the legitimacy of a social order does not require a contingent relationship
between the subjects and the order imposed that might enable us to say,
for example, that they support the order. It depends only on the fact that
the order imposed is such that it could be justified to them. In our terms it is
not a conception of legitimacy but a reformulation of the standard contractualist conception of justice.

2. LEGITIMACY AS POPULAR CONTROL

A question of freedom

What might make it the case that the state that imposes a social order on its
citizens does so legitimately? What might ensure that while citizens may not
all approve of what the state actually does in establishing laws, imposing

[15] Despite his opposition to contractualism, Bernard Williams (2005: 4) adopts a usage that is very close
to this when he says that the 'basic legitimation demand' requires the state to 'offer a justification of its
power to each subject'. Since the justification need not be accepted by each subject, this conception of
legitimacy is also distinct from that invoked here.

policies or levying taxes, still they do not have good grounds for complaint about its presumption in taking those actions? They remain obliged to accept the state as the relevant arbiter and decider of legal issues, restricting themselves to opposing laws only within the system set up by the state.

The primary reason that the state raises a question of legitimacy of this kind is that in pursuing its distinctive tasks, it assumes and exercises a presumptively unchallenged right to coercion: it brooks no opposition. People are not given an individual choice on whether or not they will have to follow the laws imposed, fall in line with the policies pursued, or pay the taxes that are levied on them. They are required by the state to do so, on pain of enduring the rigours of punishment. The problem of legitimacy is how to reconcile such political submission with personal freedom, identifying a sort of regime that can coerce citizens without depriving them of their freedom. The question, in Rousseau's (1997: IV.2.7) words, is how 'a man can be both free and forced to conform to wills which are not his own'. Or in a contemporary variant, 'How might a person be self-governing through institutional enactment of a law to which he is opposed?' (Michelman 1999: 23).

On this freedom-centred interpretation of legitimacy, the question in republican terms is whether a state can impose coercively on citizens without dominating them. We saw that in order to promote social justice the state must treat citizens well and equally in ordering their relations with one another; in republican terms it has to provide for their equal undominated status in those relations. What we now have to see is whether in a corresponding sense it can treat citizens well and equally in ordering their relations with the coercive state itself; whether it can provide for their equal undominated status in those relations.

It is worth noticing that, phrased in this way, the problem of legitimacy can be detached from ideas of the state of nature that provided a stage-setting in the heyday of the problem. Once it is granted that freedom can be compromised, not just by the social order imposed by the state, but also by the mode in which the state imposes it, the problem becomes inescapable. And the problem remains inescapable even if we reject the idea that in order to solve it we have to show how it could have been rational for people to opt for political organization from within an imagined scenario of a pre-political, natural kind. Arguably, the legitimacy problem was at the centre of concern from well before the advent of state-of-nature thinking; it assumed that place in the Roman origins of republican thought and remained at the centre throughout the period of Renaissance and modern republicanism. Roman republicanism was grounded in the claim that people's freedom would be compromised under any form of monarchy and that it was only citizenship in a suitable republic that could ensure freedom. This same thesis is present in Machiavelli's *Discourses* and in the literature of the seventeenth- and eighteenth-century tradition, inspiring a search for republican devices whereby a state might impose on people without compromising their freedom (see Richardson 2002).

There may be grounds for arguing that despite taking away people's freedom, a state can claim the authority that goes with legitimacy on distinct grounds and that legitimacy does not have to be interpreted in freedom-centred terms. Perhaps the state is successful in epistemic terms, letting people reliably identify the requirements of justice without subjecting them to the rule of others (Estlund 2007).[16] Or perhaps it enables them to live together without civil war, as a pragmatic justification might suggest (Williams 2005). Perhaps it is the only sort of state that coheres well with an assertion of the fundamental equality of human beings (Buchanan 2002). Perhaps, to invoke a broadly Confucian approach, it puts people of virtue and talent in power; it is distinctively meritocratic (Bell 2010). Or perhaps, as Ronald Dworkin (2011: 321–2) has recently argued, it manifestly strives to promote social and procedural justice, 'recognizing that the fate of each citizen is of equal importance and that each has a responsibility to create his own life'.

Such theories of legitimacy will only have plausibility, however, on the assumption that no effective state can preserve people's freedom. It would hardly make sense to invoke an epistemic, pragmatic, egalitarian or meritocratic feature – or the goodwill that Dworkin invokes – in arguing for the legitimacy of a freedom-denying regime, if there were an alternative regime available that could claim to preserve people's freedom. Why should people accept a freedom-denying state, whatever its other merits, when there is an alternative available that can play the role of common arbiter and decider without compromising their freedom? It is only if we have to despair about assessing legitimacy in terms of freedom that we will be required to explore alternative approaches. Thus we are returned to the freedom-centred version of the legitimacy issue. How can the citizens of a state be free and yet subject to state coercion?

This question, as might be expected, is going to assume a different form, depending on how freedom is understood. I look in this section at the way it will present itself, first, under the conception of freedom as

---

[16] For another broadly epistemic approach, although one inspired by a pragmatist perspective see Talisse (2007).

non-interference, and then under the conception of freedom as non-domination. I shall argue that while freedom as non-interference cannot support any plausible conception of legitimacy, republican theory can; and that under a republican conception, what legitimacy requires is shared, popular control of the state.

Legitimacy under freedom as non-interference

By the account offered earlier – and indeed by most established accounts – interfering with a choice may involve intentionally replacing, removing or misrepresenting any of the options, preferred or unpreferred, by which the choice is defined. That means that all laws take away from the freedom of subjects in at least some of their independently available choices. The point was emphasized, almost with relish, by Bentham (1843: 503) himself. 'As against the coercion applicable by individual to individual, no liberty can be given to one man but in proportion as it is taken from another. All coercive laws, therefore . . . and in particular all laws creative of liberty, are, as far as they go, abrogative of liberty.'

This means that under the conception of freedom as non-interference, there is no way in which the subjects of the law can enjoy full freedom of choice. They will be subject to state interference, and so to a loss of freedom, insofar as the state decides what laws to put in place, including laws that establish the basic liberties; enforces those laws with the threat of penalty; imposes penalties on those who offend; and taxes its subjects with a view to maintaining the system.

It is true, of course, that in a well-run society the interference that the state perpetrates in imposing laws and taxes and penalties may be less, by whatever measure is taken to be appropriate, than the interference that the state prevents. But even in that ideal event, it will remain the case that the state does indeed perpetrate interference and that in doing so it fails to preserve the freedom of citizens in their dealings with it; they are subject to its will in a way that takes from their freedom under this conception. Thus Isaiah Berlin (1969: 3) writes, in elaboration of what he takes to be a lesson from Bentham and indeed Hobbes: 'Law is always a fetter, even if it protects you from being bound in chains that are heavier than those of the law, say some more repressive law or custom, or arbitrary despotism or chaos.'

There are two reactions that these blunt observations might prompt amongst those who equate freedom with non-interference. One is to think that the concern with having a state that does not impinge on the freedom of subjects is simply misplaced and that we should give it up.

According to this view, the cause of freedom argues for a state that furthers the cause of non-interference overall – that may be thought to make for the justice of the social order imposed – but it says nothing in and of itself on how the state should be supported by the people: nothing, for example, on whether democratic or non-democratic rule is better on this count. The cause of freedom will argue for one or the other sort of rule, depending only on which is best for serving non-interference or some other value overall – which, for example, achieves the best balance between interference perpetrated and interference prevented.

This is the view adopted by Paley (2002: 314) himself, as we saw in the Introduction. 'Were it probable that the welfare and accommodation of the people would be as studiously, and as providently, consulted in the edicts of a despotic prince, as by the resolutions of a popular assembly,' he says, 'then would an absolute form of government be no less free than the purest democracy'.[17] And essentially the same view is supported by Berlin (1969: 7), when he suggests that the cause of democracy cannot be grounded in the cause of freedom as non-interference and that it has to be defended on some other basis: 'Freedom in this sense is not, at any rate logically, connected with democracy or self-government. Self-government may, on the whole, provide a better guarantee of the preservation of civil liberties than other regimes, and has been defended as such by libertarians. But there is no necessary connection between individual liberty and democratic rule' (see too Berlin 1969: 130–1).[18]

The other possible reaction to the recognition that the state inevitably perpetrates interference against its citizens, and thereby offends against their freedom as non-interference, is not to ignore or dismiss the legitimacy question in this manner but to argue that there is a special circumstance in which a state may yet be legitimate. This response draws on the idea of freedom of contract that Hobbes introduced in the seventeenth century and that became the catch-cry of classical liberal thought in the early nineteenth

---

[17] It is worth noting that unlike Bentham, Paley (2002: 312) argued that no coercive laws that promoted the common good should be regarded as reducing the freedom of subjects.

[18] As I argue in Pettit (1997c: Chapter 1), a friend of Bentham's, John Lind, used these ideas to propagandize on behalf of the British government against the American colonists in the 1770s. Drawing on Bentham, he argues against the republican Richard Price, that liberty is 'nothing more or less than the absence of coercion' and therefore that law inevitably takes away liberty since 'all laws are coercive'. And then, with those claims in the background, he asks why the rule of the British government in America is problematic, given that it imposes laws at home as well as in the colonies. The idea is that the Americans have no particular complaint since the law-making power is 'exercised by the same persons over all the subjects who reside in all the other parts of this same empire' (Lind 1776: 16, 24, 114).

century (Atiyah 1979).[19] The idea is that if someone consents to an arrangement with another under which they suffer the other's intervention, then
such an invited form of intervention does not count as interference and does
not take away from freedom. In a legal, Latin tag that was often invoked in
this connection, *injuria non fit volenti*: 'no injury, and no interference, in
the presence of consent' (Hobbes 1994a: 21.3, 1998: 3.7).

This response need not imagine a population-wide agreement to establish a political regime of the kind invoked in the state-of-nature tradition.
What it says is that the state will not count as interfering with its citizens,
even as it imposes coercively upon them, so long as the interference
practised attracts the consent of each individual subject. The consent
postulated may be prior consent or consent of a continuing character. But
in neither case can the postulate serve the purpose for which it is designed.

The consent you may have given to the state's coercion in the past is quite
consistent with that coercion's being unwelcome and frustrating at later
times in the characteristic manner of interference. So there is no hope on
that front. The continuing consent you may be thought to give to the state's
coercion offers a more promising ground for claiming that the coercion does
not constitute interference. But this possibility also turns out to be a dead
end. The problem is that it is utterly implausible to postulate continuing
consent on the part of citizens generally, however implicit or tacit the
consent may be, to the coercion of their state. People may welcome the
regime they live under but, as David Hume (1994) had already argued in
the eighteenth century, they will not consent to it in the sense of adopting it
voluntarily: that is, adopting it in preference to an otherwise acceptable
alternative (Olsaretti 2004). And it is only consent that is voluntary in that
way – and not just voluntary in the Hobbesian sense in which submission
out of fear counts as voluntary – that can make the coercion of the state
count as something less than interference.

If these observations are sound, then the conception of freedom as non-
interference raises a dilemma for understanding legitimacy in a freedom-
centred way. Either, to take the first response, legitimacy in that sense ceases
to count as an ideal that a state or social order ought to satisfy, which is
problematic. Or, to take the second, it becomes an ideal that no actual state

---

[19] I bracket the role of the monarchomach (or king-killing) tradition of thought as that is represented,
for example, in the late-sixteenth-century tract, *Vindiciae Contra Tyrannos* (Languet 1994). Adherents
of this tradition, which became an established school of thought in many European countries, argued
against absolutists that any people that is ruled by a monarch must be supposed, as a collectivity, to
have made a contract with their ruler under provisos that would allow them to dismiss that ruler –
literally or figuratively to kill the king – in the event of certain forms of injustice or tyranny.

or social order is capable of satisfying, which is equally problematic. Either the ideal is irrelevant, in effect, or it is infeasible. Things look very different, however, from a republican perspective in which freedom is cast as non-domination.

Legitimacy under freedom as non-domination

Let it be granted that the state inevitably interferes in people's lives both in establishing the basic liberties that are to be publicly entrenched, and in pursuing the taxation, coercion and punishment that is required for such entrenchment. And let it equally be granted that if the state is going to count as legitimate then it should be supported by the people in such a way that it does not take away from their freedom. How could a state that inevitably interferes in the choices of people manage to be supported in such a way that its interference does not take away from their freedom?

Under the conception of freedom as non-domination, as we saw in the first chapter, domination alone is sufficient to reduce the freedom of the dominated. That means that freedom can be reduced in the presence of domination, even if there is no interference or frustration. But, under the conception of freedom as non-domination, domination is necessary as well as sufficient for a reduction of freedom. And that means that if there is no domination involved, freedom is not reduced in the presence of either interference or frustration.

In order to illustrate the possibility of interference without domination we mentioned the scenario in which you want to reduce your drinking. In order to promote that end, you give me the key to the alcohol cupboard with instructions not to heed a request for the key except at twenty-four hours' notice. When you suffer a rebuff to a request for the key now, then you will certainly endure interference and frustration; the element of consent, contrary to the freedom-of-contract idea, does not change the fact that you want the key now and I am refusing to hand it over. But you will not suffer any loss of freedom in the presence of such interference, for while I impose a will that is hostile to your current wishes, this imposition is subject to your control. The interference you endure, as it is traditionally phrased, is of a non-arbitrary form; it does not express my will and does not reflect my *arbitrium*.

The scenario with the alcohol cupboard is a variant on the classical scenario of Ulysses and the sirens. In that story, his sailors bind Ulysses to the mast of the ship and keep him bound even as he begs them, under the seductive lure of the siren voices, to let him go. But they do so under his instructions and, presumptively, under his ultimate control. And so the interference they practise, like my interference in denying you the key to the alcohol cupboard, is not dominating. It does not impose an alien will on Ulysses, being exercised only on terms that he himself lays down.

The idea of controlled interference provides us with the core element for a republican theory of political legitimacy. It suggests that if the people governed by a state control the interference practised by government – if they control the laws imposed, the policies pursued, the taxes levied – then they may not suffer domination at the hands of their rulers and may continue to enjoy their freedom in relation to the state. A state that was suitably controlled would be legitimate in the required sense of not exercising domination over its people. It would practise interference, for sure – think about how frustrating laws and taxes can be – but it would only interfere with them on their terms, not at its own will or pleasure.

We shall be expanding on this core idea in Section 4, when we look in detail at exactly what sort of popular control over government might guarantee the legitimacy of the state. We will look there at the domain in which people have to exercise control over the state. And we will explore the nature of the control required, arguing that it must be individualized, unconditioned and efficacious. Just to spell out these requirements, the system of control must be equally shared amongst citizens; it must not be conditioned on the willingness of the government, or of any other agent, to humour the citizens; and it must score well enough in the level of control provided to ensure that even unwelcome government intervention does not provide citizens with any evidence of an alien will at work in their lives: it can come across as just tough luck.

But control may not seem so very different from consent and before getting to that discussion it will be useful to spend some time on the analysis of the idea of control and the related idea of influence. We have been invoking the idea of control at various points in the text and it is important that we be clear about what exactly is involved. The points that emerge in the course of this analysis will be of importance in later discussion.

3. THE NATURE OF CONTROL

The idea of control

To have a degree of control over a result two things are essential. First, you must have some influence over the process leading to the result. And second, you must use that influence to impose a relevant direction on the process, helping to ensure that a suitable result transpires.

The need for influence is obvious from the fact that you could not claim to have any control over a result that you merely observed as a bystander, having no capacity to make an input. Influence will not give you control, however, just on its own. Imagine the effect you will have on the traffic at a busy intersection if you play police officer and give hand signals in the usual manner, inviting the cars to ignore the lights. In all likelihood some cars will take their lead from your signals, others not; and amongst those that do not, some will try to drive quietly by, others protest with honking horns or exasperated gestures. You will certainly have an influence in such a case, making a difference to how the cars behave; you will probably create utter chaos. But will you have control? Well, if your aim was to create chaos, you may be said to have exercised control in a certain sense. But assuming that you wanted the cars to follow your signals, as they might follow the signals of a police officer, you will be a dismal failure. You will have made a difference to how the cars behave but not a difference that imposes any desired direction or pattern – not a difference that serves any identifiable end or goal.

What will be required in order for your influence to give direction to a process like the flow of cars in this example? The influence must give rise to a recognizable pattern in the process and that pattern must be one that you seek; the influence, as we say, must control for the appearance of a desired pattern. The influence must not only make a difference, as any form of influence will do; it must make a designed difference. There will be a range of ways in which you can vary your input to the process, since there are different hand-signals you can give. And for each of those inputs there will be a corresponding output: the traffic will alter in response to your signals. In the case where you take the police officer's place at the intersection this condition will not be fulfilled: there will be a more or less random correlation between how you move your hands and how the cars adjust. Were a police officer to be in your place, however, then things would certainly be different. The officer's hand-signals would reliably generate, now this sort of effect, now that; as we say, they would control for how the traffic moves.

The lesson of these observations is that there is no control without such control-for: no control without an influence-bearing input that controls for the realization of a suitably patterned output. The influential input may control for the appearance of that pattern rather than none at all. Or, if it can vary, as in the case of the traffic signals, it may control for the appearance of one pattern rather than any of a range of alternatives for which it might have controlled; in that sense, it may assume a richer form.

The paradigm case of control is the intentional control in which you exercise influence as an agent and this leads to the realization of some desired end. You act according to your beliefs for the satisfaction of your desires and you control for your actions and their effects in the sense that as your desires or beliefs change so the outputted actions and effects will change in response. This is the sort of control that a police officer will exercise over traffic. And it is the sort of control that you will exercise in the arrangement about the key to the alcohol cupboard. Your desires and beliefs will lead you to issue appropriate instructions and those instructions will lead me to uphold the arrangement you propose.

But while intentional control provides the paradigm case, control need not be intentional in every case. Purely mechanical, non-intentional mechanisms can have such an influence and impose such an identifiable direction that we happily say they exercise control; the influence exerted by the mechanism makes a designed difference but without any intentionality on the part of the mechanism itself. An example might be the cooling-heating system that keeps the temperature in a room within a certain range, coming on as the temperature climbs too high or falls too low and exercising an influence that restores it to the pre-set range. And a parallel example, drawn from the natural, rather than the artificial, domain, might be the homeostatic system that keeps the internal temperature of an animal like you or me within a biologically functional range.

But even the control exercised by intentional agents may be nonintentional. It may be like the control illustrated in Amartya Sen's (1983a) example of the patient in the coma whose wishes, thanks to family or friends, control for the treatment provided by the surgeons at the hospital. Given the form taken by the patient's wishes, the surgeons provide one sort of treatment. And had the wishes taken a relevantly different form – had that input varied – then the treatment would have been different too; at the least it would not have been of the form that the patient's current wishes generate. And yet the patient does nothing intentionally with a view to revealing or implementing those desires; they are effective by virtue of the efforts of others, not his or her own.

Whenever a system exercises control over a process, then, there will be systemically shaped inputs that control for the form of corresponding outputs. In the richer form of control, there will be influence-bearing inputs that vary depending on the state of the system and, as they vary, those inputs will determine, at least probabilistically, the direction taken by corresponding outputs. This structure will apply to all control systems, intentional or non-intentional, and amongst intentional systems – say, agents like you and me – to all modes of control, be those modes intentional or not. Hence, to take the case that interests us, it will apply to any system of control that citizens might exercise over the state. We will be examining that popular control in the next section and we will be looking at the institutional ways in which it might be realized in the two chapters remaining.

The varieties of influence

It may seem that the influence exercised in control has to be the active sort that involves a positive input on the part of the controller. But it should be noticed that there are two other forms of influence possible, which I shall describe as virtual and reserve influence. And each of these can support control just as effectively as the active variety.

Think of how I may control a horse that I ride. I may actively pull on the reins, now steering the horse in this direction, now in that. Or I may let the horse follow its head, given that it is moving in the direction I want to take. Or I may let the horse have free rein, given that I am happy for it to go wherever it wishes. The first is an example of active influence, the second a case of virtual influence, and the third an instance of reserve influence. In active influence I intervene in order to get the horse to move as I wish. In virtual influence I am poised to intervene, but only if an intervention is needed to keep the horse on track. In reserve influence I am equally poised to intervene, but only if my wishes change and an intervention is needed to satisfy them.

We have already seen examples of active, virtual and reserve forms of influence in our discussion of freedom of choice in the first chapter. If I frustrate you by obstructing a preferred option then I actively intervene in a choice. If I would have interfered with an option you might have chosen but do not interfere with the option you actually choose, as in interference without frustration, then I intervene in a virtual manner. And if I am not currently disposed to interfere but would do so if I changed my preference over how you should choose, as in domination without interference – invigilation – then I intervene in a reserve way.

Active, virtual and reserve forms of influence all serve to put a factor in place that raises the probability of a certain result: a certain patterned or designed result, as it will be if the influence mediates control. That factor consists in an actual event in the case of active influence and in a suitable disposition in the case of virtual and reserve influence. The reason for speaking of influence in the three cases is that the probabilification is effect-based in each of them, not merely evidence-based. It is not like the evidential probabilification involved when we say, for example, that your consuming an unusually large quantity of grapes – the typical hospital visitor's gift – makes it more probable that you are ill.

Thus, to return to the earlier illustration, I ensure that the horse I ride goes where I will, whether or not the influence I exercise is of the active, virtual or reserve variety. When I steer the horse, my action ensures that it goes where I will. When I give the horse its head in the manner of virtual influence, my disposition to pull on the rein should it change direction ensures that it follows my will. And when I give it wholly free rein, allowing it to go where it itself happens to want, my disposition to pull on the rein should my own wishes change in that regard ensures also that it goes where I will.

Patterns of virtual and reserve influence are as important as patterns of active influence, not just in toy examples like this, but also in the world that is tracked in natural, and particularly social, science. No inventory of the connections it is important to recognize for purposes of prediction and intervention could afford to overlook them (Pettit 2007c). They are particularly worthy of notice here since, as we shall see, there is every reason to think that the modes of influence whereby people might exercise control over government include virtual and reserve influence, as well as active.[20]

Control and consent

Control in the sense explicated here is quite different from consent, for there may be consent without control and control without consent. On the one side, you may consent to a form of interference that you do not control: once consent is given, you may have no means of calling off the arrangement to which you consented; at the limit, you may have consented to a slave contract – the bête noire of traditional republicanism – that binds you indefinitely. On the other side, you may control a form of interference to which you never gave your consent. Suppose you were born into a society where by common convention parents propose marriage partners for their children. While you go along with the system without ever having consented to it you may still exercise a good deal of control over it. You may be in control to the extent that you can opt out of the arrangement altogether

---

[20] Why not describe the three sorts of influence as causal, virtual and reserve? Two reasons. One is that virtual influence may be causal in all relevant senses, as when I now put an obstacle in the way of your choosing Y and you are independently disposed to choose X. And a second is that, the first possibility aside, virtual and reserve influence might be taken by some as examples of negative causation: cases where the absence of a certain factor can be cast as a cause.

or, short of opting out, can continue to turn down proposals until your parents propose an acceptable partner.

The divergence between consent and control remains in place even when, breaking with the standard notion of freedom of contract, we stipulate that consensual interference means interference to which you currently consent, not just interference to which you consented in the past. True, you cannot give your consent proper to a form of interference you do not control; at best you can welcome it, while being unable to call it off.[21] But while there cannot be current consent without control, you may control a form of interference to which you do not give your current consent. Amartya Sen's (1983a) example of the comatose patient whose wishes are given effect by family or friends illustrates the possibility. Their intervention empowers the patient's recorded wishes, forcing the surgeons at the hospital to conform to them. And it does this without the current consent of the controlling agent.

These observations should help to explain why thinkers in the republican tradition do not give much weight to consent, or at least to a form of consent that leaves you under a will that you do not control.[22] Such consent can play no role in guarding against arbitrary or uncontrolled interference. It ensures freedom of entry but it is quite consistent with the absence of a power of exit or of any other way of checking others: say, the power associated with having a voice. Perhaps it was for that reason that John Milton (1953–82: II, 137–58) argued so fervently that marriage could be free only if divorce was possible: that is, only if there was a possibility of release from the marriage bond – and from subjection to the rights and powers of a spouse – in the event of estrangement between the parties.

Those who cast freedom as non-interference do not treat consensual intervention as interference and so they would regard a consensual government, however unlikely the possibility, as a legitimate, freedom-compatible agency. This approach is implausible, as noticed earlier, since your past consent does not mean that my present intervention lacks the frustrating potential that is the hallmark of interference. But could those who cast

---

[21] John Rawls (1993: 222) appears to envisage this form of current consent when, having dismissed the possibility of past consent, he writes: 'we may over the course of life come freely to accept, as the outcome of reflective thought and reasoned judgement, the ideals, principles, and standards that specify our basic rights and liberties, and effectively guide and moderate the political power to which we are subject. This is the outer limit of our freedom.' For a defence of the view that such acceptance can count as voluntary, see Otsuka (2003: Chapter 5).

[22] If you bind yourself only conditionally, retaining the ability to call off the arrangement in the event of the other person breaching some conditions, you will retain a degree of control and may not be subject in a relevant sense to the domination of the other.

freedom as non-interference make use of the idea of controlled interference, joining republicans in the claim that a suitably controlled but in no way consensual government – this is the possibility explored in the next section – might be a legitimate, freedom-compatible agency?

Might they argue that controlled intervention is not really interference, to take a first possibility, as they seek to argue that consensual intervention is not really interference? No. Controlled but non-consensual intervention must count as a form of interference, since it may also be characteristically frustrating. Moreover, unlike consensual intervention, there is no sense in which it will count as invited or condoned. Thus, even if the intervention of the state in people's lives takes place under their control, there is very little plausibility in saying that it does not really count as interference. It may be extremely frustrating and in general there is no sense in which citizens need invite or condone it.[23]

Might those who cast freedom as non-interference accept this but still argue, to take a second possibility, that controlled interference does not take away freedom in the same way as uncontrolled? Again, no. Under the conception of freedom as non-interference, you are going to have freedom of choice in relation to me just insofar as I do not interfere with you: I do not intentionally remove, replace or misrepresent any option. You will suffer a loss of freedom as a result of any such interference on my part and you will suffer a loss of freedom only as a result of such interference. On this approach, then, the issue of whether I have a power of uncontrolled interference in your choice is irrelevant to whether I take away from your freedom. And equally, the issue of whether the state has a power of uncontrolled interference in the choices of citizens is irrelevant to whether it takes away from their freedom. Freedom just is non-interference, on this approach, and the issue of whether the interference is controlled or not is simply beside the point.

There may be a powerful intuition, as I think there is, that the interference you control – the interference exemplified in the alcohol example – does not take away from your freedom of choice. But in order to give countenance to that intuition, members of the opposed school of thought would have to give up on their central commitment to the idea that interference and interference alone reduces freedom. They would have to endorse the republican idea that it is domination that really matters in the

---

[23] The only plausible case in which we might want to deny the name of interference to a form of intrusive intervention is where the intervention is both consensual and controlled. It genuinely attracts the voluntary, continuing consent of the subject of the intervention.

freedom stakes. Thus the idea that a suitably controlled government might be a freedom-consistent agency is simply unavailable under the identification of freedom with non-interference. It is exclusive to the republican way of thinking about freedom.

4. THE REQUIREMENTS ON POPULAR CONTROL

We have argued for the very abstract conclusion that if the citizenry control state discretion in a suitable manner – in a way that parallels your control over the person who holds the key to the alcohol cupboard – then the imposition of a social order on those citizens will not take away from their freedom and will count as fully legitimate. But what is the nature of the control required? And what is the domain in which legitimacy requires citizens to exercise such control over the state? We will consider those questions in reverse order, looking first at requirements on the domain where citizens must control their government and then at requirements on the nature of the control that they must exercise in that domain. It turns out, according to this argument, that the domain requirements are less demanding and the nature requirements more demanding than might have been expected.

Requirements on the domain of popular control

The idea of having control in relation to the state – having an unconditioned form of directed influence – may seem preposterous. For the state, you may well say, does not give you or anyone else control over whether you are to live in political society rather than in a state of nature, or in one state rather than another. Moreover, if you live in political society, it does not give you or any other citizen, no matter how virtuous and compliant, control over whether the laws are to be coercively enforced against you; uniform coercion is the rule of the political game. So surely the republican proposal, regardless of how it is to be elaborated, is completely hopeless.

It is true that neither you nor anyone else has a choice over whether to live under a state or in a natural condition; that neither you nor anyone else has an assured choice over whether to live in one state or another; and that if you live in political society you do not have any choice over whether to comply with the law on a non-coercive basis: that is, without being exposed to penalty. But these constraints on your life raise an issue of legitimacy for the state only if they are imposed by the state itself and represent subjection to an alien will. And it turns out that they are not imposed by your state – or indeed by any other state – in the manner of a decision to interfere rather than not interfere; they materialize on an independent, unwilled basis. This means that the domain in which republican legitimacy requires civic or popular control does not include the imposition of such constraints.

It is an unintended precipitate of human history, and in particular of the mutual adjustments of different populations, that the earth is now a state-bound planet: a place where there is no inhabitable area that is free of the rule of some state. The fact that you do not have a choice between living inside a state and living outside a state is not the product of interference or domination on the part of your state. It is a historical necessity on a par with the necessity of living under the laws of physics.[24] You may think that your own state, or indeed some other state, could renounce its standing as a state and establish a stateless zone. But states are locked into a pattern where none can resign without exposing its population to the will of rivals, creating a vacuum where other states will battle for control. You may bemoan the necessity of living in a state-bound world, then, even long for a period in history or pre-history when it did not obtain. But you cannot think that because you are constrained to live in a state, you are dominated by the state under which you live, or indeed by any other state.

As historical necessity means that you have to live in one or another state, so political necessity means that in general you have no choice over whether to live in your current state or in some other. Assume that your state allows you a right of emigration and does not confine you within its boundaries; if it did, it would certainly dominate you.[25] It is still going to be the case that other states cannot guarantee you entry, given the political necessity for states to maintain their borders and disallow open access. The fact that you have no choice over whether to live under another state is not going to be a product of domination by your own state, then, only a result of how other states behave.

Does this mean that your lack of choice is due to domination on the part of those other states? Not necessarily. No state can open its borders to non-residents in general, on pain of internal malfunction or collapse; as a matter of political necessity, every state has to place limits on who can enter and in what numbers. This means that states have to institute selective policies about who to admit. Let us suppose, then, that a state adopts a policy that is

---

[24] Nor of course can you escape the deeper necessity of living in community with other people. For an extended argument that this should be regarded as a matter of more than causal necessity see Pettit (1993).

[25] I ignore the question of whether this would hold even if the very survival of the state depended on keeping you, and others like you, within its boundaries.

not discriminatory and dominating from the point of view of anyone. The policy will mean that it does not have a choice, as such, between admitting you and not admitting you, depending on its will. And if under that policy it refuses you admission, then this should not count as fully voluntary interference. It will be a by-product of an independently necessitated, otherwise unobjectionable policy: a restriction on your freedom of movement, to be sure, but one that vitiates that freedom rather than invades it.[26]

These observations indicate that you need not think of yourself as unfree – unfree in the sense of being dominated by an alien will – just because you have to live under a state and perhaps in this state rather than any other. That you have to live under these constraints is determined by historical and political necessity. Like having to live in the presence of gravity, it is a product of the existing world order, not the result of a dominating presence in your life. The existing world order may be highly undesirable, of course, and in principle there might be ways of reorganizing it – for example, ways of incorporating states into a single agent like a world state or confederation – in which there is less domination overall. But given the world order we have, it is not due to the dominating power of any state, and certainly not of your own state, that you have to live in some political society or other. And it need not be due to the dominating power of any state, and certainly not your own state, that you have to live in this political society in particular. These circumstances may be exasperating but they do not testify to the presence of a dominating will in your life.

An analogy may help to illuminate the role of historical and political necessities under these arguments. Suppose that you live in a world, however fanciful, where as a result of past adjustments the space of economic activity is entirely taken up by corporations. You could not complain of being dominated in such a world by the fact that you have to work in an incorporated company, not for yourself or for a private employer, though you might bemoan the absence of such possibilities. And you could not complain of suffering interference and domination just because you cannot change place of employment to another company; no company can afford to take on all those employees who wish to work for it. There might be reasons for the government to try to change employment practices in certain ways, and reforms might hold out the prospect of more freedom as non-domination overall. But it remains the case that in the world imagined the restrictions associated with having to work in some company, and not necessarily in the company of your first choice, do not in themselves

---

[26] There are difficult issues here that I cannot explore fully. See Abizadeh (2008).

constitute domination. The analogy is imperfect but may help to explain why you and your fellow citizens are not dominated by the historical and political necessities to which you are subject.

Back to our main theme. As historical and political necessities mean that the state is not in a position to allow you to live in a natural, rather than a political, condition, or in any other state you might prefer, so a functional necessity means that it is not in a position to grant you the privilege, no matter how virtuous you may be, of obeying the law on a non-coercive basis: that is, without fear of penalty. This is a third area where state restriction is independently necessitated and does not entail state domination.

Assume, in line with common wisdom, that in every society it is necessary to employ coercion against at least some potentially recalcitrant members. Coercion may be necessary to get those individuals to comply – lesser obstacles of shame or whatever might not work – and/or it may be necessary to provide assurance for the community that they will indeed comply – they will not free-ride on the efforts of others. But if the state imposes on some in this way, then assuming as we do that it has to satisfy the egalitarian constraint, it has no choice but to impose on all in similar manner; doing so will be a functional necessity. If the state did not impose equally on all then, by any yardstick, it would offend against that constraint, not treating citizens as equals. And if you or anyone else looked for the privilege of not being exposed to the coercive imposition of the law – if you argued for being allowed to display your virtue in voluntarily obeying the law – then you would also be in breach of that constraint: you would show yourself unwilling to live on equal terms with others. The normative constraint of expressive egalitarianism is fundamental to the approach adopted here, and to any half-plausible alternative. Accept that constraint and you cannot think that it is within the state's discretion to give you the privilege of not being coerced to obey the law.[27]

The three constraints reviewed mean that you cannot regard your state as dominating you just because you have to live in political society, you have to live in this state rather than any other, and you have to live under coercive regulation. It is true, of course, that if your state dissolved itself, then it would not impose such constraints. But its continuing to exist is necessitated by its role in protecting against foreign domination and does not represent a power of imposing on you or not imposing on you, depending

---

[27] To put the point in Kant's (1996: 393) words, each of you has a claim only to a freedom in relation to the state that 'can coexist with the freedom of every other in accordance with a universal law'.

on its will. Thus you scarcely have a reasonable complaint against your actual state. On the contrary, as we suggested, the fact that other states are poised to assume control of the territory in which you live, and therefore represent possible sources of domination, means that you would have a reasonable complaint if your state did dissolve itself. Let the state remain in place and you can avoid foreign domination: that is, a form of rule which, by definition – that is, in virtue of what it means to be foreign – is going to be uncontrolled by you and your fellow citizens, as you actually are. Let it dissolve itself and foreign domination is unavoidable.[28]

The background picture to the argument in this section is a bleak but realistic image of the world of states. Charles Tilly (1975: 42) claims that in Europe, 'War made the state and the state made war.' The idea, which applies elsewhere as well (Fukuyama 2011: 110–11), is that in a world of potential conflict, different communities are likely to find political organization attractive and that the more organization there is in other communities, the more attractive it becomes in each. States call one another into existence, in other words, as by an iron law of community competition. Short of a world-changing, game-changing challenge, I suspect that this law will continue to dictate the need for political organization, making the state into a domestically indispensable and internationally resilient institution. Not only is it necessary for the promotion of any plausible conception of justice, as we argued earlier; it is necessary on empirical grounds as well.

The world in which states protect their citizens from the threat of other states may be considerably less attractive than a world in which there are no states or – more plausibly, in view of our argument that the state is required for justice – a world in which there is only one state or federation (but see Pinker [2011]). But in any case, this world represents an equilibrium scenario where a state will not do better by its citizens, and will almost certainly do worse, by unilateral dissolution. The state-bound world might be represented, in a pessimistic analogy, on the model of a racing circuit where the cars are spread out all around the track and each is travelling at a highly dangerous speed.[29] It would be better if all the cars travelled at a more moderate pace, as it might be better if all existing states dissolved themselves. But each would do worse for itself by slowing down, as each state would do worse for its citizens by dissolving itself, since that would almost certainly cause a major pile-up.

---

[28] I am grateful to Niko Kolodny for pressing me on this issue.
[29] This is developed from an analogy presented for other purposes in Jackson (1987).

The lesson of this discussion is that while the legitimate state is required under republican theory to be controlled by its citizens, the domain of control cannot extend to the point where people are able to decide whether to live in or out of political society, whether to live in this state or another, and whether to live under coercive or voluntary fidelity to the law. No state – or at least no expressively egalitarian state – has a choice between giving or refusing its citizens control on such issues, and what legitimacy requires is that it give them control only on the range of issues where it itself has such discretion. This is the range of decision-making in which historical, political and functional necessities allow it to choose between interfering and not interfering and, where it does actually interfere, to choose between interfering in this or in that manner, to this or to that effect. Let citizens have control over this restricted domain and they will have all the control required for avoiding state domination.

On the account of domination offered in the first chapter, there are two forms of intervention in your choices that are not going to be dominating; however, they may cramp your decision-making. One is the intervention of constraints that do not reflect the will of another towards you and the other is the intervention of intentional agents who act under your control. The lesson of this discussion has two parts, corresponding to these two forms of undominating intervention. The first is that being required to live with others in a particular, coercively regulated state is the product of will-independent constraint and not a dominating imposition. And the second is that the threat of domination arises only in the area of discretion that the state enjoys – that is, in choosing to interfere with its citizens on one pattern or another – and that it is here that you and your fellows have to be able to exercise suitable control if you are to escape domination.

In the example with the alcohol cupboard that I used to introduce the idea of a controlled and undominating state, there are two ways in which you control me. First, you can suspend the arrangement under which I am required to return the key at your request although only on twenty-four hours' notice. And second, you can shape and reshape that arrangement as you will. We can see now that there is only a partial analogy between this case and the case with the state. For in the case of the state, the arrangement under which you and your fellows are subject to state coercion is not of your devising and is not subject to your suspension; it is imposed under will-independent necessity. You can only have control in the matter of how the state operates under that arrangement.

But the disanalogy between the cases is not a problem. For your freedom as non-domination does not require you and your fellows to be able to suspend the arrangement under which you live on a state-bound planet, you are confined to living under the state into which you are born, and you are required to live under a coercively imposed regime of law. Those constraints may be mediated in the actions of states, showing up in the fact that states claim a monopoly on territory and don't allow outsiders to enter at will and impose their laws coercively on all their subjects. But they derive from necessities that leave states, and your state in particular, no choice in such matters. Being required by independent necessity to impose the relevant constraints, the state does not impose them out of a will to restrict you and your fellows; necessity sidelines any will or preference it might have in the matter.[30]

Requirements on the nature of popular control

The upshot of the previous discussion is that the domain in which you and your fellow citizens have to be able to exercise control over the state is much smaller than might have been expected; it is much smaller, for example, than the domain that a state-of-nature staging of the legitimacy problem would suggest. You will want to be able to exercise control with your fellow citizens over the state that directs your lives only in the range of decision-making where the state has a capacity to take one or another approach and the power, therefore, to form and act on a will or preference as to how precisely you should be restricted.

So what might it be for you and other citizens to enjoy a suitable form of control in this domain of state discretion? What sort of control do you and they have to enjoy over the making, administering and adjudicating of law – and over related decisions – in order not to be dominated by the state or by any of the government agencies or officials who act in the name of the state? What sort of popular control do you and they have to enjoy in order for the state to count as legitimate?

---

[30] We saw earlier that an approach centred on the conception of freedom as non-interference cannot take the existence of a system of control to ensure that state interference does not count as interference. But it is worth noting, as implied in our discussion, that the approach does not have to treat the actions of the state that are necessitated in the manner described in this section – necessitated historically, politically or functionally – as instances of interference. The actions may restrict people's choices, but since they are not actions in which the state has any choice, they cannot be taken as acts of voluntary restriction – acts that are chosen over acts that would count as acceptable alternatives (Olsaretti 2004).

Any system of control, as we have seen, is going to be a system of directed influence: that is, influence exercised to a certain purpose or direction. This system of control will have to guard against the domination of individual citizens, not just the domination of the collective citizenry. But popular control of government will not ensure someone against public domination, if they have little or no part in the exercise of that control: the interference of government will continue in that case to be imposed on them by an alien will. Thus the first requirement on popular control is that it should be individualized appropriately, giving each an equal share in the control of government.

But there are two other requirements that popular control of government must also satisfy if it is to guard against the domination of the state. Not only must it be an individualized form of control, it must also count as unconditioned and efficacious in character. It must be unconditioned in the sense of being robust over changes in the will of the controlled government, or indeed of any party other than the controlling people, and it must be efficacious in the sense of being intuitively sufficient to guard those people against having to see the coercion of the state as the work of an alien will. The individualized system of control must ensure a suitable resilience and level of impact to guard people against state domination.

If a system of popular control meets these three requirements – I discuss them in greater detail shortly – then it ought to satisfy citizens that they are not dominated by the imposition of certain laws or by the way those laws are implemented by the executive or applied by the judiciary. It is true that citizens will not be able to think of themselves as exercising personal control over the state. But that they cannot exercise personal control is a by-product of the historical necessity of living in political society. And that they cannot demand a form of personal, as distinct from equally shared, control is an implication of the normative necessity of living on equal terms with their fellow citizens. No complaint about having to share control equally with others will be consistent with a claim to be willing to live on equal terms with their fellow citizens.

The requirement of sharing control equally with others might be described as a one-for-all constraint, since it means that citizens each have to accept that they do not have unilateral control over government. But the constraint is balanced by what we might call an all-for-one compensation. Under a system of equally shared control, the controlling collectivity is bound to be much more effective than any single actor could hope to be. And that agency may be expected to achieve for each whatever it achieves for any; otherwise the equality constraint would be in jeopardy.

An individualized system of popular control

A system of control will be individualized insofar as it gives a comparable role to each of the individuals involved in the exercise of control. Strictly, the system might take either of two forms. It might enable people each to exercise control in their own right, where their personal level of control is equal. Or it might enable them to exercise a form of joint control, where their share in that joint control is equal. But I see no plausibility in the first scenario. The salient way to realize it would be by giving everyone an individual veto over the doings of government – by requiring continuing, universal consent – or perhaps by giving each an equal right of exit (Warren 2011). But establishing a general right of veto or exit would be inconsistent with the state's continued existence as a corporate agent that can reliably generate and implement law, since it would put it at the mercy of individual whim.[31] Hence the only way in which the state can operate effectively and yet satisfy the demands of republican legitimacy is by giving each of its citizens an equal share in a system of joint control.

This observation will rule out a unanimity voting system, amounting as it does to a regime that gives each a veto, but all other systems of shared control will remain on the table, at least to the extent that they allow equal sharing. These candidates will include other systems of voting, whether majoritarian or super-majoritarian. But they will also include systems in which voting plays only a subsidiary part, or perhaps no part at all. We have seen that control may be exercised on the basis of active, virtual or reserve influence, for example, and that if the influence is active, it need not even have an intentional character; it may be like the influence of the comatose patient.

Popular control, by the lesson of our earlier discussion, has to involve popular influence and popular direction. Thus the requirement of equally

---

[31] There is also a normative argument against a universal veto. If people each had a veto over how the laws are made, implemented or adjudicated, that would enable a single recalcitrant individual to undo the social order, create a stateless zone and, to continue with an earlier assumption, make invasion by other states more or less inevitable. I assume that the obligation of a legitimate state to give citizens equal control over its doings would put that requirement – that normative necessity – in the way of this option. If the state has a duty to give its citizens equal control over how it performs, then to allow any individual the power of exposing their fellows to the jeopardy of foreign intervention would be quite inconsistent with that obligation. Notice that despite the opposition he would certainly want to mount against a universal veto, Kant (1996: 393–4) could not rule it out on the basis of his requirement of 'innate right' – the basic right in his political philosophy (Ripstein 2009) – that one be independent from 'being bound by others to more than one can in turn bind them'. Notice, too, that this argument against a universal veto does not carry over to a majority veto, at least not if the majority is not an incorporated agent with a will of its own (List and Pettit 2011).

shared control entails, on the face of it, that people should share equally both in exercising influence over government and in determining what direction that influence is to impose. This entailment has not always been endorsed within historical tradition. There was an extended debate in the eighteenth century, for example, as to whether equal liberty requires that all citizens – in effect, all mainstream men – should each be fully enfranchised, thereby having an equal influence, or whether equal liberty can be achieved, and so a suitable direction imposed on government, via the well-disciplined influence of the few (Reid 1988).

It should be clear, however, and it should have been clear in the eighteenth century, that there cannot be equally shared control without equally shared influence. If some people are to depend on the good offices of an elite party in order to force government in a direction they all care about – and not in a direction particularly favourable to the more powerful – then they are dependent on the goodwill of that party for their very freedom. And that, in republican logic, is anathema. Richard Price (1991: 80) spoke for the right side – and he suggested, the traditional side – when he claimed that 'every independent agent in a free state ought to have a share in the government of it, either by himself personally, or by a body of representatives in chusing whom he has a free vote'.

What, however, does equality in the exercise of influence require? It cannot require that everyone should participate equally in the system of popular influence, since some individuals may choose not to play their part in the system, whether generally or on specific occasions; they may be happy to go along with what others decide. Even under a system of compulsory voting, such as that in Australia, people may spoil their vote and are in no sense compelled to have a normal electoral input.[32] What equally shared influence requires, therefore, can only be equal access to the system of popular influence: an opportunity for participation in that system that is available with equal ease to each citizen.[33]

---

[32] But it is worth noticing that even when people do not vote – or do not contest government decisions in any active way – still they exercise some influence: they reduce the majority of the winning party or they allow government not to have to deal with their contestation. On such matters see Guerrero (2010).

[33] Richard Tuck (2008) makes an intriguing case for thinking that preferring to have a group achieve a certain effect makes it rational to prefer to play a part – even a palpably redundant part – in bringing about that effect; see too Goldman (1999). I think that the preference to play a part may be intelligible – there may be good reasons why you might want to do so – but I do not agree that the preference over the outcome rationally requires the preference for playing a part. It may be otherwise objectionable to let others bring about a result that you cherish, even when you know that your help is unnecessary, but it is surely not irrational. For a similar critique, see Brennan (2011).

What might make for equality, not in the exercise of influence, but in determining the direction that the influence imposes? Each citizen will share equally in determining the direction their influence imposes if that direction is required to be one that each is ready to accept; that each is disposed to find acceptable.[34] This requirement may not be satisfiable amongst fanatics or zealots who insist on special treatment: say, the privileging of their religion or ethnicity. But it will be enough by our normative standards if it is satisfied amongst those, as we put it earlier, who are willing to live on equal terms with others: amongst those who accept that the state should treat its citizens as equals.

To sum up the two lessons of individualization in a slogan, then, the citizens of a legitimate state have to enjoy equal access to a system of popular influence and that system of influence has to give the state an equally acceptable direction – that is, a direction that they are all actually disposed to accept. We will be looking at what might promote equally accessible influence in the next chapter and at what might promote an equally acceptable direction in the chapter after that.

An unconditioned system of popular control

In the case of the control that a people have over the state, as in all forms of control, the controller will have to exercise a certain sort of influence, and certain variations in that influence will have to correlate with certain variations in how the controlled agent behaves. There will have to be a correspondence between the inputs of the controller, on the one side, and the outputs of the controlled, on the other.

In mechanical cases of control, this correlation is more or less sufficient on its own to allow us to ascribe control. In particular, it is sufficient to allow the ascription of control even when the correlation obtains only conditionally on the goodwill of a distinct agent. Thus the cooling-heating system counts as controlling the temperature in the room, even when I remain in a position to turn it off so that the operation of the system correlates with the ambient temperature only conditionally on my allowing it to do so. This observation is important because it marks a contrast with what is required for ascribing control to one agent or set of agents over another. One agent

---

[34] Saying that something is acceptable often has a normative significance among contractualists, implying that it is such that people ought to accept it. Here and throughout this book, the word has a non-normative sense, implying that the object or policy or whatever is such that people are disposed to accept it; they find it acceptable, as we say.

will count as controlling another only insofar as the influence exercised leads to the required result independently of the will of the controlled agent, or indeed of any third party. Inter-agential control will count as control proper only to the extent that it is unconditioned on any will other than that of the controller.[35]

Suppose that you, A, are said to control what another person, B, does because B obeys your instructions or, to take a case where your control is not intentional, because B anticipates and acts on your wishes without your even being aware of this. Imagine now that the correlation between your instructions or wishes and B's actions – the inputs on your part, the outputs on B's – is contingent on B's wanting to humour you, or on my requiring B to humour you. In that case you can scarcely be held to control what B does; more colloquially, you cannot be said to have power over B. If the correlation depends entirely on B's will, no one has power over B; and if it depends on my will, then it is I who has power over B, not you. The correlation may depend on any of a variety of contingent circumstances: that B is in thrall to your charms, for example, or that you have greater physical strength or cultural clout. But it cannot depend on B's willingness to play the part, or on the willingness of any third party to make B do so.

Think of the example in which you give me the key to the alcohol cabinet, instructing me to hand it over only at twenty-four hours' notice. Suppose I go along with your instructions, but merely with a view to giving you the pleasant illusion of control; suppose that I am about to exit our relationship and think of this as a parting, somewhat sardonic gift. In that case you do not have the control you imagine; without realizing it, you are in my hands, at my mercy. So why is there control in the normal case? Why is the correlation between your instructions and my responses stable in a way that is independent of my will? Presumably because, by implicit assumption, the relationship matters to me, whether for intrinsic or instrumental reasons, and there are heavy costs associated with refusing to go along: say, with just giving up the key in blatant disregard of the arrangement, or with refusing to part with it at all.

For a further illustration of why inter-agential control has to be unconditioned, think of the case of the comatose patient, in Amartya Sen's example, whose wishes over hospital treatment are empowered by the fact that his family or friends force the doctors to abide by them. Although we did not make the point earlier, we can now register that if it is up to the

---

[35] For a congenial interpretation of related themes see N. Southwood's unpublished paper, 'Democracy as a Modally Demanding Value'.

discretion of a single person amongst the family or friends, or up to their jointly exercised discretion, to determine whether the patient's wishes should prevail, then those individuals are going to be in control, not the patient. In order for the patient to have control, it will have to be the case that the responsiveness of the doctors is not conditioned on the willingness of any single agent to speak for the patient. This requirement might be fulfilled if there were some pressure on family or friends to intervene in the patient's name – if it was not just a matter of their discretion – or if there was a queue of individuals lined up to play the role, so that the intervention did not depend on their individual or joint discretion.

We saw in the first chapter that you are not free in a choice between X, Y and Z if you can act according to your will – if you can control your actions – only insofar as I allow it. What we are now discussing is a parallel observation that bears, not on your control of your own actions, but on your control of the actions of another party. You control your own actions only insofar as you do not depend on the will of another for being able to satisfy yourself; you can satisfy yourself over changes in what any other wants you to do. You control the actions of another agent only insofar as you do not depend on the will of another – that same agent or a third party – for being able to get the other to satisfy you, acting on your instructions or wishes; you can get the agent to satisfy you over changes in what the person wants to do and over changes in what anyone else wants the person to do. As the failure of the first condition means that you do not enjoy freedom – power or control over yourself – so the failure of the second means that you do not enjoy power or control over the other. Freedom requires a robust capacity to satisfy yourself; power over another requires a robust capacity to get that other to satisfy you.

The observation made in these examples applies to the control of any agent or agency over another and so to the popular control that we want citizens to exercise over the state. The implication of the requirement in the political case is that the equally accessible popular influence that is required to impose an equally acceptable direction on government has to meet a further demanding constraint. It has to produce that effect independently of the willingness of government to go along and independently of the willingness of any other agency to have the government go along.[36]

---

[36] The other agency envisaged here might be an effectively independent army, a group of moneyed supporters or even a foreign power. The army possibility led most traditional republicans to oppose the idea of a professional or standing army; many saw the development of such an army – indeed such armies – as the factor that brought down republican Rome.

In every regime, the government, or at least the executive arm of government, is likely to be enormously more powerful than any other individuals or bodies, having special access to the means of universal coercion. But if the government is the powerful party in the relationship between people and government, then how can we expect the people to be able to exercise the independent or unconditioned form of influence that is required? It may seem that the people can hope to enjoy only the appearance of a controlling influence, not the real thing: only the trappings of power that are available when an indulgent state is willing to humour its citizenry.

The difficulty posed by this observation is real but not overwhelming.[37] For the experience of societies over the past couple of centuries, even perhaps before, shows that the control of the people over the state can be grounded in a disposition of people to rise up in the face of a government abuse of legitimacy and a disposition of government to back down in response to the fact or prospect of such opposition. This is the trump card that the people are always in a position to play, relying on any of the various measures, violent and non-violent, direct and indirect, individual and collective, that can be used to resist a regime. To the extent that the possibility of popular, successful resistance is on the cards – to the extent even that it is on the cards as a matter of common belief – the influence of the people over government can be established on a robust basis and can constitute a real form of power.

The observation that popular control of government is grounded in the actual or perceived potential for widespread resistance – people's presumptive power of rebellion – is not new. John Locke embraced the importance of the possibility in arguing for the right of people to rise up against the government, should it not be fulfilling its allotted role: as he saw it, the role of being an impartial arbiter of disputes. In his view, as on the view to which our considerations lead us, the legitimacy of a government ultimately turns on whether 'the community may be said in this respect to be always the supreme power' (Locke 1960: 11.149). The people will have to be the supreme power in any polity that has a claim to legitimacy.

Adam Ferguson, a Scottish adherent of the eighteenth-century republican creed, gave the idea memorable expression in describing the requirements

---

[37] It is taken to be overwhelming by those like Georgio Agamben (2005) who follow Carl Schmitt in arguing that even democratic governments fail the requirement. Their argument is that even such governments freely decide – that is, decide independently of any external pressure such as that which I go on to identify – that a given case is a non-exceptional one where the rule of law applies or is an exceptional or emergency case where the rule of law is suspended. In Schmitt's (2005: 5) words, 'Sovereign is he who decides on the exception.'

of liberty.[38] The liberty of the British people, he suggests, may be manifest in the fact that laws are formulated under widely accessible influence and given a widely acceptable direction. But its grounding goes much deeper: 'it requires a fabric no less than the whole political constitution of Great Britain, a spirit no less than the refractory and turbulent zeal of this fortunate people, to secure it' (Ferguson 1767: 167). This characteristically republican theme has a long history. It appears most dramatically in the idea championed in Machiavelli's (1965) *Discourses* that what enabled the citizenry of republican Rome to enjoy their freedom vis-à-vis the state was something that might appear at first sight to be a source of instability: the willingness of the plebeian poor to rise up against even the suspicion of an abuse or usurpation of power by the nobles. The price of liberty, in the hallowed republican slogan, is eternal vigilance.

It goes without saying that societies differ greatly in the extent to which this support for popular influence and control over government is available. It will be available in a measure that reflects the extent to which two factors are in place and/or are taken as a matter of common belief to be in place: on the one side, the disposition of the people to resist perceived abuses of power by the government; and on the other, the disposition of those in government to be inhibited by the fact or the prospect of such resistance. These two factors determine how resistive a society is: how far, in reality and/or perception, the citizens are resistance-prone and the government resistance-averse.[39]

We saw earlier that in order to be individualized, popular control must be grounded in an equally accessible system of influence that operates in an equally acceptable direction. But we now see that the system of directive influence to which citizens are given equal access has to be a system of unconditioned or independent or resilient influence. It must enable people to enjoy a directive influence over government that is based on the resistive character of the society, not on the goodwill of government or of any other agency.

---

[38] As a matter of passing interest, Ferguson opposed Richard Price on the issue just mentioned as to whether equal control requires equal influence: in effect, the universal franchise. See Price (1991: 80).

[39] A society might be resistive in this sense and yet not be very regularly subject to popular disturbance; the important thing is that resistance should remain a permanent possibility. John Locke may mean just to register this – and not to strike what may seem like a complacently conservative note – when he argues that since resistance is difficult to organize, and dangerous if it fails to attract majority support, it won't materialize except in the event of extreme abuse: 'such revolutions happen not upon every little mismanagement in public affairs'; they are likely to be triggered only by 'a long train of abuses, prevarications and artifices' (Locke 1960: 11.225).

An efficacious system of popular control

But popular control of government does not only require that people should enjoy equal access to a popular system of unconditioned influence and that this system of influence should push government in an equally acceptable direction. If the popular system of unconditioned influence is to ensure the popular control required for legitimacy, then it must also satisfy a further condition. It must be effective or efficacious enough to impose a popular direction on government that nullifies the intrusion of alien will. It may not reach the upper limit at which it would be as effective as possible, consistently with the equal sharing of that control. But whether it reaches or falls below that limit, it must be intuitively satisfactory.

This third condition takes us back to the requirement that the state should treat its citizens well and equally in the manner in which it imposes a social order, as well as in the character of the order imposed. The state would treat its citizens as equals if it gave them the same equal share in a system of unconditioned control. But it would not treat them well if that system of control were unnecessarily limited. In order to ensure social justice, the state must secure people's equal, undominated status vis-à-vis one another to a suitably high level or degree, as we saw in Chapter 2. And in order to achieve political legitimacy it must secure their equal, undominated status vis-à-vis the state to a similarly high level. That is the requirement registered in the demand that the system of control in which people equally share should be efficacious.

In theory, the constraints imposed under a suitable system of equally shared control might bear only on the policies and related decisions implemented by government, reducing the options in each area just to one. Such policy-centred limitations would clearly deny those in power the opportunity to evade popular control in the decisions they take. But in practice, any plausible constraints are likely in each area to leave a number of policy-options in place, not to reduce the options to just one. And so the constraints imposed on government must also include many that bear on the processes whereby ties are broken and decisions taken in each domain of policy-making.

Such constraints, too, can serve the purpose of stopping those in power from operating outside the boundaries of popular control. They might require, depending on the issue, that decisions are taken by reference to expert or impartial or judicial bodies, by a majority vote in the legislature or in a referendum, or even by some kind of lottery. The assumption is that while such process constraints will leave the final determination of policy in any area to the luck of the draw – including, for example, the draw that gives one or another side a majority in a legislature or referendum – that mode of determination can be consistent in the relevant area with popular control. If it allows the wills of some to rule on certain matters, as in giving the majority party control of various issues, it does so only because such restricted empowerment is consistent with all that popular direction and control requires; like the power that I enjoy when you give me the key to the alcohol cupboard, the power given to the majority party can only be exercised within accepted bounds and need not count as dominating.

The fact that in practice many decisions will have to be left to government under the best imaginable regime of popular control raises the spectre of abuse in this range of discretion. Abuse might consist in the authorities smuggling some self-serving candidates into the set of policies between which a decision has to be made in any area, or indeed keeping some popularly acceptable candidates out of that set. Or it might involve the authorities taking advantage of loopholes in the processes available to resolve policy disputes in any area for their own special benefit or the benefit of cronies.

These possibilities sharpen the question as to how much popular control – in particular, how much popular influence – will count as enough to banish the spectre of uncontrolled or arbitrary government. How efficacious ought the people's influence over government to be? How far ought it to be able to impose a popular direction on government, removing opportunities for the intrusion of private interest and private will? The question is akin to the issue, addressed in the preceding chapter, as to how far people need to be guarded against domination from one another for the enjoyment of freedom. Here the issue is how far people ought to be able to control those in power on an equally shared basis, if they are to enjoy freedom in relation to government. Where the earlier question asked after the degree of entrenchment required for private non-domination, this question asks after the degree of empowerment required for public non-domination.

In answer to the earlier question, I suggested that the best we can say is that entrenchment is adequate in a given society to the extent that by local standards people would display excessive timidity if they could not pass the eyeball test there – if they could not look one another in the eye without being prompted to fear or deference by the possibility of another's interference. Where the eyeball test is a good index of whether the guards against private domination are adequate, a parallel tough-luck test is a good index of whether the guards against public domination are efficacious.

Imagine that the party or personnel in government do not meet with your approval. What are you to think if they are manifestly appointed under a suitably efficacious form of popular influence and direction, in which you have an equal share? You can only think that it was just tough luck that those appointed are not to your taste; it was not the work of a dominating will, as it would be, for example, under a colonial administration. Or imagine that the government passes legislation of which you disapprove: say, legislation requiring the construction of new prisons. What are you to think if it does so, again manifestly, under the equally shared, suitably efficacious control of the people? You can only think that it was just tough luck for you that the decision went that way; it was not the result of a will at work in the public sphere that operates beyond the equally shared control of you and your fellows. Or imagine, finally, that in implementing the legislation, the government decides to your dismay that one of the prisons should be located in your neighbourhood – in your back yard. What are you to think if it manifestly makes this decision under a suitably efficacious form of control in which you and those in your area equally share? Again you can only think that it was just tough luck that the decision went against you; it was not due to the special influence of those who are richer or electorally better placed or closer to the corridors of power.[40]

The point of legitimacy is to ensure that you and your fellow citizens are not subject to an alien, controlling will, despite that fact that there may be a good deal of discretion exercised by those in power. Such legitimacy will be adequately ensured, so these observations suggest, to the extent that you and your fellows have good grounds to think that any unwelcome results of public decision-making are just tough luck. By local standards of when trust is well placed and those in government inhibited from exploiting loopholes in the constraints imposed, you need not view unwelcome results as the sign of a malign will at work against you or your kind; or at least you need not do so, assuming you are not subject to excessive anxiety or distrust. You may be exasperated by what transpires in the formation of government, or in the creation or administration or adjudication of the law, but if you really share in equal, suitably efficacious control of government, which is what republican legitimacy requires, then you will not have a reason to feel resentment at how the state performs.

You may feel resentment, of course, at how your fellow citizens behave in private or public roles, even when there is no question of popular control

---

[40] My thanks to Ben Ewing for discussion of the points in this paragraph.

being undermined; you may be indignant about the culpable ignorance or indifference, for example, that their refusal to support a certain policy seems to display. Such resentment at individuals is quite consistent with allowing that the state itself, since it enacts a will over which you enjoy shared, suitably efficacious control, is not deserving of resentment. That the state enacts an unjust policy, by your lights, will be a result of the bad luck of your having many culpably ignorant or indifferent compatriots, not a result of its harbouring an alien will. Insofar as the tough-luck test is satisfied, the will displayed by the state is under an efficacious form of control that you share equally with others in imposing. If that will fails to track the good, then you and your fellows have only yourselves to blame. And if you don't blame yourself, you can only blame your fellows.

A variant of the tough-luck test of efficacy applies, not just in the sorts of example given, but also in a case where you are charged with a crime, found guilty and sentenced to some punishment: perhaps a period in prison. If you are innocent of the crime, there will still be a great difference between the case where it really is just tough luck that all the evidence pointed against you, and that the institutions in place were incapable of registering your innocence, and the case where the system allowed some-one the power of acting against you: say, a police officer or public prosecutor who was hostile to you personally, or to those in a particular subgroup to which you belong. But what if you are guilty of the crime? In that case, a legitimate system will enable you to think, not that it was tough luck that you were sentenced to prison, but something related: that you have only yourself to blame. Knowing the rules under which you live, and knowing that you share equally in control of them, you cannot complain about what is imposed under those rules as a penalty for your breaking them.[41]

The tough-luck test offers an intuitive way of gauging how far the efficacy of democratic control over government is satisfactory. It should be noted, however, that it is only available as a plausible criterion of performance, on the republican assumption that legitimacy requires people to exercise control over the will of government, not control over everything that happens. Thus it is no problem for republican theory that in any area of policy brute

---

[41] There are difficult issues, however, that I am ignoring here. Some arise as a result of moral differences; for an excellent discussion of such cases see Talisse (2009). Other difficult issues are multi-cultural questions of the kind that Will Kymlicka (1995) in particular has put on the table; for a broadly republican approach see Nathan (2010) and for an incisive discussion of one particular issue see Laborde (2008).

chance ultimately determines what exact policy or decision the government selects under the terms imposed on it by the people.[42]

The lesson of the two previous requirements on the popular control of government that legitimacy requires was that people should have equal access to a popular system of unconditioned or independent influence that pushes government in an equally acceptable direction. Adding in the third requirement, the lesson is that popular, legitimating control of government requires equal access to a popular system of unconditioned and efficacious influence – specifically, one that imposes an equally acceptable direction on government. Putting the implications of legitimacy in a slogan, we may say that people have to enjoy an equally accessible form of influence that imposes an equally acceptable direction on the state. But it should always be understood that the directive influence to which people are given access has to be not only equal or individualized, but also unconditioned and efficacious.

5. THE DEMOCRATIC STATE

A theory of democracy

Starting from the requirements of legitimacy, understood on republican lines, we have argued that they can be fulfilled only insofar as citizens enjoy a suitable range, kind and degree of control over government. There are no other salient conditions that we might require a legitimate state to fulfil. And so we may conclude that a state will be legitimate just to the extent that in a suitable domain people enjoy equal control over government: equally accessible influence – unconditioned and efficacious influence, as I shall assume – that pushes government in an equally acceptable direction.

Any system that satisfies such conditions deserves to be described as a democracy, since it gives the *demos*, or 'people', an equally shared,

---

[42] In this as in other respects, republican theory enables us to support judgements that are independently plausible: it satisfies the test of reflective equilibrium with such judgements. This is particularly striking in the present instance, since the plausibility of the tough-luck test is not so readily established on other accounts of the role of democracy. On many other accounts the people would only enjoy control to the extent – an impossible ideal – that they controlled everything that transpires at the hands of government agencies: only to the extent that they determined the content of every law and policy, every decree and judgement. On the present account they will enjoy control to the extent that they control the will at the origin of what transpires. And they can achieve this insofar as they can impose terms that leave little or no room for the intrusion of alien will on the part of government agencies, even if they leave matters of detail to the luck of the draw. We will be looking in later chapters at examples of how such control can work.

independently supported and intuitively efficacious degree of *kratos*, or
'control', over the state.[43] And so what we have developed can count as a
republican theory of democracy. There is no one proprietary meaning of the
term 'democracy', as it is used in ordinary or philosophical or scientific
language; people often divide on what exactly the notion of democracy
connotes (Connolly 1993). Thus the theory according to which democracy
requires a popular system of individualized, unconditioned and efficacious
control does not count as analytical in character; it does not offer an analysis
of the term 'democracy' as a theory of causation might offer us an analysis of
the term 'cause'. What it offers, rather, is an ideal that democracy, at its best,
might be required to achieve or approximate.[44]

Put in other terms, what the theory offers is an account of what democratic institutions ought to do: a job specification that they ought to be
designed to implement. But such a job specification naturally raises a
question about its capacity to be implemented. The question is whether
the ideal of a regime in which people share equally in control of government
is institutionally feasible or just a utopian pipedream.

The only way to answer this question is to develop a model of how certain
realizable institutions might bring the ideal into existence, or close to
existence. Having sketched the requirements of republican justice in sections 1 and 2 of Chapter 2 – having described the job specification under
which a just social order requires the publicly entrenched enjoyment of
basic liberties – we went on in Section 3 to indicate the sorts of institutions
that might realize that ideal. We need to do the same thing for the ideal of
legitimacy or democracy, offering a model of democratic institutions in
which it might be brought to life.

I take up this task in the two chapters following. In Chapter 4, I look at
the civic or popular influence that democracy in a republican sense would
require and in Chapter 5 at the civic or popular direction that that influence
ought to impose on government. The model that emerges in those chapters
need not persuade everyone who accepts the republican theory of democracy. For all I know, there may be a better, perhaps even radically different,
alternative available. My commitment to the model goes less deep,

[43] For a popular but very useful introduction to the origin of the notion of democracy see Dunn
(2005).
[44] The conception is close to what Ronald Dworkin (2006: 131) describes as a 'partnership view of
democracy' under which 'democracy means that the people govern themselves each as a full partner in
a collective political enterprise so that a majority's decisions are democratic only when certain further
conditions are met that protect the status and interests of each citizen as a full partner in that
enterprise'. See too Dworkin (2011: Chapter 18). For a somewhat different account of the linkage
between democracy in this sense and the absence of domination see Lovett (2010: 210–20).

therefore, than my commitment to the theory. I offer it in the spirit of a realistic proposal, as I take it to be, which shows that the republican ideal of legitimacy and democracy is not other-worldly; it is an ideal that can inform politically serious contemporary debate.[45]

The appeal of the democratic state

On the assumption that the republican ideal of a legitimate and democratic regime is institutionally feasible, I would like to make some observations on the appeal that such a state ought to have for us. The democratic state, as that ideal begins to take shape within republican theory, is not just an institution that remedies or reduces some of the hardships that derive from our not being of an angelic nature. So long as it achieves republican justice, it is the source of a great and otherwise unavailable good. The necessity of the state for the achievement of this good suggests, contrary to a good deal of received opinion, that the state is not an institution about which we should be ambivalent. While it certainly requires high maintenance, as our argument should have made clear, the well-maintained state holds out the prospect of our being able to enjoy an important benefit that would otherwise escape us.

This benefit is the good of status freedom. It consists in the objective and subjective status of your enjoying freedom as non-domination, equally with fellow citizens, in the common sphere of the basic liberties and of doing so without domination by an uncontrolled, if benevolent, government. Status freedom in this sense has a horizontal and a vertical dimension, requiring independency on the will of others, as it used to be said, both in your relations with fellow citizens and in your relations with your state. It is the good, now extended to you and all your fellow citizens, that was savoured in traditional republican texts as the freedom of the *liber*, or 'free-man': the freedom of the fully and openly incorporated member of a society of fully and openly incorporated citizens.

In order to appreciate the good that a just and democratic state might provide, it may be useful by way of contrast to consider an ideal stateless society that is much celebrated in the tradition: the manifestly utopian and infeasible society associated with the Kantian idea of a kingdom of ends. It turns out that even the kingdom of ends could not provide the good of

---

[45] The republican model of democracy emerging from this account might figure among the models in David Held's (2006) standard account, but it does not coincide with the model that he describes as republican.

status freedom, at least not with the robustness that a just and democratic state might underwrite.

The kingdom of ends is a stateless dispensation in which members may differ in their levels of wealth and power but are each morally committed at the highest possible level. They are committed, first, to showing respect for others and second, perhaps going beyond Kant, to showing concern, as well. Their commitment to respect obliges members of the kingdom of ends to renounce interference in one another's basic liberties, so I shall assume, and their commitment to concern obliges them to provide any resources that others may require.

Would the introduction of a just and democratic state improve the lives of the moral paragons who inhabit the kingdom of ends? I believe it would. In all likelihood, it would provide a much more effective means of identifying the basic liberties that people are to enjoy. But, much more importantly, it would also provide in a novel way for the entrenchment of those liberties. Were people moral in the degree imagined, then the more wealthy and powerful would be disposed not to interfere with others and not to allow others to go without needed resources. But their acting on that disposition would depend on their continuing to embrace and abide by the requirements of the assumed morality. It would depend, to recall a point from the first chapter, on their displaying a good will rather than a weak will or a will to evil. In such a world, therefore, some members would have to depend on the goodwill of others for enjoying the basic liberties. And so the coercive laws of a just and democratic state would play a crucial, beneficial role, establishing external checks and supports to guard each member against dependency on the will of the more powerful. They would be a means of providing for people's enjoyment of status freedom.[46]

Would this freedom really be a benefit, however, given that the members of the kingdom of ends are vanishingly unlikely to turn ill-willed? Yes, for reasons rehearsed already. Seeing and treating one another as agents, not as pre-set, probabilistic devices, even the members of the kingdom of ends would have to recognize that whether another relatively powerful member chooses to interfere with them, or chooses not to help out in the absence of

---

[46] One qualification. In the kingdom of ends, social norms of a particularly respectful, and indeed benevolent, kind might be expected to emerge and, having emerged, might put suitable checks on interference with others or even on indifference to their needs; any such failure might trigger costs in the economy of esteem (Brennan and Pettit 2004). I ignore this here, since my only point is that the kingdom of ends as traditionally conceived would deliver more benefits if it were complemented by a democratic state. For a useful discussion of Kant's kingdom of ends that is in some ways congenial and in others uncongenial, see Van der Rijt (2012: Chapter 5).

resources, will often be up to that person. And so they would have to recognize that on one or another front they depend on the person's good-will. Thus, as we imagine the perspective of weaker parties, we see that they would be inevitably and manifestly indebted to the powerful amongst them for non-interference or for the resources they enjoy. They would be in the position of dependants, not equals, in relation to those parties.

The failure of the kingdom of ends to provide for the status freedom of its members highlights the importance of what the just and democratic state can provide. Introduced to the kingdom of ends, it would give each member protection against the accessible, if highly improbable, interference or indifference of the stronger. And in providing that benefit, it would confer a free status that would previously have been unavailable. The actual behaviour of people after the introduction of such a regime of law and coercion might not differ very much from their behaviour beforehand. The role of coercive law in providing a second line of defence against weakness or illness of will on the part of the powerful would not be visible in anything that anyone did – at least not if we assume that prior to the appearance of a state the powerful didn't ever display any weak or ill will. But the role of coercive law would still be of the utmost importance. It would mean that the non-interference and resources that the weaker enjoy come to them, not in the guise of a gift for which they should be grateful, but rather in the guise of an institutionally guaranteed claim.

As mentioned earlier, the coercive state is certainly needed to promote compliance and to assure compliers that others are complying too. But we can now see that it is needed on a third count, too. For the just and democratic state relies on coercion – the coercion involved in protecting against interference and in redistributing to those with insufficient resources – to ensure that people's enjoyment of the basic liberties is publicly entrenched. This coercive entrenchment provides people with a freedom as non-domination that is independent of the will of others as to how they should choose, including the will of government itself. And that is not something that mere morality can provide.

G. A. Cohen (2008: 148) expresses the orthodox view on the coercive state, however just and however democratic it may be, when he says that there are only two functions that it can play: 'coercion is necessary only for deviance or assurance reasons'. But this is wrong, according to the picture emerging here. Provided it is just and democratic, under the republican specification of those virtues, the coercive state can generate a good for all of us – the good of status freedom – that we cannot provide for one another on the basis of our own goodwill. We cannot provide this for one another as we actually are. And we could not provide it for one another, even if we were as angelic as the members of the kingdom of ends.

Economists characterize benefits that the private market is incapable of producing, and that appear to require collective organization, as public goods. These are goods like defence, criminal justice and public health that for reasons of psychology or organization – say, the disposition to free-ride – we would be unlikely to generate in the absence of centralized coercion. The upshot of the discussion is that the free status that republicans envisage is also a public good. Freedom requires independency on the will of others, even the goodwill of others. And for that deep and inescapable reason, free status is something that we can make available to one another as individuals only by collectively organizing ourselves in a state – strictly speaking, a just and democratic state.[47]

Back to Rawls

In introducing the model of social justice that republican theory would support, I argued that in important respects it would break with Rawls, replacing his two principles with a single principle that calls for giving people status freedom in relation to one another. While the republican theory would undoubtedly overlap with Rawls's in many of the policies supported, it would provide support on a different basis. It may be useful in concluding this discussion of the republican theory of legitimacy and democracy to sketch a parallel comparison with the approach that Rawlsian and related theory would adopt.

As we saw earlier, Rawls and others focus on comprehensive, social-cum-procedural justice in evaluating a legal order – a basic structure, in his sense – rather than breaking that evaluative task, as we have done, into the distinct issues of social justice and political legitimacy. Rawls explores the comprehensively just order by asking which basic structure or structures would satisfy his contractual eligibility or his civic justifiability test. And in answering that question he requires, unsurprisingly, that the just structure should give people certain basic political liberties and rights. The issue for

---

[47] At this point we have reason to think that it is not only good, assuming there are people around, that no one should dominate others, and that no one should vitiate anyone's undominated capacity; it is good that there should be people around who can enjoy mutual undominated relationships. This good is close to that which is celebrated by recognition theorists (Honneth 1996) and others who are influenced by Hegel's account of the status associated with freedom (Patten 2002). Adopting this view would help republican theory to deal with some of the complex issues raised in population theory as a result of the non-identity problem (Parfit 1984: Chapter 16). I am grateful to Jake Nebel for exchanges on this topic.

us, then, is whether the political rights he envisages might be sufficient to satisfy the demands of political legitimacy or republican democracy: whether they might be enough to give people an equal share in a public system of individualized, unconditioned and efficacious control.

The political rights to which Rawls (1971, 1993) directs us include all the procedural liberties associated with electoral democracy – for example, the freedom to vote or to stand for office – as well as the rights of free speech, association and movement that they presuppose. But he does not lay much emphasis on the procedural liberties, casting them at one point as 'subordinate to the other freedoms' (Rawls 1971: 233). What is important in his perspective is that if we consider impartially what society ought to provide for individuals – if we consider this, for example, from the point of view of the original position, in which none of us know how we will fare under the basic structure adopted – we must conclude that it ought to furnish them with procedural as well as more substantive liberties and rights. Those requirements are benefits that each should fully and equally enjoy, within a suitable mix of substantive and procedural rights, on pain of suffering unfairness. But they do not have a special status and may even be subordinate to their substantive counterparts.

On the republican view, things look quite different. Republican theory casts the procedural rights that people are to enjoy – together, as we shall see, with other, less formal, rights – as powers that they must each fully and equally exercise if they are not to suffer subjection and domination by an uncontrolled state. It invests the state with heavy responsibilities in the sphere of social justice, as Rawls does. But it emphasizes that nonetheless the coercive state is a real danger – a danger to the very freedom that social justice is meant to promote – and that citizens must share equally in control of political coercion if they are to enjoy the status of free persons. The spectre of the despotic and illegitimate state – even the benevolently despotic state – haunts the approach as thoroughly as the spectre of the socially unjust regime. And it inevitably gives prominence to the demand for a regime of shared, popular control.

This may explain why Rawls and others do not actually give the same standing to the requirements of legitimacy and democracy as republicans. But are they actually prevented from doing so by their focus on comprehensive, social-cum-procedural justice? Could they maintain that focus and yet be persuaded by the case for republican freedom to give a greater importance to democracy?

In principle, yes. The tests of contractual eligibility and civic justifiability on which Rawls relies can be seen as ways of operationalizing the normative demand for the state to treat its citizens as equals (Dworkin 1978). Accepting such a test, we can still go along with republican thought and take freedom as non-domination, understood in a status sense, as the good with reference to which the test ought to be applied. And if we do this, then no basic structure will appeal unless it gives citizens a suitable level of equally shared control over how it is likely to evolve at the hands of government. Let it fail to give citizens such control and their freedom is going to be jeopardized at a very deep level. They may seem to enjoy social justice under the envisaged structure but they will enjoy it only as the result of an indulgence on the part of those in power. The freedom that social justice purports to give them will not really be freedom, since it will be tainted by their dependency on the goodwill of government.

The upshot is that while the Rawlsian approach of articulating the demands of social and procedural justice in a comprehensive package may actually lead to a downgrading of legitimacy and democracy, this is not an inevitable result. It would be avoidable, at least in principle, under the assumption about the importance of freedom as non-domination that republicans make. It is certainly useful to guard against the possibility of a downgrade by distinguishing between the demands of social justice and political legitimacy, as we have done here. But that way of presenting things merely facilitates an insight into the importance of democracy that is already guaranteed by embracing the core republican ideal.

CHAPTER 4

Democratic influence

The idea in this chapter and the next is to explore the institutional possibility that the people in a polity might have such control over those who run the state that they are not individually dominated by the interference that the state practises in taxation, coercion and punishment. To the extent that they have a control that makes such interference non-dominating, the citizens will not lose out in freedom just by the fact of living within that state and, by republican criteria, the state will count as politically legitimate. A state that is legitimate in that sense may not achieve a great deal in guarding against private domination and achieving social justice, though it probably has to achieve some minimum threshold if citizens are going to be capable of exercising control over its doings.

Control, as we saw, depends on two distinct elements, influence and direction. Thus the people will achieve control over the state insofar as they attain influence, on the one side, and succeed on the other in using that influence to impose a suitable direction on government. Such popular control will be suited to republican purposes, guarding against domination, to the extent that it gives each citizen an equal share in the control, particularly an equal share in a form of control that is suitably unconditioned and efficacious. People must enjoy an equally accessible form of unconditioned and efficacious influence that imposes an equally acceptable direction on the state. In this chapter I look at how people might enjoy the required influence and I turn in the next chapter to how this influence might impose the required direction. In this chapter's discussion of the institutional means whereby people might come to enjoy the required influence I shall anticipate the discussion in the next and assume that the influence they enjoy can support a popular direction and not merely be wayward in character.

How to approach the discussion of the influence that the people might have in a polity? Should I look at utopian, perhaps fanciful ideals of how popular influence might materialize? Or should I start from democratic institutions with which we are all familiar and begin to chart the influence that they make possible? It's a hard choice. If I go the first way, I may be accused of dabbling in 'models of speculative perfection', in William Paley's (2002: 319) words, and risking irrelevance in the discussion of obtainable reforms. If I go the second way, I may be charged with lowering my sights and paying undue obeisance to the status quo.

I propose to approach the challenge as follows. I begin with a model in which the citizens gather periodically in a plenary assembly, a committee-of-the-whole, to determine the laws of the community. This model, which is reminiscent of Rousseau's assembly, offers a plausible, initial interpretation of what it might be for the people to enjoy equally accessible influence over government. Whatever its other faults, however, I argue that the model is quite infeasible, even in an electronic age in which people might assemble virtually. Having identified the problems of feasibility that a plenary assembly would confront, I go on in Section 2 to discuss the rival merits of two quite different forms of non-plenary assembly, one indicatively representative and the other responsively representative. And having argued in favour of the responsive form, I then argue over sections 3, 4 and 5 that in order to serve the cause of republican legitimacy, this assembly has to be subjected to a series of important amendments. The model to which these amendments lead promises to deliver a form of popular influence that is appropriately individualized, unconditioned and efficacious, as our ideal of legitimacy requires.

This final model does not conform to the status quo in existing systems of representative democracy but it is close enough to warrant a claim to institutional feasibility: it represents a regime we can see how to establish and stabilize. And yet the model is far enough away from the status quo to direct us to reforms that are required if our institutions are to support a form of popular influence that is individualized, unconditioned and efficacious. The model incorporates versions of the mixed constitution and the contestatory citizenry that bulk large, as we saw, in Italian–Atlantic republicanism.

1. THE PLENARY ASSEMBLY

The origin of the idea

The thesis that democracy requires an assembly of all the citizens to be the sovereign body, enjoying control over law-making, is often represented as the Athenian model – the model realized in Athens in the fifth and fourth centuries BCE – probably because of the slanted account of Athens given by

Polybius (1954) in his history of the purportedly contrasting, mixed constitution that he identified in Rome. But Athens does not conform well to
the plenary model, at least in the form it assumed from the late fifth century
on. In that period, as earlier, the courts, or *dikasteria*, which involved
hundreds of citizens, selected on the basis of a lottery, could punish someone for attempting to change the law within the *ecclesia* – the 'plenary
assembly of citizens' – and for thereby assuming some legislative authority
for themselves.[1] And while the issue of whether a law should be considered
as a candidate for revision was determined by the *ecclesia*, any actual
revisions were decided by another body of hundreds of citizens, again
selected by lot: the *nomothetai*, or 'law-makers' (Hansen 1991; Ober 1996).

Ironically, the plenary assembly model of democracy goes back in its
purest, clearest form to two thinkers who themselves defended an absolute
monarchy. They are the sixteenth-century French jurist, Jean Bodin, and
the seventeenth-century English philosopher, Thomas Hobbes (Pettit
2012b). They suggested that in casting democracy in this way, they were
being faithful to the model of classical Athens in the fifth and fourth
centuries BCE. But, mischievously or not, they were actually quite innova-
tive in the image they proposed.[2]

Bodin and Hobbes thought of law as the command of a supreme power
or sovereign. This was something of a novelty in their time, for the main
body of law that coordinated relationships between individuals and communities in the medieval world – the *jus commune*, or 'common law', as it
was known – did not have any single, centralized enforcer. Derived from
Justinian's Roman law-books, it was enunciated in scholarly glosses and
commentaries as much as in princely edicts, including the edicts of the
German-based, medieval emperor (Woolf 1913). Assuming that law was
command, however – as it must often have more plausibly seemed in their
divided, post-Reformation world – Bodin and Hobbes argued that there
had to be a single commander and a single will at its origin; there had to be a
sovereign individual or a sovereign body.

Following Aristotle's (1996) account in *The Politics*, Bodin and Hobbes
maintained that there were just three possible types of state, corresponding
to three types of sovereign: monarchy, in which the laws are handed down
by a sovereign individual – this was the strong preference of each; aristocracy, in which the laws are issued by a sovereign committee of the few; and

---

[1] The procedure under which this was possible was known as the *graphe paranomon*: it allowed for the
indictment of those proposing measures contrary to the laws (Hansen 1991; Ober 1996).
[2] For an exchange on Hobbes on democracy see Tuck (2006) and Hoekstra (2006).

democracy, in which the laws are imposed by a sovereign committee of the many. Unlike Aristotle, Bodin and Hobbes ridiculed the idea of a state that would operate under a mixed constitution. While taking different argumentative routes to the conclusion, they each maintained that because such a constitution would not identify and establish a single commander or lawgiver, it would undermine the capacity of the state to serve its purpose, ensuring order and peace in the land; it would be a recipe for civil strife and political disaster.

But if Bodin and Hobbes were the first to enunciate clearly the image of government by a plenary, legislative assembly, it was Jean Jacques Rousseau who offered the first, full-scale defence of the model. Working with the categories inherited from such absolutist predecessors, as we saw in the Introduction, Rousseau (1997: 11.2.2) rejected the idea of the mixed constitution: it would turn the sovereign, he says, 'into a being that is fantastical and formed of disparate pieces'. But he could not accept the idea of a monarchical or an aristocratic state, given his attachment to the broadly republican ideal that no one should have to live in subjection to another. And so he had little option but to argue in support of what Bodin and Hobbes would have called a democracy. He held that the people should gather periodically in a sovereign assembly to deliberate and decide upon the laws and that they should then give the job of implementing and adjudicating those laws to appointed magistrates. He himself thought of this design as republican but not democratic, since he used the term 'democracy' in a somewhat idiosyncratic manner to describe an arrangement in which the assembly would implement, as well as make, the laws (Rousseau 1997: 111.17.5).

Following Hobbes, Rousseau holds that while there has to be unanimity in the contract to enter political society – 'the act by which a people is a people' (1997: 1.5.2) – that contract makes it alright for further decisions to be taken by majority vote: 'the vote of the majority always obligates all the rest; this is a consequence of the contract itself' (IV.2.7).[3] But he breaks with Hobbes in hailing a deliberative ideal, according to which the members of his assembly should vote on the basis of the common good. They should each think as citizens, focused impartially on their common interest, and they should vote for any measure they support, whatever their personal or factional interests, on the grounds that 'it is advantageous to the State'

---

[3] He recommends that on some important matters, it may be useful to require a super-majoritarian approval: this could be introduced, presumably, by a prior majority agreement. See Rousseau (1997: IV.2.11).

(Rousseau 1997: IV.1.6); this is required if the majority vote they cast is to reflect the general will of the community, as he calls it. We shall return to a consideration of the deliberative constraint in the next chapter, when we ask how popular influence might be directed in a manner acceptable to all. In this chapter, our focus is on the prior question of how to organize a system of popular influence so that everyone has an equal share. And in discussing that question we can abstract from whether or not people should be required to exercise their collective influence under a deliberative constraint.

The discursive dilemma

Can we look to the plenary assembly as a model on which to design a system of popular influence? Many argue not, on the grounds that almost all societies are too large to allow citizens to come together in regular assembly. Rousseau (1997: III.15.12) himself seems to have recognized the problem and it became a standard observation amongst succeeding thinkers like Immanuel Kant (1996: 296) and James Mill (Lively and Rees 1978: 7). But even if the size problem could be overcome, say by resort to virtual assemblies on the Internet, there is no real prospect of enabling the citizens as a whole to establish an effective law-making body. They will confront a problem illustrated by the discursive dilemma.

The most basic requirement on any law-making assembly, acting in concert with the executive and judicial bodies that complement it, is that it should be able to promote consistency in the law and, if certain laws are shown to be inconsistent, should be capable of recognizing and responding to the problem. If the state were insensitive to challenges of consistency then, as we saw, it could not constitute an agency capable of pursuing justice or discharging any of its presumptive duties; it would be an unconversable, unreachable entity. This would be a disaster, not just from the point of view of republican justice, but also from the point of view of republican legitimacy: you and your fellow citizens could not hope to use your influence to impose any sort of direction on such a state. You can't do business with a body that finds nothing to apologize for in the fact that it upholds a number of inconsistent propositions or instructions.

The problem with the plenary assembly is that while the participants might be individually consistent in their final judgements and votes on a range of connected issues, they would be liable to generate an inconsistent body of judgements if they relied on majority voting for the aggregation of their individual sets of judgements into a common, shared set. Suppose there are just three of us in the assembly: I, A; you, B; and a third party, C;

think of us, if you like, as standing in for three distinct subgroups. And suppose that we want to form judgements on three connected issues: whether p, whether q and whether p-and-q. The proposition 'p' might be the claim that we should increase defence spending, 'q' the proposition that we should increase other spending. I, A, and you, B, might think that p, while the third party, C, rejects it. And you and C might think that q, while I reject it. In that case 'p' will be supported by a majority of members – you and me – and 'q' will be supported by a distinct majority of members – you and C. But you will be the only one to support p-and-q; I will not support it because of rejecting 'q', and C will not support it because of rejecting 'p'. Thus, despite endorsing 'p' and 'q' separately, we as a group will not endorse the combined package 'p-and-q'; indeed, under standard rules of voting, we will reject it. We will be committed, under majority voting, to thinking that we should increase defence spending, we should increase other spending, and yet we should not increase both defence and other spending.

While we will individually hold consistent views on the relevant issues, then, we will be collectively led under majority voting to adopt an inconsistent set of group views, as Table 4.1 illustrates.

Majority voting ensures that the corporate judgements are responsive to the judgements of individuals, as seems appropriate, and the problem is that such individual responsiveness makes it difficult to achieve collective rationality. There is a discursive dilemma in prospect, as I have described it elsewhere (Pettit 2001c, 2001e: Chapter 5; List 2006a).[4] The dilemma consists in the fact, broadly stated, that members can opt for individual responsiveness, in which case collective rationality is jeopardized, or for collective rationality, in which case individual responsiveness is in danger. There is no middle way, so that either individual responsiveness or collective rationality has to go.

Table 4.1 *Illustrating the discursive dilemma*

	p? Increase defence?	q? Increase other?	p-and-q? Increase both?
I, A, vote	Yes	No	No
You, B, vote	Yes	Yes	Yes
C votes	No	Yes	No
We vote	Yes	Yes	No

---

[4] The discursive dilemma is a generalization of the doctrinal paradox that arises for collegial courts; this was first properly identified and analysed by Lewis Kornhauser and Larry Sager (1992a, 1992b, 1993).

The problem, as a number of results have shown, is not specific to majority voting. It is liable to arise under a variety of interpretations of the constraints of individual responsiveness and collective rationality.[5] But it is sufficiently well illustrated for our purposes by the infeasibility of majoritarian decision-making.

The problem means that it is not going to be enough for a group, however deliberative it may be, just to rely on majority voting – or on any of a variety of such bottom-up voting procedures – to aggregate its views.[6] The group must keep track of where the accumulating commitments generated by individual rounds of voting are leading it – its members must gather feedback on whether the commitments are generating inconsistency – and it must be able to respond appropriately to that information.[7] One strategy it might adopt is the straw-vote procedure. Under this procedure, a majority vote in support of some judgement will be treated as a straw vote until the result is tested and shown to be consistent with judgements supported previously; if it fails that test then either it or some prior vote is rejected (List and Pettit 2011: Part 1). The lesson is that in order to guard against inconsistency in its group views, the group has to be able to access and process feedback on where the votes of members are leading it and, when those votes lead to inconsistency, it has to make revisions that restore consistency – or at least insulate any inconsistencies that prove recalcitrant.

A group might conduct this reflexive exercise in a mechanical way, establishing a routine whereby any later vote that proves inconsistent with earlier commitments is nullified: this would force our A–B–C group to reject the negative vote and endorse 'p-and-q', for example. But that would scarcely be satisfactory, since the recognition that prior votes require accepting a result such as the combined package might be thought by members to provide reason, not for revising the negative vote on the combined package, but for rejecting the prior, positive vote on one of the elements in the package. A satisfactory, decision-making body would have to be able to conduct

---

[5] For an initial result see List and Pettit (2002) and for a survey of later results see List and Polak (2010) and List and Pettit (2011).

[6] Some authors like to contrast aggregative and deliberative processes, as if deliberation meant that aggregation was unnecessary or unproblematic. But it is agreed on all sides among deliberative democrats that deliberation will not generally lead to consensus and that the differences which deliberation still leaves in place have to be resolved by a voting process. The discursive dilemma shows that when the issues to be voted on are logically connected, as they generally will be over any stretch of time, then there may still be a serious problem of aggregation.

[7] Those members, as Niklas Luhmann (1990: Chapter 9) argues, have to keep track in an exercise of self-reference on how under a common name – in his argument, that of the state – they are getting to be committed.

second-stage, post-feedback deliberation – for short, reflexive deliberation – as well as the basic deliberation conducted prior to first-stage voting (Pettit 2007a, 2007b). This is the sort of deliberation required under the straw-vote procedure. The group votes that p, votes that q, and, on finding that it also votes against p-and-q, deliberates about which vote to reverse.[8]

This takes us to the denouement (Pettit 2003b). No plenary assembly could be expected to be able to conduct this reflexive form of deliberation, assuming that its numbers are large. It may be possible to get members to deliberate in a basic way about a single issue – say, whether to increase defence spending or to increase education spending – and then to resolve remaining differences by voting. But what can they do to deliberate in the wake of feedback on the inconsistency of the various measures they have supported – this might be made salient by a suitable feedback committee – and on the comparative merits of resolving it in one or another manner? It is unlikely in the extreme that any large body could discharge this reflexive task satisfactorily. The consideration argues powerfully against the feasibility of the plenary assembly model and, more broadly, against any wholesale reliance on popular referenda for determining the conduct of government.[9]

One response to this critique might be to suggest that apart from the plenary assembly, there should be a body that is charged with restoring consistency whenever plenary voting generates a problem. But this body would have enormous discretion and power, since the resolution of an inconsistency could take any of a number of directions: the most recent vote might be nullified or, alternatively, any of the previous votes that are relevant to the inconsistency might be set aside. To empower such a body in this measure would undermine the rationale for the plenary assembly; it would make a mockery of the claim that the assembly gives power to the people.[10]

---

[8] Might it help if the group voted only on logically independent propositions that are fit to count as premises, allowing judgements on other propositions to be determined by the votes on the premises? No, because there is no prospect of agreement on which propositions are fit for the role of premises, and which not. See Harman (1986).

[9] Why do I concentrate on the problem of aggregating judgements, illustrated by the discursive dilemma, rather than on the problem of aggregating preference orderings, illustrated by the Condorcet paradox, that Kenneth Arrow (1963) made famous and by related results (Riker 1982)? Three reasons. One, it is easier to appreciate the problem illustrated by the discursive dilemma. Two, the Arrow impossibility can be presented as a special case of the impossibility illustrated in the results on judgement aggregation; see List and Pettit (2004) and Dietrich and List (2007). And three, the possibility of reflective deliberation, unavailable in a plenary assembly, also offers the only half-satisfactory response to the Arrovian problem. For a debunking account, however, of the Arrovian challenge see Mackie (2003).

[10] This critique of the plenary assembly depends on the assumption that the members of such an assembly are going to have to make their decisions by casting on–off votes in expression of their

2. THE RESPONSIVELY REPRESENTATIVE ASSEMBLY

Given the failure of the plenary assembly to provide a satisfactory model of how to organize a system of popular influence, where are we to turn next? I assume that any plausible alternative is going to require an assembly that represents the people in some way. In taking this line, I reject the view that representation is in any way inimical, as is sometimes said (Manin 1997), to the ideal of democracy; like Nadia Urbinati (2006) I see that as an error with Rousseauvian origins.

It turns out, however, that there are two distinct sorts of bodies that might be held to serve a representative role. One of them is representative in the indicative way in which a painting is representative of its subject; the other is representative in the responsive way in which an attorney may be representative of a client, or perhaps an actor representative of a character. The rival concepts answer to the principal metaphors that were invoked in traditional discussions of representation (Skinner 2005). In this section, I look at the indicative and responsive assemblies in turn, argue that no body can be fully representative in both ways at once, and then provide some considerations in favour of going with a primarily responsive assembly.[11]

The indicative assembly

The first sort of non-plenary assembly is envisaged as a simulacrum or likeness of the people that promises to satisfy the following condition: if it decides in favour of something, then that is good evidence that the people as a whole would make the same decision, were they capable of deliberating

---

judgements on particular issues. But that assumption is realistic (List and Pettit 2011: Part 1). It is not going to be possible to pre-package all the issues to be decided, only allowing consistent packages to come up for assembly vote, since new issues are bound to arise all the time. And when it comes to endorsing a response to any issue, members are going to have no option but to record a positive or a negative vote on each possible response. There is no feasible way, for example, in which they could record a probabilistic degree of credence in each response and then look for some method whereby their different probability distributions might be aggregated into a group distribution. There may be abstract theories in which such aggregation can be modelled but it is entirely unclear how it might be achieved in actual institutions.

[11] For a more developed account of the responsive-indicative distinction on which the following discussion draws see Pettit (2009b, 2010b). Jane Mansbridge (2009) documents the history of a closely related distinction between a sanction and a selection model of representation and establishes a range of points bearing on how the selection model may be developed. That article is broadly congenial to the viewpoint I defend here, though it is more sanguine about the possibility of combining responsive and indicative representation. For a different way of generalizing the concept of representation beyond responsive representation see Rehfeld (2006) and for a very useful discussion of the history and concept of representation, see Vieira and Runciman (2008).

together about it. The body is meant to be a microcosm of the society both in the way it is composed and in the way it operates.

In order to be a compositional microcosm this assembly will have to be statistically representative of the community as a whole, with the main communal categories being represented proportionally within it. And in order to be an operational microcosm its members will have to guard against any pressures that would lead members to behave out of character: that is, on the basis of anything other than the dispositions that make them typical of their category. Those requirements suggest that the assembly envisaged should comprise a random sample of the population that is small enough to make deliberation possible and that it should be given authority for a period that is short enough not to expose members to the warping incentives and pressures of office. It might comprise five hundred or fewer members, selected on the basis of chance, and it might hold power for at most a year or two. Given the information and leisure required for public decision-making, the resolutions of such an assembly could reasonably be expected to be indicative of the decisions that the people as a whole would support, were they able to assemble and deliberate appropriately.

The idea of an indicative assembly of citizens has good historical credentials. It was this sort of assembly that traditional institutions like the lottery were designed, wittingly or not, to establish.[12] While the *ecclesia* of Athens in the fifth and fourth centuries BCE was open to all citizens, the membership of equally crucial bodies was determined by lottery. Thus the judicial panel of about six thousand citizens was fixed on an annual basis by lot and the case-by-case membership of the courts and other smaller bodies – including the 'nomothetai', who came to have responsibility for recommending on any proposed change in the law – was fixed by a second, ad hoc lottery amongst the members of the panel (Hansen 1991; Ober 1996). A similar lottery system played a part in the constitutions of many medieval Italian city-states, where appointments to law-making and related bodies were often made by lot (Waley 1988; Dowlen 2008). And the lottery idea also had an implicit presence in the medieval development of the jury system: to be subjected to the judgement of your peers, whether in determining that there is a legal case to answer, or that you are legally liable, was

---

[12] It is unlikely that the design was witting. There were other purposes that might have been more prominent in the minds of traditional communities: for example, that lottery ensured against the excessive influence of any particular clique or faction. See Dowlen (2008). My thanks to Matteo Faini for discussion on this point.

to be exposed to a body that was meant to be indicative of the citizenry as a whole (Abramson 1994).

There are also contemporary cases of indicative bodies being put to work in place of the population as a whole. The British Columbia Citizens' Assembly is a good example, though only one of many (Sintomer 2007). A body of 160 citizens, selected on a statistically representative basis, it was entrusted by the government of British Columbia in 2004 with producing a recommendation on the voting system to be used in the province (Warren and Pearse 2008). Another example is provided by the deliberative opinion polls championed by James Fishkin (1991, 1997). These comprise fewer numbers and meet over rather shorter periods, but are also designed to make recommendations on public issues that reflect what the community as a whole would recommend, were it possible for the whole population to assemble and deliberate.

The responsive assembly

The salient alternative to having a non-plenary assembly that is a faithful, microcosmic reflection of the people as a whole is the assembly that is elected by the people to debate and enact laws on their behalf.[13] Under this arrangement the people would select those who are to serve for any period on the legislative assembly in an open, competitive exercise. That exercise may involve a single population-wide district or a number of geographically or otherwise distinct districts. It may implement any of a variety of voting systems in order to determine which of those candidates who stand for office are to be successful. And it may not only allow for the election of those who belong to the law-making assembly but also, as in the US presidential system, for the election of the head of the administration (with or without some share in law-making); this appointment, in other words, may be taken out of the hands of the assembly. I abstract for the moment, however, from such details.

Where the microcosmic body is designed to be representative in a statistical, indicative sense, the elected body is meant to be representative in a different, responsive manner. The members are appointed to office on the basis of their electoral promises and may be presumed to be responsive at

---

[13] It is quite possible for an assembly and a government to be responsive without being elected. However appointed to office, for example, it may depend on being suitably responsive to people's manifest expectations for not being faced with public outrage and uproar. While this possibility is important in looking at how far unelected governments can still be accountable to their peoples, it is not relevant to our current discussion.

some level to what they see as the wishes of their constituents. Such responsiveness will often be required in order to satisfy their electoral commitments and it will certainly be required, if that is relevant, in order to facilitate their re-election.

The members of the indicative assembly count as proxies for the people as a whole, standing in for them on the basis of their aggregate likeness to the people. The members of an elected assembly count more naturally as deputies: figures whose job it is, on pain of losing power, to be responsive to their constituents. Deputies may be required to be responsive to the more or less explicit wishes of constituents, in the manner of instructed delegates. Or they may be given a large degree of latitude on this front, being allowed, in the manner of trustees, to make their own judgements on what the presumptive interests or principles of their constituents require (Pitkin 1972). In what follows, I shall speak simply of deputies, focusing on the contrast with proxies, and generally ignore the distinction between deputies of a delegate and deputies of a trustee kind.

The lottery-based and election-based systems each serve to give members of the relevant assembly the status of authorized representatives. But they rely on quite different mechanisms to ensure that how the members are disposed to behave connects with the dispositions of the population at large.[14] Under the mechanism at work in the indicative case, the connection is evidential. Because the members of the assembly are selected to be indicative of the people as a whole, the fact that they are disposed to support this or that policy is a reliable sign that the people are similarly disposed. The responsive mechanism establishes a causal rather than an evidential connection. Because the members of the elected assembly depend on responding to popular dispositions in order to be re-elected – and more generally to satisfy electoral pressures – the fact that the people are disposed thus and so tends to cause a similar disposition in the assembly.[15]

The two mechanisms are diagrammed in Table 4.2.

[14] My discussion is simplified insofar as I do not look at responsive and indicative relationships in which there is a correlation not only between the dispositions that are present in people and representatives – for example, their beliefs in a certain domain – but also between the dispositions that are absent on the two sides: for example, their failures to believe certain things in that domain. For a treatment in which this simplification is lifted, and probabilities of correlation are introduced, see List and Pettit (2011: Chapter 4).

[15] The difference between the two modes of political representation corresponds to a distinction drawn in epistemology between two modes of epistemic representation, sensitive and safe (Sosa 2007). A responsive body will offer a sensitive representation of popular dispositions: as those dispositions change under certain inputs, so its dispositions will tend to change too in sensitive response. An indicative body will offer a safe representation of popular dispositions: as its dispositions change under

Table 4.2 *Mechanisms of representation*

People's disposition	< – – – – – evidential	Representatives' dispositions	Indicative representation
People's dispositions	– – – – – > causal	Representatives' dispositions	Responsive representation

An indicative-cum-responsive assembly

Although supporters of the French Revolution often invoked Rousseau's name as a source of inspiration, they uniformly went along with the idea that any governing assembly would have to be elected. But the general assumption was that such an electoral body would also have an indicative status, as a microcosm or model of the whole population. Thus, in an address to the French Constituent Assembly, Honoré Mirabeau maintained: 'the representative body should at all times present a reduced picture of the people – their opinions, aspirations, and wishes, and that presentation should bear the relative proportion to the original precisely as a map brings before us mountains and dales, rivers and lakes, forests and plains, cities and towns' (Pitkin 1969: 77). This opinion was widely shared amongst enthusiasts for assemblies of elected representatives. About that same time, the American anti-federalist, Melanchton Smith, could write: 'The idea that naturally suggests itself to our minds, when we speak of representatives is, that they resemble those they represent; they should be a true picture of the people' (Ketcham 2003: 342).

But the shift from a statistical to an electoral selection system inevitably makes for the diminution, even the elimination, of the indicative status of a governing assembly. The assembly that is elected may be compositionally indicative of the population as a whole, at least if the electoral system is designed, as John Stuart Mill (1964) thought it should be, to ensure a high degree of proportionality. But there is every reason to think that the assembly will fall short of being operationally indicative in any significant measure. It is unlikely to be a body such that if it votes for a certain measure, that is a sure sign that the population as a whole, were it able to assemble and deliberate, would vote for that measure.

---

certain inputs, that is a fairly safe sign that under those inputs the dispositions of the people would change too. Responsive representatives are reliable trackers of popular dispositions, so we might say, where indicative representatives are reliable mirrors of popular dispositions.

The assembly could make a good claim to be an operationally indicative status if the interests on which its members acted combined in aggregate to model the interests distributed across the population as a whole. But unlike statistically selected members, those who are elected are extremely unlikely to meet this modelling requirement. The condition on which they can be expected to be responsive representatives, as we saw, is that they will generally want to be re-elected, or to satisfy other electoral pressures, and will therefore seek to provide what their constituents and supporters are disposed to welcome. But to the extent that they pursue this goal, it is unlikely that they will mirror in aggregate the interests distributed across the population.

Seeking re-election as they do, they will each favour measures that appeal especially to more pivotal or marginal voters in their constituency or to the supporters on whom they particularly depend. And equally they will tend to strike idealistic postures that cast them in a good light as individuals – say, moralistic postures on prostitution or taxation or crime or indeed capitalism – rather than endorsing the compromise solutions that they might be otherwise disposed to support (Brennan and Lomasky 1993). A body of such electorally interested representatives is not going to act like a faithful microcosm of the society as a whole. The point was made by Benjamin Constant (2003: 387) in 1810. 'You choose a man to represent you because he has the same interests as you. By the very fact of your choosing him, however, your choice of placing him in a different situation from yours gives him a different interest from the one he is charged with representing.'

It is important to register that any representative body will tend to be less indicative of the population as a whole, the more its members are electorally responsive. But the observation does not mean that there is no point in trying to combine indicative and responsive elements in the representative status given to any body or indeed, as we shall see, any public office. Thus an indicative body might be usefully forced to be responsive by being exposed to review or challenge, if not to election; the British Columbia Citizens' Assembly was exposed, perhaps for this reason, to a referendum on its recommendation.[16] And an electorally responsive body might be more acceptable to a population to the extent that it satisfies a degree of proportionality and can claim in some respects to be indicative.[17]

[16] For the record, its recommendation for a change in the voting system in British Columbia received a little short of the 60 per cent support that it was required by government decree to receive.
[17] The very common practice of dividing a country into distinct districts might be taken to promote proportionality in a geographical dimension. Is a wish for a certain proportionality behind this practice? It is hard to believe that it did not play some role in justifying that practice but the evidence,

In favour of the responsive assembly

There is surely a useful role that indicative bodies such as the British Columbia Citizens' Assembly can fulfil in a contemporary democracy. But if we are looking for a permanent assembly to govern a society, then the electoral, responsive assembly scores decisively above it. A fairly obvious consideration in its favour is that it allows for the same members to be returned to office, thereby making for a continuity of experience and expertise across different assemblies. The indicative assembly does not promise such continuity, at least short of radical amendment, and it is hard to see how government could operate effectively if a completely new legislative body had to take over every year or so. But apart from this consideration, there are three other reasons why the electoral model ought to have much greater appeal.

The first is much cited in the literature on representative – that is, electorally and responsively representative – democracy, including in authors as different as John Hart Ely (1981), Joseph Schumpeter (1984), Juergen Habermas (1995), Stephen Holmes (1995) and Ian Shapiro (2003). A system of open, competitive, periodic election would require the satisfaction and reinforcement of a number of basic liberties, depending for its very operation on their successful exercise. But a system that was designed to facilitate indicative rather than responsive representation – or, for that matter, a plenary assembly system – would not be likely to have the same salutary impact.

The liberties I have in mind are the freedom of speech, association and travel that are required if people are to be able to stand for office, combine in parties, promote their policies and expose other parties, including the governing party, to criticism between and at the time of elections. It is only in a society where individuals have these freedoms – and, I would say, have them in the rich republican sense of escaping domination – that they can hope to continue to share equally in a system of independent influence over government. Let any of the freedoms be curtailed and the prospects for equally accessible or individualized influence are in immediate danger. Those who are exposed to any possibility of check or coercion in response to speech may not speak their piece in criticism of this or that proposal, for example. And their failure to speak will not provide default support for the proposal, as it might have done in various contexts. No matter what the

according to Rehfield (2005), is against this hypothesis. Still, districting does induce a similarity in one dimension – if, nowadays, a fairly unimportant one – between the population as a whole and the legislature that represents it.

context, people's silence will communicate nothing, since it can always be taken to reflect their lack of freedom (Pettit 1994).[18]

Let any of these freedoms be curtailed and not only does the prospect of equal, individualized access to influence decrease; so does the prospect for an unconditioned sort of influence. We saw in the last chapter that the people's influence will be unconditioned, and not granted as an indulgence of the government or the army or whatever, to the extent that the society is resistive: as a matter of actual fact and/or as a matter of common perception, people are disposed to resist any governmental abuse of power and government is disposed to respond to such resistance. It is only in a society where people actively exercise freedom of speech, association and travel – and are allowed to do so by government authorities – that these dispositions can assume the status of unchallenged facts, registered in the shared consciousness of the population. And so it is only in such a society that people can have influence over government, regardless of whether those in government – or those in any other agency – are happy to give them influence.

Where an electoral, responsive regime would require – and as it continues in existence, reinforce – a culture of freedom in the domain of speech, association and travel, the statistical, indicative regime would run the risk of failing to nurture such a culture. It might be introduced in the context of such freedoms, but its operation would not require their continuing exercise, at least outside the assembly itself. With any such freedom, it is at least likely that if you fail to use it, you lose it: your successful exercise of the freedom plays a crucial role in checking and confirming the absence of a power of interference on the part of others. Thus the statistical, indicative regime would expose a community to a very great danger that the electoral, responsive regime would actively serve to combat.

Apart from this consideration – and the consideration of continuity in office that we mentioned earlier – there is a second reason for preferring the electoral, responsive regime to the statistical, indicative one. I assume, on the basis of the argument in the last chapter, that a deliberative, democratic assembly, be it indicative or responsive, should mediate the influence of individuals in a particular direction or to a particular purpose; we postpone discussion of the required direction to the next chapter. The second consideration in favour of the responsively representative system is that it is more likely than the alternative to make it possible for people to impose a direction on government.

---

[18] For an exchange on this issue see Langton (1997) and Pettit (2007a).

A system of influence that is required to further a given purpose may fail in either of two ways. One involves false negatives, as they are called; the other false positives. False negatives consist in oversights: failures to propose or generate all the candidate policies that might promote the direction or purpose sought. False positives consist in mistakes: failures to test and filter out proposals that do not promote that direction or purpose, perhaps serving an inimical end instead. This double possibility of failure suggests that the ideal channel for popular influence will involve, first, an initial process that guards against oversights, generating an ample supply of candidates for consideration; second, a process that guards against mistakes, testing the candidates with a view to filtering out those that prove unsatisfactory; and third, a repeating sequence in which these interact in the identification of a final set of successful candidates. It will involve a complex process of a familiar generate-and-test character.

In a generate-and-test process, every element generated is tested before being allowed into the evolving product; it is incorporated in that product if and only if it passes the test (Dennett 1996). The procedure will be familiar from a variety of contexts. At one end of the spectrum of possible examples, it is illustrated by the process in which authors generate texts and editors test and filter them, so that what gets published is the joint product of both processes. At the other end it is illustrated by the process in which random mutation generates variations in existing genomes and natural selection tests the variations for whether they are adaptive – whether they increase the inclusive fitness of organisms – letting them survive only if they are.

Returning now to our two representative assemblies, it should be clear that the electoral, responsive assembly does considerably better on this count. The elected legislators have every incentive to search out policies that are likely to go down well with voters, competing as they do for voter support, so that they may be expected to generate a rich supply of candidates. And when they go to the electoral polls – and when they record voting intentions in opinion polls – the electing voters will have every incentive to scour both the policies proposed and the policies implemented to see how far they measure up to whatever metric they impose. Assuming that there is a suitable metric in operation – this, in effect, is the topic of the next chapter – the process has both of the elements required in a generate-and-test procedure.

Things are bound to be very different, however, with the statistical, indicative assembly – and indeed also with the plenary assembly. Such an assembly would not offer separate locations at which policies can be generated and tested and it would not provide actors with distinct incentives, on the one side, to generate an ample supply of candidate policies and, on the other, to test those candidates for how well they measure up to relevant desiderata. It promises a calm, smooth process of legislation, in which impartiality ought to prevail quite easily. But that promise is much less likely to deliver people from the false negatives and positives that threaten them than the two-dimensional, back-and-forth dynamic that we should expect to find in the presence of electoral competition.

The problem is made vivid in reflection on how we in a general population might feel about being governed by an indicative assembly. How would we be likely to react to being governed, this year by one contingently selected group of fellow citizens, the next year by another? We would surely want each group to be held to account for the policies it introduces in its period in office. It would seem utterly complacent to let an indicative assembly act as seems best without having to face any challenge from outside. True, the members would have to live under whatever laws they introduced and that has always been taken as an important check in republican thinking.[19] But is it check enough? Does it provide against the possibility of the group's being somewhat unimaginative or somewhat thoughtless, for example, in the decisions it makes? The answer, plausibly, is that it does not. The absence of a group of electors to whom they are answerable means that the members of an indicative assembly will not be kept on their toes in the same manner as the members of a responsive body.[20]

The two considerations just put forward for preferring the responsive to the indicative assembly will carry weight, quite independently of republican commitments. But there is a third consideration that carries particular weight from within our republican perspective.[21] This is that an indicative body, unlike a responsive, is necessarily linked with the spectre of a certain sort of domination. If such a body is given charge of the full range of legislative issues, then it will have a power to determine both the issues it considers and the resolutions that they are given. Operating as a corporate

---

[19] Algernon Sidney (1990: 571) endorses this constraint in the seventeenth century when he writes of members of Parliament: 'They may make prejudicial wars, ignominious treaties, and unjust laws. Yet when the session is ended, they must bear the burden as much as others.' Joseph Priestley (1993: 140) endorses it a century later when he raises and answers a question about the American colonists: 'Q. What is the great grievance that those people complain of? A. It is their being taxed by the parliament of Great Britain, the members of which are so far from taxing themselves, that they ease themselves at the same time.' See too Locke (1960: Section 138).

[20] This consideration is also relevant in assessing the use of lotteries defended in Burnheim (1985).

[21] I am grateful for observations on this issue to Niko Kolodny and Jake Zuehl.

agent, it will have to form a will of its own and exercise that will under few, if any, constraints. Not being subject to electoral challenges, however – or perhaps to the challenges that presuppose a vibrant, electorally nurtured culture of freedom – the assembly's will may be difficult for the people to control and render undominating. The assembly may have been chosen for the prospect of forming an indicatively representative and congenial will – a will that the population as a whole might well have formed in their place – but it will not be forced in any way to remain congenial; it will have the standing of a benevolent despot.

The lesson of this observation is that while we may rely on indicatively representative bodies to make decisions on particular issues, or particular ranges of issues, it would not be a good idea to give such an electorally uncontrolled body the open-ended authority of a legislative assembly. There may be no objection on republican grounds to a statistically representative body like the British Columbia Citizens' Assembly, which was charged with making a judgement and recommendation on the best voting system for their Province and on nothing more. But there would certainly be grounds for objecting to a statistically representative body that would have the open-ended discretion of legislature.[22]

Respresentative assemblies and assemblies of representatives

While these considerations argue strongly in favour of a primarily responsive assembly, it is important to recognize that depending on how things are otherwise organized, a responsive assembly may take either of two broad forms. To mark the distinction in perhaps too sharp a manner, it can be primarily a representative assembly or primarily an assembly of representatives.

In the case of the representative assembly, the aggregate decisions of the membership are responsive to dispositions in the electorate as a whole. In the case of the assembly of representatives, the individual decisions of members are responsive to the dispositions of their particular constituency or support base. In the first case, the assembly has the form of a corporate agent that primarily tracks the electorate in the decisions it takes as a body

---

[22] Might a non-agential collection of individuals, combining in the formation and imposition of a joint judgement on a particular issue, or a particular range of issues, still impose a freely formed will on the people as a whole? This is indeed a possibility but it is not a great danger, provided the group remains unincorporated and its members do not form a will that extends over an open range of issues. But the danger identified may still argue for guarding against the possibility of a conspiracy to dominate, as we might describe it. And the safeguard required is obviously that any policy supported by an indicatively representative assembly should be subject to an electoral check: endorsement by an independently representative body or, as in the case of a referendum, by the population as a whole.

(List and Pettit 2011). In the second case, the assembly is a collection of individuals who primarily track their own constituencies or supporters in the votes they cast within the assembly. And in this case, therefore, assembly decisions may not support a pattern that corresponds to any recognizable profile of demands in the electorate as a whole; they may be the product of ad hoc log-rolling and deal-making amongst the different members.[23]

This somewhat artificial distinction maps the difference, in broad terms, between the Westminster and Washington systems. In the Westminster system of parliamentary, non-proportional democracy, government is generally under the control of one cohesive party or alliance of parties.[24] In the Washington system of presidential democracy, government is not subject to a similar cohesive control. Because the executive in the Westminster system is upheld by the legislature, those legislators who support the government have to close ranks and vote according to an agreed programme, else the executive will fall. Because the executive is elected independently in the Washington system, members of the legislature – even members of the President's own party – are not subject to the same pressure and can operate more or less independently. Thus the main Westminster parties can go to the electorate with detailed programmes that they are in a position to implement, so that government policies are determined in good measure before the election. But Washington representatives are not in a position to do this, since government policies will be determined in one-by-one deals between members of the two houses and the administration; policies will be determined post-election, not pre-election.

The Westminster Parliament can be responsive to the electorate as a whole insofar as it implements policies that have electoral support. But the dark side of that responsiveness is that individual members of the assembly will be able to do little in response to the demands of their particular constituents; whether they belong to the government party or the opposition party they will be expected to vote in general on party lines. The Washington Congress allows individual members of the House and Senate to be responsive to the demands of their particular constituents. But again, that responsiveness has a dark side, since the system as a whole will often be

---

[23] In his famous account of how he thought democracy ought to work, Edmund Burke (1999) derided this sort of assembly as a 'congress of ambassadors'.

[24] It is important that the system I have in mind here is not only parliamentary in character, with the legislature electing the administration, but also that it is non-proportional. Where many parties have to combine to form government, as is typical of highly proportional systems, then the system will be more like Washington than Westminster. Thus, to anticipate the text, so many parties will be needed to form government that policy is mainly going to be determined post-election in inter-party deals.

unresponsive to the country-wide demands of the electorate. While both count as deputies, the members of the representative assembly are likely to behave as trustees, to invoke our earlier distinction, and the members of the assembly of representatives to behave as delegates (Pitkin 1972).

This is not the place to make a judgement on the merits of these two very different systems of responsive representation, though the Westminster system seems likely to serve republican goals more reliably. In any full-scale assessment of democratic designs it would be essential to take account of the differences between the systems and to judge on their specific advantages and disadvantages, but this book does not attempt that sort of detailed assessment. Abstracting from detailed institutional recommendations, the aim is to explore how far any democracy that is organized to broad republican specifications can ensure the legitimacy of the state.

Remedying electoral shortfalls

This extended discussion leads us to go along with common sense in making electoral institutions into a centrepiece of any democratic system. But I hope that seeing those institutions against the alternatives of the plenary assembly on the one side and the indicatively representative assembly on the other will enable us to recognize the special merits of having a body of elected, responsively representative legislators. Such a body ought to be capable, unlike the plenary assembly, of exercising the reflective deliberation needed to guard against voting up proposals that are inconsistent in logic or in practice. And when they operate well, the institutions required for the existence and operation of an elected legislature ought to ensure that the society is marked by freedom of speech, association and travel, and that it recruits ordinary electors to the interrogation of public policy.

The overall thrust of the argument in this book, as will become clear, is that democracy is defined, not by the presence of electoral institutions, but rather by the fact that the people exercise control over government, enjoying equally accessible influence in the imposition of an equally acceptable direction. There may be possible scenarios where people achieve democratic control in the absence of electoral institutions and that already means that democracy cannot be defined by reference to election. But it should be clear nonetheless that on the account adopted here, the tie between the two is very tight indeed.[25]

---

[25] Notwithstanding other differences on issues of constitutional design, I hope that these remarks will signal a deep level of agreement with Richard Bellamy (2007), who also works within the republican research programme.

Electoral institutions are necessary in practice, if not in strict logic, for giving influence and control to the people. They force people to exercise their freedoms in political action, whether as candidates or supporters, critics or activists, and they thereby reinforce the enjoyment of those very freedoms. They push political parties into exploring the space of possible policies and they require ordinary citizens to form and express their views in response. They constitute the catalyst that triggers and sustains the process whereby people may hope to gain influence over government.

But, however essential in practice, electoral institutions do not suffice on their own to maintain a suitable system of popular influence. There are serious problems that need to be addressed if an electoral system is to provide the form of popular influence that is required for democratic control in the republican sense. It is only if we can identify institutional means for remedying such electoral shortfalls, therefore, that we can hope to achieve democracy under the republican specification of what it requires.

The main requirement on a system of popular influence, as we saw in the last chapter, is that it must be equally accessible to all citizens. This parallels the requirement, to be explored in the next chapter, that the direction it imposes should be equally acceptable to all. But not only should the system of influence be individualized in this sense; it should also be unconditioned, as we put it, and efficacious. Assuming that it imposes a popular direction, as it must do in order to constitute control, its operating to a directive effect should not be conditioned on the willingness of the government, or any other party, to go along; and it should not allow for the influence of private will in public decision-making beyond what the tough-luck test would allow.

An electoral system of popular influence raises problems on all three fronts, since it might fail to be individualized, unconditioned or efficacious. I shall review these over the final three sections, making suggestions about the institutional measures that might provide remedies. My institutional suggestions are meant to be illustrative of the initiatives that might be taken and should not be treated as definitive recommendations for action; such recommendations would have to be guided, not just by philosophical analysis, but also by empirical observation and modelling. What the suggestions show, I hope, is that there is no reason to despair about the possibility of setting up a suitably democratic system of influence. All that is needed is imaginative institutional design.

3. AN INDIVIDUALIZED SYSTEM OF INFLUENCE

Individualizing electoral influence

In order for citizens to control the state in such a way that it is not a dominating force in their lives, it is not enough for them to enjoy collective control over those in power. Such collective control would be consistent with the domination of individuals who fail to go along with the collectively expressed wishes of the group. What is required, as we saw, is a system of collective control in which individuals equally share. The influence mediated by the system must be equally accessible to all and the direction imposed must be equally acceptable to all.

Here we focus on the influence that is generated under an electoral system of government. The question is whether an electoral system could give all individuals the same share in determining the impact of the influence it mediates. Under an electoral system, individuals may vote in a referendum to determine a particular policy issue. Or they may directly vote to elect members of the legislative assembly and indirectly elect the administrative and judicial authorities that the assembly is responsible for appointing. Or, as in the United States, they may even have a direct role in electing certain members of the administration and judiciary. The question we face is whether such an electoral process is enough in itself to ensure people's equal access to influence – whether it is enough to give people an equal share in determining the impact of electoral influence.

In some systems of collective influence the marginal contributions of individuals who make the same inputs are bound to be the same. Consider the simple physical system of influence constituted by a group of individuals pushing on a giant billiard ball – say, a sphere six feet in diameter – where there are differences in the direction in which they wish to move it. Let them each push in their preferred direction, assuming the optimal position for doing so, so that the direction the ball eventually takes is determined by the resultant of the different forces they constitute. Under such a system of continuous influence, as we might describe it, if all individuals contribute the same inputs – if they enjoy the same degree of strength and they each gain the same traction on the ball – then they will each make a difference of the same magnitude as others to the exact trajectory of the ball; they will share equally in determining the impact of their joint influence on that trajectory. In our terms, the system of influence will be perfectly individualized; the influence it implements will be equally accessible to each.

Under a system of electoral influence, the requirements for ensuring that all individuals control the same inputs are straightforward. Every individual should have the same voting power, access to voting should be equal for all, and votes should be aggregated in a way that privileges no voter over others; for short, every vote should have the same value. People's votes will not have the same value, and people will not have equal access to influence, if for example the more educated have extra votes, as John Stuart Mill (1964) recommended. Equally, people's votes will not have the same value if it is more difficult for some individuals to vote, due to poverty or other pressures.[26] And, of course, people's votes will not have the same value if the voting systems under which they operate are not appropriate: if, for example, the districting system allows electorally equivalent districts to vary in the size of population. But these difficulties are straightforwardly remediable, if not always easily remedied, and we may assume that the institutions in place do not offend on this count.[27]

Would the fact that people can cast equally valuable votes ensure that each has access to the possibility of sharing equally in determining the impact? Clearly not. Any electoral institutions will implement a system of discontinuous, as distinct from continuous, influence, whether in the selection of a particular representative, in the determination of who is in government, or in the resolution of a particular policy issue. In such a system there will always be winners and losers, with the relevant output satisfying the wishes of the winners and frustrating the wishes of the losers. Thus there is going to be little or no sense in which the losers can feel that, equally with the winners, they contributed to determining the direction in which things were moved on

[26] Examples of such exclusion occur in many parts of the United States, where the papers that voters have to produce in proof of their identity at the polls are not always in the possession of the poorer; or where those who are convicted felons lose their right to vote, even when they have completed their prison sentences. Such abuses argue strongly in favour of the compulsory system of voting employed, for example, in Australia. This system imposes a small fine on those who do not register at the polls, and have no independent excuse to offer, but it ensures a voter turn-out well above 95 per cent; more important, again, it ensures that those who do not turn up at the polls are a more or less random group, not a specific class. See Hill (2000) and A. Fowler's unpublished paper, 'Turnout Matters: Evidence from Compulsory Voting in Australia', for relevant background on the effects of compulsory voting. Under non-compulsory systems it is always possible, perhaps even likely, that the poorer and underprivileged will be systematically ignored in political circles; see Bartels (2008).

[27] Many systems give rise to this last difficulty when there is a second house, such as the Australian or the US Senate, to which states of different sizes elect members in equal numbers. This might not be a problem, if the second house had a distinct function from the lower house in those countries, but other things being equal it is a problem as things actually stand and it does call for reform. Other things may not be equal, as suggested in the next chapter, to the extent that apart from a norm of equal influence, people in a society like Australia or the United States also endorse a norm – perhaps for contingent historical reasons – to the effect that states should have equal senatorial representation.

any issue, whether moved in the immediate fashion of a referendum or in a manner mediated by the decisions of elected representatives.[28]

The discontinuous nature of electoral influence raises a serious problem for how we might individualize the influence mediated under an electoral system, letting it resemble the influence achieved under a continuous system where, as the example with the ball shows, individuals can share equally in determining the impact of their joint influence. Individuals will not share equally in determining the impact of any particular electoral exercise and so it may seem that they cannot be provided with individualized influence of the kind we are seeking.

But while this is a serious problem, there is a more or less salient solution on offer. Although individuals cannot share equally in determining the impact of any particular electoral exercise, it might be that with each of the issues resolved in such an exercise, they have an equal chance of sharing equally in the determination of the impact – an equal chance of being on the winning side.[29] And if they had an equal chance of winning, then we could scarcely hold that the system of influence was not appropriately individualized.

Things might be arranged, following this proposal, so that there is no *ex ante* reason to think that for any randomly chosen pair of individuals, there will be a difference between their chances of being on the winning side on any randomly chosen issue. This condition will be satisfied under a system where each person has the same vote, and each vote has the same value just so long as one further proviso is fulfilled. This is that the issues over which they vote are ones where there is no *ex ante* reason to think – no reason grounded in their identity or character, as that is determined independently of their disposition to vote – that some are bound to vote for a particular side. But this proviso, alas, is not always going to be satisfied. It will flounder on a problem that has become famous as the problem of an 'elective despotism' or a 'tyranny of the majority' (Madison, Hamilton and Jay 1987: no. 10).

The tyranny of the majority

Suppose that a group of five people meet weekly to play cards or chess and dine together afterwards at one of two local restaurants, one specializing in

---

[28] The only sense in which they might each make a contribution is in determining the size of the winning majority – and in some circumstances, the size of that majority is politically significant. See Guerrero (2010).

[29] Why not require that they have an equal chance of being decisive? Mainly because the chance of any individual's being decisive in a majority vote among a large number is close to zero. I am grateful for comments on this point from Niko Kolodny.

vegetarian food, the other not. And suppose that with a view to giving each equally accessible influence over the choice of restaurant, they let the choice be determined by majority vote on every occasion. This system will work well to the extent that the majority rotates across weeks – to the extent, in other words, that the majority is mobile. But it will work very badly if there are two people, say two vegetarians, who invariably vote for a vegetarian restaurant while the other three invariably vote for the other. In the case of such a sticky divide, the system of majority voting will continue to give each an equal vote but the voters will not have an equal chance of being on the winning side. The stickiness of the divide between majority and minority means that equal votes are not enough to ensure equally accessible influence for the different voters; those in the minority are more or less permanently locked out of the possibility of being amongst the winners.

Much has been written for and against various voting systems, whether as systems for the election of representatives by the electorate or for decision-making in a legislature or in a referendum. But whatever voting system is introduced in such a context there is always a possibility that for similar reasons it will not provide people with an equal chance of being on the winning side and so not ensure the equal access to influence that republican theory would require. On one or another range of issues there may always be a more or less sticky divide between a majority and a minority and, if there is, then on that range of issues people will not enjoy equal access to influence, not having the same *ex ante* chance of being on the winning side; the patterns of electoral or legislative voting may shut out the minority. Those of a minority religion are going to be in this situation with an issue like whether to set up the majority religion as an established church; those of a minority culture with an issue like whether to authorize only a mainstream pattern – say, the use of the majority language – in public life; and those of a minority sexual orientation with an issue like whether to give full civic recognition only to heterosexual unions.

The problem of the sticky divide is that there are independently identified individuals who, on certain issues, are more or less bound to be on the losing side. It is important that the individuals who are bound to lose are independently identified – say, identified on the basis of creed or colour, race or sexual orientation – not identified just by their disposition to vote a certain way on those issues. Otherwise we would have to say that just by being unlucky enough to choose minority views on various issues people would be deprived of access to equal influence. Otherwise, indeed, we would have to say that just by being contrarian enough always to choose views that look likely to be in the minority, people would be deprived of access to equal influence.[30] There will be no problem if individuals who are *ex ante* as likely to choose one as another side on given issues happen in general to choose the losing side or aim in general to choose the losing side. The problem is confined to the case where there is *ex ante* reason, associated with their independently fixed identity, to think that certain individuals will be in the minority on given issues: their identity pre-commits them, as we might say, on those issues.

How serious is this sort of problem likely to be? Our interest in having individuals share equally in the system whereby the people influence government derives from the fact that otherwise they will fail to share equally in control of government and will be exposed to a degree of discrimination and domination at the hands of those in power. The problem raised will certainly be serious if a sticky minority is shut out from having equal influence on any issue of significance: for example, any issue where being shut out means that they do not share equally with others in determining the basic liberties that all are to enjoy, or do not share equally in controlling the sort of resourcing or protection that is secured by the state for those basic liberties. When members of a minority group have an identity fixed by something like creed, or colour, or race, and there is an issue to be decided by majority voting on which that identity pre-commits them, then that issue is very likely to have such significance. And so the inequality of influence suffered by a sticky minority is bound to be of concern (Guinier 1994).

Beyond the tyranny of the majority

How to respond to the problem raised by sticky minority–majority divides? I see only one realistic possibility, which is to introduce a system of individualized contestation that parallels the collective challenge that elections make possible.[31] There ought to be openings for particular individuals and subgroups to test the laws or proposals for how far the process in which they are generated respects the value of equal access to influence and, more generally, the value of equal status. And those openings ought to hold out

---

[30] There is a scope ambiguity, as logicians describe it, between the characterization of the case where there is a sticky-divide problem and the characterization of the case where there isn't. In the former case we say that there are individuals such that there are issues on which those individuals are in a minority; in the latter we say that there are issues such that there are individuals who are in a minority on those issues.

[31] Electoral challenge can be seen, of course, as a form of collective contestation; on this point see McCormick (2011: 152).

the prospect of an impartial judgement on the question and, if the judgement goes in favour of the challenges, the prospect of an adjustment that
satisfies them.

Under plausible assumptions about our little group of five, the members
will be easily granted such individualized, potentially effective contestation.
The vegetarians will be free to point out the effect of majority voting and to
argue on grounds of equal access to influence for an adjustment to the
pattern. Here there is an obvious alternative: to let the members take turns
in dictating where they are to eat (Risse 2004). The ethos of any plausible
group is likely to support the egalitarian objection, and to prompt the
adoption of the alternative mode of decision-making.

As with the vegetarians in this example, people whose religious or cultural
identity pre-commits them to taking a particular side on certain issues can
enjoy equal influence over government only insofar as they are able to
contest the appropriateness of majority voting in a referendum or via a
legislature for determining such issues. They have to be able to make the
case for why majority voting on those issues ensures that they do not share
equally with others in controlling for the direction taken by government.
And they have to be able to expect that the case they make in contesting the
law or proposal receives an impartial hearing and is dealt with appropriately.

Allowing for the contestation of the results of a majoritarian voting
system – or of any comparable system of individual inputs to aggregative
decision-making – certainly makes things messy. But it is hard to see how
anyone who is concerned with giving people equal access to influence over
government could disallow it. Jeremy Waldron (1999a, 1999b) offers powerful support for majority voting on the grounds that it does better than
alternatives in the promotion of equal influence. But how could we invoke
the value of such equality in the exogenous design of a voting system
without allowing that if there is ground to argue that the system is not
actually delivering equality, then voters should be able to argue for one or
another amendment to the system (Beitz 1989)? To deny voters the right to
invoke the value of equality in critique of a system that is chosen for its
promise of delivering equality would be to fail to honour that very value.[32]

---

[32] Waldron (2006: 1364) takes a more congenial line in arguing that although the members of a
democratic society, on his assumptions, 'believe in majority rule as a rough general principle for
politics, they accept that individuals have certain interests and are entitled to certain liberties that
should not be denied simply because it would be more convenient for most people to deny them.
They believe that minorities are entitled to a degree of support, recognition, and insulation that is not
necessarily guaranteed by their numbers or by their political weight.' I am grateful to Caleb Yong for
drawing this to my attention.

When a system of influence allows individuals to invoke in criticism of its operations the very equality of influence it is designed to promote, then it counts in an established term as a recursive procedure (Benhabib 1996). It exemplifies a system that may be put into operation, not just in shaping distinct, external issues, but in shaping the very form that it assumes itself. To canonize majority rule – to give it sacred and unquestionable status – would be to deny the possibility of recursion and, inevitably, the possibility of reforming the system itself. To allow majority rule to be subject to contestation and amendment, and to keep the possibility of continued contestation and amendment alive, is to keep future developments open.

Institutional implications

In analysing how a representative assembly might operate – a responsively rather than an indicatively representative body – I abstracted from the precise details of the electoral system that ought to be introduced. This argument for allowing the individualized contestability of the assembly has been put forward under a similar abstraction from institutional detail. But it should be clear, in broad outline, what sorts of measures are likely to be required. A system that allows potentially effective, individualized contestability will have to provide, not just for contestability proper but, pre-contestation, for transparency in the decisions contested and, post-contestation, for impartiality in resolving the charges raised. The requirements are as follows.

- Transparency: the capacity of members of the society to know what proposals are under consideration and what measures have passed.
- Contestability: the opportunity for members to challenge overtures both in advance of legislation and after they have passed into law.
- Impartiality: the availability of forums in which challengers can expect an impartial assessment and, ideally, resolution.

What these measures require at a more specific level is an issue for detailed institutional design, as with the more specific requirements in a districting or voting system. According to standard thinking, often influenced by the long republican tradition, transparency will be enhanced by forcing the legislative assembly to debate its measures in public; to give recognition and exposure to the minority of legislators who constitute an opposition; to impose constraints on themselves, and on all public authorities, to justify their decisions in public; to ensure the existence of independent, potentially critical media; to allow for the formation of civic watchdog bodies that can track what is done in government; and so on.

Equally, according to this traditional body of thought, the opportunity for challenge argues for opening up channels of consultation and appeal between the public and the legislature; for establishing a system of courts and other tribunals in which challenges to laws can be heard and decided; for appointing independent officials and bodies in ombudsman or auditor roles, enabling them to raise challenges in the name of individuals; for recognizing constraints of rule of law and due process that authorities ought to be held to account for breaching; and for allowing the sorts of public meetings and demonstrations that may be necessary to muster more radical challenges to the status quo. Only in the presence of arrangements like this will the government be contestable.

And finally, so traditional wisdom goes, the need to ensure an overtly impartial system of adjudication and resolution makes a case for appointing the members of courts and tribunals, and the officials on ombudsman or auditor bodies, under constraints that give them general credibility; for establishing the independence of those authorities; and for providing plaintiffs with the opportunity to launch appeals against the decisions of those authorities themselves. This requirement of impartiality will only be capable of being fulfilled, of course, in a community where people are genuinely willing to live on equal terms with all others, even those in a perhaps recalcitrant minority. If such a spirit of accommodation and compromise is lacking, then there is very little hope of achieving the ideal envisaged here (Bellamy 1999; Margalit 2010). The best prospect for satisfying the ideal may be to allow the society to divide into two or more states or to organize itself as a federation of relatively independent regions.

How might issues of equal access to influence be resolved as a result of contestation? One resolution might be to find an alternative mode of decision-making, parallel to the resolution of the problem with our little club, which does not offend in the same way as majority voting. This sort of resolution might take any of a number of forms, ranging from giving members of the minority a special weight in the decision-making to relying on indicative assemblies or deliberative opinion polls to advise or decide on the issue, to creating special, presumptively impartial commissions to adjudicate on the matter, to establishing target quotas that ought to be satisfied in any area of decision-making.

Another resolution would be to take the issue out of the domain of popular voting altogether. Such a response would disallow the use of regular voting procedures to make the majority religion – or on similar grounds any minority religion – into an established church. And more generally, it would disallow the use of such voting procedures to give any significant privileges to those who belong to a more or less fixed majority – or, of course, to those who belong to any fixed minority. In effect, it would preserve the possibility of people's sharing equally in influencing and controlling government by denying government authority over issues where the equal sharing of influence and control is just not possible.

There is an obvious danger that a system of individualized contestation may prove unworkable, creating a build-up and backlog of endless complaints. This argues for establishing standardized ways of dealing with different types of issue where people's equal access to influence is generally agreed to be in danger. Those standardized responses might authorize appeal to special decision-making forums or routines of the kind at which we gestured. Or they might establish individual rights against majority-based decision-making. Such rights would have to be laid out in a formal or informal constitution that was not itself subject to simple majoritarian amendment. The effect of constitutionally protected rights would be to put various issues off the popular agenda, as with familiar measures that disallow majority voting on whether to set up an established religion, on whether to give special rights to heterosexuals, on whether to privilege those in a particular ethnic group, and the like. The intent of the protection, as I interpret it here, would not be to put brakes on the influence of the people, compromising democratic process. Rather it would be to ensure that the democratic system satisfies two widely recognized, democratic desiderata: on the one side, that people should have truly equal access to influence; and on the other, that the channels through which popular influence flows should not be allowed to clog up (Ely 1981).[33]

Serious exercises in institutional design are well beyond the scope of this book and these comments are not meant as contributions to such a project.[34] I make them only to illustrate in a broad way the sorts of processes that are going to be mandated once we recognize that people's equal access to influence over government requires the introduction of procedures for

---

[33] I assume that a system of rights can be made to work productively, without cramping democratic initiative (for such concerns see Schwartzberg 2007; Tully 2009).

[34] The fact that I avoid making any detailed institutional proposals may suggest that in the perspective adopted here, the status quo in most democracies is pretty well OK. I do not support that suggestion. I believe that there is much work to be done in theoretically elaborating and empirically testing the institutional requirements of republican ideals and that this work may support quite radical measures, including measures of which we may currently have no inkling. Take a proposal, then, like that which John McCormick (2011) makes for a people's lottery-selected tribunate. It would be a serious mistake to think that because I do not endorse it here, there is a deep rift between the radical republican democracy for which he looks and the image of republican democracy developed in this book. There is no necessary divergence between us, at least not on this ground; I am conducting an argument at a level of abstraction that makes it impossible to explore such proposals.

the individualized testing of any policies generated and of any processes used in the generation of policies. It requires giving people an editorial, as well as an authorial, role – a role in testing as well as generating policies – and, in particular, an editorial role that has an individualized and not just a collective dimension.[35]

4. AN UNCONDITIONED SYSTEM OF INFLUENCE

The desideratum

We assume that the influence people have under an electorally centred system is supposed to impose a certain direction on government; this assumption will be at the centre of concern in the next chapter. It is important to recognize that people might be able to use their electoral and contestatory influence to elicit such a direction on the part of those in authority, without this system of influence being unconditioned or independent. They might be able to prescribe for such a direction only because those in power, wanting perhaps to think of themselves as democrats, like to let their policies correspond to popular demands. Or they might be able to prescribe for the direction only because some background power such as a military service or a moneyed elite or an imperial overseer happens to favour government policies that are popularly satisfying.

If the people had a directive influence over government only by this sort of courtesy or connivance, then that influence would not give them control or power over government. Control requires that the correlation between popular demand and government supply should be robust across variations in the will of government or in the will of any third party. Let the correlation be contingent or conditioned in this way, and it will be the agency on which the correlation depends that enjoys power or control, not the people whom that agency chooses to benefit.

One of the main concerns that recurs in the history of Italian–Atlantic republicanism is the fear that the independence of the people as a source of directive influence on government is going to be very difficult to maintain. That independence will be jeopardized under two conditions, so Richard Price (1991: 78–9) argued. One is when a foreign state allows a people to govern itself but reserves the right to suspend the arrangement so that it is 'liable to be altered, suspended or over-ruled at the discretion of the state

---

[35] For earlier treatments in which these two dimensions of democracy are emphasized see Pettit (1999, 2000a, 2000b).

which possesses the sovereignty'. And the other is when the representatives of the people operate under a 'higher will which directs their resolutions, and on which they are dependent'. In this condition, as in the first, government acts under the influence of the people but because that influence is conditional on the acquiescence of a higher will, the government is subject to 'no controul from the people'.[36]

What measures would be likely to give an independent, unconditioned character to the system of popular influence available under an electoral and contestatory regime? I ignore the problem on the international front, since it would take us into the domain of international relations. The question we confront is, what measures might guard the system against exhibiting a domestically conditioned variety of popular influence: a sort of influence that remains in place only to the extent that government, or some collateral power, is content for it to remain in place?

In discussing this issue in the last chapter we saw that the only assured safeguard is a resistive community: that is, a community in which, as a matter of fact and/or common belief, people are disposed to resist government, should it ignore popular influence, and government is disposed to avoid triggering resistance. Just the presence of an electoral system, even one that is adjusted in a contestatory way so as to ensure individualized influence, is obviously not enough to guarantee such a resistive culture. So what initiatives might we take to promote this desideratum?

---

[36] The concern with being subject to foreign control was central to the complaints of the American colonists after the repeal of the Stamp Act in 1766. While the repeal seemed to recognize the right of colonial subjects – or at least propertied, mainstream males – to govern themselves on a more or less popular basis, it came with a sting in the tail. The Westminster Parliament did indeed withdraw an act that had seemed to violate that right but it insisted at the same time, in the so-called Declaratory Act, that it did so as matter of grace, not because of any obligation. Parliament, so it was declared, 'had, hath, and of right ought to have, full power and authority to make laws and statutes of sufficient force and validity to bind the colonies and people of *America*, subjects of the crown of *Great Britain*, in all cases whatsoever'. See the unpublished paper by J. Rakove, A. R. Rutten and B. R. Weingast, 'Ideas, Interests, and Credible Commitments in the American Revolution', and, for theoretical background to that paper, Weingast (1997).

This sort of concern was widespread in that period. Thus in 1782 the Westminster Parliament was pressed into repealing a law of 1720 under which the Dublin Parliament – not, of course, a very representative body – could have its resolutions nullified in London; this law had been designed, in its own words, 'for the better securing the dependency of the kingdom of Ireland on the crown of Great Britain' (Stewart 1993: 26). But critics protested that repeal was not enough, since it did not entail a renunciation of Westminster's right to overrule them. And then, perhaps because of the lesson learned in America, Westminster responded by passing such a renunciation in 1783. See Stewart (1993: Chapter 4). Perhaps it was for that reason that in seeking to end home rule in 1800, London did not suppress the Dublin Parliament but induced its members, largely on the basis of bribes, to dissolve the body.

I propose that two absolutely crucial measures for promoting it correspond to the two institutional elements that characterize Italian–Atlantic republicanism: on the one side, the mixed constitution and, on the other, the contestatory citizenry. If the constitution is mixed, then government is likely to be resistance-averse, and if the citizenry has a contestatory character, then the people are likely to be resistance-prone. The society, in short, is likely to be resistive.

The individualization of popular influence already argues for a degree of mixture in the constitution, for example in the separation of adjudicative power from other forms of power. And the individualization of popular influence requires people to be contestatory in the assertion of their individual and minority claims against majoritarian neglect. The best hope for making popular influence unconditioned or independent is to push for further developments on these fronts. In outlining the developments needed, as I now go on to do, I shall assume that the requirements for an electoral system in which influence is individualized are already in place. The need for transparency, contestability and impartiality has already been institutionally satisfied.

The mixed constitution

Jean Bodin and Thomas Hobbes inaugurated the assault on the mixed constitution, arguing that there could be no functionally satisfactory state – no state capable of effectively formulating and enforcing law – in the absence of a single, absolute sovereign, be that sovereign a monarch, as they each preferred, or an aristocratic or democratic assembly. This assault should not be surprising, given the concern of each with having an absolutely sovereign government that is capable of establishing peace and order in a world of deep religious and civil conflict. They each saw that the price of having such a sovereign was the exposure of the people to the whim of that individual or body. But while they thought that it was desirable for the sovereign to abide by customary and other constraints, and not to act on whim, they were each prepared to pay that price. They each held that a sovereign could breach such constraints without ceasing to be sovereign. Thus Bodin (1967: 1.8.26) held that, notwithstanding 'manifest tyranny', the 'tyrant is a true sovereign for all that', and Hobbes (1994b: Review and Conclusion) argued that 'the name of tyranny signifieth nothing more nor less than the name of sovereignty, be it in one or many men'.[37]

---

[37] One way of marking their position is to say that they were positivists about sovereignty. Just as positivists about law argue that even bad law – even law that breaches natural law – should still count as law, they argue that even the bad sovereign – even, for example, the tyrannical sovereign – should

Bodin and Hobbes adopted an antagonistic stance towards the mixed constitution, because they saw quite clearly what that arrangement, as it was characterized and celebrated by Polybius (1954), Cicero (1998) and Machiavelli (1965), was designed to do. It was meant to ensure that the state could not have the sort of power that would allow authorities to impose their own, arbitrary will on the people they govern. And so it was straightforwardly inconsistent, as Bodin and Hobbes saw it, with the sort of role that they envisaged for sovereign and state.

While traditional defenders of the mixed constitution present it in received terms as a mixture of the three pure constitutional types, monarchy, aristocracy and democracy, this rhetorical trope serves to encode straightforward institutional constraints. They divide into constraints associated with any constitutional order, on the one side, and constraints associated with the mixing of powers on the other. The constitutional constraints require that government should operate in accordance with due process, not ruling by ad hoc decree but via public, general and prospective regulations (Fuller 1971; O'Donnell 2004). They impose what has come to be known as a rule of law under which, as Cicero (1998: 151) expressed the ideal, 'a magistrate is speaking law, and law a silent magistrate'. The mixture constraints require something designed to be supportive of such a rule of law: that different governmental powers be held in different hands; that those different powers should be shared out amongst different, mutually checking agents or agencies; and that the centres of power should be designed to give all sectors of the people a fair presence or representation in the exercise of power. To put the lesson in a slogan, the mixture of the mixed constitution requires a separation of powers, a sharing of powers and a balancing of powers.

What are the powers of government that should be separated under the mixed constitution (Gwyn 1965; Vile 1967)? The answer that became standard under the influence of the Baron de Montesquieu (1989) is, the powers of legislation, administration and adjudication. But that may be over-inclusive in one way, under-inclusive in another. It may be over-inclusive in calling for the separation of legislation and administration, since the experience of Westminster systems of government is that there is no real danger – and there may be some real benefit – in not separating

---

still count as sovereign. And just as positivists take law to count as law in virtue of serving a certain function – for example, that identified in Hart (1961) – so they take the sovereign to count as sovereign in virtue of serving the function they identify as crucial: that of establishing peace and order in the society. For some cautionary remarks about the interpretation of Hobbes on this point, see Hoekstra (2001).

those branches. And it may be under-inclusive in failing to call for the separation of different branches of the armed and police forces, the separation of secular from religious authorities, and indeed, the separation of centres of political power from those in control of commerce and business. Such divisions are liable to be just as important as more formal devices in guarding against the abuse of public power.[38]

How should any power be shared under the mixed constitution? Bodin's early critics pointed out that there were many ways in which law-making might be shared amongst different individuals or bodies, or divided out amongst them (Besold 1618: 279–80; Cabot 1751; Franklin 1991). The same remains true today. Thus the legislative power might be dispersed by giving the right to propose laws to one body or official, the right to decide on the proposal to another; by having two or more legislative houses, as in standard bicameral systems; by exposing the power of those houses to the constraint of the courts, as the individualization of influence requires; and/or by giving a formal or effective veto to the administration over what laws are to stand or be enforced.[39] This is not the place, however, to discuss the relative merits of such arrangements or the virtues of combining them in different ways.

The balancing of powers complemented the required separation and sharing of powers in the traditional image of the mixed constitution (Richter 1977). The constitution was to combine the inputs of nobility and commons, as in the traditional picture, and thereby ensure that no one was excluded from influence. This requirement was interpreted in a demanding, democratic spirit by writers like Machiavelli (1965) in the sixteenth century – see McCormick (2011) – and by radical commonwealth writers in eighteenth-century England (Lieberman 2006). That interpretation emphasizes that popular acquiescence in how a regime operates is the ultimate guarantor of a constitution and that this gives the citizenry as a whole a special role in the maintenance of the regime.

[38] For an original and congenial development of this encompassing view of the separation – and also the sharing and balancing – of powers, see Braithwaite (1997). And for a consciously republican application of the view in the analysis of policy-making in an emerging democracy, see Braithwaite, Charlesworth and Soares (2012).

[39] Thus it might be worth noting that Athens shared out legislative power between the ecclesia, the courts and the law-amending body, the *nomothetai* (Hansen 1991; Ober 1996) and that among other measures Rome had distinct law-making bodies such as the tribal and centuriate assemblies (Millar 1998). This particular Roman arrangement creates different possible sources of law where most arrangements create different possible veto points. For a nice discussion of the futility of looking for which institution was really the sovereign in ancient Athens, see Ober (1996: 120–1).

Bodin and Hobbes and like-minded opponents of the mixed constitution would not have objected greatly to the separation of powers as
such, since they were happy to allow the administration of government
to be delegated to other hands. And neither would they have railed
against the balancing of powers, even interpreted radically, since they
allowed that an inclusive, majoritarian democracy was a legitimate, if not
a desirable, regime. Their real opposition would have been to the sharing
of legislative power, since it appeared, particularly in combination with a
sharing of administrative and judicial powers, to ensure that government
would be unable to close ranks and assert its authority in unruly and
divisive times.

From our point of view, of course, it is good that government should be
unable to close ranks in this way. To the extent that the agencies of
government are unable to make common cause against popular pressure,
they will be more disposed to try to avoid triggering popular resistance. Any
one governing agent or agency may be tempted to challenge popular feeling
and to face down popular resistance. But the very fact that the state acts only
when its component bodies all come into alignment – and that it is forced to
act under the constraints of a rule of law – means that the government as a
whole is less likely to be disposed to display such bravado. That government
will not be as ready as any individual part might be to ignore or push back
against popular resistance.

In concluding this discussion of the mixed constitution, it may be useful
to point out that apart from being institutionally worrisome, the absolutist
critique launched by Bodin and Hobbes – and supported in different ways
by Rousseau and Kant (Pettit 2012b) – is philosophically misconceived.
Bodin and Hobbes assume that in order to be a source of coherent law the
state has to perform as an agent or agency with a single mind – a person,
they often say – and that in order to be a source of effective sanction it has to
have absolute power. The first claim is the most relevant in the argument
against the mixed constitution. Building on the assumed need for an agent
or agency with a single mind, they each maintain that this would be
unavailable if the constitution allowed for independent centres of power,
however coordinated. 'It is impossible that the commonwealth, which is
one body, should have many heads,' Bodin (1967: VI.4.198) writes. If it were
organized in that way, Hobbes maintains, then we would have 'not one
independent commonwealth, but three independent factions; nor
one representative person, but three' (Hobbes 1994b: 29.16). And, as we
saw in the Introduction, Rousseau (1997: II.2.2) takes up the theme with

relish, arguing that under the mixed constitution the sovereign is turned into 'a being that is fantastical and formed of disparate parts'.[40]

We can agree for reasons already rehearsed that it is essential, as all thinkers assume, that the state or commonwealth should operate like a single agent or person in delivering and applying law. To be an agent in the appropriate sense is to be an individual or body that can recognize demands like those of consistency and prove responsive to them. It is to be susceptible to the constraints and challenges of reason in the adoption of ends and in the formation of judgements as to how best to promote those ends. These critics argue against the mixed constitution because they assume that in order for a state to assume such an agential or personal status, there has to be a spokesperson available to speak for it. This spokesperson may be a king or queen, they say, or an aristocratic or democratic assembly that operates under majority rule. More generally, it has to be a spatio-temporally concrete entity, not an entity that exists on the basis of how different individuals or bodies operate and coordinate. But this is sheer dogma. There is absolutely no reason why the state should not be a distributed agency that is answerable to the demands of reason, like any agent, but answerable in virtue of the rules of coordination under which distinct component parts cooperate (List and Pettit 2011).

We saw earlier that as a matter of fact an assembly that operates blindly under majority rule won't be able to live up to the demands of reason and agency and that for every candidate, law or policy generated there should be a test to determine if it is likely to induce inconsistency. This testing might clearly be done under a system of mutual checking between different houses in a legislature and under a constraint of engagement between those houses and a constitutional court. Such an arrangement, representing a simple form of mixed constitution, would give a voice to the people, as Bodin and Hobbes require. But that voice would emerge from the interaction between different bodies in the complex whole; it would not be the voice of a single body, authorized to act as spokesperson for the whole.

Why did Bodin, Hobbes and Rousseau overlook this possibility? Apart from the fact that it suited their political purposes to neglect it, they may well have been moved by what A. N. Whitehead (1997: 51) calls the fallacy of misplaced concreteness. This fallacy might have led them to think that if

---

[40] The theme routinely appears also in the long tradition on which Rousseau had a shaping influence. See for example Hegel's (1991: 308) critique of the idea that the different powers in the state should be independent: 'it is plain to see that two self-sufficient entities cannot constitute a unity, but must certainly give rise to a conflict whereby either the whole is destroyed or unity is restored by force'.

there is a mind in the commonwealth then this corporate mind must be located in a single place within the commonwealth: in the head of the monarch, quite literally, or in the forum where the assembly meets. But the purposes and judgements on which the state acts – the mind that informs its behaviour towards citizens and towards other individuals and bodies – may emerge from the interaction of distinct, separated parts within the state. They do not have to be located in any one of these concrete parts.

Gilbert Ryle (1949) tells a story about the visitor to Oxford who is taken around the colleges and, thinking that it is something equally concrete, asks also to see the University. What the visitor fails to register is that the University exists and performs as a unified agency in virtue of the way that the colleges interact; it exists in and through them, emerging as a superordinate entity, rather than consisting in something coordinate and additional. What is true of the University in relation to the colleges can be equally true of the state in relation to its constituent parts. In order to have a state that speaks with one voice and displays one mind, it is not necessary that one of those parts should be sovereign. The state may be a super-ordinate entity that exists on the basis of a sustained, disciplined form of interaction between the parts. That is the possibility that critics of the mixed constitution wittingly or unwittingly neglected.[41]

The contestatory citizenry

There are two complementary requirements for making popular influence suitably unconditioned or robust. First, as we have just seen, there must be a mixed constitution in place that disposes government to avoid triggering popular resistance. And, second, there must be a contestatory culture amongst the citizenry that disposes people to resist any governmental abuse. These two elements must not only be present in order to trigger suitable responses, they must be present as a matter of common awareness; a matter manifest to all. But this extra condition is likely to get fulfilled as a matter of course. It is hard to see how a mixed constitution and a contest-atory citizenry could be present without its being manifest that they are present.

---

[41] In contemporary philosophy of mind, the critique of the Cartesian idea that the mind or soul of the human being condenses in a particular entity – the *res cogitans* or 'thinking thing' – indicts Descartes, so we might say, for having fallen also into the fallacy of misplaced concreteness (Dennett 1992; Clark 1997). There is a nice parallel between concretist assumptions about the mind of the individual subject and concretist assumptions about the sovereign in the state.

Taking up the need for a contestatory citizenry, we should note that the individualization of power already requires people to be disposed to contest laws and policies that seem to undermine their equality of influence. But the need to ensure that popular influence is not conditioned on the goodwill of government, or that of any third party, supports the requirement independently. People must be on the watch for proposals or measures that are not suitably supported – more on this in the next chapter – and they must be ready to organize in opposition to such policies. It is only in the presence of concerted, sustained oversight of government activity – only in the presence of civic vigilance, in the old term – that we can have any assurance that government will be forced to remain responsive to popular inputs.

But what is required to ensure an appropriate form of vigilance? The freedoms of speech, association and travel that any effective electoral system presupposes must be registered in common consciousness. And citizens must regularly exercise and put those freedoms to the test in an active, engaged style of politics. While not everyone need be an activist, vigilance requires a high aggregate level of civic engagement. Numbers of people must be there to manifest an interest in every initiative of government and numbers must be there to insist on the government's justifying the initiatives it takes. Democratic life, as it is sometimes put, has to have an agonistic – better perhaps, an antagonistic – character.

Is this ideal romantic rather than realistic? It would be romantic if it required political activists and public-interest groups to keep individual tabs on everything, as in some traditional images of civic virtue (Montesquieu 1989). But contemporary states are too complex to allow such panoramic scrutiny and interrogation. What is needed, obviously, is specialization and organization: in short, a division of labour in the exercise of civic vigilance. And that ideal is scarcely unrealistic, since contemporary democracies naturally give life to watchdog, activist bodies – non-governmental organizations – that operate locally, nationally and internationally across the various domains of political life. These include bodies that specialize, for example, in consumer issues, people's working conditions, women's rights, environmental sustainability, racial equality, opportunities for the disabled, the conditions of prisoners, gay and lesbian rights, health provision and public education.

The specialization in civic vigilance and contestation that public-interest bodies make possible is desirable on two fronts. It does not only make it possible to have government more effectively invigilated by the citizenry than would be feasible under a regime of panoramic monitoring. It also makes it possible to recruit people to the exercise of civic vigilance on the basis of their particular concerns and passions; recruitment does not have to appeal merely to the abstract call of virtue. There will be no problem with a civic vigilance that is exercised on the basis of such particularistic enthusiasm and attachment, provided that it appeals to a public standard like the ideal of equal influence and that appeal is made in a public forum. It can be sourced in the divisions and resentments emphasized in the long republican tradition by Machiavelli and by contemporary writers who identify with his themes (McCormick 2011). It can be nourished just by what Adam Ferguson (1767: 167) described as the 'refractory and turbulent zeal' of ordinary people.

Not only does the activism envisaged here reject the romantic idea of each citizen's exercising a panoramic, altruistic form of oversight; it also rejects the equally romantic idea of a participatory, Rousseauvian engagement. The participatory approach is so other-worldly that it is likely to demoralize activists, not inspire them: its 'insistence on the identity of the ruler and the ruled has the effect', as one author puts it, 'of removing democracy from the pages of history and of restricting it to an ideal that has never before been realized, not even in ancient Athens' (Green 2004: 748). The engagement that is required to make popular influence robust is rather the activity of the radical social movements that offer an account of common concerns, articulate a suite of popular demands, and challenge government for its failures to recognize or reflect those demands in its policies (Young 1990; Honig 2001). While it gives people an active part in the political system, it does not pretend that politics is a matter of the people coming together in a grand, will-forming, law-making exercise.

But if the contestatory model of the democratic people is not romantic in character, neither does it have the cynical cast assumed by political realists. Thus it contrasts just as sharply with views according to which democracy requires the stabilizing effect of widespread apathy and, as by a happy fault, actually generates such apathy (Lipset 1960). If democracy is taken to consist in nothing more than the electoral assignment of governmental responsibility to a particular party or group, then it may operate best if there is little turbulence amongst the population. But if it consists in the individualized and unconditioned control of government by the people, then it must wither away in the presence of popular apathy. Let people allow themselves to become apathetic and the business of government is bound to be consigned to hands on which they have no influence and can impose no direction.

Calling for contestatory vigilance is not redundant, then, any more than it is romantic. People do have to make an effort to overcome political apathy, so that the habit of making such an effort deserves the name of virtue. It constitutes a motivated variety of virtue – a sort of virtue that is independently reinforced by personal interest and spontaneous invest-ment – as distinct from virtue of a pure, moralistic kind. However demand-ing, such motivated virtue is certainly within people's reach. And so people may be held responsible for failing to exemplify vigilance and contestation. Let them fail to display it and 'they may thank themselves', as James Harrington (1992: 20) put it in the 1650s; the failure will stem from a weakness of will for which they only have themselves to blame.

These observations show that the contestatory spirit required under a republican regime counts as a form of civic virtue, albeit virtue in a sense in which it ought to be readily achievable. But there is one other aspect of this virtue that we ought also to stress. This is that, while it consists in a willingness to challenge public proposals and policies, alleging that they are not supported by the people, or not supported in a manner that treats all members as equals, it presupposes a commitment to living under an arrangement where all members of the community can share in a system of equal popular influence. Contestatory virtue is not the sort of contrarian or sectarian disposition that opposes compromise and accommodation. It is the virtue of citizens who embrace the ideal of a republic in the community in which they happen to live – they are in that sense patriots (Viroli 1995) – and who are willing to do all that is required for realizing the ideal. Not only are they patriots in supporting their country internationally, to invoke the usual application of the idea. More relevantly for our concerns, they are also patriots at home. They are committed to establishing an undominating government in their country, just as it is, and rather than yearning or working for a land governed by their particular tribe or creed or colour, they accept that this will require accommodation on all sides, their own included.

The ideal of the contestatory citizenry that we have been describing is intimately connected with the ideal of the mixed constitution. Given that the voice of the people is meant to emerge from a process of interaction between different bodies, there is every reason to think that individuals operating in contestatory, as well as electoral, guise should constitute one of those parts. But whereas the idea of a contestatory citizenry coheres in this way with the mixed constitution, it is utterly at odds with the Rousseauvian image of a law-making assembly that speaks with the voice of a uniquely authorized spokesperson for the people. If the law-making assembly is the spokesperson that speaks with unique authority for the public or the people, as in the image that Rousseau inherited from Hobbes, then individuals cannot be allowed in their private capacity as subjects to contest that voice. Were they given rights to question the dictates of the sovereign assembly, then that assembly could not speak with the requisite authority. Thus, as we saw in the Introduction, Hobbes (1994b: 18.4) says that if subjects could 'pretend a breach of the covenant made by the sovereign ... there is in this case no judge to decide the controversy'. And Rousseau faithfully echoes that thought when he maintains that 'if individuals were left some rights ... there would be no common power who might adjudicate between them and the public' (Rousseau 1997: 1.6.7).[42]

5. AN EFFICACIOUS SYSTEM OF INFLUENCE

The dimensions of popular influence

Assuming that there is a direction it imposes, we have been looking at how far a popular, electorally centred system of influence can be unconditioned, imposing that direction independently of the will of government or of any third party. Continuing with the assumption that there is a direction that it imposes – I try to vindicate the assumption in the next chapter – we must ask, finally, about how efficacious an electorally centred system of influence can be. Are the constraints it might impose on government sufficient to enable the system to pass the tough-luck test? Are they enough to allow people within the system to think of unwelcome decisions as a matter of tough luck, not evidence of a malign will at work against them or their kind?

The influence that people might command under an electoral system that is suitably individualized and unconditioned is enormous. We can begin to appreciate its dimensions as we recognize that just as a power of interference makes three distinct forms of impact possible – frustration, interference and invigilation – so the same is true more generally of the power of exercising influence. As I put it earlier, the influence exercised may be an active, virtual or reserve form of influence.

Suppose we, the people, enjoy an individualized, unconditioned form of electoral influence over government. That puts in our hands a vast array of inputs that we may actively exploit with a view to pushing government

---

[42] Kant follows Rousseau in this image of a uniquely authorized spokesperson and elaborates a similar thought when he asks who is to decide the sort of issue that might arise between subject and sovereign under a contestatory arrangement. Envisaging an individual rather than a collective sovereign, he gives the following answer. 'Only he who possesses the supreme administration of public right can do so, and that is precisely the head of state; and no one within a commonwealth can, accordingly, have a right to contest his possession of it' (Kant 1996: 299; see too 463). It is this consideration that leads Kant to the view, mentioned in the earlier discussion of contractualism, that even should the sovereign 'proceed quite violently (tyrannically), a subject is still not permitted any resistance by way of counteracting force' (Kant 1996: 298). For an argument that still Kant could have found grounds for condemning the Nazi state see Ripstein (2009: 341–2).

policy in one or another direction. Where that policy goes will depend on how we cast our votes and on what we choose to contest as individuals or subgroups, whether via the legislature, in the courts, through ombudsman or related channels, or, of course, in the media and on the streets. The system will be set up in such a way that the actions we take individually and in aggregate ought to be capable of making a huge impact. There will be nothing to inhibit us from seeking such an impact, as we operate in a space of free speech and association and are in no way dependent on the acquiescence of a higher will. And the system will be designed under such constraints – under such checks and balances – that the inputs we deliver are transmitted smoothly, perhaps even with some amplification, to the points where they can have an effect on policy.

But these comments address only active efforts at influence and miss out on influence of other kinds. For if we, the people, have the power of exercising such active influence, whether electorally or otherwise, then we can practise a corresponding form of virtual influence on how government behaves. Without intervening when we are happy with government performance, we can remain poised to intervene should things not transpire to our satisfaction. We can ride herd on government, to return to the cowboy metaphor, wittingly or unwittingly ensuring that it does not take a policy-making direction to which we object. Without actually doing anything active, we can stop government going against our dispositions, as the cowboy who rides herd on his cattle stops them from going against wishes he has actually formed.

Apart from active and virtual influence, an electoral-cum-contestatory system will also allow us to practise reserve influence. We exercise this form of influence when we do not have formed dispositions in regard to the direction government should take on a certain issue of policy, but we remain disposed to intervene should such a disposition materialize. If we form a disposition that rules against a certain policy, then if the policy has actually been adopted we will use our active influence to combat that policy, and if it remains a merely possible option, we will rely on our virtual influence to keep it from being adopted.

Where we can command a virtual or reserve form of influence over government, it is very likely that those in power will become aware of the fact. And if government is aware of our power in this regard, then it is likely to be suitably inhibited.[43] Conscious that we would oppose the adoption of

---

[43] To be aware of the virtual interference of another agent is to be exposed to coercion; to be aware of the reserve interference of another agent – to be aware of the invigilation practised by that agent – is to be exposed to intimidation.

a certain policy, it is likely on that account to be slow to pursue it. And conscious that we might turn against a certain policy that we do not currently oppose, say as a result of seeing how it works in practice, government is likely on that account to be hesitant to introduce it. Thus we can enjoy influence over government just by being saliently disposed in this or that direction. Without raising a hand or uttering a word, we can put government in a position where it will do our work for us in acting according to our actual or likely dispositions.

These comments should make clear that under the system described so far the river of popular influence can run wide and deep. It can flow into every corner and cranny of government decision-making, imposing constraints on what decisions the different agencies reach and on how they reach them. The influence may emanate not just from how we act in general elections and in individualized contestations but, as in the virtual and reserve cases, from how we are just disposed to act on those fronts. It can enfranchise our dispositions, as well as our deeds.

Given the multi-dimensional manner in which our dispositions can impinge on government performance, there is every hope that the influence we exercise can constrain government to the point where private will is only allowed an impact that is consistent with the direction the influence is designed to impose. Assuming that there is an equally acceptable direction in which this popular influence can push government – that is the topic of the next chapter – the influence ought to be efficacious enough, other things being equal, to ensure the satisfaction of the tough-luck test.

But are other things going to be equal? Is the river of popular influence going to be allowed to flow wide and deep? Or will it be excessively diverted or diluted by the other streams of influence that can inundate the public world? I discuss that possibility in this final section, addressing three dangers in particular and arguing that none is inescapable. The first is the danger of elected politicians usurping the influence of the people under motives of self-interest. The second is the danger of private lobbies usurping that influence out of a desire to push government in a direction that does not necessarily have popular support. And the third is the danger that unelected authorities, including authorities established to counter the earlier dangers, might gain a hold over government policy that is not sensitive to popular demands.[44]

---

[44] Many of the points made in the following discussion draw on earlier arguments in Pettit (2002a, 2004b). Where I wrote there of the need to depoliticize democracy, however, I now tend to avoid this talk. It has helped to bolster the criticism that republicanism, as I interpret it, does not give people a proper, democratic role. See McCormick (2011: 155–7).

The danger from elected politicians

Benjamin Constant (2003: 387) identifies the first danger crisply when, as we saw, he observes that if you elect someone to a representative office then you thereby give 'him a different interest from the one he is charged with representing'. By electing representatives, at least in the normal run of things, we give them a special interest in being re-elected and a powerful concern to take steps that will facilitate re-election and to avoid steps that will stand in the way. This observation points us immediately to areas of policy-making in which elected politicians would have to be saintly not to be moved by their own interests, regardless of what popular influence supports – or indeed of what the preconditions for popular influence require.

The prospects of re-election are going to depend for many politicians on the voting and districting system under which they operate. A first lesson, then, is that they should not be given management of such electoral issues. But the prospects of re-election are also going to depend on how information on government performance is shaped and communicated. So a second lesson is that elected politicians should not be given command over the release of social and economic data and statistics. Again, to go to a more general matter, the prospects of re-election are going to depend most saliently on the experience of voters in the present, so that there is going to be a powerful incentive for politicians to make that experience sweet and to downplay future costs, where these are costs that electors may be presumed to care about, but to be easily led into ignoring. This last consideration argues for a number of lessons: for example, that government policies on interest rates, on energy and environmental issues, and perhaps on criminal sentencing ought not to be left entirely in the hands of the elected. Politicians, being focused on the electoral short term, are always likely to favour lower interest rates, easier energy and environmental demands, and tougher, retributively satisfying sentences. And however attractive in the short term, such policies can be very destructive and costly over the longer haul.

How to cope with such dangers? The most obvious response, and one taken in many democracies, is to put these areas of policy-making at arm's length from elected politicians. This response would argue for establishing an independent electoral commission with responsibility on districting and other electoral decisions; for introducing a body like the British Columbia Citizens' Assembly to make recommendations on some particular issues; for setting up independent, reputable authorities to gather, analyse and release publicly important data and statistics; for investing an economically informed central bank with responsibility for interest rates and related issues; and for having similar bodies make recommendations, and effectively constrain policy, on issues of energy and the environment and on matters of criminal sentencing.[45]

These comments are made on the assumption that the self-interest of politicians will be exclusively electoral in character. But we should also recognize the danger that once they occupy positions of power, politicians will be exposed to a special temptation to accept hidden payments for the favours they can do for certain individuals, corporations and other bodies. This danger argues too for the introduction and empowerment of certain unelected authorities, with a power of auditing the public books and, where required, sponsoring charges of corruption.

In dealing with the requirements for individualizing popular influence I argued that there would have to be channels of challenge, and tribunals of adjudication, that are independent of government. This requirement was further supported by our discussion of how to make popular influence unconditioned. For all we said in those discussions, however, judicial and cognate authorities might be elected in their own right or appointed with a certain arm's-length independence from government. The pressures reviewed in this section argue against election. And so they point us to yet another area – the conduct of the courts and other tribunals – where the regulation of public life should be assigned to appointed, independent authorities, not to figures who are required to keep an eye on the electoral significance of their various decisions. But does the investment of such unelected authorities itself raise a problem for the influence of the people? I turn to that question after discussing the problem raised by private lobbies.

The danger from private lobbies

Private lobbies are groups of people that constitute factions in the eighteenth-century sense of that term. They have selfish or sectional interests such that their satisfaction is not necessarily going to enjoy popular support and, to anticipate discussion in the next chapter, is not necessarily

---

[45] There is great room here for institutional innovation. For a recent proposal in this spirit of innovation, see the proposal for a Citizen's Council in California at http://berggruen.org/files/thinklong/2011/blueprint_to_renew_ca.pdf. This council would be appointed on the basis of expertise, experience and presumptive impartiality and would have the authority to make constitutional and legislative proposals, as well as making recommendations on proposals emanating from other quarters.

consistent with the direction that popular influence would ideally impose on government. They are private in the sense that they seek either to sideline popular influence, looking for an inside channel to government, or to mobilize popular influence on the basis of deception or manipulation or just the threat or power of inflicting harm: say, the harm to a neighbourhood that a corporation can inflict by moving elsewhere, or the harm that unions can impose by calling a general strike. In this respect, they contrast with public-interest groups of the kind invoked in the last section. Such organizations count as public-interest groups just insofar as they seek to mobilize popular influence without resort to under-handed tactics or strong-arm measures.

Private lobbies, so understood, may achieve influence by making politicians financially dependent on their support in electoral campaigns. Or they may achieve influence by being able to do harm to politicians, whether in the manner of the print or electronic media that can create a lot of electorally adverse publicity, or in the manner of the corporation or union, or indeed the foreign power, that can hold out a prospect of action that is bound to hurt the country and be electorally damaging. Whether a foreign power or a multinational corporation is capable of being resisted will depend on the international order and takes us beyond our concerns in this book. But what measures might be taken to combat more domestic kinds of private lobby?

Combating the influence of private media is a challenge for every democracy, and the only response, which may or may not be available under a given constitution, is to establish such a variety of universally accessible media that misinformation and manipulation is readily identified. That is particularly difficult, however, in the contemporary world, where different sectors of the political electorate can tune into broadcasters of their choice, opting only to hear the voices of those with whom they are independently primed to identify: those in their comfort zone (Sunstein 2009). Perhaps the most promising remedy is for government to establish a publicly funded, politically independent broadcaster like the BBC, where this broadcaster achieves such prominence and credibility that no one can ignore it.[46]

How to combat the influence of private campaign supporters? This is a particularly powerful challenge in presidential systems like the US, where

---

[46] One of the first policy changes introduced by President Zapatero of Spain, as he sought to follow a republican agenda, was to put the national broadcaster at arm's length from the control of the government. See Marti and Pettit (2010).

there is no governing party or coalition whose members have to close ranks on pain of allowing the administration to fall (Lessig 2011). In such systems, legislators can vote independently of party and, while that sounds attractive, it means that they can be exposed to enormous financial pressure to vote in this or that manner on particular issues. Limiting private campaign finance, providing public funds to match private campaigning funds, and restricting the use of expensive advertisements on the electronic media are all possible modes of dealing with the problem. But unfortunately such steps are sometimes not possible under received and difficult-to-amend constitutions. Thus they would be very hard to implement in the US, since the courts treat money spent on elections as protected political speech, arguing that the more speech there is, the better; and put few restrictions even on essentially self-interested bodies like commercial corporations (Bakan 2004).

It is generally easier to deal with this particular problem in parliamentary democracies. Not only do most parliamentary regimes allow the use of independent regulators to impose restrictions on campaign finance; when they are not so proportionally elected as to put very loose coalitions in power, these regimes offer an inbuilt, though only partial, safeguard against the influence of private lobbies that seek to buy favours. The members of the majority party in the legislature have to vote together on major issues, since the administration is liable to fall if they do not close ranks in this way. And that means that in order to influence what happens in government, private lobbies have to buy over the whole party or couple of parties in power; they cannot concentrate, as in the US system, on buying off individual, more or less pivotal figures.

The danger from unelected authorities

In exploring how to deal with the previous two dangers I have been suggesting that there must be unelected authorities established in political life, side by side with those who are elected. These may be particular officials such as judges or ombudsmen, statisticians or auditors or regulators; bodies like an electoral commission, a central bank, a budgeting office or a food and drug administration; a media organization like the BBC; or indeed, a temporary, advisory assembly such as the British Columbia Citizens' Assembly.[47] While they may serve in primarily executive, contestatory or

---

[47] Pierre Rosanvallon (2006: 240) treats the Interstate Commerce Commission, established in the United States in 1887, as one of the first examples of an 'independent institution', 'shielded from the direct authority of executive power'.

adjudicative roles, they have a distinctive independence in common. They are appointed to their offices by elected officials rather than being elected themselves but they do not serve as functionaries of those officials; they are appointed to serve for fixed or open terms, not at the pleasure of those who appoint them.

The last question we need to confront is whether such unelected authorities constitute a source of influence that is independent from the influence of the people, undermining the regime of popular influence for which we are looking. The existence of these authorities may cause less of a problem for a system of popular influence than the dangers they are designed to combat. But the question is whether nevertheless they are a problem: whether they represent a current of influence that dilutes the stream that originates with the people.

The question is easily answered in the case of the statistically or indicatively representative assembly that is charged, like the British Columbia Citizens' Assembly, with giving advice on the decision to be taken on a particular policy or set of policies. Such a body does not adopt initiatives in causal response to the dispositions of people in the manner of electoral, responsive representation. But that it takes one or another initiative is good evidence that the people as a whole would adopt that sort of initiative, under suitable information and deliberation. The intentional empowerment of such an indicatively representative body, then, can be seen as a way of giving influence to the dispositions of people in the domain where it operates. Certainly it can be seen in this way, if there is a safeguard against the body assuming a dominating role in its own right; this will be in place, for example, when its recommendations are subject to independent review – for example, by a referendum of the kind required in the British Columbia case. The existence of such an advisory body is not an obstacle to the influence of the people, but rather a means of channelling that influence.

I suggest that if other independent, unelected officials and bodies are appointed under suitable conditions, and are forced to operate under suitable constraints, then they too may have a claim to serve the people in the same indicative way. Suppose that a judge or court, an electoral commissioner or commission, a central banker or a central bank are selected on the publicly contestable grounds of scoring well on experience, expertise and impartiality. Suppose, second, that they are exposed to incentives of professional esteem to show themselves to be experienced, expert and impartial in the way that they resolve different issues (Brennan and Pettit 2004). Suppose, third, that they are given a brief that has presumptive popular support: a brief to interpret and apply the law impartially, to set up district boundaries and voting rules that maximize electoral competition, to establish interest rates that guard against inflation or unemployment. And suppose, finally, that they can be forced to operate under conditions of such publicity, and such exposure to criticism and challenge, review and censure – in brief such contestation – that they face serious costs if they fail to live up to their brief. In that case, the decisions they make are likely to be ones that the people, individually or collectively, would make or approve if they had all the relevant information and expertise. And this is not just a happy result of how they are independently disposed: it is a pattern that is more or less imposed on them by the contestatory pressures to which they are subject.

In our earlier picture, electorally responsive officials and bodies are representative of the people in virtue of being responsive and are forced to perform appropriately by the individualized contestation to which they are exposed. In the picture I am sketching here, unelected authorities have a complementary profile. They are indicative officials and bodies as a result of the basis on which they are selected, the incentives to which they are exposed, and the briefs they are given. And like elected authorities they are forced to perform appropriately by the individualized contestation to which they are exposed. They are proxies for the people who serve a crucial representative role in complementing and containing the people's elected deputies.

The unelected authorities to which this analysis applies are not limited to those in official roles of the kind illustrated. Any system of individualized contestation requires particular individuals or groups to be ready to bring charges against those in government, elected or unelected, whether in the courts, in the press, or on the streets. What gives such contesting parties – such private attorneys general, as they are sometimes known – the right to speak, as they generally claim to do, in the name of the people? I think we can cast them as indicative representatives who are subject to such constraint and contestation that they are bound to enact a brief, as we might think of it, that they are given by the people. The brief is provided implicitly in the fact that a popularly approved constitution allows private attorneys general to mount arguments in the courts or other forums against new laws and other decrees. The rationale behind the brief is to ensure that those in any potentially disadvantaged sector of society can be represented by one of their kind, or someone sympathetic, in challenging and testing the measures at issue. And those private attorneys are more or less bound to enact their brief, and honour its rationale, by being required to follow established channels, arguing their case in a publicly accessible forum on publicly available and contestable grounds.

To gesture at the possibility of making unelected authorities into indicative, suitably controlled representatives of the people is not to design the incentives and briefs, the appointment procedures and operating constraints that might promote that ideal. Here, as in the other cases reviewed in this chapter, we have to be content with being able to see in the abstract how the people might enjoy a system of equally accessible influence that meets republican constraints. I think that the considerations offered do support the claim that this is a feasible possibility in the current case – and in the other cases rehearsed – even if the rehearsal of such considerations falls well short of the hard work required in institutional design.

The picture emerging from the discussion requires an electoral and contestatory democracy that is established on a constitutional basis, written or unwritten. The system envisaged is a form of constitutional democracy insofar as it combines familiar democratic devices with more or less familiar constitutional elements. But it is not a system in which these devices and elements are just added together as independent components. And it is not a system in which the constitutional elements are fixtures that resist democratic control. The constitution is there to facilitate democratic influence – that is, an equally accessible form of unconditioned and efficacious influence – not just to complement it as an independent factor. And the constitution is going to remain there only to the extent that the democratic influence it facilitates is not exercised for purposes of revising it. In view of these features, the picture we have been led to adopt might be cast in James Tully's (2009: 1, 4) phrase, as democratic constitutionalism: an approach in which 'the constitution and the democratic negotiation of it are conceived as equally basic' (see too Mueller 2007; Espejo 2011).

I said at the beginning of the chapter that our discussion would lead us to a model of equally accessible popular influence that is far enough away from the status quo to direct us towards reforms, yet near enough to assure us of its feasibility. I hope that this promise seems to have been borne out in the picture that has emerged from our critique of the plenary assembly, our endorsement of an electoral assembly, and our introduction of amendments to ensure that the popular influence it mediates is suitably individualized, unconditioned and efficacious. With that picture in place, we turn in the next chapter to ask how such a system of equally accessible influence – equally accessible, unconditioned and efficacious influence – might push government in an equally acceptable direction and establish the popular control that republican democracy requires.

CHAPTER 5

Democratic control

According to the argument developed in Chapter 3, a state will be legitimate to the extent that the order it imposes on its citizens is imposed under popular control. But, so the argument continued, people will control the state just insofar as they have an individualized, unconditioned and efficacious influence that pushes it in a direction that they find acceptable. First, the people must have an influence on government that is individualized, unconditioned and efficacious. And, second, they must exercise this influence to a purpose or direction that individuals – or at least those who are prepared to live on equal terms with one another – find acceptable. People must have such a power over government that the regime can be described, in a rich, egalitarian sense of the term, as democratic: a regime that establishes the *kratos*, or 'control', of the *demos*, or 'people'.

This conclusion gave us the task of spelling out how the institutions of a society might meet this design specification and implement a republican conception of democracy. We took up that task in the previous chapter, when we looked at how the people might be given individualized, unconditioned and efficacious influence over government. Without being able to go into detail, we saw that that job specification was likely to require an open electoral system under which individualization would be achieved by the possibility of individualized contestation; unconditioned independence by the resistive character of the citizenry; and efficacy by the insulation of the channels of popular influence against the distorting effects of electoral pressures and private lobbies. Under this image, the political institutions would require many amendments in even the best-practice democracies today; but they would not be so distant from current arrangements as to seem utterly infeasible or utopian.

We turn in this final chapter to the parallel task of exploring how such a system of popular influence might push government in a direction that is equally acceptable to all and thereby come to constitute a system of popular control. The task is to identify an equally accepted purpose that the system of popular influence, individualized, unconditioned and efficacious, might be organized to promote. The discussion is in three sections. In Section 1, I look at two familiar candidates for this role, finding reason to be unhappy with each. In an extended Section 2, I introduce an alternative candidate – the dual-aspect model of democracy, as I call it – show how this might play the required role, and discuss its attractions. And then in Section 3, I look at the implications of endorsing the dual-aspect model for our view of the state, the people and the constitution – in short, for our political ontology – arguing that under this model, government can live up to Lincoln's requirements: it can truly be government of the people, by the people and for the people.

1. TWO FAMILIAR MODELS OF DIRECTED INFLUENCE

Influence without control

The main point to register in taking up the task of the chapter is that a democracy of popular influence need not count as a democracy of popular control; it may not direct government appropriately, establishing the undominated status of the people. Even if the system of influence were rich enough to be capable of imposing a popular direction in an individualized, unconditioned and efficacious way – surely a high ideal – it might still fail in actual fact to give government such a direction. It might impose a large range of constraints, but only with the effect of inducing a series of showdowns and stalemates in the interaction of people and government. In the event of such gridlock, the government might be frustrated in its own ambitions, defensible or otherwise, but it would still dominate the people in particular decisions; it would impose on them coercively, without the coercion being suitably controlled.

The decision-making of a gridlocked government might be wholly chaotic in character, undermining the agential status of the state to which it is ascribed and certainly failing to satisfy people generally. Or it might display a pattern that allows us to extrapolate from past to future performance, but not a pattern for which the people plausibly control. The pattern might be the publicly unwelcome precipitate of individual acts of publicly constrained decision-making. Or it might be a precipitate that is welcome in some sectors but unwelcome in others. In either case, it would not be a pattern that counts as equally acceptable to all the people, even to all who are willing to live on equal terms with others.

For many theorists of democracy today, particularly in economic and political science, the democratic ideal is one of popular influence – indeed a form of popular influence that need not be deeply constraining – and nothing more. This representation of the democratic ideal appears clearly in the influential work of the Austrian–American economist and political theorist, Joseph Schumpeter. In his discussion of democracy in *Capitalism, Socialism and Democracy*, first published in 1942, Schumpeter presented an argument for thinking that while democratic government depends importantly on the influence of the people, it need not be given – and, as a matter of fact, is not given – any particular direction by that influence.

Schumpeter assumes, reasonably, that any plausible democratic system is going to involve open, periodic, electoral competition, with different parties seeking to attract enough support to win office. He is sceptical on a number of counts about the possibility that the results of such a democratic process would be 'meaningful in themselves – as for instance the realization of any definite end or ideal would be' (Schumpeter 1984: 253). The people do not form systematic views that they might impose on leaders; under the influence of popular pressure and party propaganda, they display only 'an indeterminate bundle of vague impulses loosely playing about given slogans and mistaken impression' (Schumpeter 1984: 253). And even if they did form such views, they would not be able to impose them. The political decisions produced from 'the raw material of those individual volitions' (Schumpeter 1984: 254) might take any of a variety of forms, depending on the initiatives of the party boss and the party machine. Parties and leaders are primarily committed to keeping office, not to representing any standing principles, and no matter what the input from the electorate, 'the pyrotechnics of party management and party advertizing' will deliver whatever response promises to serve best in 'the competitive struggle for political power' (Schumpeter 1984: 283). Thus, while the people choose between parties at election time, they do not otherwise 'control their political leaders' (Schumpeter 1984: 272).

In view of his scepticism about the idea that democracy might serve any popularly imposed purpose, Schumpeter defines it by the process it employs; it is nothing more or less than 'that institutional arrangement for arriving at political decisions in which individuals acquire the power to decide by means of a competitive struggle for the people's vote' (1984: 260). This definition has been popular with political scientists ever since his time, because it makes democracy into a workable category in the descriptive characterization of regimes (Przeworksi 1999). In Schumpeter's words it provides 'a reasonably efficient criterion by which to distinguish democratic governments from others' (1984: 269). In this respect it certainly scores well above the republican conception of democracy. There can be little controversy about whether the politicians in a given system compete for the people's vote in order to attain power. But there is bound to be controversy about how far in a particular society people rely on their individualized, unconditioned and efficacious influence to exercise equally shared control over government.[1]

But we ought not to allow taxonomic considerations to outweigh normative concerns in deciding what democracy ideally requires. The real question for us is how attractive a democracy of influence-without-control is likely to be, especially from a republican perspective. It has some clear attractions, as Schumpeter (1984: 269–73) himself stresses. It promotes interaction between rulers and ruled, for example, requires considerable freedom of discussion amongst the electorate, and gives people a power of evicting government which guards against the possibility of dynastic rule. These virtues may give us reason to think that democracy is a lot better than dynastic or other systems – that it is the worst form of government, as Winston Churchill is reputed to have said, except for all the others. But a democracy of influence-without-control would not establish the legitimacy of government in the republican sense. Its presence would not entitle us to say that people have such an individualized, unconditioned and efficacious degree of control over government that its interference in their lives does not constitute domination. Schumpeterian democracy is a second-grade ideal from our point of view, not the sort of arrangement for which we have been looking.

The system of popular influence described in the last chapter will underpin a system of popular control insofar as it serves to impose a direction on government that is equally appealing for all those citizens who are willing to live on equal terms with one another. The task in the remainder of this section is to review the standard ends or purposes that the people's influence on government might be thought capable of advancing, and to assess them for plausibility. These candidates divide into two categories, depending on whether the idea is that people might knowingly and intentionally seek their promotion or might produce them without necessarily being aware of doing so: this, in the way in which people are said to produce competitive pricing, as by an invisible hand, in the open market. I shall look at these two categories in turn, finding fault

---

[1] For an overview of various attempts to define democracy with a view to characterizing actual regimes see Tilly (2007: Chapter 1). Given the account in this book of the institutions required for a republican democracy, it ought to be possible to adapt one of these approaches in developing an audit of democracy. The Economist Intelligence Unit offers a congenial index of democracy at www.eiu.com/public/democracy_index.aspx.

with the standard approaches associated with them. That will lay the ground for introducing a third, more promising candidate that I go on to explore in Section 2.

The intentional direction of government

If people are to participate within a system of influence that imposes a certain direction on government, then according to many thinkers they must implicitly or explicitly endorse the purpose that they want government to fulfil. They must each articulate that purpose or end and, intending to cooperate with others in its promotion, they must each assume that everyone can do this, recognize that others can do it, and so on. And then they must each take steps that make sense as a contribution to the presumptively general enterprise of advancing that purpose.

Rousseau (1997: IV.I.6) thinks that this is the approach that the members of his assembly will take, at least if they are operating properly; they will each cast any vote on the basis that 'it is advantageous to the State . . . that this or that opinion pass', not on the factional basis that that is 'advantageous to this man or this party'. In that respect, the intentional-control model of popular control has close affinities with the general-will model. But how might the idea apply in the representative regime envisaged here?

Schumpeter (1984: 269) assumes that under an electoral regime a similar form of intentional control might materialize, though he himself thinks it won't. It might be, as he takes 'the classical theory' to maintain, that '"the people" hold a definite and rational opinion about every individual question and that they give effect to this opinion – in a democracy – by choosing "representatives" who will see to it that that opinion is carried out'. In this picture, the people identify suitable policies first and then choose representatives on the basis of their endorsing those policies.

The view that the people intentionally impose a purpose on government, however, might not take this policy-first form. For all that the approach strictly requires, the people might cast their votes for certain representatives, not on the grounds that they are likely to see to it that the independently formed opinions of voters are implemented, but on the grounds that those deputies are intellectually and motivationally reliable and are likely to form a sound opinion about the matters they deal with (Montesquieu 1989). In this context the sound opinion might be taken by voters to be the opinion that they themselves would be likely to form, if they had the time and information and expertise that representatives may be expected to enjoy. This approach might be described as a deputy-first version of the theory, as distinct from the policy-first version that Schumpeter ascribes to the classical theory.[2]

The purpose that representatives are supposed to advance, whether in a policy-first or deputy-first way, might plausibly be identified, in traditional phrases, with the common good, the public interest or the welfare of the society. Whether it generates an agenda that people articulate for themselves, or an agenda that they rely on suitable representatives to articulate, it answers to the sort of thing that such phrases are generally taken to identify. But how should we best interpret the phrases? How should we understand the public interest, to favour one particular phrase, that people might plausibly endorse and seek to impose on government?

In one interpretation of the public interest, it is nothing more or less than the intersection of people's private interests: that is, the interests that they bring to society – the interests that they have, independently of their having to live together with each other. This is not a satisfactory account of the public interest, however, since there may be only a very small degree of overlap between such pre-social interests. You may have an interest in hunting for a living, I in farming; you may want one religion supported, I another; you may want clean water where you live, I may want to build a factory that will pollute it. And even if there is a considerable overlap in pre-social interests, that overlap is going to be unstable, since a change in even one person's interests is liable to disrupt it. Such a goal would shift unpredictably and make an unsuitable purpose to assign to government.

Is there a better version of the common good or public interest that people might plausibly endorse and seek to impose? An obvious improvement will come with the recognition that there is a difference between the interests people have independently of having to live in society and the interests they have, given that they have no option but to live with others – and, to reiterate a basic normative presumption, to live on equal terms with others. You may be of one religion and I another and neither of us may have an independent interest in supporting, or even in tolerating, the other's creed. But if we have to live with one another, and live under a collectively coercive state, then we each have an interest – a post-social rather than pre-social interest – in establishing a regime under which the freedom of our respective religious practices is assured. This will be better than allowing no

---

[2] Under the policy-first version, deputies are cast as delegates, in Hannah Pitkin's (1972) phrase; under the deputy-first they are cast as trustees. As we saw in the last chapter, deputies of either sort are responsive representatives and should be distinguished from proxies, or indicative representatives. The view of the American founders was clearly that elections would serve in the first place to select out suitable deputies (see too Madison, Hamilton and Jay 1987: no. 57; Herreros 2006).

freedom of religion to anyone, which would unnecessarily restrict the range of basic liberties. And it will be better than privileging one religion, since this would reject people's claim to equality; as we saw in the last chapter, it would effectively ensure that people did not have an equal share in the electoral system of popular influence.

What obtains in the religious domain holds also in a range of other domains. As we have a shared individual interest in freedom of religion, so we will have such a shared interest in having a regime that allows you to hunt and me to farm, you to have clean water and me to build a factory, and so on. The public interest, conceived in this way, is composed of those goods that anyone who accepts the necessity of living on equal terms with others is likely to want to have collectively guaranteed or promoted. It consists in the interests that people are going to share insofar as they have equal status as members of a polity (see Goodin 1996; Pettit 2004a).

While this account distinguishes the public interest from the intersection of private interests, it also makes it distinct from what might be described as the good of the nation or people, considered as a corporate entity. Considered in a corporate role, a nation survives over many generations and its good may have little to do with the good of the individuals who make it up at any time. The nation or people may prosper in terms of international power relations, for example, without that prosperity making for an aggregate gain amongst members; maintaining the hegemony may be extremely costly and provide most members with only the dubious benefit of being able to take pride in their state. To identify the goal that the people might intentionally impose on a state as the maintenance of such a corporate performance would be counter-intuitive, though a certain sort of nationalism might support the line. It would be to reject Aristotle's (1996: 2.5) common sense when he argues in *The Politics* that while a set of odd numbers may add up to an even sum, a population of unhappy people cannot add up to a happy *polis*: 'the whole cannot be happy unless most, or all, or some of its parts enjoy happiness'.

If these observations are sound, then the most plausible version of this first account of popular direction would say that the people exercise popular control insofar as they intentionally use their influence to force government to pursue public-interest policies, where the public interest is understood in a post-social but non-corporate manner. The people may be held to do this either in a policy-first or deputy-first manner: either by first identifying suitable policies and then selecting representatives who support those policies; or by first identifying suitable representatives and then relying on them to formulate public-interest policies. But in either version, as we shall see, the theory is less than satisfactory.

The elected representatives in each version may deliberate with one another before casting their votes on the policies to be put in place. But despite each endorsing a consistent set of policy judgements, the effect of aggregating their votes may be to support an inconsistent package; that is the lesson of the discursive dilemma, as we saw in the last chapter. This means that the body of elected representatives will have a good deal of discretion in deciding on their policies, whether they decide on them one by one, as under the Washington system of deal-making, or in the overall programme that parties typically present to the electorate in the Westminster alternative.

The availability of such discretion accentuates a deep difficulty for the intentional-direction approach. The politicians in the system – and to some extent the people too – must be virtuous enough to make impartial judgements on what is in the public interest and then to introduce policies that promote that interest. In particular, they must be virtuous enough to do this, even when electoral or other private interests – and no system of popular influence can completely silence these – argue strongly for warping the judgements or the policies in another direction and, of course, for representing that redirection as itself required by the public interest. Indeed, they must be virtuous enough to do this, even when all we know of cognitive frailty suggests that private interest can delude them into seeing the redirection as a requirement of public interest; it can enable them to hide their misrepresentation from themselves (Gilovich, Griffin and Kahneman 2002; McGeer and Pettit 2009).

The virtue required of people and representatives under the intentional-direction story, unlike the virtue we ascribed to those who identify with certain watchdog groups and social movements, is likely to be unmotivated. There need not be any elements of personal interest or spontaneous commitment to support it, so that the virtuous performance required may only be forthcoming in the presence of something close to moral perfection. That is a problem, for two reasons. One, such virtue is not an assured commodity and a system that requires it is not guaranteed to be sustainable. And two, even if people and politicians were generally disposed to be virtuous, they might not be confident about one another's virtue, and, lacking assurance on the point, might fail to display virtue themselves; they might each look after their own interests, fearing the prospect of being made a sucker by others.

We can be concerned about this problem, I should mention, without going to the extreme of adopting the so-called knave's principle. We need not assume, in Bernard Mandeville's (1731: 332) words, that the best sort of constitution is the one which 'remains unshaken though most men should prove knaves'. We can reject the principle, in David Hume's words (1875: 117–18), that in 'fixing the several checks and controls of the constitution, every man ought to be supposed a knave, and to have no other end in all his actions than private interest'. The knave's principle may be counter-productive, as some empirical evidence suggests; it may argue for institutions that crowd out whatever virtue is available, say by triggering resentment and defiance (Pettit 1996b; Brennan and Pettit 2004: Chapter 14). Without embracing any such dubious principle, however, we can still see good reason to reject any design that would make unmotivated virtue into a prerequisite for the proper performance of an institution; we can see good reason to economize on virtue (Brennan and Hamlin 1995).

The intentional-direction model fails on precisely this count. It requires politicians to put aside their private concerns – including their characteristic concern with re-election – in formulating the policies that promise to promote the public interest. And it requires ordinary electors to be disposed to demand and respond to policies that succeed in doing this. Politicians and electors must each form judgements about what the public interest requires. They must do so in full sensitivity to the range of relevant concerns, however altruistic. They must use their discretion in aggregating those judgements without letting private interest or other pressures warp the exercise. And they must then live up to those judgements – if you like, those public-spirited preferences – in their performance on different fronts: at the polls, in the party room, and in Parliament or Congress. O brave new world that hath such people in it.

If this response seems somewhat cynical, I might add in conclusion that it is fully in line with the long tradition of republican thought. Amongst republican thinkers across different periods, it has been a constant refrain that human beings are universally corruptible if often – thanks perhaps to supportive institutions – actually uncorrupt (Pettit 1997c: Chapter 7). Public office is a particular source of corruption, according to the tradition, since it gives bearers a special opportunity to benefit from evil-doing and often a special capacity to avoid being caught. It enables them, like the ring of Gyges, to further their self-interest without having to run the usual risks of detection and punishment. Thus, as Richard Price (1991: 30) puts the recurrent theme, 'There is nothing that requires more to be watched than power.' To entrust politicians with the articulation and advancement of the public interest, regardless of their private concerns, would fly in the face of this caution.

The non-intentional direction of government

We saw in Chapter 3 that it is possible for a person to control a process without exercising control intentionally. The example we gave, drawn from Amartya Sen, was that of a patient in a coma whose wishes dictate the treatment provided, thanks to the intentional efforts of family and friends. The wish of the patient has an influence on the treatment adopted by the hospital, due to the influence of family and friends; it controls for the treatment that the patient receives. And the connection between influence and effect, input and output, is suitably robust or unconditioned: while it depends on one of the family or friends coming forward, for example, any of a number are willing to do so. Thus if the wish had been absent, then the hospital would not in all likelihood have provided that treatment; and if a different wish had been in its place, to mark a richer possibility, then the hospital would have provided that alternative instead.

In this example, the purpose effected by the system of influence and direction is truly a goal or desideratum of the agent: it corresponds, after all, to a wish. It is because of the influence of that wish that the treatment assumes a certain form. But the causal mechanism whereby the wish generates the treatment involves, not the intentions and efforts of the agent, but rather those of family and friends. The lesson of the example, then, is that direction and control may be non-intentional as well as intentional. That lesson applies in collective, as well as individual, cases, as we shall now see, and directs us to a second way in which popular influence might be recruited to serve a popular purpose.

Consider the invisible hand whereby, under standard economic assumptions, the behaviour of consumers in an open market ensures the satisfaction of the wish on the part of each to be able to buy goods and services at the lowest feasible price. Consumers are each disposed to buy something of a given quality as cheaply as possible, thereby displaying that wish, and to shop around in order to achieve this. Producers of the commodity or service are disposed to undercut one another's prices in order to maximize revenue; if they are not, then others will have an incentive to enter the market and challenge them. And the effect of the interaction between the dispositions of the two groups is to push producers to sell at the competitive price: that is, at the lowest price that is consistent with their remaining in business. Consumers do not cooperate on the basis of a shared intention or wish to establish competitive pricing – certainly they need not do so. But they do each wish to be able to buy what they want at competitive prices – although not perhaps under that description – and the effect of their each acting on those wishes is that, as by an invisible hand, the wishes are satisfied.

The notion of an invisible-hand mechanism became widely known and celebrated in the wake of Adam Smith's economic theories, as presented in *The Wealth of Nations* in 1767 (1976). Unsurprisingly, it was soon adapted for use in political theory. A compatriot of Smith's, James Mill, argued in 1819, in a small treatise entitled *An Essay on Government*, that if we only design the electoral system appropriately, then we can rely on an invisible hand to promote the public interest (Lively and Rees 1978). Mill had rallied behind Jeremy Bentham's new philosophy and he argued that in a suitable electoral system we can rely on an invisible hand to promote a utilitarian version of the public interest: in the popular slogan of the time, the greatest happiness of the greatest number.

Mill begins from an assumption that all human beings pursue their own interest-satisfaction, where this is understood as the satisfaction of their selfish preferences – in brief, their own happiness (Lively and Rees 1978: 5). This gives him a utilitarian conception of the public interest; it consists in 'that distribution of the scanty material of happiness, which would insure the greatest sum of it in the members of the community, taken together' (Lively and Rees 1978: 5). How then is a community of such individuals to rely on government – government by a small number of their members, as he assumes it has to be – to promote the public interest? 'The community itself must check these individuals, or else they will follow their interest' (Lively and Rees 1978: 22) – their 'sinister interest', as he also describes it (25). And how is the community to do this? By relying on 'that grand invention of modern times, the system of representation' (Lively and Rees 1978: 21). Specifically, by relying on a system under which, first, electors are inclusive enough to exemplify the range of interests in the community as a whole (Lively and Rees 1978: 22) – Mill thinks that all older males will be enough (27); and second, the period between elections is as short as possible, consistently with allowing representatives to get on with their job (25).[3] The idea is that this system will force representatives to reflect the interests of constituents in their voting, and that with such 'an identity of interest' (Lively and Rees 1978: 34) between electors and elected, the decisions reached will reflect a compromise that is going to promote the greatest aggregate satisfaction of essentially self-interested agents. This satisfaction is what he takes to constitute the public interest.

---

[3] I am ignoring the fact that for Mill that job was mainly to keep an eye on the government exercised by the King and his ministers.

If Mill's picture is sound, then those in government will promote the public interest of the community, in the utilitarian sense in which he understands the public interest, and do so under the popular influence of voters. That popular influence will generate the public interest, however, not via an intention on the part of electors as a whole to let the public interest have a dictating role, but rather via a mechanism that operates behind their backs. With electors each voting for policies or deputies that promise to satisfy their own self-regarding preferences, and with deputies seeking to track the preferences of their constituents, the aggregate, unintended effect is supposed to be that the interests of electors are maximally satisfied overall.

Not many contemporary thinkers embrace Mill's account of the popular, invisible-hand direction of government that can be achieved under a responsively representative picture. Whether interpreted on a basis that gives priority to policies or deputies, it is open to the obvious objection that for all that he says, electors and elected may form coalitions to impose particular sectional interests in a way that is unresponsive to minority interests within the society. Forming on the basis of common ethnic or religious, commercial or regional priorities, such interest-groups could systematically warp the laws and policies of government in their own favour.

But though Mill's specific proposal no longer attracts many supporters, there are loose relatives of the proposal that have been given some support in more recent times. One is interest-group pluralism. It would suggest that while interest-groups would certainly upset Mill's individualist scheme, they themselves might compete for influence over government in such a way that the authorities can be expected, on pain of not being re-elected, to look for the highest possible aggregate satisfaction of those competing interests. According to this view, as one commentator puts it, 'influence over political decisions is diffused over a host of organized groups – trade unions, business organizations, churches, societies for the promotion of this or the protection of that – which express a variety of views and interests' (Lively 1975: 58). And the idea, at least in some interpretations, is that if people are generally represented in such interest-groups, then the influence of those groups over government, proportional as it is likely to be to their numbers, can be expected to be utilitarian in its overall effect: that is, to lead to something like maximal preference-satisfaction overall.

This alternative, invisible-hand account of how the people might direct government is open to even more salient objections than James Mill's own. For as many commentators have argued, there is absolutely no reason to think that the influence of the different groups will be proportional to their numbers (Connolly 1969). It is much more likely to be proportional to their power over government, where that power is going to reflect a range of possible factors: their level of organization and their financial resources, their potential for campaigning against government or disrupting government performance, and their usefulness at election time.

Starting afresh

The discussion of existing proposals for the popular direction of government, whether intentional or non-intentional, seems to give credibility to Schumpeter's scepticism. There may be ways of establishing popular influence, even ways of making it into a very rich and penetrating form of influence, as we saw in the last chapter. But going on the official record, there appears to be very little prospect of using that popular influence to impose a suitably popular direction on government.

The first of the two broad approaches sketched would organize government around people's public-interest judgements: their impartial preferences over what happens to the society as a whole. The second would organize it under a mechanism designed to make government responsive to more particular attitudes: people's partial preferences over what happens to them and theirs. But there seems to be little chance of arranging things so that either socially oriented or self-oriented preferences can rule appropriately in the corridors of power. The view that socially oriented preferences might rule requires a dubious faith in the reliability of people's virtue. The view that self-oriented preferences might rule – that is, rule in a more or less inclusive and fair fashion – requires an equally dubious faith in the capacity of society to guard against the effects of unequal power.

Notwithstanding these criticisms, however, each of the approaches discussed has an appealing aspect. The first is attractive in focusing us on a plausible goal for popular direction: that of the public interest, understood in a post-social, non-corporate manner. The second is attractive in directing us to a plausible means for popular direction: an invisible-hand mechanism that does not require people to maintain monitoring and control of government on an intentional basis. This raises the question as to whether there might not be a third arrangement with both appealing aspects: a way of directing government towards something like the public interest, as that is understood in the first approach, that is implemented by something like an invisible-hand process, as that is exemplified in the second.

As it happens, I think that this scenario is a real institutional possibility. It will materialize, so I argue, insofar as two conditions are fulfilled. First, people come to support certain norms of public policy-making, whether or not this is something they intend, in virtue of pursuing popular influence over government. And, second, these norms come to direct public decision-making, whether or not this is something that people intend, thereby establishing a popular purpose that government serves.

I look at how these two conditions can be fulfilled in Section 2 and at the merits of the system of popular direction that this would install. And then in Section 3 I explore the implications of the system for political ontology – for our view of the nature and the relationships between people, constitution and state – arguing that it allows us to think that in a distinctive sense government satisfies Lincoln's three demands: it is of the people, by the people and for the people.

I describe the picture emerging from our considerations as a dual-aspect model of how popular influence can impose a popular direction. This is because democratic politics works in two timescales, according to that picture. In day-by-day policy-making, the people exercise an equally accessible form of electoral and contestatory influence over public decision-making. And by means of doing this in the short haul, they manage over the long haul to impose an equally acceptable direction on the performance of government.

2. A DUAL-ASPECT MODEL OF DEMOCRACY

Games of acceptance and acceptability

The best way of introducing the core idea in the dual-aspect model is to consider the difference between two ways in which a group of people who have to organize some common enterprise might resolve conflicting differences of interest and opinion in the formation of policies. I describe one of these approaches to organized decision-making as the game of acceptance, the other as the game of acceptability.

Consider the group of people who own apartments in a condominium and who face the task of organizing the condominium's affairs.[4] And suppose that the group confronts a policy-making decision in some domain: say, the decision about how much the owners of different apartments, some more expensive, some less, should have to pay into the funds of the body corporate.

---

[4] My use of the model of the condominium for thinking about republican political theory, which I pursue here and later in the text, is mirrored in an intriguing way by a recent set of studies that look at how far condominiums and related organizations live up to republican expectations in post-Soviet Russia. See Kharkhordin and Alipuro (2011).

In an acceptance game, the parties each seek to influence others in favour of this or that policy by announcing the minimal concession that they are willing to make, by revising their offers or bids in face of a failure to secure convergence, and by going through successive rounds or revisions until convergence is achieved. The drive in this exercise is to identify an arrangement that each is willing to accept – in that sense, it is an acceptance game – assuming that they each wish to grant the smallest concession that they can get away with; they each want to make the smallest sacrifice possible to the interests or indeed the opinions that they stand for. This exercise might be conducted without any discussion in a round of bids akin to the bids made in opening a game of bridge. But if discussion is allowed, then it will consist in self-serving arguments by the different parties. Those on lower, less expensive floors might argue, for example, that they are unable to concede further in view of their relative poverty, that their interest in securing convergence is less than the interest they are being asked to sacrifice – for example, unlike those on higher floors, they can live without an elevator service – or that the remaining concession required from the better off is really quite trivial.

In the acceptability game, things are done in quite a different fashion. The parties are required to propose the policy that they favour in the domain of group choice – or perhaps to suggest a novel candidate – and to present considerations to one another that should count as relevant by the lights of all. The idea is that any considerations adduced should help to make the policy acceptable to everyone, given shared assumptions about the dispositions of each; they should engage with those dispositions and help to make the policy congenial to each. The exercise is much more demanding than one in which they each just announce what they are prepared to accept. And equally it is more demanding than one in which each puts forward considerations that, as they claim, others morally ought to accept: considerations that they ought to accept, for example, assuming that they ought to share the speaker's religious faith or ethical vision. The considerations adduced should count as relevant according to everyone's views but according to everyone's views as they actually are or can be brought to be, not according to everyone's views as in some sense they ought ideally to be.

The participants in the acceptability game, being required to treat others as equals, will debate with one another on broadly the sort of model envisaged by deliberative democrats.[5] They cannot present considerations that some subset of the group are bound to regard as irrelevant from their

---

[5] The thinker who has done most to emphasize the potential of the acceptability game, though not in that phrase, is Juergen Habermas (1984–9). Jon Elster (1986) gives an insightful presentation of the

point of view; certainly they cannot do so and expect to carry others with them. Willingly or unwillingly, they are required to obey the old principle of law and rhetoric (Skinner 1996: Part 1): *audi alteram partem*, 'hear the other side'.[6] The only considerations they can invoke are ones that argue on all sides – though perhaps with a varying force or weight – for accepting the policy supported; they must count with everyone as grounds that it is at least relevant or pertinent to adduce in arguing for or against a policy. Being presented as considerations that everyone licenses in this way, or can at least be expected to license, the rival parties offer them as reasons for why everyone ought to be ready to accept the policy proposed.

The acceptability game is governed, in the nature of the case, by a norm to the effect that participants should only offer considerations for or against a policy that all can regard as relevant. On the account adopted earlier, a norm is a regularity of behaviour amongst the members of a group such that, as a matter of shared awareness, almost everyone complies with it, almost everyone expects others to approve of compliance and/or disapprove of non-compliance, and this expectation helps to keep the regularity in place. Under the pressures of the acceptability game, it is inevitable that participants will generally comply with the regularity of seeking out considerations that all others, no matter what their interests or opinions, can treat as relevant in collective decision-making; else they will have little impact. And it is equally inevitable that participants will register this fact in common awareness as well as registering at the same time that any failure of compliance will attract the inhibiting derision or disapproval of others. Those who present considerations that can only carry weight with a particular subgroup will be laughed out of court.

---

approach that distinguishes it usefully from alternatives. Although the participants in an acceptability game are required to be willing to operate on equal terms with others – that is built into the game – the considerations that are likely to be valorized there should be distinguished from the 'public reasons' that John Rawls (1999) associates with 'reasonable political conceptions of justice' (133). Unlike Rawls's public reasons, the considerations endorsed may be context-bound in three distinct senses. They may pass muster only because of the history of the group: an example, used later in the text, might be the consideration, licensed in a history of federation, that argues for the equal representation of states with different population levels. Unlike Rawls's reasons, they may be required to pass muster at any time with current members, not to be such that they would pass muster under any feasible change in or of the membership; this limitation is not objectionable insofar as a change of that type, for example a change in degree of religious uniformity, would generate a revision of accepted considerations under the discipline of an acceptability game. And unlike Rawls's reasons, they may be specifically tied to particular issues about whether to adopt this or that policy or to endorse this or that process of decision-making; they may not generalize into any easily formulated principles. For a good account of Rawls on public reason see Larmore (2003).

[6] For a recent psychological argument that this is an important and productive discipline on human reasoning see Mercier and Sperber (2011).

This general, guiding norm – this norm of norms – does not require that participants only offer considerations that have already been tried and tested. It will prime them to search out considerations in any domain of policy-making that people can be brought to endorse, given their existing commitments. Suppose people are committed to the high-level principle of equality in all possible domains. Or suppose, more plausibly, that they are committed to equality in an area that is distinct from the domain under discussion. On the basis of such prior commitments, the supporters of a certain sort of policy in that domain may invoke the consideration of equality, arguing for its relevance on the basis of the general commitment to equality or the commitment to equality in a distinct but purportedly parallel domain. They may or may not be successful in gaining such acceptance for the relevance of the equality consideration in the domain addressed, certainly not on the first round. But if the consideration really does cohere well with the existing commitments of participants, then sooner or later it is very likely to win acceptance as a relevant coin in the currency of acceptability debates.

If people abide by the norm of norms in debates with one another – if they invoke only considerations that may be expected to count as relevant by all lights – then this should ensure the emergence of more specific norms amongst them. Let participants be successful in getting the pertinence of certain considerations accepted by all. That means that there will be evidence to hand that makes it manifest to all that everyone accepts their pertinence; manifest to all that this is manifest to all; and so on in the usual hierarchy associated with common or mutual belief (Lewis 1969). Over time, then, the considerations will come to constitute points of reference that are manifestly pertinent or relevant, by everyone's lights, to issues of public policy.[7] For any accepted consideration, C, it will be true, and true as

---

[7] Does the dichotomy of acceptance and acceptability game neglect a third alternative in which it is required that people all be able to see proposals as acceptable but not necessarily on the same grounds, only on their own personal grounds? For a sophisticated development of such an approach see Gaus (2011), and for a related approach that privileges religiously motivated, doctrinally specific reasons see Stout (2004). My own view, which I cannot fully defend here, is that no such approach can point us to a genuine alternative, in view of the following dilemma. If people do not have to defend the personal grounds on which they require public policies to be acceptable – if, in a term introduced later in the text, those personal grounds do not have to answer to concordant interests – then the proposal is likely at best to support a version of the acceptance game, as participants seek to make compromises with one another and avoid a destructive stalemate. If people do have to defend those grounds at a higher level, however, on the basis of concordant interests – for example in the way that people might appeal to religious freedom in defence of their own sectarian right of practice – then the proposal amounts to a version of the acceptability game. For an illuminating discussion of this and related positions see the unpublished paper by S. Macedo, 'Why Public Reason?'

a matter of common awareness, that almost everyone treats it as a relevant factor in political argument, almost everyone expects others to approve of this treatment and to disapprove of a refusal to grant such treatment, and almost everyone is motivated by this expectation to grant it this treatment themselves.

Specific norms of argument and deliberation will emerge, on this account, as an inevitable by-product of the successful, continuing use of the acceptability game: that is, by robust adherence to the norm of norms associated with the game. Participants will learn that as a matter of common awareness this or that consideration is going to count as relevant – to pass muster – in arguing for or against a policy. And with the approval or lack of disapproval attending such a practice, they will learn as a matter of common awareness that to reject the relevance of the consideration will earn the inhibiting disapproval of others. Thus the consideration will be reinforced by its own specific norm, coming to wear the tag: deny my relevance – however you weight me – at your peril!

The considerations that an acceptability game is likely to valorize in this way fall into two broad categories: considerations of convergent, and concordant, interests. Convergent considerations will point participants to universal benefits that all take to be relevant, or can be brought to see as relevant, in matters of shared decision-making. Examples in the political world would certainly include the benefit of equality or cohesion, prosperity or peace and, of course, the corresponding harms of inequality or divisiveness, poverty or conflict. If you can show that only one of a number of competing policies in any area promises to provide such a benefit or avoid such a harm, then you will have registered something that ought to carry weight on all sides, though perhaps heavier weight on some sides than on others.

Concordant, as distinct from convergent, considerations point the participants in an acceptability game to benefits that accrue only to this or that individual or subgroup. Despite the partiality of their relevance to people's fortunes, these considerations will command a following on all sides to the extent that everyone accepts that it is a matter of convergent interest that the group as a whole should confer that benefit on the sort of individual or subgroup favoured. No group can accept that the interest of each in securing a certain advantage, regardless of the cost to others, provides a relevant consideration in joint policy-making. But a group may well accept, for example, that none of its members should have to suffer the sort of inequality that majority voting would impose on the vegetarian members in the dining-club example of the last chapter. More generally, the group may accept that members have a concordant interest in being protected against any such inequality, or against any of a variety of misfortunes. Thus a likely harm to one or another member on this front may pass as a relevant consideration in joint policy-making. And something similar may hold with a suitable benefit. For example, the fact that a benefit would help some while not doing any harm to others – the fact that it would represent a Paretian improvement – may argue on all sides for a policy that promises that benefit.[8]

Whether they reflect convergent or concordant interests, the more specific norms of policy-making will direct participants in any acceptability game to an evolving body of arguments that they can safely draw upon in supporting this or that proposal. But they will also provide resources that participants can exploit in supporting this or that process or procedure for resolving the differences that remain in place after deliberation. Differences will almost always remain in place, since the considerations presented on different sides of a policy debate will rarely underpin unanimous agreement; they will only reduce the number of candidates on the table. And so it will be necessary at some point to bring the deliberative exercise to an end and achieve resolution by recourse to some independent procedure: say, by voting amongst the remaining alternatives, by selecting between them on a lottery basis, or by referring the issue to an agreed umpire. Thus, as specific norms of policy-making will bear on different policies, so they will also bear on the suitability in a given case of resorting to one or another process of final resolution.

The specific norms that emerge in any group will never constitute a closed set, fixed once and for all (Young 1990, 2000; Honig 2001). They will be subject to constant development, as deliberative innovators manage to gain acceptance for novel sorts of argument, perhaps by extending the reach of recognized arguments to new domains, perhaps by coming up with new arguments that gain acceptance by others. Such innovations are likely to be triggered by changes in the dispositions of the existing membership and, of course, by changes of membership that occur at any time and across different times. As new norms evolve in this way, others may decay and lose potential, say because they are not acceptable to some members in the changed society. But in general we would expect the norms that are given

---

[8] Notice the difference between the following claims. One, the subgroup should not be expected to bear a certain cost by criteria that no one in the society who is willing to live on equal terms with others would reject. Two, the subgroup should not be expected to bear the cost by criteria that no one could reasonably reject: by criteria that no one could reject while counting by some independent standards as a reasonable person. It is the first claim that is relevant in this discussion, not the second.

countenance to increase in number and application, being laid down like a sediment deposited by the flow of debate and exchange.

Returning to our earlier example, imagine the policy-making norms that are likely to gain hold amongst the owners in a condominium of apartments. Some of those norms will be established in advance under contracts of purchase, but even if they are not pre-established, we can easily imagine them emerging and multiplying as members of the condominium come together to work out the terms on which they are to live together. As owners talk, try out proposals and then vote on remaining candidates, they will inevitably establish norms that rule their communal life together. These will determine:

- The reasons why they should collectively organize the servicing of elevators, the tending of common areas, the maintenance of a sinking fund, and such endeavours.
- The features of collective decision-making that are acknowledged on all sides as desirable: openness, consultation, deliberation, efficiency, and the like.
- The duties of individuals in relation to the group in the matter of body corporate fees, committee participation, general civility, etc.
- The equality of individuals in collective decision-making, despite the variations in the fees paid by the owners of different apartments.
- The rights of individuals to furnish and decorate their apartments internally to their own taste.
- The benefits that individuals can expect to be able to claim from the group corporate in dealing with particular problems like ground-floor flooding.
- The penalties that ought to be meted out to apartment owners who breach commonly established procedures.
- The value of giving authority to an elected committee, while allowing for challenges by other members to its resolutions.
- The utility of outsourcing certain decisions to independent advisers and auditors, given possible conflicts of interest.

The fact that a group operates under an acceptability regime in which certain norms of argument dictate the terms of argument and association does not mean that members will always behave in a saintly, or even a salutary, manner. Members may enter public debate and decision-making only reluctantly, preferring to allow things to get determined in many areas by default. When they enter debate or register dissent, members may not be moved by an impartial concern for the common good; so long as they are disciplined by the rules of the acceptability game, their fundamental motivations may be more or less self-seeking. And in debating or communicating with one another about different measures, members need not argue in the formally correct manner appropriate to a seminar. Thus, to elaborate on this last point, the arguments in which common norms are invoked may be implied in the particular observations that people make, in analogues from other areas that they suggest, or just in the unflattering cast that they give to the claims of opponents. The long tradition of political rhetoric shows us how any of a variety of such interventions, ranging from the wittily inverted phrase to the shaft of irony, to the hyperbolic gloss on an opponent's claim, to the subtle recasting of negatives and positives, to the interjection of a vivid example, even to the use of outright mockery, can activate accepted norms – perhaps fairly, perhaps unfairly – and provide support for one or another policy or process.[9]

But while the operation of an acceptability regime in a group like the condominium does not mean that things will be done in the most saintly or salutary fashion, the very fact of adopting the acceptability game does testify to a commitment to seeking solidarity in collective decision-making. The members of the condominium must be prepared to make their local community work, and work in a manner that gives each a role in community governance. By their very participation in deciding on common policies, or in revising the processes under which policies are decided, they show that they are ready to accommodate themselves to others in various ways, making whatever compromises and concessions are required. They are willing to think from the point of view of the group as a whole, rather than living in isolation and resentment or seeking after a community that is more congenial to their tastes. This commitment to the group amounts to a local counterpart of what would count as patriotism at the national level.

The acceptability game in the public world

Is politics going to generate games of acceptance, or games of acceptability, or a mix of both? In particular, which sort of game is it likely to favour if a regime of popular influence is established on the lines described in the previous chapter? Games of acceptance may play a subsidiary role in any political context, as when political parties negotiate on such a basis within a parliamentary context. But if a regime is designed to facilitate an

---

[9] For a good introduction to many traditional styles of rhetorical argument see Skinner (1996); on the potentially benign use of rhetoric see Garsten (2006) and McGeer and Pettit (2009).

individualized, unconditioned and efficacious form of popular influence, as our model requires, then it is bound to give a prominent role to games of acceptability and is bound therefore to generate a range of commonly accepted norms of policy-making.

The dominant, unifying theme in the system of popular influence that we sketched in the last chapter is that there must be room at many institutional sites for challenge and contestation, discussion and decision-making. We argued for a responsive, as distinct from an indicative, legislature on the grounds that it would allow the collective interrogation of elected authorities, reinforcing the freedom of speech, association and travel that this presupposes. We argued that in order to guard against the possibility that votes would not have equal value, so that the system would fail the requirement of individualized influence, this system of collective challenge has to be complemented by a system of individualized contestation, allowing individuals and groups of individuals to challenge any problematic measures proposed or imposed by government. We argued that in order to give this system of popular influence an unconditioned or independent character, government would have to be constituted out of distinct, mutually checking or contestatory parts, rather than having the power of an absolute sovereign, and the people would have to exhibit the deep, contestatory power – premised on a patriotic commitment to the success of the community – that specialized public-interest groups might provide. And we argued, finally, that in order to make popular influence efficacious, it is essential to guard against the electoral motives of politicians, establishing independent, indicative authorities in their place, to guard against the influence of private-interest groups by using such authorities to constrain their operation, and to guard against abuse on the part of those authorities by subjecting them to contestation in their own right.

The multi-dimensional, multi-centred pattern of contestation required for a suitable system of popular influence ensures that the acceptability game must dominate the operations of that system. Contestation is possible within an acceptance game as one or another party digs in on the concessions it is willing to make, relying on its wealth or size, or just its reputation for dogged intransigence, in order to oppose a resolution supported by others. But this sort of contestation would privilege the individuals and groups with greater bargaining power and expose political life to the chaos of random power plays. The only hope of getting individuals to share equally in a system of popular control is to organize the influence they exercise under the protocols of an acceptability game.

The acceptability game is quite consistent, as we saw, with an eventual resort to voting, or to any similar mechanism of resolution. But wherever it is in place, it will force people to interact in a manner that gives rise to shared policy-making norms. We may expect such common norms to get established at the multiple sites of opposition and contestation envisaged in the system of influence described. These sites include electoral campaigns and debates, judicial and cognate hearings, parliamentary discussions, exchanges between branches of government, public justifications of policy, disputes between watchdog bodies and government agencies, interactions in the press and other media, judgements or opinions offered by independent authorities, and popular campaigns for constitutional change. At each of these sites the final resolution of an issue may depend on a blunt instrument like voting and may be determined by the numbers available on any side. But the requirement for the parties on each side to defend their partisan proposals in multi-partisan terms ensures that as they construct their different programmes, they will lay down a foundation of common ground between them. The dissensus with which they end may be a failure in one dimension but it is going to represent an achievement in another: it will secure or reinforce the norms of argument that the disagreement drives the different sides to identify.

Not only will policy-making norms begin to emerge and crystallize at each site where contestation is brought or heard, answered or adjudicated. Those sites will naturally be accessible to one another, so that norms endorsed in one context are always going to be available for trialling, and acceptance or rejection, at another. The identification of an accepted norm in one context is going to present the parties who operate in any other with a potential resource for making their case on this or that question. And so we should naturally expect every candidate that proves acceptable at one site to become rapidly available for testing at other sites where government decisions are exposed to challenge. Norms accepted at one site, of course – say, amongst the members of a particular church or culture – may not prove to be acceptable at others. But the multiple connections between sites – connections enforced in a public, electoral culture – ought to ensure the identification of norms that have society-wide credentials.

There is little prospect of differences running so deep that few if any norms of that kind emerge.[10] Or at least there is little prospect of this to the extent that people on all sides of the society remain committed, on a patriotic basis, to making their community work. Patriotism of the kind

---

[10] For a different point of view see Gaus (2011).

envisaged here requires people not to allow their more personal or partial attachments – say, those centred on religious affiliation, ethnic identity or geographical location – to undermine their commitment to the larger community.[11] Let patriotism prevail and there are unlikely to be divisions of the kind that would undermine the emergence of society-wide norms.[12]

What are the norms that we might expect to emerge under a regime where things are organized to give people individualized, unconditioned and efficacious influence over government? A first is a norm, broadly speaking, of equality of influence. The very possibility of individualizing influence, as we saw in our earlier discussion, requires a recognition on people's part of the relevance of any argument, based on the need for equal access to influence. If people are to guard against the possibility that a sticky minority will be deprived of all influence, for example, then they must be required to recognize the importance of avoiding the marginalization of such a minority. The very possibility of a system of individualized influence – and so the very possibility of a legitimate government – turns on the extent to which such a norm of argument has a hold on people's imaginations and dictates their responses. People must be committed to the possibility of their particular community being governed under a regime of equally shared influence – in that sense they must be patriotically motivated – and they must be willing to take the electoral and contestatory steps required to uphold such a regime. Otherwise, by the line of argument developed here, legitimacy in government is going to be an unattainable ideal.

But if people's claim to equally accessible influence – equal respect in collective decision-making – is recognized on all sides, then so, plausibly, will be a more general claim to equal respect in how they are treated under collective decisions. This claim to equal respect will be registered as a reference point in public contestation and argument (Beitz 1989). And the acceptance of the claim is likely then to generate a series of more specific egalitarian norms, as ongoing exchanges and institutions establish interpretations of the demands of equal respect in schooling opportunities, conditions of employment, the operation of the courts, the organization of public facilities, and so on. These interpretations may vary across societies, of course, and indeed across eras. Thus the interpretation of the demands of equal respect shifted

---

[11] For an illustration of such a breakdown in a small corporate body, amounting to what I describe as collective akrasia, see Pettit (2003a).

[12] As noted earlier, however, recent changes in broadcasting create a danger that those in different political parties will only listen in on news and debates in their particular niche (Sunstein 2009).

dramatically in the United States with the rejection of the idea that races could be separate but equal. And that shift of interpretation released a cascade of changes in the way things were done in public life.

As there are likely to be various norms of equality under the system of influence described in the last chapter, so there are likely to be various norms of freedom. The idea of having a system of popular influence that is individualized, unconditioned and efficacious goes naturally with recognizing the need for each to have a sphere of personal choice and with an interpretation of the freedom that people should have in that sphere. As with equality, the demands of freedom may be differently interpreted in different polities and different periods, but they are likely in any society to enforce some boundary between the domain where people ought to be able to make their own decisions and the domain where government or other authorities can rule; to establish some sense of what is required for people to be able to make their own decisions in this way, enjoying a relative independence from others; and to license this or that level of government resourcing and protection as a means of establishing such independence for all.

A dispensation for ensuring a suitable degree of popular influence has to assume institutional form at some point, with the introduction of measures that provide for election, challenge and interrogation; that limit the authority of elected officials and regulate the activities of private lobbies; and that delineate possibilities of legitimate opposition and contestation. And as the institutions required emerge and stabilize, they are bound to gain acceptance and to license associated norms of argument. Those norms will support appeals to the principles and precautions that the institutions embody, such as importance of the separation of powers, the independence of the judiciary, the transparency of government decisions, and so on. The precise institutions introduced in any society may vary from the institutions introduced in others, of course, and as they vary, the corresponding institution-specific norms will vary too.

Apart from the equality-based, freedom-based and institution-specific examples just canvassed, a host of independent norms are going to emerge in any society with growing convergence on the question of what the state ought to do and with institutions that implement such convergence. The business that government is charged with taking up will certainly include the defence of the country, the identification of the basic liberties, the enforcement of law and order, and the facilitation of industry, commerce and employment. But in most societies it will also extend, under this or that interpretation, to the provision of education for the young, the regulation of various markets, the insurance of communities against catastrophe, and the insurance of individuals against urgent or pressing need, medical, legal or economic. The list is more or less open-ended.

I have been speaking about the variety of norms that we might expect to develop in any society, particularly in any society with a system of popular influence that is designed to be individualized, unconditioned and efficacious. There is a common character that we might expect such democratic norms to display, as I have stressed, but the precise content they assume will always depend on contingencies of local culture and development. But I should not suggest that democracy will be free of faults and fetters. The norms that emerge in any society, reflecting some perhaps questionable beliefs and values, may often be deficient, judged from the point of view of this or that conception of justice or legitimacy.

While the history of a democratic society will typically offer a rich and appealing set of norms to invoke in public life, it can also saddle those who live in the society with unwholesome constraints and unwelcome fetters. Every developed democracy will have evolved along a certain trajectory, being built upon a tradition of letting government take charge of such and such matters and being associated with more or less settled institutions and arrangements. This can put a society in a bind, locking members out of the possibility of arguing for what by most of their shared norms of argument would constitute an improvement. Thus, to give a simple example, it was essential in the founding of the United States, and at the time of Australian federation, that large and small states were given equal representation in the Senate; this is unsurprising, since they were the parties responsible for creating the new political order. This pattern of representation would be unlikely to command much support in either country today, if the constitution were being redrafted from scratch. The citizens of distinct states within both the United States and Australia are geographically mobile and probably do not identify as strongly with their local states as their predecessors would have done. But nonetheless, there is no immediate prospect of an alteration in either regime. The norm of equal state representation has a pedigree that puts it beyond effective interrogation.

Deliberative regulation by policy-making norms

These observations support the idea that in any regime that implements something like the popular system of influence that democracy requires, there are going to be norms of public policy-making that get to be accepted on all sides. The question we now confront is whether those democratic norms might exercise a directive or shaping role over policies. Might popular influence serve to promote compliance or compatibility with policy-making norms?[13]

The policies adopted in different regimes of popular influence, and the processes under which they are adopted, are likely to vary greatly from one another. Thus the norms that are endorsed across different regimes, shaping the policies and processes adopted, may diverge significantly. Again, empirical assumptions are required to determine the implications of any set of norms for the actual policies or processes put in place and these, too, may vary across societies. And the mechanisms of final resolution that inevitably play a role in determining policies may also push societies in different directions: resolution by majority voting or an impartial umpire can be as indeterminate as resolution by lottery.

But consistently with such variation it can still be the case that the policies and processes adopted in any regime are subject to the constraining or guiding effect of policy-making norms. Those norms will constrain and guide policy-making to the extent that their presence more or less ensures that two conditions are fulfilled. First, a policy-condition: no policies are left on the table as possible candidates for adoption in any domain, if they are in violation of the norms. And second, a process-condition: no process for selecting between candidates that survive that first cut – and no process for selecting between rival processes – is employed, if its employment in that domain would be in violation of the norms.[14]

Assuming that policy-making norms impose effective constraints, as they are surely capable of doing, the dispensation depicted here is going to give them a substantial directive role. Going back to the example of the condominium, we can imagine a regime emerging in which things are reliably done to the satisfaction of the norm-based expectations of owners. Under the impact of those norms, the owners come to establish certain decision-making processes and, invoking relevant norms, to build up an accumulating body of policies. The organization will run under the influence of those members – and, as we may assume, their individualized, unconditioned and efficacious influence – and that influence will have the effect of imposing compliance with the norms that they endorse. The members will disagree strongly on particular issues, of course, perhaps dividing into bitterly opposed factions. But to the extent that their differences continue to be debated and resolved without offending against any of the norms they hold in common, the members will have succeeded in establishing a common norm-based order.

Suppose that one party wants to allow some of the apartments in the building to be rented out to a nearby hotel and the other party is strongly opposed to this development. And imagine that they make the decision in a way that conforms to shared norms. Whichever party wins in that case, the members of the condominium will have achieved an important goal together: the compliance of their policies and policy-making with norms that are shared amongst them. They may not come to a common mind on the particular issue on hand but that will not be a problem so long as the final decision is made on the basis of norm-compatible process. Suppose that the numbers for and against the hotel proposal break even and the decision is made on the basis of a coin-toss, where this process of decision-making is itself consistent with the accepted norms. The result of such a chance device will not undermine the common achievement of norm-compliance. And neither would the victory of one or the other side under any other accepted process – say, voting on the committee, or in a referendum. One party will prevail on the issue, and perhaps on a range of related issues, but at a deeper level it is the members of the condominium as a whole that rule. Their common norms, not the norms of any particular faction, shape the direction in which the organization moves.

As the norms emerging amongst the members of a condominium can shape the policies and processes that prevail there, forcing whatever decisions are made to conform to a template they impose, so we might expect the norms of a political community to have the same directive impact on the operation of government. The decisions taken by government may vary enormously, depending on what particular norms have been endorsed, on who happens to occupy elected or unelected office, and on what those officials come to decide on specific issues. But if the emergent norms are truly effective, as they ought to be in the presence of a suitable constitution and citizenry, then they should put a directive and controlling stamp on what is collectively done in the community. They should filter out offending policies and processes, making room only for modes of decision-making, and actual decisions, that fit with accepted standards.

The regulation its members impose on their condominium, or its citizens on their government, can be described as deliberative regulation, since the norms that they deploy all emerge as the by-product of deliberation within the organization. But the deliberative regulation of the condominium or government is not likely to come about as a result of every decision being taken on an explicitly deliberative basis. Since the presence of public deliberation on a number of occasions at a number of sites is enough to generate the required norms, that is all it presupposes. And since it will equally be enough that the norms have been generated and have come to be generally accepted, even such episodic deliberation will be less and less required as the condominium or society develops. The regulation will operate, not on the basis of continuing, ubiquitous deliberation, but rather as the product of institutional constraints that reflect deliberative norms. The decisions the body eventually reaches will have to flow along so many channels, skirt so many potential checks and obstacles, and avoid floundering on so many contestatory hazards that they are more or less bound to satisfy the requirements of deliberatively generated norms.

How distinct is this ideal of deliberative regulation from that of deliberative democracy? It is built out of the same observation, familiar in particular from the work of Juergen Habermas (1984, 1989), that when people debate with one another about what they should combine to do, then they have little option but to seek out considerations that all can see as relevant to a joint enterprise (Elster 1986). As we know, these may be convergent considerations identifying benefits they can all share in, such as safety or prosperity or cohesion. Or they may be concordant considerations licensing the provision of benefits for a subgroup in a recognized sort of predicament, as when its members suffer a deprivation that is seen as problematic on all sides, or are in a position to improve their lot without doing any harm to others.

But while the approach taken here is deeply continuous with the spirit of deliberative democracy, there is a break at two distinct levels. At a foundational level, the approach is inspired by the republican insight that people must share equally in their control of government if they are to avoid domination, and not by a foundational commitment to the value of deliberation as such (Cohen 1989).[15] At the operational level, it is organized around the idea that it is the deliberative regulation of public business – that

---

[15] Jake Zuehl has persuaded me that in the later papers in Cohen (2009), the foundational commitment to the value of actual deliberation gets to be qualified in a contractualist way, as the reasons that are taken to count get to be indistinguishable from the Rawlsian public reasons mentioned in an earlier footnote.

is, regulation by deliberatively tested norms – that is essential, not the deliberative conduct of decision-making at every site and on every occasion.

The difference of perspective and practice between the two approaches shows up in the fact that whereas dissensus always represents a second-best for deliberative democrats, it is entirely acceptable, even desirable, within the present approach. It is the experience of dissensus, after all, that drives the different sides to identify common policy-making norms, as they try to make sense of their respective views to one another. And it is those norms that constrain the policies that they are willing to entertain and the processes of decision-making they are ready to employ.

The fact that the deliberative regulation of collective decision-making does not entail a great deal of deliberative conduct also has a further implication. It means that the members of a deliberatively regulated group, unlike the members of a group that conducts all its business in explicit exercises of deliberation, may not always be conscious of the deliberative regulation under which they operate. The impact of deliberative norms may be elusive, indeed almost invisible, if the system is working well. Assuming that it is working at its best, the institutions established will not be called into question; the arguments put forward at various sites will be weighed differently but admitted as relevant on all sides; the proposals made by one or another side will be opposed by others but not condemned as normatively objectionable; and the final resolution of differences will be achieved under undisputed processes of decision-making. In short, the conduct of public business will run along straight and even tracks without any evidence of being directed onto those paths by a body of popular norms.

The direction of public business by popular norms will become salient only when things do not go so well in one or another forum and participants launch norm-based objections to the content of a policy or to the process by which a policy is determined. But since participants will presumably want to avoid such objections, they have an incentive to stay within limits that keep them safe from such retort. And when they do genuinely stay within such boundaries, the system will be working fairly well; it will be displaying a high level of compliance with policy-making norms.

Although popular norms may not have a salient presence in a system that is working well, however, this is not to say that they do not have an impact there. The impact that they will have under such an ideal scenario, to return to an idea already introduced in other contexts, will have a virtual or even reserve character. To take the virtual case, it will be like the impact of the cowboy who rides herd on his cattle. The cowboy may do little or nothing by way of guiding the cattle; he lets them have their head, given that they are on the right path. But he clearly has a determining influence on the path they take because he is ready to intervene effectively if any of them should wander off the track. The same is going to be true of the influence that policy-making norms have in the scenario presented. As policies are proposed, defended and challenged, and as they are finally selected under one or another process, there will be players within the system who are ready to cry foul if a policy or process looks to be in breach of accepted norms. And so even when those norms do not play an active role in the shaping of what transpires, they can still have a powerful effect. They can ride herd, as it were, on the process of policy-formation.

Consider the condominium example again. As insiders or outsiders contemplate what happens in the day-to-day working of the organization, the salient features will be the routines that are more or less unthinkingly followed, the ways in which members come to differ on various aspects of policy, the arguments that they each invoke in support of their views, and the mechanical resolution to which most of their differences are eventually subjected. Nowhere in this manifold of observations will there be positive evidence of the role of the norms to which members subscribe. And yet those norms will be in place to outlaw any norm-incompatible routines, and to rule out any arguments – and any proposals based on arguments – that do not satisfy the norms. The eye-catching exchanges will all take place within a field of interaction that is shaped by the norms, but the impact of the norms themselves may be close to invisible. Even when the waters of politics run at their most turbulent within the condominium, the turbulence will be consistent with the existence, beneath the surface, of a common stream of influence and direction.

Dual-aspect democracy

We have argued that any regime of suitable popular influence will give a powerful role to acceptability games; that such games will give rise to widespread adherence to policy-making norms; that those norms will tend to shape policy-making by putting norm-incompatible policies and processes off the table; that they may operate to this effect without a great deal of explicit deliberation taking place within the system; and that when they operate well in achieving the effect, their impact will often be hard to discern: the influence they support may often have a virtual or reserve character.

The lesson of these observations is that a regime that is deliberatively regulated is likely to operate in two time-scales, whether it materializes in a private association like the condominium or in the political community at large. It will require the short-haul, highly charged process of campaign and election, proposal and counter-proposal, debate, division and contestation. But it will achieve its signature impact in the long-haul process, as silently as gravity, whereby participants are wittingly or unwittingly led to establish only such policies and processes as conform to the norms of argument and association that prevail amongst them. Over this long haul, a deliberatively regulated politics will generate and regenerate a supply of publicly valorized considerations. These will serve at any particular time to keep an indefinite number of policies and processes off the table, rendering them unthinkable and invisible. And they will combine from time to time to make certain existing policies or processes suddenly seem intolerable and in urgent need of repair.

This image of a deliberatively regulated regime constitutes what I describe as a dual-aspect model of democracy. Apart from the fast democracy of election and contestation that commands most attention amongst political participants, observers and theorists, it directs us to a slow democracy that works under suitable forms of popular influence to impose a distinctive stamp on what government, over the long haul, effects.

In the nature of the case, evidence that a political regime conforms to the dual-aspect model, constituting a deliberatively regulated democracy, is going to be hard to identify. The claim that the regime imposes deliberative norms on government is going to be particularly difficult to establish, given that such regulation will only be evident over the long haul. In order to overcome this problem, and illustrate the operation of something like the dual-aspect model, I must resort to history, in particular the sort of history that looks at the *longue durée*.

I think the reality of slow democracy, and the viability of the dual-aspect model, is well supported in the work of Oliver MacDonagh (1958, 1961, 1977) on the massive shifts in the activities of British government over the half century or so after the debates about the Great Reform Bill of 1832. I pick this example for two reasons. One, it is distant enough in time and culture to allow us to get a clear view of what transpired. And two, it was a period in which the rise of democracy meant that there was much to achieve – not just, as is now often the case, much to maintain or recover – in order to keep the government in line with popular norms. While the franchise was not greatly extended in 1832, electoral democracy became more and more established as a guiding ideal in nineteenth-century Britain and later extensions of the franchise were heralded by an enormous rise in public petitions and public demonstrations (Knights 2005).

The nineteenth-century transformation took England, and Britain more generally, from a state that had become minimal by any standards to a regime in which government assumed responsibility for regulating a great swathe of social behaviour, establishing offices that imposed strict inspection and control over such matters as the employment of children, the treatment of women, the preparation of food and drugs, the operation of the civil service and, relatedly, the conduct of affairs in mines, mills, factories, ships, railways and public offices. I do not argue here that this growth in the administrative responsibility of the state was desirable, though to my eye much of it clearly was. Drawing on MacDonagh's work, my only aim is to use this shift to illustrate the depth at which policy-making norms can operate in a broadly democratic context to impose a slow, long-haul direction on government – and often, as in this case, on a deeply resistant, even resentful administration.

The early nineteenth century in England was a period of enormous social problems. These were occasioned by a number of connected factors: the introduction of steam-based industrialization, the vast increase in population, the capacity of people to move into new areas, even across oceans, and the ensuing concentrations in industrial cities and towns; in the first quarter of the nineteenth century, many towns in Yorkshire and Lancashire grew by a factor of three or four. With these developments, a more or less paternalistic tradition of management in agriculture and village industry gave way to the ruthless discipline of Blake's dark satanic mills. As Sir Walter Scott wrote in 1820: 'the manufacturers are transferred to great towns, where a man may assemble five hundred workmen one week and dismiss them the next, without having any further connexion with them than to receive a week's work for a week's wages, nor any further solicitude about their future fate than if they were so many old shuttles'.[16]

While the problems that arose in the new industrial world were daunting and varied, the doctrine of laissez-faire individualism that prevailed in official circles might well have left them unaddressed. As democratization increased, however, the pressures brought to bear on government pushed it slowly and reluctantly into becoming something unimagined at the beginning. In MacDonagh's (1958: 57) words, they occasioned a 'transformation, scarcely glimpsed till it was well secured, of the operations and functions of government'.

The transformation was effected now in the mines, now in the factories, now in ocean-going ships, having an impact that affected the lives of men,

---

[16] Quoted by MacDonagh (1977: 2).

women and children across the society. In each case, the transformation was prompted by the same factors and developed along the same lines.

The factors that drove the changes, according to MacDonagh (1958: 57–8), were 'the increasing sensitivity of politics to public pressures' that we would expect with growing democratization and 'the widespread and ever-growing influence of humanitarian sentiment and of stricter views of sexual morality'. The humanitarianism was particularly important, bubbling up in 'the raw and immediate reactions of a variety of ordinary and thoroughly representative people', for it managed to overcome the resistance of laissez-faire doctrine and commercial self-interest: 'the general level of compassion in contemporary England overswept policy and commerce' (MacDonagh 1961: 330). This was not just a dumb, pre-conceptual sort of compassion; it was organized around concepts and norms that had deep roots in the political culture. Many of the abuses condemned were cast as abuses against freedom, for example, and as analogues of enslavement. In a famous newspaper letter of 1830, a reformer, Richard Oastler, could write: 'Thousands of our fellow-creatures and fellow-subjects, both male and female, the miserable inhabitants of a Yorkshire town ... are this very moment existing in a state of slavery, more horrid than are the victims of that hellish system colonial slavery. These innocent creatures drawl out, unpitied, their short but miserable existence.'[17]

The different changes that occurred in nineteenth-century England were generally prompted, then, by a democratically empowered humanitarianism. But not only did the changes have a common source, according to MacDonagh, they also evolved under a similar dynamic and in parallel stages.

In each case the change began with the revelation by newspapers or reform organizations of just how scandalous conditions were in this or that domain; in each case this scandal led to a degree of public outrage amongst the population at large; and in each case that outrage prompted a reaction from government, in particular an initiative designed to put things right. 'Once it was publicized sufficiently that, say, women on their hands and knees dragged trucks of coal through subterranean tunnels, or that emigrants had starved to death at sea or that children had been mutilated by unfenced machinery, these evils became "intolerable"; and throughout and even before the Victorian years "intolerability" was the master card' (MacDonagh 1958: 58).

[17] The letter is to the *Leeds Mercury*, 16 October 1830; see www.makingthemodernworld.org.uk.

The dynamic that called for such reform never played itself out in a single round. Almost invariably it transpired some years after the first initiative that the law had been ineffective and that the scandal remained. And with that second revelation the dynamic ran its course again, leading to the appointment of executive inspectors and officers who were charged with putting the law into effect. Nor was that all. The reports of these administrators fuelled yet further developments, as it became clear that problems were proving recalcitrant, and this third iteration of the dynamic generated a progressively more professional and better-organized public service. The culmination of such transformations across a variety of domains was the slow emergence of a new and characteristically modern sort of state.

The impact that popular pressure can give to policy-making norms is well illustrated, I believe, in this narrative. The norms had a background presence in people's attitudes, which survived ideological and party differences. And they had a slow, relentless effect on how government operated, pushing it inexorably towards a certain destination. The direction in which a gradually democratizing government was pushed in Victorian England is particularly salient to us, given the contrast, at least in the developed world, between those times and ours. But I believe that it illustrates the sort of purpose that democracy can serve everywhere in imposing accepted norms on government. It shows that the dual-aspect model described here is not necessarily a pipedream.

No illustration of the model is going to be ideal, of course, and there are a number of particularities about this example that we should note. One is that while it exemplifies the role of accepted norms in putting certain issues on the agenda of government and in prompting improvements to a clearly imperfect practice in that domain, it does not illustrate the less salient role of norms – so important in any advanced democracy – in maintaining improvements already in place. A second is that while it exemplifies the role of accepted norms in putting certain policies off the table – those, for example, that would allow for the employment of children in mines – it does not illustrate their equally important role in putting certain processes or procedures of decision-making off the table. And a third is that it does not make clear that the satisfaction of humanitarian norms achieved in the long-haul development described was a by-product of debates that were focused on rather more specific, short-haul policies. Those norms had a slowly mounting impact, not because humanitarian norm-compliance was a target at which anyone aimed, but because it was a common, barely recognized constraint on the concessions and adjustments that politicians were forced to make under the pressures of day-to-day politics.

Notwithstanding these features, the MacDonagh studies serve us well in illustrating how popular pressures can empower norms, impose them on government and make them into a more or less fixed feature of how things get to be done. They display the workings of a more or less deliberatively regulated democracy, as the various individuals and bodies involved in its short-haul operations are pushed under the pressure of popular influence to adopt a discernible, long-haul direction.

The sort of thesis that MacDonagh defends is borne out in other contexts too. Thus, to mention one important example, William Eskridge and John Ferejohn (2010) argue in a detailed examination of cases that popular pressure in the United States has led to the statutory implementation and effective entrenchment of norms of equal citizenship, market openness and personal security. In an uncanny parallel to MacDonagh's narrative, they describe a process in which a social movement or other pressure creates a demand for state action; publicly supported legislation generates a statute embodying a new norm; the statute is administered and expanded with feedback and pushback from various sectors of the community; the norm is revisited and reaffirmed by the legislature in face of opposition; and this is followed by further administrative elaboration, further feedback and pushback, and further legislative revision (Eskridge and Ferejohn 2010: 19–20). Like MacDonagh, they illustrate the slow emergence and impact of popular norms that I see as evidence for what democracy is capable of achieving over the long haul in imposing a direction on government.

Our discussion points us towards a popular purpose or direction that might be imposed on government under the system of popular influence described in the last chapter. That purpose is compliance with policy-making norms, whether they be norms that put policies or processes off the table, norms that are associated with the agenda of government, the status of citizens or the conduct of government, or norms that are encoded in particular institutions and in laws or conventions that have a less formal existence amongst members of the community. That purpose can be systematically promoted, so it appears, as the long-term effect of short-term attempts to exercise influence within the constraints imposed by an acceptability game.

With this image of dual-aspect democracy in place, we can turn finally to considering its attractions. I promised at the end of Section 1 that the dual-aspect model would combine the appeal of each of the existing models of popular control: in the first of these, government is under the intentional control of the people and in the other under their non-intentional control. It is time now to make good on that commitment.

Combining the attractions of existing models

The first of the existing models of popular control would organize government around people's public-interest judgements – their impartial preferences over what happens to the society as a whole. The second would organize it under a mechanism designed to make government responsive to more particular attitudes: people's partial preferences over what happens to themselves. The first is attractive, we saw, in focusing us on a plausible goal for popular direction: that of the public interest, understood in a post-social, non-corporate manner. The second is attractive in directing us to a plausible means for popular direction: an invisible-hand mechanism that does not require people to maintain control in an intentional manner.

The dual-aspect model has the virtue of combining the respective attractions of these competitors. To the extent that the policies pursued in government satisfy policy-making norms, they may be expected to further the public interest, as that is understood in the first of these competing models. And to the extent that they are forced to satisfy those norms as the long-term effect of people's short-term attempts to influence policy-making, they promise to materialize as the result of an invisible-hand mechanism akin to that envisaged in the second competing model.

As a plausible example of a matter of public interest – that is, a matter of the post-social and non-corporate interest of all – we mentioned the interest that the followers of different religions are likely to have, assuming they are willing to live on equal terms with each other, in the freedom of religious practice. But the assumptions that show freedom of religion to be a public interest show equally that there is likely to be a norm requiring people to acknowledge the relevance of invoking freedom of religion as a reason to favour certain policies and oppose others. The general norm of invoking only considerations that can carry weight with all would permit this consideration to have a place in public debate. And assuming that there is occasion to invoke the consideration – assuming, in other words, that there are religious issues that arise in politics – we can expect to see a specific norm emerge under which people are required, on pain of the disapproval of others, to acknowledge its relevance.

This example helps to show how the dual-aspect model is likely to promote a version of the public interest associated with the intentional-control picture of democracy. But while it promises in this way to display the same appeal as that particular model, it is not subject to the same disadvantage. The intentional-control model supposes that a democracy will promote the public interest only insofar as politicians and citizens more generally display a high level of unmotivated virtue in the judgements they endorse and the policies they support. The dual-aspect model suggests, by contrast, that a democracy can promote the public interest under an invisible-hand mechanism of the kind that makes for the appeal of the standard alternative to the intentional-control model: that is, the model of democracy, illustrated in James Mill's theory of representative government, on which democracy works like the market.

The participants in a dual-aspect democracy will be involved at any time or context in supporting a decision on this or that policy, or this or that process of decision-making, and will be required by the rules of the acceptability game to identify considerations that can pass muster on all sides. But as this game continues in a society, now in one domain of policy, now in another, now in one context of policy-making, now in a second, the participants are bound to generate a range of policy-relevant norms as a by-product of the process in which they are involved. And as they narrow down the candidates between which they have to decide on any occasion, and let the final resolution be determined by a mechanism like voting, they will ensure that process-relevant norms have a constraining role on the mechanism used. Thus if all goes well, the policies and processes adopted are likely to satisfy the demands of the norms in play. That result will materialize without being something that any of them explicitly pursues.

The people under this model each have a wish not to have to live under government policies or processes that breach received norms, as evidenced in the political arguments they advance and accept. And by each acting on the basis of that self-regarding desire, they combine to ensure an aggregate result under which they each achieve satisfaction of that desire. The desires that drive their efforts lead to a pattern of behaviour that satisfies the desires without anyone necessarily foreseeing or intending this – that is, as by an invisible hand. The citizens of a dual-aspect democracy control for their government's satisfaction of accepted norms, to revert to the analogue used earlier, in the same way that the consumers in an ideal market control for the competitive pricing of available goods. The dual-aspect democracy gives effect to the political wishes of citizens, as the ideal market gives effect to the economic wishes of consumers. Each mode of organization has an empowering effect, helping to ensure that the relevant desires of the parties, economic or political, get to be satisfied.[18]

---

[18] Not only is a pattern of competitive pricing, as generated in the ideal market, going to be attractive to all. It is going to be a stable equilibrium: a pattern such that no one has an incentive to depart from it

The non-intentional control that citizens exercise over government in the dual-aspect model contrasts with the sort of control that members of a group might exercise as a matter of jointly intentional action. For an example of jointly intentional action, consider how people sitting on a beach can act together to save a swimmer who is having trouble in the water. There are many analyses of what can support joint action, but one clear possibility would materialize when it is manifest to members of the group:

- that they together can save the swimmer by forming a chain into the water;
- that they each want the group to adopt that strategy and achieve that result;
- that they are each disposed to play their part so long as others join them; and
- that others are going to join anyone who takes the initiative.

Under such conditions someone is bound to take the initiative, triggering the cooperation that promises to save the child. And when cooperation occurs, then it is going to be natural to say that the members of the group perform a joint action with a joint effect: they intentionally control for the desired outcome.[19]

It may well be the case in a democracy that people act out of a joint intention to influence government; that would certainly fit with the model of the last chapter. But it is not the case, under the model of this chapter, that people act out of a joint intention to control government as the intentional-control model envisages.[20] The collective control for which the dual-aspect model programmes is generated in quite a different manner. People combine under that model to ensure that the policies and processes of government conform to popular, equally acceptable norms. But it need not be manifest to members of the group – that is, it need not be a matter of common belief amongst them – that they together can achieve that aggregate, cumulative result, and so it need not be a matter of explicit desire or intention – it need not be in any sense a general will – that they should do

unilaterally, and if anyone does, then the pattern is likely to be quickly restored. The same is true, I believe, of the pattern of norm-satisfaction that a deliberatively regulated, dual-aspect democracy would generate. No one would have an incentive to depart from it unilaterally, at least given the repercussions that this is likely to have on others. And in the event of a departure, those repercussions would be likely to restore the pattern.

[19] There is a large literature on what it is for people to cooperate in forming such a joint intention and pursuing such a joint action. See for example Bratman (1987); Searle (1995); Tuomela (1995); Gilbert (2001). My own preference follows broadly the lines taken by Bratman; see also Pettit and Schweikard (2006); List and Pettit (2011).

[20] For a paper that outlines the form that such a model might take see Bratman (2004).

so. They generate the effect by each looking after their own efforts: they each seek to support their own arguments in accepted terms, and they each require others to do the same. And they each have a reason to welcome that effect, given the desire at the origin of those efforts. But the effect itself eventuates by a hand that is likely to be hidden from them; it materializes behind their backs.

The critique of the intentional-control model combines with the defence of the dual-aspect model to suggest that the promotion of policy-making norm-satisfaction may be possible only on the basis of the invisible-hand mechanism described. In Jon Elster's (1979, 1983) phrase, such norm-satisfaction may constitute an essential by-product. It may be a result that can be reliably secured only as a side-effect of people's pursuing some other aim. Let people explicitly try to agree in identifying and implementing common norms and they are likely to recognize the costs that the satisfaction of appropriate norms can impose on them and theirs. And as they recognize those costs, high virtue is liable to fail them and leave them at irreconcilable loggerheads with one another.[21] The only dependable path to establishing a regime of norm-satisfaction may be the one charted in the dual-aspect model.

In the account emerging from these observations, the participants in a dual-aspect democracy will struggle with one another, and perhaps divide quite antagonistically, over particular matters of policy. But however adversarial their struggle, they will honour the demands of the acceptability game, and generate norms that have a double effect of cutting down the policies treated as potential candidates for implementation and of cutting down the processes to be employed for resolving disputes over candidate policies. This double impact means that the policies generated ought to make a plausible claim to be in the common or public interest, where that interest is understood in a post-social, non-corporate manner. Plausibly, indeed, the policies might even begin to answer to the demands of justice, as those are understood under republican or related conceptions. Being policies supported by considerations acceptable on all sides – supported in their own right and via the support given to the processes under which they are selected – they promise not to be too far out of kilter with what might be expected to promote justice.

----

[21] There is every reason to think, of course, that as people pursue this norm-identifying exercise under an acceptability regime, they will establish higher-order norms amongst themselves. The lesson follows by an argument that parallels Lewis Carroll's argument in his classic paper on Achilles and the Tortoise (1895).

The citizens who play their part under the dual-aspect model will each have their own particular conceptions of justice, of course, differing on at least some of the policies that they think justice requires. And so in making proposals, offering objections and generally contesting how things are evolving under government, they will be guided by those conceptions, looking for commonly acceptable considerations by which they can hope to draw others to their side. While no side can expect a full victory in a society where plurality rules – the republican side included – they may each still expect that the policies and processes that get established are not going to offend too radically against their more central principles. And they may each even hope that as debates and decisions evolve, the most compelling conception of justice – their own, as they will each take it to be – will come eventually to prevail.

This is an optimistic vision of how things can transpire under a dual-aspect democracy and I hasten to add that it will only materialize under quite demanding conditions. It is a commonplace in economics that few markets live up to the demanding conditions laid out in textbooks: most are affected by a variety of economic distortions, ranging from restrictions on entry to natural monopolies to collusion amongst producers. And it is equally a commonplace that competitive pricing will not generally materialize in the presence of such distortions. It is important to recognize that a parallel observation holds in the democratic case. The dual-aspect model of democracy is only going to work when there is a properly individualized, unconditioned and efficacious system of popular influence, and when the rules of the acceptability game have a sufficient presence to ensure the deliberative regulation of public business. To the extent that distortions warp the system of popular influence and exchange, there will be a shortfall from the ideal we have been describing. And the greater the distortions, plausibly, the larger that shortfall will be.

This observation serves to underline the critical edge of the model developed here. The dual-aspect model offers us a picture of a system in which the *demos*, or 'people', enjoy *kratos*, or 'control', over government. But the model is only going to materialize under the sorts of conditions at which we have been gesturing in this chapter and the last. Let those conditions fail and there will be democratic distortions that parallel the market distortions of which economists speak. While the conditions will often fail to be satisfied, however – while they will call for revision to existing practices – the prospect of their fulfilment is not a utopian pipedream. The dual-aspect model supports a programme of reform and renovation that is well within the bounds of feasible achievement.

3. THE PEOPLE, THE STATE AND THE CONSTITUTION

Government of the people, by the people, for the people

One of the most widely accepted characterizations of democracy was offered by Abraham Lincoln in his Gettysburg address when he described it as government of the people, by the people and for the people. Under a plausible interpretation, the characterization requires that government be for the people in assuming a pattern or direction answering to people's wishes or needs; that it be by the people in being directly or representatively implemented by the citizenry; and that it be of the people insofar as the people are in ultimate control: they do not depend on the willingness of any other agent or agency for their capacity to shape the government they live under. The dual-aspect model of democracy ensures that all three clauses are satisfied.

The effect of a system of popular influence in forcing government to comply with accepted policy-making norms is bound to be equally acceptable to all participants. And in that sense the system of control and direction valorized under the dual-aspect model will ensure that government is for the people. It imposes significant restrictions on the will of government, although it may leave a good deal to the effects of chance; as we saw in the last chapter, chance will appear in the processes that happen to be chosen for resolving policy ties, for example, and in the results to which those processes happen to lead. And the restrictions it imposes will answer equally to the concerns of all citizens who deserve a hearing – all those who are willing to live on equal terms with others – since these will reflect considerations that have to be relevant, by all lights, to the enterprise of collective decision-making. Thus the policies adopted and the processes employed in selecting them must all pass muster by universally endorsed criteria; the will that guides the generation of laws and other measures has to operate on terms that reflect an outlook common to all relevant members of the society.

The dual-aspect model of government is also bound to ensure that government is by the people. It requires the system of popular influence that imposes an equally acceptable direction on government to be individualized, unconditioned and efficacious. And in developing an institutional model under which this requirement can be satisfied it argues for an electoral-cum-contestatory regime in which the influence that shapes government emanates directly or indirectly from the people themselves. Everything done under this system of government is going to be done by the people themselves, whether this involves their collective presence in election or their collective representation by suitably responsive or indicative agents. Their agents will act in the people's name insofar as they are suitably appointed and they will act under the people's control insofar as they have to discharge their representative roles under a suitable form of popularly imposed constraint and review.

Finally, government will be of the people insofar as the directive influence exercised by the people is not exercised at the discretion or by the permission of any distinct agency: not the government itself, not any power elite within the society, and not any foreign power. The dual-aspect model ensures the fulfilment of this final clause in requiring that the influence of the people should be unconditioned in character, mediating a form of control that is truly the people's own. This condition will be breached under any form of colonial or neo-colonial rule, even a rule that allows the domestic polity to do business in an electoral fashion. And equally it will be breached in any regime where the people succeed in putting government through electoral and contestatory hoops only when this accords with the desires of the governing authorities, the wishes of the army or police, the dictates of a priestly caste, or the interests of the very wealthy.

We developed the dual-aspect model with a view to identifying a government with claims to republican legitimacy: a government that would interfere in the affairs of its citizens, as all governments have to do, but that would interfere under their equally shared control and so without domination. But the model does not only have good republican credentials in that sense – the satisfaction of the Lincoln triad shows that by almost any benchmark it is also going to have excellent credentials as a model of democracy. A system that met the specifications it lays down would ensure the sort of self-rule or self-control that Lincoln's characterization requires.

The self-control that the people secure under the dual-aspect system is relatively indeterminate, of course, since, as we know, it leaves much to the operation of chance. This may be the chance whereby a particular majority governs parliament, the decisions of a court or tribunal or commission take a certain shape, the vote in a particular referendum goes a certain way, or indeed a lottery mechanism generates one or another result. But the indeterminacy of the control that people exercise over themselves in the dual-aspect model is paralleled by an indeterminacy in the personal self-control that individuals enjoy under various interpretations of autonomy.

Take the interpretation of autonomy as orthonomy, which was mentioned in the first chapter. Orthonomy involves the sort of self-rule in which you guide what you believe and desire, intend and do, by the values that you endorse, however valuation is construed (Pettit and Smith 1996).

Displaying a high degree of orthonomy, you may be faithful in your belief-processing to the value of hearing all sides of a question, in your desire-formation to the value of looking beyond the moment, and in your actions to the various claims you recognize in others. But while proving orthonomous in that sense, you may be led to embrace any of a number of beliefs and desires and to take any of a variety of actions; the constraints of the relevant values will leave a lot of slack or indeterminacy in place. That is fine, so long as the indeterminacy is resolved by more or less contingent or chance factors, without any inconsistency with the values that are meant to be in control.

Just as self-government in the personal case is not jeopardized by the fact that the factors in control – your values – leave a lot of slack in place, so the same is true of self-government in the democratic context. The presence of slack or indeterminacy is no problem for the ideal whereby the civic or constituting people govern themselves in their life together by the norms they accept, imposing those norms on the practice of policy-making. Or at least it is no problem, provided that the slack is taken up in an appropriate, norm-compatible way: that is, without the unlicensed intrusion of any alien will.

The role of the state under the dual-aspect model

Not only does the dual-aspect model offer us an intuitive sense in which the *demos*, or 'people', exercise *kratos*, or 'power', it also gives us the wherewithal to analyse that claim in more exact terms. It provides the materials for a political ontology in which the notion of the people is given more precise reference and the idea of a popular government is spelled out more properly. I shall focus on this ontology in the remainder of the chapter, beginning with the role of the state, then turning to the more important issue of the role of the people and concluding with six principles of political ontology that the dual-aspect model supports.

No matter how multi-centred and multi-dimensional a political system – no matter how mixed a constitution – we have seen that the state that it establishes will have to be capable of satisfying constraints of rationality in its commitments and actions and displaying sensitivity to the charge of failing to satisfy them. Without such a mode of organization the state could not effectively discharge its duties under any plausible account of those duties. And in particular it would not be an entity that we, the citizens, could challenge on the basis of common norms of policy-making. Unable to respond to rational expectations, the state would not be an entity with which it was possible to do business. It would not be a corporate agent or person – a conversable body that is active and answerable in the manner of a single agent (List and Pettit 2011) – but just a site of random, potentially incoherent, response.

How can the people who impose a norm-complying direction on government, now in this domain, now in that, ensure that the state will be rationally sensitive and suitably conversable under collective and individual challenge? How can they guard against the possibility that the commonwealth they constitute might be a many-headed beast, an amalgam of conflicting voices, that sovereigntists like Bodin, Hobbes and Rousseau associated with the mixed constitution? I suggested in the last chapter that there is no reason why a mixed constitution should not be able to support a coherent government and state and I charged sovereigntists with falling to the fallacy of misplaced concreteness in thinking otherwise. But it will be useful to expand a little on why the particular mixture prescribed under the dual-aspect model is perfectly compatible with coherence in government.

If the democratic state is to constitute a popular but coherent entity, according to sovereigntists, then it must be incorporated in the form of a majoritarian assembly of all its members. Ironically, as we saw earlier, they were wrong in this since, as the discursive dilemma illustrates, a majority of individually consistent and conscientious members may vote in a way that supports an inconsistent set of assembly views. In order for such a group to be able to incorporate coherently – incorporate in a way that makes the resultant body capable of registering and responding to rational constraints like consistency – the members must gain feedback on the corporate attitudes that evolve on the basis of individual contributions, for example individual votes, and must be able to adjust as a group so as to avoid failures like inconsistency. An assembly of the sort imagined in the tradition might do this, as we saw, by relying on a device such as the straw vote. Under this procedure the group would check on whether the result of any majority vote generates an inconsistency with previous votes, and if it does then the group would go through further rounds of reflective deliberation in order to determine how best to restore coherence.

The constitution envisaged in the dual-aspect model is a mixed constitution insofar as it lets final decisions on law and policy be determined, whether simultaneously or sequentially, on the basis of interaction between different centres, civic and official, executive and legislative, constitutional and judicial. How can a constitution of that kind allow for the emergence of a suitably coherent and contestable state?

The discursive dilemma is avoidable in the assembly case on the basis of a straw-vote approach, because this requires members to keep track of any inconsistencies arising from majority voting and to decide together on how best to resolve them. Generalizing from that example, we can see that the coherence and contestability of what any state does in making law and policy can be ensured to the extent that similar conditions are fulfilled. First, there are some points at which the system allows for feedback about how far candidates for commitment, however they are individually generated, make a coherent whole. And second, the system distributes authority to some body or bodies to make adjustments in light of that feedback that can help to ensure coherence in the evolving body of law and policy.

There are many different ways of designing a political system, even a system with competing centres of control, so that it meets these constraints. Any design will be satisfactory so long as it requires relevant agents to keep track of the attitudes that the state counts as upholding, in virtue of their individual contributions, and to make sure that those attitudes amount to a more or less consistent, and otherwise rational, package (Pettit 2007b). They cannot just look to how they themselves perform in their different roles, as voters in an assembly might just consider their own votes. They must act with a conscious, continuing reference, not just to themselves, but to the state in whose name, and for whose sake, they are enjoined to act (Luhmann 1990).

Two examples of satisfactory but contrasting constitutions are provided by the Washington and Westminster systems that we mentioned in the last chapter, where the first organizes the state's business around an assembly of representatives, as we described it, the other around a representative assembly.

In the Washington system, policy is mainly made in the deals struck amongst individual representatives elected to office: members of the House, members of the Senate, and the President. Since no one knows in advance what such deal-making will support, no one at election time is in a position to commit credibly to a detailed programme. And so no one works out such a programme in advance, submitting it for scrutiny at the time of election. This raises a problem, since the hurly burly of negotiation and accommodation that an assembly of representatives allows may lead to laws and decisions that are incoherent in various ways with one another or with constitutional provisions. But the courts can come to the rescue in the case of any such difficulty, interpreting the emerging dictates in a way that restores internal and constitutional coherence. The system recruits the courts, side by side with the Congress and Administration, in the process of decision-making and it helps to ensure thereby that the state – the government considered as an encompassing set of agencies – speaks with one coherent voice.

In the Westminster system, the courts play a less important role than in the Washington one, because there is not a similar need for judicial interpretation and shaping under this system – even under a version of the system in which Parliament is not a sovereignist authority, as it is sometimes held to be in the British case.[22] The Parliament at any time is subject to the control of a single party, or a close alliance of parties, where members are required to close ranks in maintaining the executive in power. This being a matter of common knowledge, each party or alliance is required to commit in its electoral campaigning to a fairly detailed programme of legislation, submitting that programme to electoral scrutiny. And so the main laws and policies enacted by any government will have been determined pre-election and tested for coherence by members of the party itself, by the opposition and the punters in electoral debate, by the electorate at the polls, and indeed by independent or statutory authorities. While they may be subject to amendment or rejection by the courts, as happens routinely in the Australian and Canadian versions of the Westminster system, those laws and policies are likely to achieve coherence independently of judicial intervention.

These examples show why the operation of a dual-aspect democracy, and the implementation of the mixed, contestatory constitution that it presupposes, is quite compatible with the emergence of the state as an agent with which it is possible for its citizens, and other bodies, to do business. The state in prospect is a legal person to which it will be perfectly appropriate to attribute attitudes of judgement, desire and intention, as we might attribute them to an individual agent. It will be an agent or agency that we can see as the ultimate source of law and policy in the country where it rules.

The role of the people, constituting and constituted

The system of influence and direction associated with the dual-aspect model gives a networked set of electoral and other roles to ordinary members of the populace and to those who represent them, whether in a responsive or

[22] See for example Goldsworthy (1999). Without going into the debate about whether Parliament is sovereign in Britain, so that there is not strictly a mixed constitution in that country, it should be clear that a Westminster-style constitution might not give Parliament such uncontested authority, if only by allowing for a system of judicial review, as in Australia and Canada. For an insightful case for the merits of such a constrained parliamentarianism see Ackerman (2000).

indicative way. The people are present or represented at each of the mutually checking centres whose interaction within a mixed constitution generates the public laws and policies under which everyone lives. The river of their influence washes into every corner where decisions are taken in their name and it has the effect of directing those decisions towards the satisfaction of popular policy-making norms.

The existence of such a multi-dimensional, multi-centred system of popular interaction and decision-making entitles us to say that the people rule themselves, as we have seen. But what we can now add is that it allows us to say this in each of two distinct senses. The existence of the system means, in the first place, that the people considered as a plurality govern themselves and, in the second, that the people considered as a singular, corporate entity is also self-governing.

The plural people are the individuals who play various parts, electoral and contestatory, in establishing their representatives and in sustaining and operating the processes that secrete the laws and policies under which they have to live. This is the civic people or, better, in a phrase borrowed from the Abbé Sieyes (2003), the constituting people: that is, as I shall understand the phrase, the members of the population acting as citizens to determine how things are set up and run. The people in this sense rule themselves to the extent that it is their influence and their direction that shapes how they are governed.[23]

The constituting people assume a direct presence in elections and referenda and a represented presence in the authorities who run the government and in those private attorneys and social movements who contest government proposals and decisions. They rule themselves, in the first place, to the extent that their influence is present on all sides in the mutual checking and balancing of these elements within a mixed constitution – in the interaction between the elements out of which, in one way or another, all political decisions emerge. And the people rule themselves, in the second place, to the extent that as a result of these often contrary tides of popular influence a norm-complying direction is imposed on the policies and processes that gain political support. The constituting people have a double role in their self-government, then, as we might expect under the dual-aspect model. Whether directly or representatively, they are active on the one side in the short haul of day-to-day, policy-by-policy decision-making. And at the same time they are active on the other side in the long haul of shaping government policies to the requirements of commonly endorsed norms.

[23] On the background to Sieyes's work see Hont (1995).

But while the plural, constituting people are the agents of a republican democracy, exercising individualized, unconditioned and efficacious control over government, they establish conditions under which it is appropriate to posit the existence of a people in a distinct, singular sense of the term. This, in a complementary phrase from Sieyes, is the constituted people: the people considered as an entity that we can take to be answerable, as an individual agent might be answerable, for the range of commitments supported in the laws and policies of government.

In order to be effective in the imposition of policy-making norms, as we saw, the people in their constituting role must establish a state that serves as a corporate agent, responsive to rational desiderata. But if the state is sustained and operated by the constituting people, then its commitments as an agent are all going to be shaped by those people. And so it can be depicted as the people in incorporated form: the people, operating in the manner of a singular, corporate entity. Where the civic or constituting people are the people qua organizing, the constituted people are the people qua organized.[24]

The constituted people, understood in this way, is just the state and the state is just the people: in John Rawls's (1999: 26) words, it is 'the political organization of the people'. Thus whenever something is done on a political basis, we can say either that the state or the people – the people in the singular voice – performs the relevant action (Pettit 2006b). As we attribute the laws and policies in any country to the state that enacts them so, under the dual-aspect model, we will be able in the same way to attribute them to the people (Kelsen 1961, 1970).

If the constituted or corporate people is indistinguishable from the state in this manner, then we can say in particular that not only do the constituting people govern themselves through the state, the constituted people governs itself in a corresponding sense of self-government. While we may regret this ambiguity in speaking of the self-government of the people, we should note that it has long pedigree. It may go back to Aristotle's use of 'demos' in *The Politics* (1996), but in any case it is certainly present in an important fourteenth-century author.

In one of the first theoretical articulations of a democratic ideal, Bartolus of Sassoferrato argued that the independent city-republics of fourteenth-century Italy, such as his own Perugia, did not lack a prince and were not exposed, on account of lacking a prince, to the will of the

---

[24] For an account of the emergence of the idea of the state, in an early version of our current conception, see Brett (2011). On the development of the idea of the state see Skinner (2009).

Holy Roman Emperor; the assumption had been that the Emperor's writ did not run within cities that were governed by princes (Canning 1983; see too Ryan 1999). In the city republic, Bartolus said, the people is a corporate entity, a legal person, and for all practical purposes a prince; the people, in his memorable phrase, is *sibi princeps*, 'a prince unto itself' (Woolf 1913: 155–60).[25] But who exactly does the word 'people' or *populus* refer to? Bartolus's answer is, the *civitas*. In giving this answer, he gave life to the ambiguity that haunts us still. For the term *civitas* may refer either to the constituting or to the constituted people. It may direct us to the citizenry that rule in a popular regime – in a regime where, in Bartolus's phrase, things are done *secundum vices et secundum circulum*: 'by representation and rotation' (Woolf 1913: 180). Or it may refer us to the state that the incorporating citizenry establish when they operate in that manner. The *civitas* as citizenry is the 'constituting people'; the *civitas* as state is the 'constituted people'.

Six principles of political ontology

It is quite useful to be able to think of the corporate, constituted people as self-governing. Doing so highlights the fact that the people do indeed incorporate as a group agent under the sort of democratic arrangements described and, more specifically, that they incorporate in a way that gives control to its citizens and its citizens equally; the incorporation is not like that of a typical commercial corporation or a hierarchical church. The corporate people in this sense is akin to the membership in a democratically organized condominium and is indistinguishable from the state in the way that the membership in such an organization is indistinguishable from the condominium. As we may say either that the condominium or the membership takes such and such measures, so we may say either that the state or the people adopts such and such initiatives; in each case, the two ways of speaking have much the same import.

But notwithstanding the utility of this language, talk of the self-governing, incorporated people should not blind us to the more important role under the dual-aspect model of the civic or constituting people. It may be useful to set out some principles that guard against this danger. The principles affirm the priority of the constituting over the constituted people, downplay the capacities of the constituted people in a number of respects, and show how the emerging picture enables us to dissolve a familiar

[25] For further commentary on Bartolus see Canning (1983); Ryan (1999).

constitutional paradox. They help to flesh out the picture of people and state – if you like, the basic political ontology – associated with the dual-aspect model.[26]

The priority of the constituting people

The first principle is that it is only in virtue of the role of the several, constituting people in establishing and continuing to maintain the state that the constituted or incorporated people exist, figuring as an agent that can be relied upon to adjust and act in suitably rational ways, or at least to be sensitive to the demands of agential rationality (List and Pettit 2011).[27] This prioritization of the constituting people contrasts with the view developed by Hobbes, and endorsed by Rousseau, under which the incorporated or constituted people displaces the several, constituting people in importance. They hold that a people become self-ruling only insofar as they are constituted in an assembly, and operate according to majority rule. It is true that the constituting people have to vote unanimously to set up this incorporated entity – this public person – as they each say. But once that vote is cast, according to this picture, the constituting people have no further role to play: qua several they amount to nothing more, in Hobbes's terms, than an 'aggregate' or 'heap' of agents (1994a: 21.11), 'a disorganized crowd' (1998: 7.11), a 'throng' (1994b: 6.37). Following this line of thought, as we saw, Rousseau (1992: 11.6.7) denies a continuing voice to contestatory citizens – in our terms, the constituting people – on the grounds that if they were allowed a hearing then, absurdly, there would have to be a further arbiter to determine whether they or the incorporated body speaks for the people.

The dependent sovereignty of the constituted people

Does the constituted people, in our sense, count as a sovereign? It will certainly be sovereign in the external sense that, things going well, it can operate in the international arena as an agent with its own ends, its own

---

[26] The discussion that follows is germane to many debates. It is relevant, for example, to the debate between the view, associated with Hans Kelsen, that prioritizes constituted power in conceptualizing the state and the view, associated with Hannah Arendt, that puts much greater emphasis on the constituting power of the people. Hans Lindahl (2007: Section 1) offers a very illuminating account of the divergence on this issue. It should be clear that my sympathies lie broadly on the side that he associated with Arendt.

[27] This represents a perhaps surprising point of continuity with Negri (1999), Hardt and Negri (2000) and Kalyvas (2005). For an interesting, broadly congenial view of the people as a constitutionally shaped process see Espejo (2011).

views and its own resources. But will it be a sovereign on the internal or domestic front, vis-à-vis its own citizens? Yes, in the sense that it can be identified as the source of the laws imposed, to invoke Bodin's founding conception of a sovereign, and indeed as an entity that is not itself subject to the laws. No, in any sense that might reduce the importance of the constituting or civic people.[28] In the dual-aspect model, the corporate or constituted people is an agent that emerges under the norm-imposing control of its constituting members, not an entity that can push back against those very individuals; it is dependent on them for its continued existence and for the manner of its operation. Again, this observation marks a contrast with Rousseau, for whom the constituted people – in his story, the popular assembly – has absolute power over the individual citizens, considered as a plurality. Each citizen may be independent of others in the Rousseauvian theory, but they are all required to be 'excessively dependent on the City', where the City is just the people in assembly, the people qua incorporated (Rousseau 1997: 11.12.3).[29]

The undominating will of the constituted people
The third proposition, related to the other two, is that while the constituted people is a corporate agent and can be said to express its will in the laws and policies it imposes, that will is undominating in relation to citizens. This is because the will of the constituted people is formed on the basis of the processes of interaction and decision-making that obtain amongst the constituting people, materializing under the direction of the norms they endorse at the different centres at which they and their representatives operate. Given these norm-governed processes of will-formation, the will of the constituted people is bound to answer to the individualized influence and direction of individuals; things going well, it is pre-tested case by case for whether it is suitably controlled and non-arbitrary. Here, too, there is a sharp contrast with the Rousseauvian picture. The will of the assembly, assuming it expresses the general will,

---

[28] The ambiguity was used by many, of course, to identify the sovereignty of the people with the sovereignty of the state, thereby depriving the idea of popular sovereignty of any bite it might have had. Thus Hegel (1991: 318) writes that 'sovereignty lies with the people, but only if we are speaking of the whole' – that is, as he goes on to clarify, only if we are speaking of the sovereignty that 'belongs to the state'. In tones that hark back to Hobbes, he says that apart from the state 'the people is a formless mass' (Hegel 1991: 319).

[29] My view is consistent, however, with that which Nadia Urbinati (2006: 223) expresses as follows: 'Popular sovereignty, understood as an *as if* regulating principle guiding citizens' political judgement and action, is a central motor for democratizing representation.'

is supposed to be a will that is present in each of the members. It is meant to be non-dominating, not because it is controlled by suitable norms, but because it is part of the person's own will.

The corporate will is not the general will

The will of the constituted people may look similar to Rousseau's general will, but the difference is more important than any similarity. The general will is supposed to be a will that is present in each of the citizens, side by side with their particular wills. In our terms, it is a will that is meant to be common to the constituting people. But there need not be any will that is common to the constituting people, as we saw, let alone a will to which they might subject government. All that may be in common is a network of norms that people impose on government as the unintended consequence of pursuing influence under the discipline of an acceptability game. The corporate will of the constituted people is the will of an artificial entity that the constituting people create and, emerging under the interplay of rival bodies, it need not have any place in their individual hearts. They may be individually willing that it should emerge from that process of interaction, but neither the ways in which it operates, nor the policies to which it leads, have to answer to anything like a personal will or intention or desire on their part.

The replaceability of the constituted people

The corporate people emerges as a group agent insofar as citizens subscribe to an organizational structure – broadly a constitution – that generates out of their interactive contributions a generally coherent and coherently evolving set of commitments: a profile of attitudes that can be ascribed to that agent. But this means that if the constitution is rejected by the constituting people – if the constitution is changed but not under any existing articles of amendment – then the constituted people ceases to exist and, assuming a new constitution emerges, is replaced by a distinct corporate entity. The point was made by Aristotle (1996: Book 1) when he noted that a *polis*, or 'city', is individuated by its constitution and is replaced by a different city, albeit a city with the same inhabitants, when the constitution is replaced (see too Rubenfeld 2001). But, contrary to what Hobbes and Rousseau think, the replacement of the constituted people need not return people to the state of nature that they imagined – a scenario in which the people dissolve into a mob – since the constituting people can retain enough coordination as a set of individuals to manage a smooth transition to a new constitution. This, arguably, is what happened when the people of the United States rejected the Articles of Confederation in favour of the 1787 Constitution.[30]

Beyond the paradox of constituent power

There is a paradox raised about the relation between people and constitution, but it is more or less readily resolved under the dual-aspect model (Lindahl 2007; Shapiro 2011: 37–40). The corporate people comes into existence only in virtue of the constitution or organization that establishes it as an agent. And yet it appears, paradoxically, that the corporate people must also be causally responsible for the constitution, at least in a democratic society. But in our account there is no paradox here. First of all, it is the constituting people who are primarily required under democracy to be causally responsible for the constitution. And in any case, causal responsibility does not require the temporal precedence that would give rise to a paradox (*pace* Kalyvas 2005). Both the constituting and constituted people can be responsible for a constitution that was set up by a particular individual or group, insofar as they have the power to change it and choose not to do so; that is why there can be a democracy without a founding, democratic moment. The constituted people will be responsible for the shape of the constitution to the degree that they can change it under constitutional rules of amendment. The constituting people will be responsible for it to the degree that not only can they change it under those rules of amendment, they can also change it by non-constitutional means: they can replace the old constitution with a new one, thereby establishing a novel state and a novel constituted people. Under the dual-aspect model, the constituting people are paramount in this respect, as in so many others; in John Locke's (1960: II.149) phrase, they continue 'to be always the supreme power'.[31]

---

[30] Akhil Amar (1988) argues that the current US Constitution might be constitutionally amended – say, by a straight majoritarian vote – and yet not in accordance with Article 5; his surprising claim is that that article does not identify the only constitutional ways of changing the Constitution. The motivation for his argument is removed in the viewpoint adopted here, for it would not have to represent a major democratic crisis for the constituting people of the country to decide unconstitutionally against sticking with the existing Constitution. Rejecting the Constitution in that way would change the identity of the constituted people, but not the identity of the constituting people. And so there is no logical difficulty in imagining that one and the same people – one and the same constituting people – might reconstitute themselves under a new arrangement.

[31] In Locke's view, however, the people – in our sense, the constituting people – play just a remote standby role, as noted earlier, being ready to intervene only at the extreme where things go quite bad. The interventions he envisages 'happen not upon every little mismanagement in public affairs', he says; they are likely to be triggered only by 'a long train of abuses, prevarications and artifices' (Locke 1960: II.225).

Conclusion. The argument, in summary

The argument of this book has taken us over a wide terrain, introducing the republican perspective, traditional and contemporary; presenting the ideal of freedom that lies at its core; sketching a theory and model of the social justice that this ideal would support; defending a matching, republican theory of political legitimacy; and then outlining a model of the democratic institutions that might be thought to satisfy that theory. In conclusion, I think the best thing I can do is to provide a summary of the claims maintained in the development of the argument. While the summary is inevitably sketchy and inexact, I hope that it will help to facilitate readers in finding their way through a book that I wanted to make shorter and simpler than it has turned out to be.

INTRODUCTION. THE REPUBLIC, OLD AND NEW

1. The main ideas in the republican tradition are: freedom as non-domination, the mixed constitution and the contestatory citizenry. Appearing in the Roman republic, in medieval and renaissance Italy, in seventeenth- and eighteenth-century Europe and Britain, and eventually in revolutionary America, they suggest that the state should enable its citizens – however inclusive – to act as free, undominated persons in the sphere of the fundamental liberties, being protected under a mixed, contestatory constitution.
2. This republican tradition came under sustained attack at the hands of Jeremy Bentham and William Paley in later eighteenth-century England, as they introduced a theory of freedom as non-interference. They argued that while the state should cater for the freedom of all citizens – now understood more inclusively – it should do so with only this less demanding ideal in view.
3. Italian–Atlantic republicanism was also challenged in the late eighteenth century by the communitarian republicanism of Jean Jacques Rousseau.

293

While he continued to think of freedom as non-domination, he followed Jean Bodin and Thomas Hobbes in giving up on the mixed constitution and the contestatory citizenry. He argued that there had to be a single sovereign in any well-functioning state and thought that in a republic this should be the assembled, incorporated people.

4. The aim of this book is to build philosophically on the main republican ideas, developing a theory of social justice and, in particular, political legitimacy, where justice governs people's relations with one another, legitimacy their relations with the state. The republican theory of legitimacy gives the state a democratic job specification, requiring it to operate under equally shared, popular control.

5. The methodological requirement on these republican theories of justice, on the one side, and of legitimacy or democracy on the other, is that they can pass the test of reflective equilibrium, as John Rawls described it; they combine with empirical facts to support independently plausible normative judgements.

6. Even the interpretation of freedom as non-domination is guided by the method of reflective equilibrium. There are a variety of context-bound, apparently conflicting uses of the notion of freedom, and the republican interpretation is justified as a regimentation of the idea that plays a useful role in grounding a plausible normative theory.

7. The republican theory of democracy developed here contrasts with Isaiah Berlin's views in tying democracy to freedom; with Joseph Schumpeter's views in requiring popular control rather than popular influence; and with William Riker's in treating constitutional measures as means of popular control, not as constraints on its operation.

8. What relative importance should be given to justice and democracy? The question is not directly addressed in the book, but the republican approach would naturally treat democracy as the more important ideal. Any compromise to democracy will represent a deeper challenge to the robustness with which non-interference has to be guarded under the republican ideal of freedom.

CHAPTER I. FREEDOM AS NON-DOMINATION

1. Assuming that you are able to choose between certain options, as metaphysical free will requires, how might you fail to enjoy freedom in that choice? That is the question addressed here, with the issue of the freedom of a person, which was actually more central in republican thought, being postponed to the next chapter.

2. One issue raised by the question is whether freedom in a choice might be reduced by a hindrance to any option or only by a hindrance to the option you prefer: only by actual preference-frustration. Where Hobbes thought the latter, Berlin argues persuasively for the former. In a free choice, all the doors must be open, not just the one you push on; otherwise you could make yourself free in a choice by adapting so as to make sure that what you want you can get: what you want is an open door, not a closed one.

3. Freedom in a choice requires consciously having the resources, personal, natural and social, to be able to satisfy your will as between the options. There are two ways in which those resources may be affected and the choice hindered; one is by invasion, the other by vitiation. Invasion is a hindrance that is triggered by your trying to satisfy your will, whereas vitiation is a hindrance that comes about for independent reasons. In effect, invasion comes about via the imposition of the will of another, vitiation via unwilled forms of hindrance.

4. Both forms of hindrance are important but invasion has a particularly inimical quality. In invading a choice, another agent or agency usurps your control of what you do, whether totally or partially, and such invasion naturally gives rise to resentment and outrage. Vitiation does not give control in that sense to another agent; it may involve just the limitation imposed by natural obstacles.

5. The difference between vitiation and invasion, and the complex character of each form of hindrance, make the measurement of freedom a very challenging task. This book generally avoids measurement problems, relying instead on tests of intuitive sufficiency. Thus, as we shall see, it invokes the eyeball test to determine a threshold at which people should enjoy equal freedom as non-domination in relation to one another.

6. Freedom of choice, as it is discussed here, depends on how far you can act according to the will or preference you form over the relevant options. As this freedom is distinct from metaphysical free will, so it is distinct from freedom of the will in the psychological sense in which this requires that you form your will autonomously, however autonomy is understood.

7. The republican theory of freedom as non-domination argues for two theses. The first is that there is no invasion of choice without domination, the second that there is no domination of choice without invasion. B dominates A in a choice to the extent that B has a power of interfering or not interfering in that choice, in particular a power that is not controlled by A. And B interferes in A's choice insofar as B removes, replaces or misrepresents an option.

8. There is no invasion without domination, because interference may be conducted under the control of the interferee. It may be like my interference in denying you the key to the alcohol cupboard, except on twenty-four hours' notice, when this is an arrangement that you set up and can suspend.

9. There is no domination without invasion, because my having a power of uncontrolled interference in a choice, even a power I do not exercise, means that whatever you choose, you choose in subjection to my will; you depend on my will remaining a good will for being able to act according to your wishes. Domination without interference may involve me in invigilating what you do and/or, if you believe you are invigilated, in intimidating you. And it may also be willed or unwilled.

10. Berlin argues that freedom can be reduced without actual frustration – by interference with an unpreferred option – on the grounds that otherwise you could make yourself free by adaptation: that is, by adjusting your preferences. It is possible to argue that freedom can be reduced without interference – as in the pure domination just discussed – on the parallel grounds that otherwise you could make yourself free by ingratiation: that is, by softening up the powerful. Freedom requires, not only that all doors be open, but also that there be no door-keepers.

11. Assuming an absence of vitiation, freedom can be equated on this account with non-domination. But consistently with holding by this equation, we can allow that domination without interference or frustration is better than domination with interference and without frustration; and that it is better again than domination with both interference and frustration. We need not rule on whether it is better in terms of freedom or in other terms.

12. How can we ensure your freedom in a choice? We must make sure that you have the required resources, guarding against vitiation. And we must protect you against invasion, guarding against anyone else's domination. Protecting you is distinct from making interference improbable, which might be achieved by giving rewards for non-offences. It requires obstructing interference, not probabilifying non-interference.

13. Interference may be more or less serious, whether it involves removing, replacing or misrepresenting an option. And at whatever level of seriousness, interference may be available with greater or lesser ease to others: it may be more or less eligible. Protection requires obstructing interference so as to make it at least ineligible and to do this in a greater measure, the more serious the interference is. The criterion of adequacy in such protection is subjective and will be fixed later by the eyeball test.

14. Will a failure to resource and protect you in a certain choice count itself as a form of interference? And will the power not to resource and protect count as domination? Not necessarily. But often there is a fuzzy line in this area between action and omission: a failure may count as interference once the resourcing and protection has been established as a matter of standard expectation.

CHAPTER 2. SOCIAL JUSTICE

1. Taking citizens to be all the more or less permanent, adult and able-minded residents of a state's territory, and taking the state to be an agency that operates via different government branches, two questions arise. What policies should the state be required in social justice to impose? And what processes of decision-making should it be required to follow if it is to constitute a politically legitimate decision-maker? Both may get a hearing in standard theories of comprehensive justice, but it is better to give them separate tags and keep them clearly apart.

2. Two assumptions guide this and almost all discussions of justice, social and comprehensive. Justice requires the state to establish a proper balance between the competing claims of citizens in the social order it establishes. And in pursuing the goals to which people have claims, the state should be expressively egalitarian: it should treat all its citizens as equals – and, looking at this from the other side, all its citizens should be willing to live on equal terms with others. The state is required to treat its citizens well, advancing suitable goals, and in doing so to treat them as equals.

3. Theories of justice diverge on what goals the state should pursue in an expressively egalitarian fashion – resources, utility, capability, or a mix of these goods. And they differ on the issue of what expressive equalization entails. Some strategies would involve a substantive form of equality, whether in opportunity or outcome, others not.

4. A republican theory of justice would seek the expressive equalization of freedom as non-domination: the promotion of freedom as non-domination on the basis of an equal concern for each citizen. How should we interpret this goal in more concrete terms? The ideal of the free citizen, central to the tradition, provides a useful heuristic, at least on the assumption that the society is operating within the circumstances of justice and can enable each, in principle, to enjoy the status of a free citizen.

5. The ideal suggests that citizens should be guaranteed resources and protections in the same range of choices – the basic liberties – on the basis of public laws and norms and up to the limit dictated by the eyeball

test: absent timidity, each should be able by local standards to look others in the eye without reason for fear or deference. Social justice, so interpreted, would require each citizen to enjoy the same free status, objective and subjective, as others. It would mandate a substantive form of status equality.

6. This egalitarianism does not fall foul of the levelling-down objection, for it does not imply that it might be desirable to reduce the level of the well-off just for the sake of achieving equality. If everyone has, or can access, an undominated status, there will be no call to level down. And if it is impossible for all to achieve such a status then the circumstances of justice fail and the expressive equalization of freedom as non-domination will not argue for substantive status equality.

7. But the egalitarian ideal of equal status may seem to fall foul of another objection. While requiring a free status for all, it allows inequalities in people's private wealth and power and in the private resources and protections they can command. Are these inequalities likely to prove objectionable? No, they are not. The ideal of equal status freedom is social in character, requiring each to be able to command the respect of others, and it puts significant constraints on how large material inequalities can be.

8. How to identify the range of choices in which republican justice requires people to be safeguarded? Assume that the range should be as large as possible. The guiding idea, derived from the ideal of the free citizen, is that only choices that are co-exercisable and co-satisfying should be entrenched in this way: these are choices that all can exercise at once, while each still enjoys the standard reward associated with the choice.

9. The co-exercisability constraint rules out choices that individuals cannot perform individually, even with plausible state resourcing, or cannot perform at one and the same time, whether for reasons of logic or scarcity. On a similar basis, the co-satisfying constraint rules out choices in which individuals cannot find satisfaction or choices – harmful, over-empowering or counter-productive choices – in which the satisfaction of some entails the dissatisfaction of others.

10. Some choices that are not co-exercisable or co-satisfying in themselves can be reconstituted under social rules so that they do pass the two constraints. Not everyone can take possession of things just as they wish but all can take possession as they wish under suitable rules of ownership. Not everyone can enjoy speaking to an audience if everyone is speaking at the same time, but everyone can enjoy doing so under *Robert's Rules of Order* (Robert 2011).

11. For this and other reasons the basic liberties are likely to assume a different cast in different societies; they are not a natural kind. Amongst any set of basic liberties, the only ones that need attention are the most distal and the most general that meet the two constraints; look after these and you will automatically look after others.

12. The republican assumption is that if people are publicly entrenched in their enjoyment of the basic liberties, understood in this way, then they will be positioned to live meaningful lives. It is possible to be as free as a full and meaningful life requires and yet only to be as free as your fellow citizens.

13. Republican justice requires entrenching people in the exercise of the basic liberties, whereas Rawlsian justice requires protecting them in the basic liberties (first principle) and, in addition, guarding them against certain material inequalities (second principle). This observation does not tell against the republican theory, since the entrenchment of freedom involves securing resources as well as protections and the freedom entrenched is freedom as non-domination, not freedom as non-interference. Built on a strong counterpart of Rawls's first principle, it has no need of a counterpart of his second.

14. Republican justice would require a rich infrastructure for social life with developmental, institutional and material aspects. It would argue for insuring people on social, medical and legal fronts, rather than letting them depend on the goodwill of philanthropists. And it would provide for their insulation against others both in special, asymmetrical relationships and on the generic front.

15. The insulation of people on the generic front requires a criminal justice system. Republican theory provides a clear account of what criminalization is, why criminalization is necessary, what acts should be criminalized, and how criminalization should proceed.

16. This republican theory of justice operates with a modest, broadly consequentialist principle that can serve in ideal or non-ideal theory. It supports a rich and intuitive set of demands on the social order. And it is quite distinctive in linking justice with a social status that people enjoy in virtue of the laws they live under and the norms that come into existence to support those laws.

CHAPTER 3. POLITICAL LEGITIMACY

1. Where justice is a virtue of social institutions that imposes demands on the horizontal relations between citizens, legitimacy is a virtue of political institutions that imposes a demand on the vertical relations between the

citizenry and the state. Justice and legitimacy in this sense can come apart, as illegitimate states may provide well for justice and legitimate states badly. Empirically, the legitimacy of a state might require a measure of justice and justice a measure of legitimacy, but they still make distinct demands.

2. The state is an agency, operating via government officials and bodies, that is capable of making commitments to citizens and others and then living up to them. Only an agency of this kind, and not for example an impersonal rule of communal norms, can advance the cause of justice. And in order to advance that cause it must be able to coerce its citizens, claiming a right against any competitors. Hence the problem of legitimacy. What entitles the state to impose a social order, just or unjust, on its people – particularly on a people who may themselves differ in their views of justice? What gives it a claim to the role of arbiter and decider in these matters?

3. The justice of a state's laws would provide a pro tanto reason for complying with them, the legitimacy of a state – judged by whatever benchmark – would provide a pro tanto reason for accepting it. The meaning of acceptance shows up in the fact that while the injustice of any laws would allow citizens to try to change them, if not perhaps to ignore them, the legitimacy of the state would oblige them to try to change the laws only within the system.

4. The political obligation that goes with political legitimacy, then, is the conditional obligation of citizens, if they oppose any laws on the grounds of injustice, or indeed on other grounds, to oppose them only within the system. Opposing some laws within the system is consistent, however, with a campaign of civil disobedience in which campaigners do not challenge the right of the courts to try them and penalize them.

5. Whether justice fails or not, there is a fall-back, content-independent reason to comply with the law: that it provides a basis on which people form mutual expectations about their behaviour. And even where legitimacy fails there is a similar reason for opposing laws only within the system: that this offers a promising way of inducing and maintaining legitimacy over the longer term. This is an important observation, since many actual states fall short of legitimacy, but it won't play any role in the argument of this book.

6. What makes for legitimacy in the sense introduced? Hobbes, Locke and Rousseau argued that a state can be legitimate only if it is set up with the consent of citizens and continues over time to attract that consent. More recent political philosophies, utilitarian, contractualist or what-ever, have tended to ask after the performance of states in delivering justice, whether social or more comprehensive justice, ignoring the issue of whether they have a legitimate pedigree.

7. The question of whether a state is legitimate is best taken as the question of whether state coercion of citizens is consistent with their continuing freedom. Whatever its failures in other respects, a regime that preserves this freedom would be bound to count as more legitimate than a rival that doesn't.

8. If freedom means non-interference, then no state can preserve the freedom of its citizens; every state imposes taxes and laws and penalties and thereby interferes with its citizens. Adherents of this notion of freedom must focus on the performance of states, neglecting their pedigree, or argue that interference with consent is not interference. The first approach would ignore the problem of legitimacy; the second would make it insoluble.

9. If freedom means non-domination, however, another possibility opens up. This is that if the citizenry control the interference of the state, as you control my interference in the alcohol example mentioned in Chapter 1, then that interference will not count as dominating and the state will not deprive people of freedom.

10. Control in the sense envisaged here would require the people not just to have an influence on government behaviour but to have an influence that imposes a welcome direction on that behaviour. They must not just make a difference to how government behaves, since the difference made might be chaotic or wayward; it might be like my influence on the traffic, if I tried to play traffic cop. People must make a difference that is in some sense designed.

11. Such control is quite distinct from the consent that figures in other theories of the legitimate state. You might have consented to an arrangement without controlling what it allows to happen, as under a slave contract. And you might have grown up under an arrangement without your consent and still control what it allows: you might retain the right of exit or the right to dictate the terms on which it operates in your case.

12. What form of control on the part of the citizenry could make the state into an undominating force in their lives, ensuring its legitimacy? The question bears first on the domain where people ought to control the state and second on the nature of the control that they ought to be able to impose in that domain.

13. The state you live under does not constrain you to live in political society, since that constraint is imposed as a necessity of history. It does not constrain you to live in this state rather than any other so long as it allows emigration; that constraint derives from the political necessity whereby other states deny a right of open immigration. And, finally, it

does not constrain you to live under coercively applied, as distinct from voluntarily accepted, laws; the requirement on the state to treat all its citizens as equals combines with the fact that some citizens have to be coerced to support the functional necessity of universal coercion.

14. These observations show that the popular control that would give a state republican legitimacy does not have to enable citizens to live out of political society, or to live in a society of their choice, or to live under a regime where they are not coerced to obey the law. It has to give them control only in a domain where the state has discretion: that is, in the matter of how it interferes in imposing taxes and laws and other measures.

15. But what is the nature of the control that the citizens would have to exercise in this domain if the state is to count as legitimate? There are three distinct and important requirements: the popular control exercised has to be suitably individualized, unconditioned and efficacious.

16. Control will be individualized if the people enjoy an equally accessible system of popular influence that imposes an equally acceptable direction on government. Control will be unconditioned if their directed influence materializes independently of any other party's goodwill: the threat of popular resistance is enough to fasten it in place. And control will be efficacious if their influence imposes that direction so unfailingly that when decisions go against particular citizens, they can take this to be just tough luck, not the sign of a malign will at work in their lives.

17. The requirements of republican legitimacy, then, are that the people control their state in the domain where it has discretion and do so in an individualized, unconditioned and efficacious way. This is a theory of democracy insofar as it identifies an intuitive job specification for a democratic system: a specification of what a system must achieve if it is to give a distinctive form of *kratos*, or 'power', to the *demos*, or 'people'.

18. This theory of democracy motivates a search for the institutions that might implement that job specification. It pushes us to devise a republican model of the system of popular influence and direction that would ensure legitimacy and establish a proper democracy.

19. The just and democratic state that is held out in prospect here is an attractive ideal. It would provide for people's enjoyment of the free status of the citizen in the horizontal dimension of relations between people and in the vertical dimension of their relations to the government.

20. Even the virtuous dispositions of the members of Kant's kingdom of ends would not ensure this status, since the less powerful members would depend on the goodwill of the more powerful for escaping interference; they would suffer domination. Thus the laws of a just

and democratic state can secure for people a public good that even the highest level of individual morality cannot bring about.

21. It may be useful to distinguish, as we have done, between social justice and political legitimacy, since it emphasizes the importance of democracy. But even an approach that treats justice as a comprehensive, social-cum-procedural ideal, as Rawls's does, will be forced to recognize the importance of democracy, provided that it endorses the core republican ideal of freedom as non-domination.

CHAPTER 4. DEMOCRATIC INFLUENCE

1. In order to enjoy equally shared control over government, as republican democracy requires, people must enjoy an equally accessible form of suitably unconditioned and efficacious influence that imposes an equally acceptable direction on the state. We look in this chapter at how such a system of popular influence might materialize and ask in the next about how it might impose a suitable direction on government.

2. A plenary legislative assembly might seem to promise a powerful system of popular influence and a model of democracy. Ironically, it was first introduced in that role by supporters of absolute monarchy, Jean Bodin and Thomas Hobbes. They opposed the mixed constitution, arguing that there had to be an absolute sovereign. While preferring a king, they conceded that in principle the sovereign might be an elite committee or, however implausibly, a committee of the whole.

3. But the idea of the empowered plenary assembly, endorsed most fulsomely by Rousseau, runs into trouble with the discursive dilemma. Any system of voting by individually consistent members is liable to generate inconsistent policies and the most plausible way of remedying this is by members considering case-by-case what the body as a whole should do to restore consistency. A plenary assembly would be incapable of the reflective exercise in deliberation that this would require.

4. The salient amendment is to opt for a representative assembly. But there are two candidates for this role: an indicatively or statistically representative body, whose members have dispositions that mirror those of the population, or a responsively representative body, whose members are chosen, say electorally, to have dispositions that are sensitive to how the people are disposed as a whole.

5. Mixing these models is not very plausible, since the electorally induced motivations of responsive members are likely to undermine their claim to indicative status. It may be an attractive idea to have a proportional

electoral assembly, but the grounds of the attraction cannot be the hope of making the body representative of the people in both modes.

6. The responsive, electoral assembly is the more appealing alternative. It should foster the use, and therefore the presence, of freedoms of speech, association and travel amongst the people. Embodying a generate-and-test methodology, it should eliminate both the false negatives and false positives that can misdirect public policy. And the threat of electoral sanctions should help to keep it under popular control.

7. An electoral assembly of the kind envisaged might be a representative assembly, answering as a whole to the expectations of the people, or an assembly of representatives, each answering primarily to their own constituents. The divide corresponds broadly with that between a Westminster and a Washington assembly, but while the issue of which is preferable is bound to be important in more fine-grained institutional design, we have to ignore it here.

8. Whatever form it takes, however, an electoral system of influence is not guaranteed to provide for the individualized, unconditioned and efficacious system of directed popular influence that republican democracy requires. Elections may be necessary for democracy, at least in practice, but they are very unlikely to be sufficient.

9. Elections can give each citizen a vote with the same value, but that is not sufficient to ensure that they each have equal access to influence, as individualization requires. Equal access would require an equal chance of being on the winning side on any randomly chosen issue and this requirement is not going to be satisfied when there are sticky minorities whose identity fixes how they are likely to vote on various questions. This is the old problem of majority tyranny.

10. The only hope of remedying the problem is to allow individuals or subgroups to contest various decisions on the grounds that the majoritarian procedure does not give them an equal chance of influence in the relevant area. Individual contestability has deep institutional implications, requiring transparency in public decision-making and impartiality in the resolution of contestations. The resolutions of particular issues might take any of a number of forms, including putting some issues off the regular electoral agenda.

11. An electoral system will fail to give the people an unconditioned sort of influence if the power of government itself, or of an agency like the army or police or of any powerful elite, is such that electoral and contestatory inputs are only allowed to have an impact when this suits that body. In order to guard against such a danger the people must be ready to resist

measures that compromise their influence – they must be resistance-prone – and the government must be disposed to back down: they must be resistance-averse. But how to ensure the fulfilment of such conditions?

12. A good way of making government resistance-averse is to embrace an arrangement like the traditional mixed constitution. This would ensure the separating of the many powers of government, the sharing of each of those powers by different authorities, and the recognition of popular acquiescence as the ultimate guarantor of the constitution. It would restrict the ability of those in power to close ranks against the people and dispose government to avoid triggering popular resistance or doing battle against it.

13. Under a mixed constitution, the voice of the people emerges from coordination amongst distinct, interacting individuals and bodies, rather than being identified with the voice of a single spokesperson, as sovereigntists like Hobbes, and indeed Rousseau, thought it had to be. They were guilty of the fallacy of misplaced concreteness in thinking that there could be no coherence or unity in the voice of the people, short of establishing a single individual or corporate sovereign.

14. Turning to the second condition, the people will be resistance-prone, ensuring that their influence is not conditional on any other party's goodwill, insofar as they are disposed to contest what government proposes or decides on various fronts. This vigilance requires the virtue displayed by those who identify with social movements that make their arguments in public, on purportedly publicly acceptable grounds. This is a motivated form of virtue, deriving from personal interest or spontaneous commitment, and ought not to be in short supply.

15. The ideal of the people's sovereign assembly, as embraced by Rousseau, implies that it is only this body that can speak for the people. Thus it would challenge the right of individual contestation on the grounds, derived from Hobbes by Rousseau, that if individuals were allowed this right, then a further authority would be required to judge between those individuals and the people as a whole, in which case that authority would be sovereign. This shows how tight is the connection between the twin republican ideas of the mixed constitution and the contestatory citizenry.

16. The final requirement that an electoral system of influence has to satisfy is that it be suitably efficacious: whatever direction it serves to impose on government – the topic of the next chapter – it does so with such an effect that individuals who do not like what government does, either in general or in its dealing with them, can see this as tough luck, not the result of their subjection to an alien will.

17. The influence of the people under an electoral system is potentially enormous, consisting in their actual electoral and contestatory inputs, in their dispositions to make such inputs should government take a line they do not like, or in their dispositions to make such inputs should their own wishes shift in light of government policy. It may take an active, a virtual or a reserve form.

18. Still, this influence is likely to be diluted if elected politicians are allowed to dictate policy in domains where their electoral, party-political motives are dominant or if private interest-groups are allowed to have a covert or manipulative influence on government, forcing it to respond to their special concerns.

19. The only hope of guarding against such influences requires setting up unelected agencies that are appointed by elected representatives but do not serve at their pleasure. These will include executive authorities like electoral commissions or central banks, contestatory authorities like ombudsman or auditor bodies, and, of course, the judicial authorities represented in various courts and tribunals. These can help ensure against the problems mentioned.

20. But will such authorities themselves dilute popular influence? Not if they operate with publicly dictated briefs, under publicly imposed constraints, exposed to public challenge and review. In that case they can count as suitably constrained indicative representatives of the people.

CHAPTER 5.   DEMOCRATIC CONTROL

1. No matter how powerful a system of popular influence, it will not support republican democracy unless it serves to impose a popular direction on government. Democracy requires more than popular influence, contrary to the image promulgated in the work of Joseph Schumpeter and accepted in most branches of political science.

2. There are two models of how popular influence might put a directive stamp on government policy, thereby giving the people control. Under one, the people would intentionally impose the required direction; under the other, they would act in a way that has the unintended but welcome effect of imposing a certain direction.

3. The intentional model suggests that people can form and then impose their view of the public interest, which is best interpreted as the interest that they each have in how things should be done, given that they are required to live on equal terms with others. The trouble with the model, however, is that it would require a great deal of unmotivated virtue in

both the people and their representatives; it would be vulnerable to any failure of virtue on their part.

4. The non-intentional model, classically illustrated in James Mill's proposal, suggests that if people just vote for their private preferences, and if representatives have to answer for how they serve those interests in very frequent elections, then, as by an invisible hand, those in power will tend to maximize overall satisfaction: a utilitarian version of the public interest. This model is equally problematic, because it would be vulnerable to the efforts of special coalitions of voters or representatives to serve their own particular ends.

5. But however problematic, these models have complementary attractions. The first directs us to an appealing conception of the public interest, the second to an appealing, invisible-hand mode, in which the public interest might be promoted by popular influence. And it turns out that there is a third model, to be developed here, in which those separate attractions can be combined.

6. In order to introduce this model, we must distinguish between two different procedures whereby people might try to identify and secure a collective, universally beneficial arrangement. In the game of acceptance they each seek to make the minimal concession required, perhaps in a series of bids and counter-bids. In the game of acceptability they each seek to move the group by appeal to considerations that all find acceptable; they are all ready to recognize them as relevant in public decision-making, even if some weight them more heavily than others.

7. In the acceptability game the considerations that make a plausible claim to relevance, as participants abide by the norm of making an appeal to all, are going to be supported by special norms. Each emerging consideration will be such that, as a matter of common belief, everyone treats it as relevant, everyone expects everyone to approve of this treatment and to disapprove of the refusal to grant it, and everyone will be moved by this approbative pattern to grant such treatment themselves.

8. The considerations that are supported in this way by norms may mark out the convergent interests of the members of the group in some general benefit or the concordant interests of individual members or subgroups in receiving special treatment: like the interests subgroups have in being treated as equals with others, these will be special interests that it is in the convergent interest of all to recognize as important for each.

9. The currency of public policy-making norms that ought to emerge in any group that operates under the acceptability game will put various policies off the table, reducing the eligible candidates in any domain. But

they will also put various processes for selecting between eligible candidates off the table in any domain. The approved process in a particular domain might involve election amongst members, a lottery device of some kind, reference to another body, or whatever.

10. The acceptability game is clearly present in the operation of private associations like a condominium of apartment owners. But it ought also to have a presence under the sort of electoral-cum-contestatory regime described in the last chapter. It will make room for the emergence of policy-making norms at the various, mutually accessible, sites of debate, formal and informal, that the system sets up.

11. The sorts of norms that we might expect to emerge will license the importance of equal influence and associated aspects of equal status, register the demands of personal space and freedom, establish desiderata on how public decision-making is to be conducted, and help to fix the range of duties that the state is expected to promote. And they will also identify historically inherited features of the system as fixtures that, fortunately or unfortunately, are not up for revision.

12. Such emerging norms of policy-making are bound to serve a constraining and regulatory function, ensuring that while different policies are identified and decided in ways that suit different factions, they are all fixed in a way that conforms to the requirements of the commonly endorsed norms. Not everything will be decided in a deliberative way but everything will be done under a form of deliberative regulation.

13. This regulation may not be very salient when it is working well. Its effect will be to put off the table an indefinite range of policies and processes, making them more or less unthinkable for members of the relevant community. That effect may be quite important and yet not be much remarked within the community.

14. If a political system operates under the sort of popular influence described in the last chapter, imposing norms of the kind described in this, then it will have a dual aspect, each with its own temporal register. In the short haul, the system will engage people in electoral and contestatory exercises of a familiar kind. But over the long haul it will engage them in the exercise of ensuring the compliance of public policy-making with the norms that get established amongst citizens, or at least amongst citizens who are willing to live on equal terms with others.

15. This dual aspect of a functioning democracy can be illustrated in actual-world politics. Oliver MacDonagh's studies of the changes in government policy as Britain democratized over fifty years or so in the nineteenth century serve this purpose nicely. They reveal a pattern whereby publicity

given to what are scandals by contemporary norms, now in this domain, now in that, generates popular outrage and then forces government to respond with remedial measures. These measures become progressively more substantive as renewed publicity reveals the failure of existing interventions to rectify the problem.

16. The dual-aspect model of democracy combines the attractions of the intentional and non-intentional pictures. In this model, government is forced to promote the public interest, conforming to public norms in the policies adopted and the processes used to decide them. And in this model it does so via an invisible hand akin to that which is held to operate in the open market, not by the formation and imposition of a general will or intention. Where the market harnesses people's economic influence so as to support competitive pricing, this model would harness their political influence – ideally, their individualized, unconditioned and efficacious influence – so as to ensure compliance with policy-making norms.

17. The model makes sense of how government can satisfy Lincoln's three demands. Government will be for the people insofar as it is forced to satisfy accepted norms. It will be by the people insofar as the influence that forces it to do this originates, directly or indirectly, with the people. And it will be of the people insofar as this influence, being unconditioned, is independent of the goodwill of any other party; it prevails regardless of the wishes of those in government, a local powerful elite, or indeed a foreign country.

18. The dual-aspect model allows the emergence of a state that has a single voice, operates to a coherent set of ends, and can reliably incur and discharge commitments to its citizens and other national or international bodies. It allows the state to take on the conversable form that, as we saw, any state must assume if it is to be able to discharge standard duties.

19. The people under the dual-aspect model appear in two roles. The people as a plurality establish and maintain the state insofar as it is their influence, directly or indirectly applied, that shapes policy-making and imposes a norm-complying pattern on it. But in establishing the state, those people incorporate as a group entity, taking the form of a singular agency rather than a plurality of many agents; the people in this sense just is the state.

20. In the first role they may be described, in Sieyes's term, as the constituting people; in the second as the constituted people. Both as constituting and constituted, the people rule themselves, satisfying Lincoln's triad. This ambiguity in talk of popular self-rule has an ancient pedigree,

appearing in the medieval use of *civitas* to refer either to the citizenry or to the state.

21. Under the dual-aspect model, as distinct from the sovereignist picture, the constituting people have a priority over the constituted. While the constituted people counts as a law-making sovereign that is not itself subject to the law, as in Bodin and Hobbes's ideal, it exists only by virtue of the constituting people; being formed by the constituting people, it cannot dominate them; and it can be replaced by the constituting people as they set aside the constitution under which it comes into existence.

22. Under the dual-aspect model, finally, there is no paradox in the claim that the people are causally responsible for the constitution, yet exist only in virtue of the constitution. It is the constituting people who are responsible historically for the constitution and they do not require the constitution in order to exist. And both the constituting and constituted people are responsible in the sense of being able to alter the constitution at any time. The constituted people can alter it by acting within the rules for amendment and the constituting people can alter it even without conforming to those rules.

References

Abizadeh, A. (2008). 'Democratic Theory and Border Coercion: No Right to Unilaterally Control Your Own Borders'. *Political Theory* 36: 37–65.

Abramson, J. (1994). *We, the Jury: The Jury System and the Ideal of Democracy.* New York, Basic Books.

Ackerman, B. (2000). 'The New Separation of Powers'. *Harvard Law Review* 113: 633–729.

Adams, J. (1776). *Thoughts on Government Applicable to the Present State of the American Colonies.* Philadelphia, John Dunlap.

Agamben, G. (2005). *State of Exception.* Chicago University Press.

Alexander, J. M. (2008). *Capabilities and Social Justice: The Political Philosophy of Amartya Sen and Martha Nussbaum.* Aldershot, Ashgate.

Amar, A. R. (1988). 'Philadelphia Revisited: Amending the Constitution outside Article V'. *University of Chicago Law Review* 55: 1043–104.

Anderson, E. (1999). 'What is the Point of Equality?' *Ethics* 109: 287–337.

Anscombe, G. E. M. (1957). *Intention.* Oxford, Blackwell.

Appiah, K. A. (2010). *The Honor Code: How Moral Revolutions Happen.* New York, Notrons.

Arendt, H. (1958). *The Human Condition.* University of Chicago Press.
    (1973). *On Revolution.* Harmondsworth, Pelican Books.

Aristotle (1996). *The Politics,* ed. S. Everson. Cambridge University Press.

Arneson, R. (1989). 'Equality and Equal Opportunity for Welfare'. *Philosophical Studies* 56: 77–93.

Arrow, K. (1963). *Social Choice and Individual Values.* New York, Wiley.

Atiyah, P. S. (1979). *The Rise and Fall of Freedom of Contract.* Oxford University Press.

Bailyn, B. (1967). *The Ideological Origins of the American Revolution.* Cambridge, MA, Harvard University Press.

Bakan, J. (2004). *The Corporation: The Pathological Pursuit of Profit and Power.* New York, Free Press.

Baldwin, T. (1984). 'MacCallum and the Two Concepts of Freedom'. *Ratio* 26: 125–42.

Barry, B. (1995). *Justice as Impartiality.* Oxford University Press.

Bartels, L. M. (2008). *Unequal Democracy.* Princeton University Press.

Beitz, C. (1989). *Political Equality: An Essay in Democratic Theory.* Princeton University Press.
    (2009). *The Idea of Human Rights.* Oxford University Press.

Bell, D. (2010). *China's New Confucianism: Politics and Everyday Life in a Changing Society*. Princeton University Press.

Bellamy, R. (1999). *Liberalism and Pluralism: Towards a Politics of Compromise*. London, Routledge.

(2007). *Political Constitutionalism: A Republican Defense of the Constitutionality of Democracy*. Cambridge University Press.

Benhabib, S. (1996). 'Towards a Deliberative Model of Democratic Legitimacy' in *Democracy and Difference: Contesting the Boundaries of the Political*, ed. S. Benhabib. Princeton University Press.

Bentham, J. (1843). 'Anarchical Fallacies' in *The Works of Jeremy Bentham*, ed. J. Bowring. Edinburgh, W. Tait, vol. II.

Berlin, I. (1969). *Four Essays on Liberty*. Oxford University Press.

Besold, C. (1618). *Politicorum Libri duo*. Frankfurt, J. A. Cellii.

Besson, S. and J. L. Marti (2008). *Law and Republicanism*. Oxford University Press.

Bodin, J. (1967). *Six Books of the Commonwealth*, ed. M. J. Tooley. Oxford, Blackwell.

Bohman, J. (2007). *Democracy Across Borders: From Demos to Demoi*. Cambridge, MA, MIT Press.

Braithwaite, J. (1997). 'On Speaking Softly and Carrying Big Sticks: Neglected Dimensions of a Republican Separation of Powers'. *University of Toronto Law Journal* 47: 305–61.

(2002). *Restorative Justice and Responsive Regulation*. New York, Oxford University Press.

Braithwaite, J., H. Charlesworth and A. Soares (2012). *Networked Governance of Freedom and Tyranny: Peace in East Timor*. Canberra, ANU Press.

Braithwaite, J. and P. Pettit (1990). *Not Just Deserts: A Republican Theory of Criminal Justice*. Oxford University Press.

Bramhall, J. (1658). 'The Catching of Leviathan or the Great Whale' in *Castigations of Mr Hobbes ... Concerning Liberty and Universal Necessity*, J. Bramhall. London, John Crooke.

Bratman, M. (1987). *Intention, Plans, and Practical Reason*. Cambridge, MA, Harvard University Press.

(2004). 'Shared Valuing and Frameworks for Practical Reasoning' in *Reason and Value: Themes from the Moral Philosophy of Joseph Raz*, ed. J. Wallace, P. Pettit, S. Scheffler and M. Smith. Oxford University Press, pp. 1–27.

(2007). *Structures of Agency*. New York, Oxford University Press.

Brennan, G. and A. Hamlin (1995). 'Economizing on Virtue'. *Constitutional Political Economy* 6: 35–6.

Brennan, G. and L. Lomasky (1993). *Democracy and Decision: The Pure Theory of Electoral Preference*. Oxford University Press.

(2006). 'Against Reviving Republicanism'. *Politics, Philosophy and Economics* 5: 221–52.

Brennan, G. and P. Pettit (2004). *The Economy of Esteem: An Essay on Civil and Political Society*. Oxford University Press.

Brennan, J. (2011). *The Ethics of Voting*. Princeton University Press.

Brett, A. S. (2011). *Changes of State: Nature and the Limits of the City in Early Modern Natural Law*. Princeton University Press.

Brettschneider, C. (2007). *Democratic Rights: The Substance of Self-Government*. Princeton University Press.

Brugger, W. (1999). *Republican Theory in Political Thought: Virtuous or Virtual?* New York, Macmillan.

Buchanan, A. (2002). 'Political Legitimacy and Democracy'. *Ethics* 112: 689–719.

(2004). *Justice, Legitimacy and Self-Determination: Moral Foundations for International Law*. Oxford University Press.

Burke, E. (1999). 'Speech to the Electors of Bristol' in *Select Works of Edmund Burke*. Indianapolis, Liberty Fund.

Burnheim, J. (1985). *Is Democracy Possible?* Cambridge, Polity Press.

Cabot, V. (1751). 'Quod Non Omnis Status Reipublicae Simplex Est' in *Novus Thesaurus Juirs Civilis et Canonici*. G. Meerman. Amsterdam, Pieter de Hondt. 2: 622–3.

Canning, J. P. (1983). 'Ideas of the State in Thirteenth and Fourteenth Century Commentators on the Roman Law'. *Transactions of the Royal Historical Society* 33: 1–27.

Carroll, L. (1895). 'What the Tortoise said to Achilles'. *Mind* 4: 278–80.

Carter, I. (1999). *A Measure of Freedom*. Oxford University Press.

(2008). 'How are Power and Unfreedom Related?' in *Republicanism and Political Theory*, ed. C. Laborde and J. Maynor. Oxford, Blackwell.

Christiano, T. (2008). *The Constitution of Equality: Democratic Authority and its Limits*. Oxford University Press.

Christman, J. (2009). *The Politics of Persons: Individual Autonomy and Socio-historical Selves*. Cambridge University Press.

Cicero, M. T. (1998). *The Republic and the Laws*. Oxford University Press.

Clark, A. (1997). *Being There: Putting Brain, Body and World Together Again*. Cambridge, MA, MIT Press.

Cohen, G. A. (1979). 'Capitalism, Freedom and the Proletariat' in *The Idea of Freedom*, ed. A. Ryan. Oxford University Press.

(1993). 'Equality of What? On Welfare, Goods, and Capabilities' in *The Quality of Life*, ed. M. C. Nussbaum and A. Sen. Oxford University Press, pp. 9–29.

(2008). *Rescuing Justice and Equality*. Cambridge, MA, Harvard University Press.

Cohen, J. (1989). 'Deliberation and Democratic Legitimacy' in *The Good Polity*, ed. A. Hamlin and P. Pettit. Oxford, Blackwell, pp. 17–34.

(2004). 'Minimalism About Human Rights: The Most We Can Hope For'. *Journal of Political Philosophy* 12: 190–213.

(2009). *Philosophy, Politics, Democracy*. Cambridge, MA, Harvard University Press.

(2010). *Rousseau: A Free Community of Equals*. Oxford University Press.

Cohen, M. (1933). 'The Basis of Contract'. *Harvard Law Review* 4: 553–92.

Coleman, J. (1974). *Power and the Structure of Society*. New York, Norton.

(1990). 'The Emergence of Norms' in *Social Institutions: Their Emergence, Maintenance, and Effects*, ed. M. Hechter, K.-D. Opp and R. Wippler, Berlin, de Gruyter, pp. 35–59.

Connolly, W. E. (1969). *The Bias of Pluralism*. New York, Atherton.
  (1993). *The Terms of Political Discourse*. Oxford, Blackwell.
Constant, B. (1988). *Constant: Political Writings*. Cambridge University Press.
  (2003). *Principles of Politics Applicable to All Governments*. Indianapolis, Liberty Fund.
Cornish, W. R. and G. d. N. Clark (1989). *Law and Society in England 1750–1950*. London, Sweet and Maxwell.
Costa, M. V. (2007). 'Freedom as Non-Domination, Normativity and Indeterminacy'. *Journal of Value Inquiry* 41: 291–307.
Dagger, R. (1997). *Civic Virtues: Rights, Citizenship, and Republican Liberalism*. Oxford University Press.
Demosthenes (1939). *Against Meidias*, trans. A. T. Murray. London, Heinemann.
Dennett, D. C. (1992). *Consciousness Explained*. New York, Penguin.
  (1996). *Darwin's Dangerous Idea: Evolution and the Meanings of Life*. New York, Simon and Schuster.
Dietrich, F. and C. List (2007). 'Arrow's Theorem in Judgment Aggregation'. *Social Choice and Welfare* 29: 19–33.
  (2008). 'A Liberal Paradox for Judgment Aggregation'. *Social Choice and Welfare* 31: 59–78.
Dowlen, O. (2008). *The Political Potential of Sortition*. Exeter, Imprint Academic.
Dryzek, J. (2003). *Deliberative Democracy and Beyond: Liberals, Critics, Contestations*. Oxford University Press.
Duff, R. A. (2001). *Punishment, Communication, and Community*. Oxford University Press.
Dunn, J. (2005). *Democracy: A History*. New York, Atlantic Monthly Press.
Dworkin, G. (1988). *The Theory and Practice of Autonomy*. Cambridge University Press.
Dworkin, R. (1978). *Taking Rights Seriously*. London, Duckworth.
  (1986). *Law's Empire*. Cambridge, MA, Harvard University Press.
  (2000). *Sovereign Virtue: The Theory and Practice of Equality*. Cambridge, MA, Harvard University Press.
  (2006). *Is Democracy Possible Here? Principles for a New Political Debate*. Princeton University Press.
  (2011). *Justice for Hedgehogs*. Cambridge, MA, Harvard University Press.
Eisgruber, C. L. (2001). *Constitutional Self-Government*. Cambridge, MA, Harvard University Press.
  (2002). 'Constitutional Self-Government and Judicial Review: A Reply to Five Critics'. *University of San Francisco Law Review* 37: 115–90.
Elster, J. (1979). *Ulysses and the Sirens*. Cambridge University Press.
  (1983). *Sour Grapes*. Cambridge University Press.
  (1986). 'The Market and the Forum: Three Varieties of Political Theory' in *Foundations of Social Choice Theory*, ed. J. Elser and A. Hillard. Cambridge University Press.
  (1999). *Alchemies of the Mind: Rationality and the Emotions*. Cambridge University Press.

Ely, J. H. (1981). *Democracy and Distrust: A Theory of Judicial Review*. Cambridge, MA, Harvard University Press.

Eskridge, W. N., Jr and J. Ferejohn (2010). *A Republic of Statutes: The New American Constitution*. New Haven, CT, Yale University Press.

Espejo, P. O. (2011). *The Time of Popular Sovereignty: Process and the Democratic State*. University Park, Pennsylvania State University Press.

Estlund, D. (2007). *Democratic Authority: A Philosophical Framework*. Princeton University Press.

Ferguson, A. (1767). *An Essay on the History of Civil Society*. Edinburgh, Millar and Caddel (reprinted New York, Garland, 1971).

Fishkin, J. (1991). *Democracy and Deliberation: New Directions for Democratic Reform*. New Haven, CT, Yale University Press.

(1997). *The Voice of the People: Public Opinion and Democracy*. New Haven, CT, Yale University Press.

Fleurbaey, M. (2008). *Fairness, Responsibility and Welfare*. Oxford University Press.

Forst, R. (2002). *Contexts of Justice: Political Philosophy beyond Liberalism and Communitarianism*. Berkeley, University of California Press.

Frankfurt, H. (1969). 'Alternate Possibilities and Moral Responsibility'. *Journal of Philosophy* 66: 829–39.

(1987). 'Equality as a Moral Ideal'. *Ethics* 98: 21–43.

(1988). *The Importance of What We Care About*. Cambridge University Press.

Franklin, J. (1991). 'Sovereignty and the Mixed Constitution: Bodin and his Critics' in *The Cambridge History of Political Thought 1450–1700*, ed. J. H. Burns and M. Goldie. Cambridge University Press.

Fukuyama, F. (2011). *The Origins of Political Order: From Prehuman Times to the French Revolution*. New York, Farrar, Straus and Giroux.

Fuller, L. L. (1971). *The Morality of Law*. New Haven, CT, Yale University Press.

Garsten, B. (2006). *Saving Persuasion: A Defense of Rhetoric and Judgment*. Cambridge, MA, Harvard University Press.

Gaus, G. (1983). *The Modern Liberal Theory of Man*. London, Croom Helm.

(2011). *The Order of Public Reason: A Theory of Freedom and Morality in a Diverse and Bounded World*. Cambridge University Press.

Gauthier, D. (1986). *Morals by Agreement*. Oxford University Press.

Geuss, R. (1981). *The Idea of Critical Theory*. Cambridge University Press.

Gilbert, M. (2001). 'Collective Preferences, Obligations, and Rational Choice'. *Economics and Philosophy* 17: 109–20.

(2006). *A Theory of Political Obligation*. Oxford University Press.

Gilovich, T., D. Griffin and D. Kahneman, eds. (2002). *Heuristics and Biases: The Psychology of Intuitive Judgment*. Cambridge University Press.

Goldberg, J. (2005–6). 'The Constitutional Status of Tort Law: Due Process and the Right to a Law for the Redress of Wrongs'. *Yale Law Journal* 115: 524–627.

Goldman, A. (1999). 'Why Citizens Should Vote: A Causal Responsibility Approach'. *Social Philosophy and Policy* 16: 201–17.

Goldsworthy, J. (1999). *The Sovereignty of Parliament*. Oxford University Press.

Goodin, R. E. (1996). 'Institutionalizing the Public Interest: The Defense of Deadlock and Beyond'. *American Political Science Review* 90: 331–43.

Goodin, R. E. and F. Jackson (2007). 'Freedom from Fear'. *Philosophy and Public Affairs* 35: 249–65.

Green, J. E. (2004). 'Apathy: The Democratic Disease'. *Philosophy and Social Criticism* 30: 745–68.

Guerrero, A. (2010). 'The Paradox of Voting and the Ethics of Political Representation'. *Philosophy & Public Affairs* 38: 272–306.

Guinier, L. (1994). *Tyranny of the Majority: Fundamental Fairness in Representative Democracy*. New York, The Free Press.

Gutmann, A. and D. Thompson (1996). *Democracy and Disagreement*. Cambridge, MA, Harvard University Press.

Gwyn, W. B. (1965). *The Meaning of the Separation of Powers*. Nijhoff, The Hague.

Habermas, J. (1984–9). *A Theory of Communicative Action*. Cambridge, Polity Press, vols. I and II.

(1994). 'Three Normative Models of Democracy'. *Constellations* 1: 1–10.

(1995). *Between Facts and Norms: Contributions to a Discourse Theory of Law and Democracy*. Cambridge, MA, MIT Press.

Hansen, M. H. (1991). *The Athenian Democracy in the Age of Demosthenes*. Oxford, Blackwell.

Hardt, M. and A. Negri (2000). *Empire*. Cambridge, MA, Harvard University Press.

Harman, G. (1986). *Change in View*. Cambridge, MA, MIT Press.

Harrington, J. (1992). *The Commonwealth of Oceana and a System of Politics*. Cambridge University Press.

Hart, H. L. A. (1955). 'Are There Any Natural Rights?' *Philosophical Review* 64: 175–91.

(1961). *The Concept of Law*. Oxford University Press.

(1973). 'Rawls on Liberty and its Priority'. *University of Chicago Law Review* 40: 534–55.

Hayek, F. A. (1988). *The Fatal Conceit: The Errors of Socialism*. University of Chicago Press.

Hayward, C. (2011). 'What Can Political Freedom Mean in a Multicultural Democracy? On Deliberation, Difference and Democratic Government'. *Political Theory* 39: 468–97.

Hegel, G. W. F. (1991). *Elements of the Philosophy of Right*, ed. A. W. Wood. Cambridge University Press.

Held, D. (2006). *Models of Democracy*, 3rd edn. Cambridge, Polity.

Herreros, F. (2006). 'Screening Before Sanctioning: Elections and the Republican Tradition'. *European Journal of Political Theory* 5: 415–35.

Hill, L. (2000). 'Compulsory Voting, Political Shyness and Welfare Outcomes'. *Journal of Sociology* 36: 30–49.

Hobbes, T. (1994a). *Human Nature and De Corpore Politico: The Elements of Law, Natural and Politic*. Oxford University Press.

(1994b). *Leviathan*, ed. E. Curley. Indianapolis, Hackett.

(1998). *On the Citizen*, ed. and trans. R. Tuck and M. Silverthorne. Cambridge University Press.

Hobbes, T. and J. Bramhall (1999). *Hobbes and Bramhall on Freedom and Necessity*, ed. Vere Chappell. Cambridge University Press.

Hoekstra, K. (2001). 'Tyrannus Rex vs. Leviathan'. *Pacific Philosophical Quarterly* 82: 420–46.

(2006). 'A Lion in the House: Hobbes and Democracy' in *Rethinking the Foundations of Modern Political Thought*, ed. A. S. Brett and J. Tully. Cambridge University Press.

Holmes, S. (1995). *Passions and Constraint: On the Theory of Liberal Democracy*. University of Chicago Press.

Honig, B. (2001). *Democracy and the Foreigner*. Princeton University Press.

Honneth, A. (1996). *The Struggle for Recognition*. Cambridge, MA, MIT Press.

Honohan, I. (2002). *Civic Republicanism*. London, Routledge.

Honohan, I. and J. Jennings, eds. (2006). *Republicanism in Theory and Practice*. London, Routledge.

Hont, I. (1995). 'The Permanent Crisis of a Divided Mankind: "Contemporary Crisis of the National State" in Historical Perspective' in *The Contemporary Crisis of the Nation State?*, ed. J. Dunn. Oxford, Blackwell, pp. 166–231.

Hume, D. (1875). *Of the Independence of Parliament. Hume's Philosophical Works*, ed. T. H. Green and T. H. Grose. London, vol. III.

(1994). *Political Essays*. Cambridge University Press.

Husak, D. (2008). *Overcriminalization*. Oxford University Press.

Jackson, F. (1987). 'Group Morality' in *Metaphysics and Morality: Essays in Honour of J. J. C. Smart*, ed. P. Pettit, R. Sylvan and J. Norman. Oxford, Blackwell, pp. 91–110.

James, S. (1997). *Passion and Action: The Emotions in Seventeenth-Century Philosophy*. Oxford University Press.

Joyce, J. M. (1999). *The Foundations of Causal Decision Theory*. Cambridge University Press.

Kalyvas, A. (2005). 'Popular Sovereignty, Democracy and the Constituent Power'. *Constellations* 12: 223–44.

Kalyvas, A. and I. Katznelson (2008). *Liberal Beginnings: Making a Republic for the Moderns*. Cambridge University Press.

Kant, I. (1996). *Practical Philosophy*, trans. M. J. Gregor. Cambridge University Press.

(2005). *Notes and Fragments*, ed. Paul Guyer. Cambridge University Press.

Kaufman, A. (2006). *Capabilities Equality: Basic Issues and Problems*. London, Routledge.

Kelly, E. (2009). 'Criminal Justice without Retribution'. *Journal of Philosophy* 106: 440–62.

Kelsen, H. (1961). *General Theory of Law and State*. New York, Russell and Russell.

(1970). *The Pure Theory of Law*. Berkeley, CA, University of California Press.

Keohane, N. O. (1980). *Philosophy and the State in France: The Renaissance to the Enlightenment*. Princeton University Press.

Ketcham, R., ed. (2003). *The Anti-Federalist Papers*. New York, Signet Classic.

Kharkhordin, O. and R. Alipuro, eds. (2011). *Political Theory and Community Building in Post-Soviet Russia*. London, Routledge.

Knights, M. (2005). *Representation and Misrepresentation in Later Stuart Britain: Partisanship and Political Culture*. Oxford University Press.

Kornhauser, L. A. (1992a). 'Modelling Collegial Courts. I. Path-Dependence'. *International Review of Law and Economics* 12: 169–85.

(1992b). 'Modelling Collegial Courts. II. Legal Doctrine'. *Journal of Law, Economics and Organization* 8: 441–70.

Kornhauser, L. A. and L. G. Sager (1993). 'The One and the Many: Adjudication in Collegial Courts'. *California Law Review* 81: 1–59.

Kramer, M. (2003). *The Quality of Freedom*. Oxford University Press.

(2008). 'Liberty and Domination' in *Republicanism and Political Theory*, ed. C. Laborde and J. Maynor. Oxford, Blackwell, pp. 31–57.

Kukathas, C. (1989). *Hayek and Modern Liberalism*. Oxford University Press.

Kymlicka, W. (1995). *Multicultural Citizenship*. Oxford University Press.

Laborde, C. (2008). *Critical Republicanism: The Hijab Controversy and Political Philosophy*. Oxford University Press.

Laborde, C. and J. Maynor, eds. (2007). *Republicanism and Political Theory*. Oxford, Blackwell.

Langton, R. (1997). 'Disenfranchised Silence' in *Common Minds: Themes from the Philosophy of Philip Pettit*, ed. H. G. Brennan, R. E. Goodin, F. C. Jackson and M. Smith. Oxford University Press.

Languet, H. (1994). *Vindiciae, Contra Tyrannos*. Cambridge University Press.

Larmore, C. (2003). 'Public Reason' in *The Cambridge Companion to Rawls*, ed. S. Freeman. Cambridge University Press, pp. 368–93.

(2012). 'What is Political Philosophy?' *Journal of Moral Philosophy* 9.

Lessig, L. (2011). *Republic, Lost: How Monday Corrupts Congress – And a Plan to Stop it*. New York, Hachette.

Levin, M. (1984). 'Negative Liberty'. *Social Philosophy and Policy* 2: 84–100.

Lewis, D. (1969). *Convention*. Cambridge, MA, Harvard University Press.

Libourne, J. (1646). *The Legal Fundamental Liberties of the People of England, Asserted, Revived, and Vindicated*. London.

Lieberman, D. (2006). 'The Mixed Constitution and the Common Law' in *The Cambridge History of Eighteenth-Century Political Thought*, ed. M. Goldie and R. Wokler. Cambridge University Press, pp. 317–46.

Lind, J. (1776). *Three Letters to Dr Price*. London, T. Payne.

Lindahl, H. (2007). 'The Paradox of Constituent Power: The Ambiguous Self-Constitution of the European Union'. *Ratio Juris* 20: 485–505.

Lipset, S. M. (1960). *Political Man: The Social Bases of Politics*. New York, Doubleday.

List, C. (2004). 'The Impossibility of a Paretian Republican? Some Comments on Pettit and Sen'. *Economics and Philosophy* 20: 1–23.

(2006a). 'The Discursive Dilemma and Public Reason'. *Ethics* 116: 362–402.

(2006b). 'Republican Freedom and the Rule of Law'. *Politics, Philosophy and Economics* 5: 201–20.

List, C. and P. Pettit (2002). 'Aggregating Sets of Judgments: An Impossibility Result'. *Economics and Philosophy* 18: 89–110.

(2004). 'Aggregating Sets of Judgments: Two Impossibility Results Compared'. *Synthese* 140: 207–35.

(2011). *Group Agency: The Possibility, Design and Status of Corporate Agents.* Oxford University Press.

List, C. and B. Polak (2010). 'Symposium on Judgment Aggregation'. *Journal of Economic Theory* 145 (2): 441–66.

Lively, J. (1975). *Democracy.* Oxford, Blackwell.

Lively, J. and J. Rees, eds. (1978). *Utilitarian Logic and Politics: James Mill's 'Essay on Government', Macaulay's Critique, and the Ensuing Debate.* Oxford University Press.

Locke, J. (1960). *Two Treatises of Government.* Cambridge University Press.

Long, D. C. (1977). *Bentham on Liberty.* University of Toronto Press.

Lovett, F. (2001). 'Domination: A Preliminary Analysis'. *Monist* 84: 98–112.

(2010). *Justice as Non-domination.* Oxford University Press.

Lovett, F. and P. Pettit (2009). 'Neo-Republicanism: A Normative and Institutional Research Program'. *Annual Review of Political Science* 12: 18–29.

Luhmann, N. (1990). *Essays on Self-Reference.* New York, Columbia University Press.

MacCallum, G. C. (1967). 'Negative and Positive Freedom'. *Philosophical Review* 74: 312–34.

McCormick, J. P. (2011). *Machiavellian Democracy.* Cambridge University Press.

MacDonagh, O. (1958). 'The 19th Century Revolution in Government: A Reappraisal'. *Historical Journal* 1: 52–67.

(1961). *A Pattern of Government Growth 1800–60.* London, MacGibbon and Kee.

(1977). *Early Victorian Government.* London, Weidenfeld and Nicolson.

McGeer, V. and P. Pettit (2009). 'Sticky Judgment and the Role of Rhetoric' in *Political Judgment: Essays in Honour of John Dunn*, ed. R. Bourke and R. Geuss. Cambridge University Press, pp. 48–73.

McGilvray, E. (2011). *The Invention of Market Freedom.* Cambridge University Press.

Machiavelli, N. (1965). *The Complete Works and Others.* Durham, NC, Duke University Press.

Mackie, G. (2003). *Democracy Defended.* Cambridge University Press.

McLean, J. (2004). 'Government to State: Globalization, Regulation, and Governments as Legal Persons'. *Indiana Journal of Global Legal Studies* 10: 173–97.

McMahon, C. (2005). 'The Indeterminacy of Republican Policy'. *Philosophy and Public Affairs* 33: 67–93.

Madison, J., A. Hamilton and J. Jay (1987). *The Federalist Papers.* Harmondsworth, Penguin.

Mandeville, B. (1731). *Free Thoughts on Religion, the Church and National Happiness.* London.

Manin, B. (1997). *The Principles of Representative Government.* Cambridge University Press.

Mansbridge, J. (2009). 'A "Selection Model" of Political Representation'. *Journal of Political Philosophy* 17: 369–98.

Margalit, A. (2010). *On Compromise and Rotten Compromises*. Princeton University Press.

Markell, P. (2008). 'The Insufficiency of Non-Domination'. *Political Theory* 36: 19–36.

Markovits, D. (2005). 'Democratic Disobedience'. *Yale Law Journal* 114: 1897–952.

Marti, J. L. and P. Pettit (2010). *A Political Philosophy in Public Life: Civic Republicanism in Zapatero's Spain*. Princeton University Press.

Maynor, J. (2003). *Republicanism in the Modern World*. Cambridge, Polity Press.

Mercier, H. and D. Sperber (2011). 'Why Do Humans Reason? Arguments for an Argumentative Theory'. *Brain and Behavioral Sciences* 34: 57–111.

Michelman, F. I. (1999). *Brennan on Democracy*. Princeton University Press.

Mill, J. S. (1964). *Considerations on Representative Government*. London, Everyman Books.

(1978). *On Liberty*. Indianapolis, Hackett.

Millar, F. (1998). *The Crowd in Rome in the Late Republic*. Ann Arbor, University of Michigan Press.

Miller, D. (1984). 'Constraints on Freedom'. *Ethics* 94: 66–86.

Milton, J. (1953–82). *Complete Prose Works of John Milton*. New Haven, CT, Yale University Press, vols. I–VIII.

Montesquieu, C. d. S. (1989). *The Spirit of the Laws*. Cambridge University Press.

Morris, I. (2010). *Why the West Rules – For Now: The Patterns of History, and What they Reveal about the Future*. New York, Farrar, Straus and Giroux.

Mueller, J. W. (2007). *Constitutional Patriotism*. Princeton University Press.

Murphy, L. and T. Nagel (2004). *The Myth of Ownership*. New York, Oxford University Press.

Nagel, T. (1987). 'Moral Conflict and Political Legitimacy'. *Philosophy and Public Affairs* 16: 215–40.

(1991). *Equality and Partiality*. Oxford University Press.

Nathan, G. (2010). *Social Freedom in a Multicultural State: Towards a Theory for Intercultural Justice*. New York, Palgrave Macmillan.

Negri, A. (1999). *Insurgencies: Constituent Power and the Modern State*. Minneapolis, MN, University of Minnesota Press.

Nelson, E. (2004). *The Greek Tradition in Republican Thought*. Cambridge University Press.

Niederberger, A. and P. Schink, eds. (2012). *Republican Democracy: Liberty, Law and Politics*. Edinburgh University Press.

Nozick, R. (1974). *Anarchy, State, and Utopia*. Oxford, Blackwell.

Nussbaum, M. (1992). 'Human Functioning and Social Justice'. *Political Theory* 20: 202–46.

(2006). *Frontiers of Justice*. Cambridge, MA, Harvard University Press.

O'Donnell, G. (2004). 'Why the Rule of Law Matters'. *Journal of Democracy* 15: 32–46.

O'Neill, M. (2008). 'What Should Egalitarians Believe?' *Philosophy and Public Affairs* 36: 119–56.

O'Neill, O. (1979–80). 'The Most Extensive Liberty'. *Proceedings of the Aristotelian Society* 80: 45–59.

Ober, J. (1996). *The Athenian Revolution*. Princeton University Press.

Olsaretti, S. (2004). *Liberty, Desert and the Market*. Cambridge University Press.

Otsuka, M. (2003). *Libertarianism without Inequality*. Oxford University Press.

Paley, W. (2002). *The Principles of Moral and Political Philosophy*. Indianapolis, Liberty Fund.

Parfit, D. (1984). *Reasons and Persons*. Oxford University Press.

   (2000). 'Equality or Priority?' in *The Ideal of Equality*, ed. M. Clayton and A. Williams. New York, St Martin's Press, pp. 81–125.

Patten, A. (2002). *Hegel's Idea of Freedom*. Oxford University Press.

Pettit, P. (1986). 'Free Riding and Foul Dealing'. *Journal of Philosophy* 83: 361–79.

   (1990). 'Virtus Normativa: A Rational Choice Perspective'. *Ethics* 100: 725–55; reprinted in P. Pettit (2002) *Rules, Reasons, and Norms*. Oxford University Press.

   (1991). 'Decision Theory and Folk Psychology' in *Essays in the Foundations of Decision Theory*, ed. M. Bacharach and S. Hurley. Oxford, Blackwell; reprinted in P. Pettit (2002) *Rules, Reasons, and Norms*. Oxford University Press.

   (1993). *The Common Mind: An Essay on Psychology, Society and Politics*, paperback edition 1996. New York, Oxford University Press.

   (1994). 'Enfranchising Silence: An Argument for Freedom of Speech' in *Freedom of Communication*, ed. T. Campbell and W. Sadurksi. Aldershot, Dartmouth, pp. 45–56.

   (1996a). 'Freedom and Antipower'. *Ethics* 106: 576–604.

   (1996b). 'Institutional Design and Rational Choice' in *The Theory of Institutional Design*, ed. R. E. Goodin. Cambridge University Press.

   (1997a). 'A Consequentialist Perspective on Ethics' in *Three Methods of Ethics: A Debate*. M. Baron, M. Slote and P. Pettit. Oxford, Blackwell.

   (1997b). 'Republican Theory and Criminal Punishment'. *Utilitas* 9: 59–79.

   (1997c). *Republicanism: A Theory of Freedom and Government*. Oxford University Press.

   (1998). 'Reworking Sandel's Republicanism'. *Journal of Philosophy* 95: 73–96.

   (1999). 'Republican Liberty, Contestatory Democracy' in *Democracy's Value*, ed. C. Hacker-Cordon and I. Shapiro. Cambridge University Press.

   (2000a). 'Democracy, Electoral and Contestatory'. *Nomos* 42: 105–44.

   (2000b). 'Minority Claims under Two Conceptions of Democracy' in *Political Theory and the Rights of Indigenous Peoples*, ed. D. Ivison, P. Patton and W. Sanders. Cambridge University Press, pp. 199–215.

   (2001a). 'Capability and Freedom: A Defence of Sen', *Economics and Philosophy* 17: 1–20.

   (2001b). 'The Capacity to Have Done Otherwise' in *Relating to Responsibility: Essays in Honour of Tony Honore on his 80th Birthday*, ed. P. Cane and J. Gardner. Oxford, Hart, pp. 21–35; reprinted in P. Pettit (2002) *Rules, Reasons, and Norms*. Oxford University Press.

   (2001c). 'Deliberative Democracy and the Discursive Dilemma'. *Philosophical Issues* (supp. to *Nous*) 11: 268–99.

   (2001d). 'Non-Consequentialism and Political Philosophy' in *Robert Nozick*, ed. D. Schidmtz. Cambridge University Press.

(2001e). *A Theory of Freedom: From the Psychology to the Politics of Agency.* Cambridge and New York, Polity and Oxford University Press.

(2002a). 'Is Criminal Justice Politically Feasible?' *Buffalo Criminal Law Review*, Special Issue ed. Pablo de Greiff, 5(2): 427–50.

(2002b). 'Keeping Republican Freedom Simple: On a Difference with Quentin Skinner'. *Political Theory* 30: 339–56.

(2003a). 'Akrasia, Collective and Individual' in *Weakness of Will and Practical Irrationality*, ed. S. Stroud and C. Tappolet. Oxford University Press.

(2003b). 'Deliberative Democracy, the Discursive Dilemma, and Republican Theory' in *Philosophy, Politics and Society Vol. 7: Debating Deliberative Democracy*, ed. J. Fishkin and P. Laslett. Cambridge University Press, pp. 138–62.

(2004a). 'The Common Good' in *Justice and Democracy: Essays for Brian Barry*, ed. K. Dowding, R. E. Goodin and C. Pateman. Cambridge University Press, pp. 150–69.

(2004b). 'Depoliticizing Democracy'. *Ratio Juris* 17: 52–65.

(2005a). 'The Domination Complaint'. *Nomos* 86: 87–117.

(2005b). 'The Elements of Responsibility'. *Philosophical Books* 46: 210–19.

(2005c). 'On Rule-Following, Folk Psychology, and the Economy of Esteem: Reply to Boghossian, Dreier and Smith': contribution to Symposium on P. Pettit's *Rules, Reasons, and Norms. Philosophical Studies* 124: 233–59.

(2006a). 'The Determinacy of Republican Policy'. *Philosophy and Public Affairs* 34: 275–83.

(2006b). 'Rawls's Peoples' in *Rawls's Law of Peoples: A Realistic Utopia*, ed. R. Martin and D. Reidy. Oxford, Blackwell.

(2007a). 'Joining the Dots' in *Common Minds: Themes from the Philosophy of Philip Pettit*, ed. H. G. Brennan, R. E. Goodin, F. C. Jackson and M. Smith. Oxford University Press, pp. 215–344.

(2007b). 'Rationality, Reasoning and Group Agency'. *Dialectica* 61: 495–519.

(2007c). 'Resilience as an Explanandum of Social Theory' in *Contingency*, ed. I. Shapiro and S. Bedi. New York University Press.

(2007d). 'Responsibility Incorporated'. *Ethics* 117: 171–201.

(2007e). 'Free Persons and Free Choices'. *History of Political Thought*, Special Issue on 'Liberty and Sovereignty', 28: 709–18.

(2008a). 'The Basic Liberties' in *Essays on H. L. A. Hart*, ed. M. Kramer. Oxford University Press, pp. 201–24.

(2008b). 'Freedom and Probability: A Comment on Goodin and Jackson'. *Philosophy and Public Affairs* 36: 206–20.

(2008c). *Made with Words: Hobbes on Language, Mind and Politics.* Princeton University Press.

(2008d). 'Republican Liberty: Three Axioms, Four Theorems' in *Republicanism and Political Theory*, ed. C. Laborde and J. Manor. Oxford, Blackwell.

(2008e). 'Value-mistaken and Virtue-mistaken Norms' in *Political Legitimization without Morality?*, ed. J. Kuehnelt. New York, Springer, pp. 139–56.

(2009a). 'Corporate Responsibility Revisited'. *Rechtsfilosofie & Rechtstheorie*, Special Issue on 'Philip Pettit and the Incorporation of Responsibility', 38: 159–76.

(2009b). 'Varieties of Public Representation' in *Representation and Popular Rule*, ed. I. Shapiro, S. Stokes and E. J. Wood. Cambridge University Press.

(2010a). 'Legitimate International Institutions: A Neorepublican Perspective' in *The Philosophy of International Law*, ed. J. Tasioulas and S. Besson. Oxford University Press.

(2010b). 'Representation, Responsive and Indicative'. *Constellations* 3: 426–34.

(2010c). 'A Republican Law of Peoples'. *European Journal of Political Theory*, Special Issue on 'Republicanism and International Relations', 9: 70–94.

(2011a). 'The Hedgehog's Fantasies': review of Ronald Dworkin, 'Justice for Hedgehogs'. *Times Literary Supplement*. London, News International.

(2011b). 'The Instability of Freedom as Non-Interference: The Case of Isaiah Berlin'. *Ethics* 121: 693–716.

(2012a). 'The Inescapability of Consequentialism' in *Luck, Value and Commitment: Themes from the Ethics of Bernard Williams*, ed. U. Heuer and G. Lang. Oxford University Press.

(2012b). 'Two Republican Traditions' in *Republican Democracy: Liberty, Law and Politics*, ed. A. Niederberger and P. Schink. Edinburgh University Press.

(in press). *Just Freedom*. New York, W.W. Norton and Co.

Pettit, P. and D. Schweikard (2006). 'Joint Action and Group Agency'. *Philosophy of the Social Sciences* 36: 18–39.

Pettit, P. and M. Smith (1996). 'Freedom in Belief and Desire'. *Journal of Philosophy* 93: 429–49; reprinted in F. Jackson, P. Pettit and M. Smith (2004) *Mind, Morality and Explanation*. Oxford University Press.

Pinker, S. (2011). *The Better Angels of our Nature: Why Violence has Declined*. New York, Viking Penguin.

Pitkin, H. (1972). *The Concept of Representation*. Berkeley, University of California Press.

Pitkin, H. F., ed. (1969). *Representation*. New York, Atherton Press.

Pocock, J. (1975). *The Machiavellian Moment: Florentine Political Theory and the Atlantic Republican Tradition*. Princeton University Press.

Pogge, T. (1990). *Realizing Rawls*. Ithaca, NY, Cornell University Press.

Polybius (1954). *The Histories*. Cambridge, MA, Harvard University Press.

Prentice, D. A. and D. T. Miller (1993). 'Pluralistic Ignorance and Alcohol Use on Campus'. *Journal of Personality and Social Psychology* 64: 243–56.

Price, R. (1991). *Political Writings*. Cambridge University Press.

Priestley, J. (1993). *Political Writings*. Cambridge University Press.

Przeworksi, A. (1999). 'A Minimalist Conception of Democracy: A Defense' in *Democracy's Value*, ed. C. Hacker-Cordon and I. Shapiro. Cambridge University Press.

Quiggin, J. (2011). *Zombie Economics: How Dead Ideas Still Walk Among Us*. Princeton University Press.

Raab, F. (1965). *The English Face of Machiavelli: A Changing Interpretation 1500–1700*. London, Routledge.

Raventos, D. (2007). *Basic Income: The Material Conditions of Freedom*. London, Pluto Press.

Rawls, J. (1955). 'Two Concepts of Rules'. *Philosophical Review* 64: 3–32.

(1971). *A Theory of Justice*. Oxford University Press.

(1993). *Political Liberalism*. New York, Columbia University Press.

(1995). 'Political Liberalism: Reply to Habermas'. *Journal of Philosophy* 92: 132–80.

(1999). *The Law of Peoples*. Cambridge, MA, Harvard University Press.

(2001). *Justice as Fairness: A Restatement*. Cambridge, MA, Harvard University Press.

Raz, J. (1986). *The Morality of Freedom*. Oxford University Press.

Rehfield, A. (2005). *The Concept of Constituency: Political Representation, Democratic Legitimacy, and Institutional Design*. Cambridge University Press.

(2006). 'Towards a General Theory of Political Representation'. *Journal of Politics* 68: 1–21.

Reid, J. P. (1988). *The Concept of Liberty in the Age of the American Revolution*. Chicago University Press.

Reidy, D. (2007). 'Reciprocity and Reasonable Disagreement: From Liberal to Democratic Legitimacy'. *Philosophical Studies* 132: 243–91.

Richardson, H. (2002). *Democratic Autonomy*. New York, Oxford University Press.

Richter, M. (1977). *The Political Theory of Montesquieu*. Cambridge University Press.

Riker, W. (1982). *Liberalism against Populism*. San Francisco, W. H. Freeman and Co.

Ripstein, A. (2009). *Force and Freedom: Kant's Legal and Political Philosophy*. Cambridge, MA, Harvard University Press.

Risse, M. (2004). 'Arguing for Majority Rule'. *Journal of Political Philosophy* 12: 41–64.

Robbins, C. (1959). *The Eighteenth Century Commonwealthman*. Cambridge, MA, Harvard University Press.

Robert, H. M., H. M. Robert, III, D. H. Honemann, T. J. Balch, D. E. Seabold and S. Gerber (2011). *Robert's Rules of Order Newly Revised*, 11th edn. Cambridge, MA, Da Capo Press.

Roemer, J. (1998). *Equality of Opportunity*. Cambridge, MA, Harvard University Press.

Rosanvallon, P. (2006). *Democracy, Past and Future*. New York, Columbia University Press.

Rousseau, J. J. (1997). *Rousseau: 'The Social Contract' and Other Later Political Writings*, trans. Victor Gourevitch. Cambridge University Press.

Rubenfeld, J. (2001). *Freedom and Time: A Theory of Constitutional Self-Government*. New Haven, CT, Yale University Press.

Ryan, M. (1999). 'Bartolus of Sassoferrato and Free Cities'. *Transactions of the Royal Historical Society* 6: 65–89.

Ryle, G. (1949). *The Concept of Mind*. University of Chicago Press.

Sandel, M. (1996). *Democracy's Discontent: America in Search of a Public Philosophy*. Cambridge, MA, Harvard University Press.

Sanyal, S. (forthcoming). 'A Defence of Democratic Egalitarianism'.

Scanlon, T. M. (1998). *What We Owe to Each Other*. Cambridge, MA, Harvard University Press.

Scheffler, S. (2005). 'Choice, Circumstance and the Value of Equality', *Politics, Philosophy and Economics* 4: 5–28.

Schmidtz, D. and J. Brennan (2010). *A Brief History of Liberty*. Oxford, Wiley-Blackwell.

Schmitt, C. (2005). *Political Theology: Four Chapters on the Concept of Sovereignty*. Chicago University Press.

Schumpeter, J. A. (1984). *Capitalism, Socialism and Democracy*. New York, Harper Torchbooks.

Schwartzberg, M. (2007). *Democracy and Legal Change*. Cambridge University Press.

Searle, J. (1995). *The Construction of Social Reality*. New York, Free Press.

Sellers, M. N. S. (1995). *American Republicanism: Roman Ideology in the United States Constitution*. New York University Press.

Sen, A. (1970). 'The Impossibility of a Paretian Liberal'. *Journal of Political Economy* 78: 152–7.

(1983a). 'Liberty and Social Choice'. *Journal of Philosophy* 80: 18–20.

(1983b). 'Poor, Relatively Speaking'. *Oxford Economic Papers* 35: 153–68.

(1985). *Commodities and Capabilities*. Amsterdam, North-Holland.

(2002). *Rationality and Freedom*. Cambridge, MA, Harvard University Press.

(2009). *The Idea of Justice*. Cambridge, MA, Harvard University Press.

Shapiro, I. (2003). *The State of Democratic Theory*. Princeton University Press.

Shapiro, S. (2011). *Legality*. Cambridge, MA, Harvard University Press.

Sharp, A., ed. (1998). *The English Levellers*. Cambridge University Press.

Shiffrin, S. (2000). 'Paternalism, Unconscionability Doctrine, and Accommodation'. *Philosophy and Public Affairs* 29: 205–50.

Sidney, A. (1990). *Discourses Concerning Government*. Indianapolis, Liberty Classics.

Sieyes, E. J. (2003). *Political Writings*. Indianapolis, Hackett.

Simmons, A. J. (1976). 'Tacit Consent and Political Obligation'. *Philosophy and Public Affairs* 5(3): 274–91.

(1979). *Moral Principles and Political Obligations*. Princeton University Press.

(1999). 'Justification and Legitimacy'. *Ethics* 109: 739–71.

Sintomer, Y. (2007). *Le Pouvoir au Peuple: Jurys citoyens, tirage au sort et democratie participative*. Paris, Edition la Decouverte.

Skinner, Q. (1974). 'The Principles and Practice of Opposition: The Case of Bolingbroke versus Walpole' in *Historical Perspectives: Studies in English Thought and Society in Honour of J.H. Plumb*, ed. N. McKendrick. London, Europa Publications.

(1978). *The Foundations of Modern Political Thought*. Cambridge University Press.

(1996). *Reason and Rhetoric in the Philosophy of Hobbes*. Cambridge University Press.

(1998). *Liberty Before Liberalism*. Cambridge University Press.

(2005). 'Hobbes on Representation'. *European Journal of Philosophy* 13: 155–84.

(2008a). 'Freedom as the Absence of Arbitrary Power' in *Republicanism and Political Theory*, ed. J. Maynor and C. Laborde. Oxford, Blackwell.

(2008b). *Hobbes and Republican Liberty*. Cambridge University Press.

(2009). 'A Genealogy of the Modern State'. *Proceedings of the British Academy* 162: 325–70.

Slaughter, S. (2005). *Liberty beyond Neo-Liberalism: A Republican Critique of Liberal Government in a Globalising Age*. London, Macmillan Palgrave.

Smith, A. (1976). *An Inquiry into the Nature and Causes of the Wealth of Nations*. Oxford University Press.

(1982). *The Theory of the Moral Sentiments*. Indianapolis, Liberty Classics.

Smith, M. (1994). *The Moral Problem*. Oxford, Blackwell.

Sober, E. and D. S. Wilson (1998). *Unto Others: The Evolution and Psychology of Unselfish Behavior*. Cambridge, MA, Harvard University Press.

Sosa, E. (2007). *A Virtue Epistemology*. Oxford University Press.

Spitz, J.-F. (1995). *La Liberté Politique*. Paris, Presses Universitaires de France.

Steiner, H. (1994). *An Essay on Rights*. Oxford, Blackwell.

Stewart, A. T. Q. (1993). *A Deeper Silence: The Hidden Roots of the United Irish Movement*. London, Faber.

Stilz, A. (2009). *Liberal Loyalty: Freedom, Obligation, and the State*. Princeton University Press.

Stout, J. (2004). *Democracy and Tradition*. Princeton University Press.

Strauss, L. (2000). *On Tyranny*. Chicago University Press.

Strawson, P. (1962). *Freedom and Resentment and Other Essays*. London, Methuen.

Sugden, R. (1998). 'The Metric of Opportunity'. *Economics and Philosophy* 14: 307–37.

Sunstein, C. R. (2009). *Republic.com 2.0*. Princeton University Press.

Talisse, R. B. (2007). *A Pragmatist Philosophy of Democracy*. London, Routledge.

(2009). *Democracy and Moral Conflict*. Princeton University Press.

Tan, K.-C. (2008). 'A Defense of Luck Egalitarianism'. *Journal of Philosophy* 105: 665–90.

Taylor, C. (1985a). *Philosophy and the Human Sciences*. Cambridge University Press.

(1985b). *Philosophy and the Human Sciences: Philosophical Papers 2*. Cambridge University Press.

Temkin, L. (1996). *Inequality*. Oxford University Press.

Thaler, R. and C. Sunstein (2008). *Nudge: Improving Decisions about Health, Wealth and Happiness*. London, Penguin Books.

Tilly, C. (1975). 'Reflections on the History of European State-Making' in *The Formation of National States in Western Europe*, ed. C. Tilly. Princeton University Press.

(2007). *Democracy*. Cambridge University Press.

Tomasi, J. (2012). *Free Market Fairness*. Princeton University Press.

Trenchard, J. and T. Gordon (1971). *Cato's Letters*. New York, Da Capo.

Tuck, R. (2006). 'Hobbes and Democracy' in *Rethinking the Foundations of Modern Political Thought*, ed. A. S. Brett and J. Tully. Cambridge University Press.

(2008). *Free Riding*. Cambridge, MA, Harvard University Press.

Tully, J. (2009). *Public Philosophy in a New Key*. Cambridge University Press, vols. I and II.

Tuomela, R. (1995). *The Importance of Us*. Stanford University Press.

Tyler, T. R. (1990). *Why People Obey the Law*. New Haven, Yale University Press.

Urbinati, N. (2006). *Representative Democracy: Principles and Genealogy*. University of Chicago Press.

Vallentyne, P. and H. Steiner, eds. (2000a). *Left-Libertarianism and its Critics*. New York, Palgrave.

(2000b). *The Origins of Left-Libertarianism*. New York, Palgrave.

Van der Rijt, J.-W. (2012). *The Importance of Assent: A Theory of Coercion and Dignity*. New York, Springer.

Van Gelderen, M. and Q. Skinner (2002). *Republicanism: A Shared European Heritage*, 2 vols., Cambridge University Press.

Van Parijs, P. (1995). *Real Freedom for All*. Oxford University Press.

Vatter, M. (2011). 'Natural Right and States of Exception in Leo Strauss' in *Crediting God: Sovereignty and Religion in the Age of Global Capitalism*, ed. M. Vatter. New York, Fordham University Press.

Vieira, M. B. and D. Runciman (2008). *Representation*. Cambridge, Polity Press.

Vile, M. J. C. (1967). *Constitutionalism and the Separation of Powers*. Oxford University Press.

Viroli, M. (1995). *For Love of Country*. Oxford University Press.

(2002). *Republicanism*. New York, Hill and Wang.

Waldron, J. (1999a). *The Dignity of Legislation*. Cambridge University Press.

(1999b). *Law and Disagreement*. Oxford University Press.

(2006). 'The Core of the Case Against Judicial Review'. *Yale Law Journal* 115: 1346–1406.

(2007). 'Pettit's Molecule' in *Common Minds: Themes from the Philosophy of Philip Pettit*, ed. G. Brennan, R. E. Goodin, F. Jackson and M. Smith. Oxford University Press, pp. 143–60.

Waley, D. (1988). *The Italian City-Republics*, 3rd edn. London, Longman.

Walzer, M. (1981). 'Philosophy and Democracy'. *Political Theory* 9: 379–99.

(1983). *Spheres of Justice*. Oxford, Martin Robertson.

Warren, M. E. (2011). 'Voting with Your Feet: Exit-based Empowerment in Democratic Theory'. *American Political Science Review* 105: 683–701.

Warren, M. E. and H. Pearse, eds. (2008). *Designing Deliberative Democracy*. Cambridge University Press.

Watson, A. (1985). *The Digest of Justinian, Four Volumes*. Philadelphia, University of Pennsylvania Press.

Watson, G. (2003). 'Free Agency' in *Free Will*, 2nd edn, ed. G. Watson. Oxford University Press.

(2005). *Agency and Answerability: Selected Essays*. Oxford University Press.

Weber, M. (1947). *The Theory of Social and Economic Organization*. London, William Hodge.

Weingast, B. (1997). 'The Political Foundations of Democracy and the Rule of Law'. *American Political Science Review* 91: 245–63.

Weinstock, D. and C. Nadeau, eds. (2004). *Republicanism: History, Theory and Practice*. London, Frank Cass.

White, S. and D. Leighton, eds. (2008). *Building a Citizen Society: The Emerging Politics of Republican Democracy.* London, Lawrence and Wishart.

Whitehead, A. N. (1997). *Science and the Modern World.* New York, Simon and Schuster.

Williams, B. (2005). *In the Beginning was the Deed: Realism and Moralism in Political Argument.* Princeton University Press.

Williamson, T. (2000). *Knowledge and its Limits.* Oxford University Press.

Winch, D. (1978). *Adam Smith's Politics: An Essay in Historiographic Revision.* Cambridge University Press.

Winch, P. (1963). *The Idea of a Social Science and Its Relation to Philosophy.* London, Routledge.

Wirszubski, C. (1968). *Libertas as a Political Ideal at Rome.* Oxford University Press.

Wolf, S. (2010). *Meaning in Life and Why it Matters.* Princeton University Press.

Woolf, C. N. S. (1913). *Bartolus of Sassoferrato.* Cambridge University Press.

Young, I. (1990). *Justice and the Politics of Difference.* Princeton University Press.
    (2000). *Inclusion and Democracy.* Oxford University Press.

Zucca, L. (2007). *Constitutional Dilemmas: Conflicts of Fundamental Legal Rights in Europe and the USA.* Oxford University Press.

Name index

Abizadeh, A. 162
Abramson, J. 197
Ackerman, B. 285
Adams, John 134
Agamben, Georgio 173
Alexander, J. M. 79
Alipuro, R. 252
Amar, Akhil 292
Anderson, E. 91, 93
Anscombe, G. E. M. 53
Appiah, K. A. xii, 128
Arendt, Hannah 12, 18, 289
Aristotle 6, 189–90, 291
Arneson, R. 79
Arrow, Kenneth 194
Atiyah, P. S. 151

Bailyn, B. 6–7
Bakan, J. 116, 235
Baldwin, T. 48
Barry, Brian 143
Bartels, L. M. 210
Bartolus of Sassoferrato 287–8
Beitz, Charles xii, 143, 146, 214, 262
Bell, D. 148, 151
Bellamy, Richard 3, 207, 216
Benhabib, S. 215
Bentham, Jeremy 8, 9, 10, 123, 149,
    249, 293
Berlin, Isaiah 9, 17, 22, 29, 30–5, 39, 41–3, 48,
    64–7, 149, 150, 294, 295
Berntson, Daniel 42
Besold, C. 222
Besson, S. 3
Bodin, Jean 12–13, 14–15, 189–90, 220–1, 223–5,
    290, 293–4, 303
Bohman, J. 3, 128
Bolingbroke, Viscount 6–7
Braithwaite, John xii, 3, 117, 119, 121, 222
Bramhall, Bishop J. 29, 142
Bratman, M. 48, 277

Brennan, Geoffrey xii, 12, 15, 20, 117, 121, 128, 169,
    182, 200, 236, 247
Brett, A. S. xii, 287
Brettschneider, C. 265
Brugger, W. 3
Buchak, Lara 32
Buchanan, A. 146, 148, 151
Burke, Edmund 206
Burnheim, J. 204

Cabot, V. 222
Canning, J. P. 288
Carroll, Lewis 278
Carter, Ian xii, 44, 46, 51
Charlesworth, H. 222
Christiano, Thomas 145
Christman, J. 48
Churchill, Winston 242
Cicero, M. T. 6, 88, 221
Clark, A. 115, 225
Cohen, G. A. 20, 79, 96, 183–4
Cohen, Joshua 13, 14, 15, 23–5, 79, 123, 126,
    144–5, 267
Cohen, M. 111
Coleman, J. 84, 115
Connolly, W. 180, 251
Constant, Benjamin 16, 200, 232–3
Cook, Maeve 44
Cornish, W. R. 115
Costa, M. V. 58

Dagger, Richard 11
Demosthenes 135
Dennett, D. C. 203, 225
Dietrich, F. 106, 194
Dowlen, O. 12, 196
Dryzek, John 145
Duff, R. A. 118
Dunn, J. 180
Dworkin, Ronald 11, 20, 48, 78, 79, 148,
    180, 186

329

Subject index

For EU product safety concerns, contact us at Calle de José Abascal, 56–1°,
28003 Madrid, Spain or eugpsr@cambridge.org.

www.ingramcontent.com/pod-product-compliance
Ingram Content Group UK Ltd.
Pitfield, Milton Keynes, MK11 3LW, UK
UKHW020341140625
459647UK00018B/2251